MW01129978

THE MOTHMAN'S PHOTOGRAPHER

II

THE MOTHMAN'S PHOTOGRAPHER II

MEETINGS WITH REMARKABLE WITNESSES

TOUCHED BY PARANORMAL PHENOMENA, UFOS,

AND THE PROPHECIES OF WEST VIRGINIA'S

INFAMOUS MOTHMAN

Andrew B. Colvin

METADISC BOOKS
THE SEATTLE CONCEPTUAL ART MUSEUM | SEATTLE
GARUDA TRUST

Books by Andy Colvin

The Mothman's Photographer: The Work of an Artist Touched by the Prophecies of the Infamous Mothman

The Mothman's Photographer II: Meetings With Remarkable Witnesses Touched by Paranormal Phenomena, UFOs, and the Prophecies of West Virginia's Infamous Mothman

The Mothman's Photographer III: From Animal Mutilations, Mind Control, and the Men in Black to Manson, Montauk, and the Mahabharata – Further Meetings With Remarkable Witnesses Touched by the Phenomenon Known As "Mothman" (2008)

The Mothman's Photographer II

Meetings With Remarkable Witnesses Touched by Paranormal Phenomena, UFOs, and the Prophecies of West Virginia's Infamous Mothman

ISBN 1-4196-5266-4

© 2007 by Andrew B. Colvin, All Rights Reserved

PUBLISHED BY: Metadisc

IN ASSOCIATION WITH: Garuda Trust and The Seattle Conceptual Art Museum

SERIES ART DIRECTION: The Cincinnati Gallery of Conceptual Art

SCIENCE/TECHNICAL SUPPORT: Wikimoth

SERIES CONTACT/IMAGERY/PRODUCT: www.andycolvin.com

FRONT COVER ILLUSTRATION: "Anomalous Shapes That Appeared on Photographic Negative Prior to 2001," by Andy Colvin

BACK COVER ILLUSTRATION: "Terrorists and Birdmen That Appeared On Triple-Exposed Image For The Mothman's Photographer DVD Series" by Andy Colvin

CONTENTS

NOTES

You hold in your hands a portion of a larger body of work called *The Mothman's Photographer*. This body of work presents narrative and non-narrative information in the form of sound recordings, visual images, and spoken and written words. The information was gathered via synchronous coincidences seemingly related to the notorious Mothman and one of his major prophecies: the 9/11 tragedy.

Due to my background in documentary photography and Native studies, I have relied on the spirit of those traditions. To me this involves seeing objectively by being conscious of the subjective. This means that the still photography, audiovisual footage, and recordings presented in this series were captured intuitively – with as few preconceived notions as I am capable – and altered as little as possible thereafter. Extraneous subconscious cues caused by post-production "sweeteners" have been removed from the equation.

For example, the photographs presented in book one, *The Mothman's Photographer: The Work of an Artist Touched by the Prophecies of the Infamous Mothman* were not altered in any way other than slight cropping. The video footage presented in *The Mothman's Photographer Reality Series* is presented almost exactly as it occurred, without the use of dramatic alterations such as background music, crossfades, and subtitles. Likewise, the words of witnesses and experts presented in the books *The Mothman's Photographer II* and *Mothman's Photographer III* are presented just as they were spoken, except for the removal of redundancies and seemingly unrelated material. The only liberty taken was the cleaning up of my own language, in order to better convey intent and to fill in factual details that I couldn't remember on camera.

Another aspect of this work to which I was committed was the role of the Heyoka, or artist-priest, or sacred clown. According to Native Americans, the Heyoka is anyone who has seen the Thunderbird. In my opinion this includes someone, like myself, who has seen the Mothman or Garuda. Having this responsibility required that I wholeheartedly "wear the head" and consider the most profane, outrageous Mothman conspiracies and supernatural explanations. I'm not sure if anyone else has written songs from the point of view of a mind control doctor, or compiled an ethnographic photography book featuring "paranormal conspiracy theory." I *am* sure that no one else has made a 32-hour Mothman reality series, and then transcribed it and added explanatory notes. In this sense, the Mothman II and III books are unique.

Mothman II is about my adventures in West Virginia, from the point of view of a fascinated experiencer willing to look at many angles, from the scientific to the supernatural to the conspiratorial… Mothman III is about my West

Coast and Southwest adventures with people I have met since leaving WV, examined from a slightly more spiritual, less conspiratorial, point of view. Together they comprise a written version of the "director's commentary" section of my *Mothman's Photographer* DVD release.

My original goal with the reality series and the books was to pay homage to the oral storytelling traditions of Appalachia. Those of us who grew up there understand the emotional importance of hearing our elders tell stories while whittling on the porch in their rocking chairs. That is why these projects are comprised mostly of interviews, and why I have printed most of the interviews in their entirety – or close to it.

After running into certain difficulties trying to figure out how to structure this book, we tried putting the material in alphabetical order, according to the name of the person being interviewed. To our surprise, this seemed to be somewhat consistent with the actual timeline of events, and also allowed for the historically key Barker and Berlitz material to come first. Hopefully it should also make it easier for readers to find information.

Unfortunately, I was unable to use the real name of my childhood friend back in WV who discovered the "9/11 vision spot." Alas, "Timothy Thomas Burnham" is a pseudonym. Burnham and his mother did not want to participate in this project, which is understandable due to their association with agencies like NASA. I felt it best to protect their privacy. Any investigator seriously wishing to find out more need only travel to Pleasant Dell, up Woodward Drive, in Mound, WV, and ask neighbors there about the Vampire Boy. Last time I was there, he was still vivid in the memories of many. Amazingly, his real last name just happened to synchronously appear onscreen – off to the side for just a second – while we were filming a clip about "the name game" so prevalent in Mothman lore. The superspectrum had once again spoken…

There is some repetition in the text due to me saying similar things in different contexts (i.e. on camera, over the airwaves, or on the computer). For this, I apologize. However I imagine that some people might welcome the repetition. The synchronicities and linkages *do* start to pile up and become challenging to remember.

Looking back, it is amazing how different life was when the phenomenon was active. The period from late 2001 to late 2006 was a sort of educational hallucination – a revolving time capsule inside a spinning vortex, gyroscopically floating weightless before one's mind-eye. My apologies to anyone I bumped into as I was spinning. So much was going on that it would probably take five *more* years – or maybe 50 – to figure it all out.

Andy Colvin, Lincoln City, Oregon, June 12, 2007

ACKNOWLEDGMENTS

Thanks to Dave Scott for his artistic, paranormal, and generally radical sensibilities.

Thanks to Keith Hansen of "The Grassy Knoll" for suggesting that we transcribe the interview material and add notations. Our friends Carlos Allende, Carlo Ardo, and the VARO and AVRO Corporations would be proud. Thanks to the entire conspiracy crowd, in general.

Thanks to Farrah Karapetian for making the transcription happen.

Thanks to my wife Andrea for her support, as well as that of her Protector Bug.

Thanks to The Gibsonian. I am always available, regardless of molecular composition.

Thanks to Gray Barker for his contributions, regardless of intent. I still suspect that somewhere along the way, he unwittingly contacted Mothman and began channeling.

Thanks to Jeff Wamsley for encouraging me at an appropriate time.

Thanks to John Keel for discouraging me at an appropriate time. His warnings were not unwarranted. But without Keel, this book would not exist. Nor the concept of doing it…

Thanks to Adam Gorightly for his kindly support, and for his exemplary research on Charles Manson, the JFK assassination, and Montauk.

Thanks to Manson for the many insights gained from his liberal use of mountain codespeak.

Thanks to Sara Jane Moore for trying to do the right thing at least once her life.

Thanks to Mom for sending me to see Harriet.

Thanks to Dad for sending that message to Harriet from the other side.

Thanks to Medula and all the great mystics, channelers, and psychics.

Thanks to Mothman for just being… As McLuhan never said, "The medium is the Mothman."

Most especially, thanks to all of those who contributed interviews to this series. Many of you didn't feel totally comfortable with it. But you did it anyway, probably because you sensed that I was truly interested… You trusted, or hoped, that I might do something worthwhile with it. I hope that I have lived up to that trust.

RELEARNING REALITY

As toddlers, we bite and touch everything to test our surroundings. As we mature into young adults, most of us are taught by our elders that there are certain things that are real, and others that are not. This real; this is not. This is fact; this is not. There it is; you can see it. See the giraffe? Giraffes must be real… Our brains are very complicated instruments, capable of sorting through all of this data in order to determine and define our personal reality. After this lengthy programming period, our perception is then limited to what we have been taught and what we have had the opportunity to test for ourselves. Our concepts about the nature of reality become permanently solidified.

What then about those other things? The monster under the bed? The bogeyman? Ghosts and goblins? No, we know they are just stories. They're not real because people have told us they aren't real. And we have never seen them. They can't be real! People who believe in things like that are superstitious or delusional. Right? We know certain things are impossible because we have been programmed to think that way. And our life experiences have reinforced these beliefs.

For the sake of our own sanity, we break the world into two camps: the real, and the not real. The possible and the impossible… If we encounter anything new, our brain automatically filters it through our "reality filter" and tells us whether or not it is real.

What happens, then, when we actually encounter one of these "impossible" things, and no matter how hard we try to discount it, no matter how carefully we examine the evidence, we are unable to dismiss it? It can't be real, but it is! What happens if we discover that Bigfoot is real, or UFOs, or Mothman, or ghosts? If just a single "impossible" thing turns out to be "possible," what does this do to our view of reality?

If we are open-minded enough to move through the trauma of having our view of reality re-programmed, we are opened up to a whole new world of perception. If ghosts are real, then what about fairies, or elves, or all of the other things we have been taught to ignore as superstition, as figments of our imaginations? Maybe some of them are real, too.

When creative individuals are opened up to these new realities, there is a natural drive to tell other people. We feel a need to expose this hidden world to the disbelievers. The shock of discovering this new reality transforms us in some way, and expands our creative abilities. We become messengers. Even prophets… We use whatever abilities we have to let other people know that there is more to the world than what we have been led to believe. If only we experience it with open minds…

The word "truth" becomes a bit bigger. Some of us struggle to share this bigger version of the truth. And at least one of us becomes The Mothman's Photographer.

-David A. Scott
Curator, Cincinnati Gallery of Conceptual Art

FIREWORKS AND FURY

The 17 shows that Andrew Colvin did on "Vyzygoth's Grassy Knoll" represent the longest thematic interview series I've ever done. This is ironic because, before we did the first show, I was just hoping we could do a decent hour and be done with it.

Once we got started, though, I realized Andrew had some kind of story to tell. One that gave rise to countless—and I mean countless—other stories deserving of extensive research for the truths waiting to be revealed... There are literally not enough hours in an individual's life to fully track down the leads and stories Andrew offered listeners.

As best I remember, this whole saga sprang from a conversation that my wife and I had with her parents in late 2005. My mother-in-law had asked me if I knew anything about the Mothman, a movie about which she had just seen. (I haven't seen the movie or read Keel's book.) She went on to mention that Mothman was connected in some way with the December 1967 collapse of the Silver Bridge that connected Kanauga, Ohio, and Point Pleasant, West Virginia.

Ah, now that rang a bell! About 25 years earlier, I had read something of the event as it pertained to a lawsuit filed by the family of one of the 46 people who died in the tragedy. The case was explicated in a communications law book I obtained for a graduate journalism program. I had been accepted to Ohio University in the summer of 1979. OU is in Athens, not that far from the site of the collapse. During that summer semester, I would spend many of my weekends around the Kanauga-Point Pleasant area.

Soon after arriving in Athens, I was reunited with a number of fellow high school classmates from Teaneck, New Jersey, who, for whatever reasons, had gravitated to Athens in the early seventies. Before we even finished our first beer together, they advised me that I was a member of their softball team. Throughout the next eight weeks, we traveled to towns along the Ohio River that hosted cash-prize, high-arc softball tournaments.

More interesting, though, is that a principal in the lawsuit I studied was author Joe Eszterhas, then a reporter for the *Cleveland Plain Dealer*. Eszterhas, who had been a student at OU, was found by a jury to have published reckless and calculated falsehoods about a member of the plaintiff's family. Therefore, Forest City Publishing Company, which owned the Plain Dealer, lost the suit (Cantrell v. Forest City Pub. Co.).

What was laughable in all of this was the contempt the Commlaw professor displayed for Eszterhas, whom she referred to as "the Ohio University non-graduate." It became his title of ignobility. I think it was a case of "the professor doth protest too much" since Eszterhas had gone on to make it as a screenwriter – proving that a pedigree from OU wasn't essential for success. By the way, I share one distinction with Eszterhas: I didn't graduate from OU, either. But I did make some money playing softball.

This anecdote may seem a digression, and it is, but it's just a minor example of the kind of phenomena that occurred in each of Andrew's interviews: the creation of a stream of synchronicities—and perhaps some coincidences as well—that, in turn, led to endless other branches just as alluring and mysterious. Although Andrew focuses on Mothman and the Garuda, my major interest was his research into myriad events, clandestine projects, prominent places, personages, institutions, corporations, organizations, and agencies.

Among all that Andrew and I discussed, what I found most compelling were "the usual suspects" he brought up – those very same individuals who I had come to identify as the Illuminists, who have ruled this nation for over a century. Owing to the constraints placed on Andrew by both work and family, we understood that our time was short and that the protracted series must come to an end. Therefore, in our last three hours, Andrew, with a palpable urgency in his voice, shared with the listeners nearly the whole of his research notes on topics that, regrettably, we'd likely never have the chance to cover.

He was understandably driven to get this all out. Though I couldn't help but want to linger awhile on certain topics, he pressed on, unfurling a dizzying number of provocative facts that left us much to contemplate and much to remember him by. For me, this informational concatenation was the equivalent of a fireworks finale. When it was over and I bid Andrew goodbye, I felt the very same way I had as a child, on so many Fourths of July: saddened and rendered inanimate by the sudden silence and emptiness in the wake of such sound and fury.

What made the void left by Andrew a bit more difficult, however, is that I couldn't console myself with the thought we could do it all over again, come another year. I mean could I ever get that lucky again?

-Keith Hansen, aka "Vyz"
July 2, 2007

UNRAVELING MOTHMAN

You hold in your hands the musings of a modern day shaman, Andy Colvin, who began his odyssey at an early age, when he and some childhood chums experienced a series of life-changing adventures in the West Virginia woods with a "monster" named Mothman. Pop history instructs that The Mothman was some sort of malevolent manifestation; a diabolic conjuration from the darker side of human nature; a devil sent to earth to wreak havoc and cause panic, making bridges collapse and people to go batty.

But, of course, things aren't always as they seem, and the mythos surrounding Mothman may in part be a misrepresentation by some of what is actually a guardian angel in devil's clothing, come to warn mankind of imminent doom and disaster. Seeing beyond the pop media conception of Mothman has taken Colvin deep into his past to revisit those strange and seminal experiences that formed his psyche and set him on a path of discovery.

Included in this volume is a series of in-depth interviews – conducted by Keith Hansen, host of "Vyzygoth's from The Grassy Knoll" – in which Colvin begins to unravel not only the Mothman mythos, but as well the many strange doings which lurk behind the tranquil façade of the West Virginia countryside and its confluence of weird creature sightings, secret military installations, and apparent MK-Ultra mind control operations. Enter Charles Manson and Sara Jane Moore, who grew up together on the very same West Virginia street where The Mothman stretched his shadow long on many a moonlit night.

Such are the dark dots that Colvin connects throughout his ongoing investigation, using his intuition to guide him and tie together many seemingly disparate threads and, in the course, transcend the pop Mothman legend to paint a picture perhaps more unsettling than the one illustrated in John Keel's *Mothman Prophecies*.

It is to this end that the shaman in Colvin emerges, as he seemingly channels clues and hidden codes that reach to the heart of this mystery that has transformed his life. A journey you will now join in, with a turn of the page.

If you so dare...

-Adam Gorightly

INTRODUCTION

This project came into my life like a wave. Immediately following the 9/11 attacks, I suddenly remembered that 34 years earlier, my best friend at school had predicted that such an event would occur in the year 2001. He had said that it would be the start of "World War III." My friend stated that his knowledge had come from his personal visits with "space aliens" and a flying birdman that was being seen in the area. In the media, the birdman was dubbed "Mothman." The story of the Mothman sightings later became the focus of a best-selling book and motion picture called *The Mothman Prophecies*.

Central to the Mothman tale is that there appears to be shapeshifting creature that can communicate with people either telepathically, or through dreams and visions. The Mothman is an enigmatic subject that has confounded mainstream "cryptozoologists" and UFO researchers for decades, as it incorporates things that go far beyond typical creature sightings or UFO encounters. According to author John Keel, who popularized the story, the Mothman was communicating with people about events completely unrelated to UFOs. The Mothman's prophetic messages had to do with things like political assassinations, energy blackouts, and industrial sabotage. Keel noticed an odd mix of seemingly unrelated phenomena such as highly gifted children, missing teenagers, "lightning-strike" victims, "intelligent" balls of light, Bigfoots with glowing eyes, occult activity, fake military officers, fake clergy, fake photographers, fake spacemen, and fake Smithsonian vans, as well as entirely real stalkers, serial killer activity, cattle and human mutilations, and threatening operatives like the Men in Black. Underneath one finds links to the military-industrial complex, to international banking, terrorism, narcotics, petrochemicals, pharmaceuticals, atomic energy, biowarfare, secret societies, and religious organizations. Occult historian Peter Levenda seems to think that the clues, correspondences, and synchronicities prevalent around Mothman point damningly to the occultic wings of fascism and neo-Nazism, as evidenced by the cover-ups surrounding Charles Manson and Sara Jane Moore.

Birdmen such as the Mothman are present in the lore of almost all cultures on earth, including the ancient Sumerians, Greeks, Hebrews, Buddhists, Muslims, Christians, and Native Americans. The Greek letter Psi is based on the Phoenix, a derivation of this winged being. There are obvious connections between ancient birdmen and symbols like the caduceus (now the logo of the American Medical Association), the chakra system (on which Eastern medicine is based), and the "eagle and ribbon" imagery so prevalent in various governmental offices around the world. Some connections, like the Great Stone Owl of Moloch worshipped annually by elite Republican leaders at Bohemian Grove,

CA, are less obvious – yet still quite intriguing. The Old and New Testaments connect flying beings with Ezekiel's Wheel and the messianic Christ whose symbolic cross, or "tree," is eerily similar to the symbologies of the Thunderbird and the Garuda, Asia's fearsome protector deity. There also seems to be some sort of code embedded with the Mothman encounters, similar to the daVinci Code. This code may reflect the ancient Hindu belief that the Garuda's role is to systematically root out those who commit heinous crimes. In this sense, the Mothman phenomenon and its attendant "prophecies" may be a naturally occurring social mechanism for tracking political crimes, harmful military and/or governmental operations, and predatory business behaviors – especially those that harm the young and innocent. The concept of a messianic protector or crime-fighting deity is an old one. Researchers have counted several messiahs prior to Christ. Each one seems to have utilized "prophecies" given to ordinary humans.

After 9/11 had occurred and I realized that my friend had been correct in his prediction, I began to look differently at everything that had transpired in my youth. The events started to have a real context. I began reading everything I could find on related subjects. I went back to the Ohio and Kanawha Valleys several times, and interviewed people from my childhood. I produced a Mothman video series, and began writing and doing interviews on the subject. As I traveled, I shot several thousand photographs, approximately 300 of which appeared in my first book. I searched for the places where people had seen the creature, and familiarized myself with the "energy" of these places. I looked for that energy in other places. Along the way, the phenomenon seemed to interact with me, placing obvious synchronicities in my path, as a kind of validation that I was going in the right direction.

During the course of the investigation, I began to wonder if I had subconsciously been following a life-course influenced by my original interactions with the phenomenon. I began to suspect that my photos, songs, poems, drawings, paintings, and video footage might contain pieces of "Mothman Code." I began to realize that I might be acting as an unwitting cipher for Mothman. Naturally, this led me to look more closely at anything I could remember about my early encounter with Tommy's 9/11 vision. Through the haze, I could remember a generalized sense that some important things would happen in the 5-yr. period between the time of the destruction seen (9/11/01) and my 47th birthday, which was in October of 2006. Lo and behold, not long after my 47th birthday – and a string of minutely detailed synchronicities far too precise to be mere coincidence – it just so happened that my life changed in unexpected ways. Suddenly, the phenomena ceased. As a result, I more fully understood the helpful intent in Mothman's warnings. I realized that the 5-yr. period following 9/11 could be interpreted as some kind of cosmic setup or timeloop – albeit one where my decisions still mattered despite falling within a pre-ordained context. Those 5 years were, frankly, among the most difficult years of my life. But although they were extremely challenging, they were also unbelievably rewarding...

Once the spell was broken and I was free, I understood that the 2002 "energy field event" described herein may be interpreted as showing that Mothman presents electromagnetic mirrors to us, to see ourselves and other parts of the human matrix. Occasionally, a veil might be used. He/she/it observes our responses, and reports back to what seems like another part of the matrix. That he might be doing this synchronously occurred to me on 7/1/07. I was being given an energy healing by a psychic who had "cleared" my house, who had not been asked at all about Mothman. While treating me, she had a strong vision of the very memory I was having at that moment, of my house on Woodward Drive. I was 10 years old, and had just come to realize that humans were mortal. I looked out at a sea of dandelions and experienced brief enlightenment, or satori. I then got the sense that trees were alive. When the session was over, the psychic told me that she had missed one visual detail: there had been a "man-bat" that could "morph" watching from the trees.

To little Verplanck

Without whom the full meaning of "The Mothman's Photographer"
would have gone undiscovered…

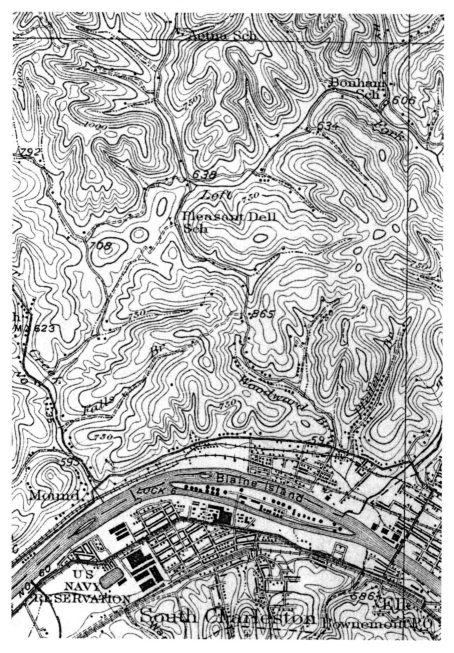

1929 revision of a 1907 U.S. Interior Survey of west Charleston, WV. Mound and Naval base are in lower left. Elk City, where the Elk River flows into the Kanawha, is in lower right. Woodward Dr. runs north from Blaine Island, up through Pleasant Dell to Aetna School (top center), which burned down. Aetna is where aliens, Mothman, UFOs, and MIBs were seen. One can see from this map that Blaine Is. was speedily covered with Carbide's huge chemical storage tanks in less than 5 yrs. The 1925 photo of Blaine (page 70) shows it still untouched.

CHAPTER 1

"Hold-Hold, still my hand.
Steady my eye, chill my heart,
And let my gun sing for the people.
Scream their anger, cleanse with their hate,
And kill this monster."

-Sara Jane Moore

"When you review the ancient references, you are obliged to conclude that the presence of these objects and beings is a normal condition for this planet. They (the ultraterrestrials) are not from outer space. There is no need for them to be. They have always been here. Perhaps they were here long before we started bashing each other over the head with clubs. If so, they will be here long after we have incinerated our cities, polluted all the waters, and rendered the very atmosphere unbreathable. Of course, their lives – if they have lives in the usual sense – will be much duller after we have gone. But if they wait around long enough, another form of so-called intelligent life will crawl out from under a rock, and they can begin their games again."

-John A. Keel, "The Mothman Prophecies"

"By this time, my suitcase was getting very heavy, so I rested on a grassy knoll and took a peek inside. As I opened it, out burst a fountain of many-colored butterflies, rainbows, chess pieces, laughing cups, tiny jasmine tables, and flying plates covered with exotic fruit..."

-Grassy Knoll conspiracy show intro

Colvin, Andy – Grassy Knoll radio interview 1 – Feb. 1, 2006

"Vyz" at Grassy Knoll Radio (GK): Welcome to another segment of the Grassy Knoll. You're hearing this probably on the stream or on local Tampa radio, on AM1610 WDCX. This is Vyz, and with us today is Andrew Colvin. This is kind of a different topic for us. It's something that you folks may have come across. Some of you may know it very well. I'll confess I don't… But it is intriguing. Andrew is going to be here with us for this next hour and hopefully in subsequent days or weeks, to speak to the topic of the Mothman. Andrew, welcome to the Grassy Knoll. Thanks for spending some time with us.

Andy Colvin (AC): Hi. Thanks.

GK: You're welcome. What is the Mothman? What is the history behind all of this?

AC: The modern history starts in 1966 with the first sighting of the Mothman flying along the Elk and Kanawha Rivers in WV. Soon there were several sightings that occurred in Point Pleasant, West Virginia, which is on the Ohio River. The Ohio River joins with the Kanawha River at Pt. Pleasant. There were a lot of sightings up the Kanawha in Charleston, West Virginia, about 30 miles from Point Pleasant. That was the second main area of sightings. But there was a precursor back in the 1790s in terms of the Mothman. A lot of people believe that Shawnee Chief Cornstalk put a curse on the town of Pt. Pleasant, and that the Mothman was somehow an outgrowth of that curse.

GK: The chief put a curse on what I would expect is a European settlement?

AC: Yes. Point Pleasant at that time was an important fort. It was at this juncture of the rivers. The Kanawha River was really important because it was about the only way you could get from Virginia to Ohio. There were a couple of other ways to go as well, but this particular river had salt mines on it. These were really important to the settlers and to the Indians. There were also some asphalt or oil pits that the Indians used for healing and things. Later on, when oil was discovered in the 1850s – with the Rockefellers – the oil drilling started in West Virginia and Pennsylvania.

GK: I think it's interesting you mentioned it, because when the Rockefellers first started to mess with oil and market it, they did it as some kind of health benefit. So the Indians were using this for the same purpose?

AC: They were rubbing themselves with it.

GK: And I guess it was working…

AC: The pharmaceutical industry is an outgrowth of the oil industry. That tradition of co-optation has carried on…

In his early years as a traveling salesman, Rockefeller clumsily – or perhaps ruthlessly – tried to copy the Indians' healing methods by selling raw petroleum in jars, as a cure-all. Of course, this made many people very sick when they ingested it. For a time, Rockefeller was forced to stay on the move to avoid prosecution. Along the way, he was reportedly accused of pursuing young women in a highly aggressive manner. This helped feed the legend of the quack doctor whom no one should trust, selling bogus treatments from the back of a wagon. Although they had to clean up his image a bit, Rockefeller was more or less the inspiration for the Wizard in "The Wizard of Oz." Rockefeller's early interest in quack medicine led to his vigorous interest in pharmaceuticals.

As an example of mild synchronicity... When I was studying acting and performance art in college, I often played a messianic character named "Wiz." I had initially gotten this name from a food product made by Kraft. Kraft makes an array of products with unusual names that seem to allude to parts of the Mothman story. Some of these names would be Gummy Roadkills (mutilated animals), Jello (made from bone, which the ancient Moorish peoples of WV ground up and ritually ingested at mound sites similar to those occupied by Mothman), Knox Gelatin (reminiscent of Ft. Knox and that missing gold that is perhaps connected to the collapse of the "Silver" bridge), Kool-Aid (the deadly beverage at Jonestown and at the Heaven's Gate mansion), Crystal Light (seen by everyone from UFO abductees to enlightened masters, New Agers, and fundamentalists), and Shake & Bake (what happens to people when they are hit with either a Mothman-inspired kundalini experience, lightning, "deathray" laser, UFO beam, crop circle beam, or high-frequency mind control beam such as the one supposedly pointed at Pt. Pleasant).

GK: Getting back to the origin of the Mothman... This tribal chief put a curse on this particular settlement because, I'm assuming, we (the colonists) got in the way?

AC: I'm not an expert on that particular battle, but apparently it was the last large battle between the Indians and US Army in the east. Cornstalk evidently was murdered in cold blood while in captivity, by an Army intelligence unit. One of the themes I've looked at in terms of the modern sightings is whether or not they have any sort of connection to Army Intelligence. Army Intel is sort of where it all started.

GK: You say that there is some kind of documentation or lore that substanti-ates that the being known as Mothman existed as far back as the late 18th century?

AC: Well, Cornstalk didn't actually say, "The Mothman is coming," or anything like that. But we have – worldwide – a long, long history of birdman creatures in every culture, going back as far as the Sumerian legends. It's been with us for centuries... Millennia...

GK: Are there Moth*men*? Is this some kind of species?

AC: It's hard to prove, one way or another. You certainly have your cryptozo-ology crowd who wants to see it as a large, undiscovered bird. However the more you look into it, the more you find that there really *is* a supernatural quotient in it, especially in terms of the Indians. I mean they didn't believe the Thunderbird was just a plain, big bird. They believed it was a deity, a supernatural bird. It's the same for the Garuda, which is what this kind of creature is called in Asia.

GK: That is "Garuda?"

AC: Yes, Garuda. John Keel actually subtitled his book *The Mothman Prophecies* as *An Investigation of the Mysterious American Visits of the Infamous Feathery Garuda*. He initially had more of an emphasis on the Garuda in the book, but about half of the book was edited out. The other half subsequently made its way into his (rare) book called *The Eighth Tower*. If you want to read about the Mothman, it is best to read both books.

GK: You've done a documentary as well, haven't you, about this Mothman?

AC: Yes, it's called *The Mothman's Photographer*...

GK: Are you primarily a photographer?

AC: Yes, I'm a documentary photographer, but I have a background in fine art. Art history, painting, design, performance, sculpture, and video... I also took a lot of psychology, philosophy, and theosophy courses. I was in graduate school for years. At some point I sort of settled into a straight documentary approach, using photography and video. Most of my photography these days falls into one of two categories: "urban" and/or "landscape." At the age of eight, I suddenly was able to draw and paint, and for a while I did portraits at county fairs around West Virginia. I went to art school at the Art Academy of Cincinnati. Then I went to the University of Texas at Austin for graduate school. There I studied film, photography, and art history – mostly of Native American art.

I also took some dance courses, but they didn't like my working-class attitude very much.

GK: I'm looking at your website on the home page. That image of the WTC is from the Brooklyn Bridge, isn't it?

AC: Yes, that was a picture I took of the World Trade Center six weeks before the 9/11 disaster. Something we can get into later, once we've gotten through the basic Mothman story, is the fact that I had a childhood friend in WV who came to me and said that he had seen a vision of this disaster coming in 2001, of exploding buildings. He (and I) actually had a brief precognition of it back in 1967. There seems to be a connection of some kind between the 9/11 tragedy and the Mothman.

GK: This precognition, this is from your friend. Is that correct?

AC: Yes. I actually experienced it, though, because he was claiming that it came from merely standing in a certain spot on his property. He dared me, "If you stand in this spot, you will be able to see it." So I stood in the spot, and I did indeed see something. And it scared the hell out of me. I jumped out of that situation. We sort of had a falling out after that.

GK: Are you a West Coast guy?

AC: Since college, yes.

GK: Are you an Easterner by birth?

AC: Yes. My father is from upstate New York. He is part of the Colvin clan that produced Verplanck Colvin, who surveyed the Adirondacks and turned it into a state park. When my father was in the military, he was stationed in Norfolk, VA, right at the time of the Philadelphia Experiment (1943).

Photograph of the World Trade Center Towers taken by the author, just 47 days before the Sept. 11th, 2001 tragedy, a vision of which was first seen by author's best friend in 1967. Note the oddly shaped dark mist hanging over the towers - a random film development anomaly. The number 47, a sacred measurement used in the construction of the Great Pyramid at Giza, kept coming up in the years following the disaster. One example was in the author's fight to protect a 47-foot long strip of property that once housed an old schoolhouse in an Indian village. Another was the author's hazy, precognitive memory from 1967 that certain things would happen in 2007, when he was 47 yrs. old - things which later turned out to be true.

He met my mother at Virginia Beach. She was from West Virginia. She's from a county in WV that feeds the national security apparatus. I've been finding out that there are a lot of women from this county who have psychic abilities. Some of them have been recruited for government service. But my parents met at Virginia Beach, then got married and lived in New York for a few years. My oldest sister was born there. Then they moved to West Virginia, where I was eventually born.

GK: I lived for two years on the western side of Vermont. In the town of Poultney, there are a whole load of Colvins. Until I encountered your name, the only other encounter I've had with it is the town of Poultney. The Colvin clan is kind of generational there. At any rate, I grew up across the river from Manhattan. I watched the Trade Towers being built. That your friend would say something like that in 1967 is very curious because, really, they weren't all that tall at that time... Yet we *knew*. We knew where they were going [in terms of height]. As we watched them get built Andrew, I'll tell you, all of us said "they're going to fly a plane into that some day." I mean it almost *begs* it, if you know what I'm saying. That your friend said that – *that* early on – is quite interesting.

AC: The interesting thing about that vision is that it was from water level in the Hudson. I'm not sure what that means... I've been to New York many times. But I only went to the towers and looked at them a couple times prior to photographing them in July 2001. I had forgotten about this precognition of 9/11 for many years. I wasn't thinking about it. Anyway the vision we had in 1967 was from the New Jersey side, looking over to Manhattan.

GK: I got caught up in NYC that day [of 9/11]. I was actually visiting, walking, and not plugged in to any media. I walked and walked, visiting old sites as I'm given to do. I didn't know until 2:30 what had taken place. Then I was just absolutely taken aback. And I heard some strange things that day. One of them was probably one of the jets that came upon the area. It's a sound you don't usually hear there so it was very, very telling. At any rate, we'll jump back to the Mothman. Going back to the curse from Cornstalk, was there anything that you could uncover between the late 18th century and 1967, where others had encounters [with] or saw this creature?

AC: Yes, there's an account in one of WV folklorist James Gay Jones' books, from 1895, somewhere up the Elk River. The Elk River also plays into this. It flows into the Kanawha River, which then goes on down to the Ohio River. Actually the first Mothman sighting was near the Elk River, a few miles Charleston. There were some guys digging a grave. They saw something fly over. Then there were these contacts that started occurring in Point Pleasant the next day or so. This would have been in mid-November, 1966.

There were sightings of a large bird in Webster County, WV in 1895 that were described in the Feb. 24th St. Louis Globe Democrat as a Roc (also known as Piasa, or Thunderbird). A hunter was severely mauled by the bird. A dog, some sheep, and a 10-yr. old girl were completely carried off by it, and apparently eaten. There were also similar sightings in Wyoming County, WV, in 1978, during a UFO flap.

Cryptozoologists claim that there is a migration pattern for "giant birds" that can be mapped from appearances in the last two centuries. When the birds fly north in the Spring, they seem to pass through WV, Pennsylvania, and NY, on their way to Quebec. Many people apparently see birds with 15 to 35-foot wingspans, year after year. Cryptozoologists believe Pennsylvania to be a place where the birds linger and "spend the warmer months of the year." In the 1940s, Robert R. Lyman Sr., a witness from Coudersport, PA, collected the bird stories into two volumes called "Strange Events in the Black Forest." Lyman, who was from a family of psychics, recounted many sightings that seemed unexplainable or even supernatural. One witness said that the giant birds seemed to be able to fly straight through tangled mazes of branches far too dense for a flesh-and-blood bird of that size. Like the sand-hill crane and the mythical Thunderbird, these giant birds appear more frequently before and after thunderstorms. Some consider cranes to have supernatural powers. Crane-human hybrids are a staple of Egyptian occultism. Arabian djinn, or genies, are said to manifest physically as large, cranelike birds emanating from caves.

According to Claude Schaeffer of the Museum of the Plains Indians in Browning, Montana, "White Bear" of the Cree tribe was snatched up and carried away to Devil's Head Mountain by one of these large ghost birds in the mid-1800s. White Bear happened to be a "conjurer" (occult practitioner) and trapper of eagles. White Bear was dropped into a nest that contained two young birds. Supposedly, he later escaped with their aid. As a side note, when my nephew was 3 years old, he had a dream that I had been carried off by "hairy white bears." My sister has recurring nightmares about a white bear creature trying to get into our old house in Mound, WV.

The New York area has seen both early and modern sightings, with creature reports filed on Sept. 27, 1894 (in the Essex County Republican) and again in the mid-1970s by Dr. Eric Berthold Schwartz and Judith Diliberto. When I was a boy, I remember hearing stories about birdman sightings at Coney Island, where we vacationed.

GK: Alright, what did the Mothman do? Why do we talk about him? What was the fallout from the Mothman? *Was* it the prophecies, and their uncanny coming to fruition?

AC: There were a couple of different things that were happening. There were these prophecies that people were having, visions they were seeing. And there were other paranormal things that were sort of going on, for which no one quite knows if the Mothman was responsible. Things such as animal and human mutilations, Men in Black sightings, UFO sightings... These kinds of thing were also going on. My interest with the documentary has mostly been to look at what happened to the witnesses *after* they had had their experiences. You find a lot of psychic things happening to them afterwards. They're basically able to *know* when things are going to happen – on an ongoing basis – for the rest of their lives. They also undergo creative changes, lifestyle changes, and that sort of thing.

GK: Alright, so those who had visually encountered this creature were touched in a certain way. Did they have any kind of enhanced powers? Did they have any kind of unusual circumstances, after the fact? Did this necessarily lead to their, shall we say, untimely death?

AC: There is actually very little to go on in terms of people dying. I think it was alluded to in the movie that there were Mothman witnesses on the Silver Bridge when it collapsed. That's another aspect of this story, that this bridge collapsed 13 months after the sightings started. People seemed to feel that the bridge collapse was connected to the Mothman, because Mothman was supposedly seen flying over the bridge that day. However a week before that, there had been men seen on the bridge, tinkering around with it. So whether or not the Mothman brought it down is an open question. I personally don't think the Mothman brought the bridge down. I think he was alerting us to something about the bridge. But it's really never been proven, as far as I know, that there were any more than a few people on the bridge that had seen Mothman, or had some connection to him. There's been a lot made of this, of course, with the Mothman Death Curse that Loren Coleman has been talking about... I think that this kind of morbid speculation may lead to some people believing that the Mothman caused all this. And that's certainly *not* what I think. If you look at the history of these birdmen throughout different cultures, they are generally seen as a positive force that is only scary when people first encounter it. Whenever we are forced to jump through hurdles in our lives, or cross obstacles in order to change for the better, there's almost always some perceived difficulty. Positive change usually seems scary at first. I think there is a symbology of that going on in the Mothman. There was also a third child involved directly with the sightings on the Burnhams' property. She's actually in my film quite a bit, doing different psychic readings and things. She's a very psychic person. In 2002, I was with her and my niece, who has also had a Mothman sighting. We went to this Mothman shrine spot and encountered an energy field. This is, again, at the same spot where we once had this precognition of 9/11. I tend to think that this spot has a history that goes way before us. But we encountered an energy field of some kind that you could see, very subtly. It was moving. There were lots of different physical effects that occurred, and we recorded everything. You can tell that there were some odd things going on, listening to the tape. We had a lot of sightings in Charleston in the 1960s and '70s that didn't make it into the newspaper. Lots of things were on TV, on the nightly news. I had fairly liberal parents, so I was able to watch the news at night. I would wait with baited breath to hear about the recent sightings. The TV reports wouldn't necessarily be in the newspaper. Nor are they in Keels' book. There are a couple of sightings from the area that *are* in Keels' book, but certainly not all of them. The total number of "official witnesses" is about 100. This is simply the number of witnesses Keel interviewed. Jeff Wamsley, who has written the book *Mothman: Behind the Red Eyes*, estimates another 100 in Point Pleasant who saw the Mothman but didn't report it. So we have at least 200 in Point Pleasant alone. I would imagine that many more saw it in Charleston.

GK: Has anyone ever captured any kind of photographic or videographic evidence?

AC: There have been a couple of photos that have been floating around that appear to be hoaxes – at least to me. There's one of a birdlike thing jumping off of a bridge in Huntington, West Virginia. There's a shot of something flying off of the World Trade Center as the planes hit, or after the planes hit. In the one I'm thinking of, the building is on the right and this thing is flying towards the left. To me it just looks like someone cut and pasted a flying man image.

GK: That's the same one I've seen. I think it's pretty much a hoax.

AC: Yes, but I think that there's something to this other photo, that my sister took. The nice thing about it is that it can be verified. It's not a digital file. It's an old photo from the 1970s that can be verified by Kodak…

GK: With all these sightings, does it seem to necessarily pertain to geographical West Virginia? I mean hasn't it been seen in Ohio, Virginia, Pennsylvania, and Maryland?

AC: Yes, and there were some sightings in 2002 in Western Pennsylvania, which got some press. There have been reports coming into the different Mothman discussion lists of sightings up the Ohio River towards Pittsburgh, and in Eastern Kentucky and Southeastern Ohio… We had a guy that I interviewed for the documentary who saw Mothman on the border of Florida and Georgia right after the 9/11 tragedy. I speculated in the documentary about what that might mean in terms of vote fraud links between FL, GA, and OH. There was a voting machine-linked murder near the location of the Mothman sighting.

GK: In ancient Indian lore and perhaps in other cultures, when one saw an owl, it was not a portent of good things to come. Is Mothman connected to this at all? Is it good that one should *not* see the Mothman?

AC: Well, this sort of gets back to the dichotomy I was talking about before, which is that it only *appears* to be something scary, that we should be afraid of… It is scary, yes, but it affects us differently later. I think there's some kind of interplay happening with this entity. Especially if it's an interdimensional entity, as John Keel believes, that interacts with the human mind... It changes you. I think that change is for the better. Once you get into looking at the Hindu cosmology of the Garuda, you see it in a different light. I think some of the other things that people tend to confuse with the Mothman are actually more linked to the death experience. These would be Men in Black, the large black dogs that people see, the black panthers... Historically, if you look at the Celtic lore, those entities are more related to the death experience.

GK: When you talk about Men in Black, we always think about men in suits. Is that what you're referring to?

AC: Yes, for the most part… The problem is that there has been a purposeful muddying of the waters. I think that some of these guys are government agents, and some are paranormal. For instance, when my father died (there's a whole story with my father and this phenomenon), he saw a Man in Black outside the hospital window. But my sister couldn't see the MIB. So my father was having a *vision* of the MIB. Now *that's* a definite death connection. However, I think these MIB that were seen in Point Pleasant – the ones wired for sound – were flesh and blood. They had wires running up their legs, and electronic equipment in their cars. They were probably Men in Black involved in some sort of covert operation.

GK: West Virginia is an extremely interesting state. I think there's a reason why the X-Files used it as a location for a lot of interesting governmental stuff. Like a lot of their predecessors (H.G. Wells and such), they wove into it some fiction, some ludicrous turns. That way, people would just dismiss it *all* as fiction. But what the [X-Files seemed to] center on in the state of West Virginia – the connection to the Rockefellers – is pretty [non-fictional] isn't it?

AC: Yes, it sure is. I think a lot of that goes back to the oil industry and how the Rockefellers controlled the state. The state got involved in chemical production very early on, prior to the turn of the 20th century. They were already building these large chemical plants in the 1890s, and forming the modern corporation. This is really where the state-capitalist corporate model was pioneered. The process of taking tax revenue and finding ways to funnel it through a corporation and into private hands… In the case of West Virginia, a lot of these corporations were owned not just by the Rockefellers, but also by their European partners. A lot of this money was going out of the country. Those who know anything about the coal industry know that a lot of the coal mines were owned by the British.

GK: Is that right? Are we talking about going back to the 18th century and such, or are you talking about even more modern day like the 19th century and the 20th century?

AC: I'm more or less talking about the beginnings. It's hard to find out who owns what today. It really is… If you look at the mergers and acquisitions that occur in the energy and chemical industries, it's just mind-blowing. There are hundreds and even thousands of transactions each year, with these companies trading parts of themselves to others. So if you were to go into Charleston now, and try to find out who owns the plants, you could never figure it out. That's sort of the Standard Oil model. It's a really secretive company, or series of companies. Some have said that it's more secretive than the CIA.

Some say that Standard is the "parent" of the CIA. That the CIA is an outgrowth of Standard and the (earlier) Dutch East India Company…

GK: I'll go along with that, no problem… You know, you talk about the Mothman Prophecies and it sounds like there was a particular person who elicited all these prophecies. But that's not necessarily so, is it? When one hears about the Mothman Prophecies, you're thinking about some kind of supernatural entity, a singular person or creature who is getting [or giving] these portending and ominous looks into the future. But that really isn't the case. The prophecies that are associated with the Mothman are not generated from a Mothman. Or are they?

AC: Well, that's a good question. If you look at the history of the Garuda and the way it's viewed, it is generally seen as a crime-fighting deity. So I've tried to use that model to sort of lay over the events, and see if it makes any sense. And it does... If you look at the various prophecies chronicled by Keel, a lot of them have to do with these great crimes, assassinations, and even terrorist events. I just started trying to figure out a theoretical progression. If the Mothman is a crime-fighting deity, maybe he's sending coded messages by appearing in certain places and at certain times. Perhaps he's encouraging people to have these visions... It appears to be an otherworldly process. Garuda is supposed to show up at critical times in mankind's history. I think a lot of us feel that we're sort of at this point where we could destroy ourselves with nuclear weapons and pollution. This could be a healing process in action, trying to reverse negative trends.

GK: Has there been a "latest" sighting, to your knowledge?

AC: There was one last year that was near the Willow Island Nuclear Plant, so maybe there is some sort of connection to a nuclear event coming up. But you know, it's difficult sometimes to know how far away some of these prophecies are. In the case of the 9/11 prophecy, it was experienced 34 years before the actual event happened... There was also a prophecy in 1967 of a blackout in New York City that everyone thought came true soon thereafter (the night Pres. Johnson lit the White House Christmas tree). But as I told Keel, that 1967 prophecy may have actually been a prophecy of the recent blackout that occurred in New York, just a couple of years ago. The 1967 blackout prophecy may relate to the "terror programming" we are now receiving via seemingly manufactured events such as 9/11, anthrax, DC Sniper, bird flu, and suspicious bombing scenarios recently in Madrid, London, and India.

When former Nazi Otto Skorzeny was interviewed in S. America (an interview which appeared in the Feral House book "Secret and Suppressed"), he stated that the postwar Nazi "Odessa" group likes to use Madrid and London as bases for modern terrorist actions. He claimed that they make big money on the stock market changes such events cause. The American and United Airlines "put options" sold on the NY stock exchange the day before 9/11 (involving Deutschebank and AIG) were never actually investigated, even though the national media repeatedly claimed that they "would get to the bottom of it."

GK: By the way, what was your take on Keel? I mean, his work is one that we have to consider fiction, is it not?

AC: The Mothman book and the movie are completely different animals. I think they had some real budget crunches happening with the movie. The movie is good, but is essentially a work of fiction.

GK: What about the book, then?

AC: The book is definitely *not* fiction.

GK: How did you take to Keel? Did you find him very passionate about this, and serious? I would assume so...

AC: He's passionate about a lot of things. He did a series of talks in the 1990s, about one a year. He would just sort of report on what he was studying. He covers a wide array of phenomena. As far as the Mothman goes, he's been pretty tight-lipped about it. I think he's only given about four talks on it. It was an honor to be able to interview him at length about it. It's not something he does very often.

GK: Did you live in West Virginia for any particular amount of time, or was your being there based directly on your doing a documentary?

AC: Oh yes, I lived there as a kid. I was born there and raised there until I left for college. I lived on the west edge of Charleston. It was actually called Mound in the early days, if you can believe that. There's a whole interesting history there with Mound. I've researched this, looking at the history of the valley. It turns out that the Kanawha Valley is the oldest valley in North America. The Ice Age changed most of the landscape 10,000 years ago. It changed the Ohio River, but it didn't affect the Kanawha. So you've got the oldest gorges there, and Mound was a gorge. It's now been damned up. I've looked at the history of the damning process for the river and that's a pretty fascinating story... They were planning these chemical plants back in the 1800s. They were bringing in French and German technicians to build the dams, and these dams were state-of-the art, modern dams. They were doing things on them that they hadn't even done in Europe. But they dammed up the river. And in the middle of the river, there at Mound, was an island that at one time must have been 100 feet high. It must have been just a big, tall spike in the middle of the river. This area had hundreds of Indian mounds. Some mounds were for the dead, but other mounds were not. Regardless of the mounds' function, the Indians would have been canoeing upstream. Once you got to Charleston, the falls in the river became so high that you couldn't go up any further. So if they were looking for a sacred spot, Mound would have been as far as they could go easily to deposit any bodies, or have major ceremonies...

GK: I've heard about the mounds out in the Midwest as well. I've known people that have lived there. Have you heard the piece of lore that a tornado will never touch down on an Indian burial ground? That's what they say out there. They say that in Ohio, too. But when they talk about the prophecies, where do the prophecies come from? Why is that always connected to the Mothman?

AC: Well, if you look again look at the history of the Garuda, you have a Messiah-like deity that came before Christ, which has a lot of similarities to Christ actually (and I've gotten into some heated debates over this issue with Christians). There appears to be a paranormal source from which all these religions spring. There's a book, by a theologian named Kersey, called *The Sixteen Saviors*. Apparently there were 16 "messiahs" that came before Christ. Like Christ, the Garuda is there to change things for the better… Of course, the Garuda would most likely have to use human agents for that betterment process, just as Christ used his disciples. All of these ancient messiahs are connected with prophecies. So there's a long, long history of prophecies being used to change the direction of the human race, via human agents who receive the messages. I think that seeing this Birdman could, depending on the level of interaction one has with it, be that kind of process happening.

GK: Can you give us a little bit of a thumbnail of what took place on that bridge back in what was it, December of '67? First of all, tell us what happened on that night or that evening... It was, I guess, right after 5:00 PM?

AC: Yes, the bridge was full with Christmas shoppers. It was a very cold night. I remember that quite well. I remember when it happened, when the news came over… It was shocking. Most of the shoppers drowned. Strangely, there were some locals who had had visions of floating packages in the water, prior to the event. People had had various prophetic dreams in advance. One was Mary Hyre, who was the reporter there. She wrote most of the original articles. She was writing for the Athens (Ohio) Messenger newspaper. She had dreamed of these floating packages. There were other oddities. People were on the bridge as they were every day at rush hour, but on this day, the stoplight was "broken." So the traffic was moving very slowly…

GK: So that meant that there were probably more vehicles on the bridge than might normally have been?

AC: Yes, but we had men tinkering with the bridge a few days before. This makes me wonder if this light wasn't out for a reason, perhaps to monitor the bridge and see who was on the bridge at any given time. They might have been looking for a particular vehicle to be on the bridge. If somebody did actually sabotage this bridge, then that light being out could be a clue.

GK: In other words, it would have been part of the whole scenario.

AC: It could be... That would explain why Marcella Bennett's uncle saw Mothman flying above the bridge just prior to the collapse.

GK: Alright... So [assuming] that it's a benign creature, it was [only] trying to alert. It was not necessarily responsible for [the collapse]. If anything, it was perhaps trying to tell people "something's up." Is that correct?

AC: Yes.

GK: Now, I'm going to ask you two questions. The first one is, exactly what was the official story about what happened to the bridge to cause its collapse on that December 15th evening?

AC: The 13th I-beam bolt failed. That was the official explanation.

GK: And nobody had any idea beforehand that there was any kind of stress occurring, that would result in this catastrophic failure?

AC: Well, that's hard to know because, first of all, we don't know who it was that was inspecting the bridge – if that's what they were really doing. One would think that if the bridge were inspected, that there would have been some report of that. On the other hand, it could be a cover-up in that the bridge was indeed inspected and found to have problems, yet nothing was done. In order to not have a big uproar, they just sort of covered that up. That could be another explanation.

GK: All right, now the other thing that peaked my interest, given the fact that we deal with conspiracies... After four years of dealing with people who commit suicide with three self-inflicted gunshot wounds, I have to ask you: who might have been targeted for a hit on that bridge that night?

AC: Looking at the context of what was happening at that time in West Virginia, you had a lot of labor unrest. My father was on strike at the time. He worked for Union Carbide, and there was a lot of pretty radical talk going on in union circles then. He actually told me that there were guys talking about blowing up the chemical plant. So you have a really serious situation... I think there had to have been a response to that from the owners of the company, in one form or another. There were a lot of suspicious deaths that occurred. There were disappearances and suppression... It doesn't necessarily mean that worker sabotage is what occurred with the Silver Bridge. It may have been someone with a financial interest in building the new bridge. For background on who that might have been, there was a famous economist who worked on JFK's staff. His name was Peter D. Beter. He wrote a book back in the 1970s called *The Conspiracy Against the Dollar*. He died in the 1980s. He was a conspiracy theorist of sorts, who had a radio program at the time. He was the father of the Fort Knox gold conspiracy. He actually ran against Jay Rockefeller for governor of West Virginia. My mother loved Beter because she loved his name and his whole conspiracy angle. He believed that the gold was being shuffled out of Fort Knox by some organizations connected to the Rockefellers. If that were the case, then that gold might have been moving up the Ohio. It is possible that there was a truck full of gold on the Silver Bridge that made it collapse, or someone who needed to be silenced about the gold or the MIBs. There are a lot of different possibilities that one could go into...

GK: Honestly, I don't think Beter was [simply] a theorist. I think he probably had it pretty well down. I don't think there's anything in Fort Knox these days anyway, but of course that's just what I think.

AC: Beter did a wonderful tape cassette series that he mailed out to people. He was a lot like Gray Barker. He had a following of people around the country, and he would produce these tapes and send them around. You can actually find transcripts of them on the web if you do a search. They're fascinating... He brings in some angles that are rarely covered by other researchers, such as theories about the White Russians in league with the Israelis...

This belief is also echoed in the work of JFK researcher Michael Collins Piper, who argues that Meyer Lansky and the Jewish mob managed the gambling and drug trades. According to Piper, back in the 1950s and '60s, a healthy percentage of "skim" monies from the casinos and rackets flowed to the secret atomic bomb project of the fledgling state of Israel. JFK's refusal to support Israel and the huge "oil depletion allowances" flowing to Big Oil ultimately led to his assassination.

AC: Beter was really intent on looking at the influence of this power bloc, which certainly was in play in the Ohio Valley. We had a lot of spy activity going on in Ohio and West Virginia then. The FBI had a KGB general on their payroll. His name was Alexander Orlov, and he was in Cleveland. There are a lot of connections to Cleveland in some of these Mothman conspiracies. In fact the famous Man in Black, Indrid Cold, who supposedly was from the planet Lanulos, is now said to have actually *moved* to Cleveland! Taunia Derenberger, the daughter of Woody Derenberger (the famous contactee involved in the Mothman story), has recently stated on discussion lists that Mr. Cold moved to Cleveland after the Mothman events. To me, this sort of implies that maybe Cold wasn't *really* from Lanulos.

GK: How did this capture you? Was it because you lived there? I mean you're now decades removed from it. What has kept you so involved in what took place in West Virginia four decades ago?

AC: It started with a friend who had this 9/11 precognition. He claimed that the Mothman was coming to his home. He also said that aliens were coming to his home, and that the aliens had predicted parts of his life in advance. He claimed that he *knew* what he was going to do when he became an adult. And it turns out that he did know! He was supposed to work for NASA (according to the aliens) and it turned out that he *did* work for NASA. His mother later worked for NASA, too. This kid had really special qualities. He was extremely intelligent. He tested as a genius at age eight (with a score of 172). We all seemed to have increases in our IQ levels after this stuff happened. We had half a dozen geniusy kids in my fourth grade class. So I always remembered that. It was very odd. Then we had a UFO superflap in the early seventies that resulted in my sister taking a possible photo of Mothman. We had another superflap in the late '70s that seems to have been a vehicle, of sorts, for my dead father (or some other entity) to make a ghostly appearance in a crop circle. I was going to school at Marshall University in Huntington, West Virginia in the late 1970s. There were some strange things there, too, that seemed related to Mothman. There's a whole Manson clan that reportedly hangs out near Huntington. In the early '80s, we had a resurgence of things occurring. I found out that Charles Manson and Sara Jane Moore had both lived on our street, and that the two had known each other as children. They may have even dated. There was actually a guy interviewed on TV about this. This is what sparked my interest in it as an adult. I saw this guy on TV say, "Yes, Sara Jane Moore and Charlie Manson used to come into my store holding hands." His store was right at the end of our street. This got me going again. I started reading up on Manson, UFOs, and that whole paranormal genre. But it wasn't until '93 that I found Keel's book, so I've only been aware of Keel's angles on it for a few years.

GK: Can you imagine living in a neighborhood with Charlie? What a hoot that would be...

AC: Sara Jane Moore lived right next to our grade school where, like I said, we had all these genius kids. The military actually came and checked out our progress to some degree. We had a very radical school for the time period. It was given funds by RFK, via something called the Appalachian Project. We were given a bunch of money to have an experimental school. One day a "documentary" crew came to interview us all, and there was an Air Force officer supervising the process. So there's more there than meets the eye. There were some odd things going on there...

"In the Acts of the Apostles, the story of Paul's conversion describes a series of manifestations that have occurred repeatedly in modern times with only minor variations. Surprisingly, these manifestations are largely ignored today, even by the theologians who complain that "God is dead" and that the wonders of biblical times have long since ceased. We are, in fact, surrounded by the same kind of happenings that were once regarded as miracles. Saul of Tarsus set out on the road to Damascus to join a battle against the growing Christian cult. At high noon on the desert, a blinding light "above the sun" appeared suddenly, and Saul fell flat on his face, possibly going into a trance. The men traveling with him reportedly heard a voice but saw nothing. When Saul arose, or regained consciousness, he was blinded. He remained blind for three days. Then Ananias, a Christian who had visions, was guided to Saul, touched him, and cured his blindness instantly. Impressed, Saul gave up his hobby – killing Christians – and changed his name to Paul. He was instrumental in spreading Christianity…

"Blinding aerial lights from an unknown source still appear hundreds of times each year, and thousands of witnesses have suffered temporary conjunctivitis similar to the eyeburn you can experience on a beach if you don't protect your eyes from the sun. This is caused by the ultraviolet actinic rays, which can also tan your skin. Loyal flying-saucer fans around the world have documented innumerable cases of this. An even more curious effect of these "meandering nocturnal lights," as the U.S. Air Force calls them, is temporary deafness, probably caused by high-frequency ultrasonic waves generated by rapid pulsation. It is not unusual for witnesses to such lights to lapse into epileptic-type trances and experience elaborate hallucinations. Some see horrible monsters, while others see space creatures, angels, and great luminous godlike beings.

"All great religions and countless fringe cults began with the exposure of a single person to this phenomenon. Saul, Daniel, and other biblical personages saw luminous phenomena at the outset of their adventures, usually falling on their faces or passing out. While in this condition they received messages and accurate prophecies. Later, when they passed the prophecies on to their friends and followers, and those predictions came true right on the nose, they felt the holiness of their condition had been proven. The ranks of their followers grew. It was this process that inspired the spread of Christianity."

-John A. Keel, "The Eighth Tower"

Note: On Feb. 24, 2007, after editing this chapter, I noticed the name "Ananias" in the Keel quote above. This is coincidentally the name of someone I mentioned in a post that same day. He was a Catholic friend of mine from Charleston who had made skeptical public comments about the Mothman saga. Interestingly, this name is very similar to "manaia," the Maori name for the Garuda. It comes from the same etymological root as "man," "mound," "mania," "manic," "monster," and so forth. If we etymologically reinterpret the Apostle Paul story, we see Saul or "Sol" (the sun) of "Torus" (the building block dodecahedron shape undergirding our physical universe) having his "blindness" removed by "manaias" (the Garuda). Garuda cools the fires of Indra. Man soaks up the rays of the sun. This "light of language" inside symbol — as represented in shapes like the torus — is seen in the very fabric of nature, and is indestructible. You can see it in the shapes inside of a honeycomb, or on the back of every turtle (my childhood obsession).

Oddly, as I was writing to this, I misspelled "manaia" as "mananaia." Just as I was typing the misspelling into the computer, I heard a phrase being sung from the song "Rakim" by Dead Can Dance. It was that very word, "mananaia," the misspelling! The song is sung in some Asian language, so I'm not sure what the song is about. The next song after that (on a live DCD album recorded Oct. 1, 2005) is called "The Black Sun." The Black Sun is the feminine earth force emanating from the center of the earth. It was worshipped by the Nazis and lies at the root of the Montauk mystery, according to Peter Moon. Before starting the Black Sun song, the DCD singer makes a reference to trance programming by saying, "Your wish is my command." Incredibly, the first line of the song is "Burn! Man on fire!" This is exactly what happened to the sailors at the Philadelphia Experiment, who had soaked up the wrong rays. The Mandaeans of ancient Iran/Iraq, whose name is similar to "manaia," worshipped a Peacock Angel later referenced by Aleister Crowley and the Ordo Templi Orientis. I was also obsessed with peacocks as a child - in addition to the turtles. The Peacock Angel was known to help people, not unlike Philip K. Dick's earth-orbiting VALIS, which he claimed helped him regain monies from uncollected book royalties.

CHAPTER 2

As a prelude to understanding how the Mothman saga connects to the Philadelphia Experiment of 1943, we transcribed the following rare audio reports from Gray Barker, West Virginia's famous UFO publisher of the 1950s and 60s. Barker holds the honor of being the first writer to popularize the Men In Black. He also was responsible for keeping the Philadelphia Experiment lore alive following the death of Morris K. Jessup in 1959. Today, Barker materials are very rare, selling for incredible prices when they happen to come up for sale. As an example, worn copies of Barker's Mothman "hoax" book, "The Silver Bridge," often sell for well over $300. Interestingly, the most rare Barker book is the highly conspiratorial "Men In Black: The Secret Terror Among Us," written in 1983. This was Barker's last book, coming well after the Senate investigations of the 1970s exposing black ops and mind control. One gets the clear sense that Barker was coming around to the government conspiracy angles later in his life. Perhaps he felt it safer to wait until the very end before pointing at the dangerous truth?

Barker, Gray – Report on the Philadelphia Experiment – 1981

Well, hello to my friends and correspondents everywhere. This is Gray Barker, and this tape is being made available as a part of the dissemination of my research into the mysteries of the Allende letters, the apparent suicide of Doctor M.K. Jessup in 1959, the "annotated edition" of Jessup's *The Case for the UFO*, and other matters that still remain mysteries and are of great interest to serious students of ufology. Now this recording is just being made informally. It's not being read. It's just from a few notes, so I hope you will pardon the way it's made. It's just as if I would be sitting here talking to you about this… That is how I would like to proceed.

Some of you listening to this tape have already read the annotated edition of *The Case for the UFO* by Dr. M.K. Jessup. The facsimile edition that I reprinted, and have been distributing, for some years now… Those of you who have read this, I'm sure this tape will mean a great deal more to you than those who haven't. To those who are thoroughly familiar with Jessup, Allende, the alleged disappearing ship, etc., I would hope that you pardon me while I just sketch out a few things, briefly (in case the person listening to this tape is not too familiar with these things).

The mystery of the annotated edition started back in 1955, when Bantam Books published a paperback of Dr. Jessup's book *The Case for the UFO*.

Well, that wasn't too mysterious... But it *was* [mysterious] when a copy of this book was mailed into Washington, to the Office of Naval Research. There was a lot of peculiar scribbling in this book in three shades of blue ink, evidently written by three different mysterious people, calling themselves Mr. A, Mr. B, and Gemi. These annotations were almost alien in their character, very strange, and we don't know how they came about. But for some reason, possibly because of his allusions to a secret naval experiment, this book surfaced in a very peculiar edition, sometime afterward.

A company in Garland, Texas was given this annotated edition by the military, and in the office of this firm (which manufactured electronic gear for the military) it was laboriously typed on offset stencils. The annotations that were written in it were printed in a different color of ink. If you've seen the annotated edition, you know what I mean. Then, a limited number of copies of these were distributed.

> *These books were labeled as being made by the VARO Corporation,*
> *a defense contractor specializing in infrared devices. Could there be a*
> *connection to the Canadian AVRO Corporation? As can be readily seen*
> *in archival footage recently aired by the Discovery Channel, AVRO built*
> *Nazi-inspired flying saucer designs in the 1960s.*

Also in this book were reproduced some very strange letters that Jessup had received from a Carl M. Allen, or Carlos Miguel Allende, previous to the annotations being sent in. The most interesting thing about these letters was that they described an experiment that allegedly took place at sea, during which a destroyer – with all its crew – became invisible (due to the utilizing of the principles of Einstein's Unified Field Theory). According to these letters, the experiment went wrong in some ways. Some of the crew froze and were unable to recover from the invisibility imposed by the strange field. [Some] could be brought back [only] by a strange "laying-on of hands" ceremony by crewmembers, or by sophisticated equipment hurriedly readied after the experiment went awry.

For years, people had heard about copies of this book but had never seen one. After I obtained a copy and reprinted it, however, it's more generally known. A great many questions began to surface. For one thing, who was Carlos Miguel Allende? Did he actually exist? Was he one of the people who annotated the strange copy of the paperback sent into Washington? Well, no one could prove anything because no one could locate Allende. The mystery just went along. However, during the last couple of years, Allende (or at least a man claiming to be Allende) suddenly surfaced and began to show up and talk to people, and write letters to people. Finally, I was able to have a meeting with Allende in the company of fellow researcher James W. Moseley. We asked him some questions and he consented that we record his answers on a tape. One of the amazing revelations that came from Allende was that he did the *complete* annotations (so he claimed) by being able to write in three different handwriting styles. I don't know if this proves that this man we're going to hear is the actual Allende. The mystery of that, and the research that has been done, would take up far too much time…

What actually *did* happen at the Philadelphia Naval Yard in 1943, and possibly in continuing experiments? We cannot be absolutely sure because, evidently, this has been a matter carried out in utmost secrecy. [It is] a matter protected by [probably more] secrecy than the A-bomb when it was being developed. Let's try to review what we can deduce from several sources. First of all, of course, are the letters from Allende to Dr. Morris K. Jessup (which we will talk about just a little later), which first broke the story about the experiment. Since that time has come the research of William Moore and Charles Berlitz. Moore has uncovered some actual witnesses to this thing and, although some of them will not permit themselves to be identified, a lot of things are falling into place. I think that we can pretty well get a picture of what actually happened there.

According to all of this evidence, the Navy evidently was conducting an experiment in which they were attempting to attain radar invisibility. [This is] somewhat like the project that has been leaked recently, called Project Stealth, whereby an aircraft is not maybe [totally] invisible to radar, but at least partially invisible to radar. They were trying to build some sort of a radar shield to protect their ships from Nazi [attacks] in our shipping lanes. The way they set about to accomplish this apparently was to use principles of Einstein's Unified Field Theory, and to construct huge degaussing devices to possibly create a shield of invisibility to radar. But apparently when this [degausser] was turned on, more happened than what the scientists and the military authorities had reckoned. According to witnesses, a blue sort of haze first seemed to engulf the ship, and then it suddenly became invisible. Only its imprint in the water was visible. Apparently, the people conducting this experiment were rather shocked by all this and turned it off as quickly as possible, but not before severe psychological damage was done to the crew aboard the ship. This may be the thing that has led the military to clamp the secrecy lid on this, because this could be a very embarrassing thing to reveal. Men may have suffered irreparable psychological and physical damage.

According to what we can learn, the crewmembers suddenly saw some very frightening phenomena. According to Allende in one of his letters, this electromagnetic field was effective "in an oblique, spheroidal shape extending 100 yards out from each end of the ship." Any person within that sphere became vague in form. He observed others aboard the ship [who] appearing to be walking upon *nothing*. Apparently what the crew saw was very, very weird. Their fellow crewpersons [were] apparently walking on thin air. Some rumors even have it that while in this invisible state they became involved in some other dimension, and that they saw strange creatures that were not human, that possibly had something to do with the UFO phenomena. Of course these rumors have a way of growing but, according to Allende (and other sources), even after the device was turned off, the crewpeople suffered not only the psychological shocks of entering this invisible state, but also the after-effects. According to Allende, without warning, these people – maybe for weeks and months afterwards – would suddenly become invisible. Some are said to have disappeared even permanently. One of them walked right through the wall of his house and [was] never seen again.

Now, I know you're holding onto your hats, and this is very difficult to believe. It's very difficult for me to believe. I can't help but think that maybe this has been built up too much, that the rumors have grown so far that what we get is a very distorted picture. Especially the [next] part of the story, which is *really* too fantastic to be believed... It is said that while the ship was in the invisible state at the Philadelphia Naval Yard, it showed up at another naval yard in Norfolk, Virginia. It suddenly reappeared there – where it shouldn't be – to the amazement of several observers who happened to be looking at that portion of the bay. Then, almost as suddenly as it appeared at Norfolk, Virginia, it disappeared. According to Allende, who is the main source for this rumor, the ship was actually teleported not through design, but through some accidental affect of the experiment that no one predicted. A vessel weighing thousands of tons, according to this rumor, was just picked up and made to vanish and to reappear, almost instantly, several hundred miles away – almost something out of Star Trek or science fiction movies.

But despite the terrific unbelievability of all of this, the rumor has persisted and proof has grown, particularly in the last few years. Researchers have become interested in this again, after not believing there was anything to it for several years. They also apparently believed that Allende didn't exist and was a hoax of some sort. I disproved this by locating Allende and getting his voice on a tape...

Barker, Gray – Interview with Carlos Allende – 1978

Gray Barker (GB): Doubt has been expressed as to whether there is an Allende, or whether Allende has disappeared. What I would like for you to do is identify yourself on the tape, so that people can be sure that they are indeed hearing Allende.

Carlos Allende (CA): Mi nombre es Sr. Carlos Miguel Allende de Allende, de ciudad Guadalajara, estado de Jalisco, Mexico, senor. At your service…

GB: Excellent… Now, Allende has been associated in the minds of a great many ufologists as the author of certain annotations in the book *The Case for the UFO*. Would you identify yourself as the author of those annotations?

CA: I can, and I will. See here on my right long finger… It is hard, as you two witnesses here, James Moseley and Gray Barker, can see. It is hard and the top of it has been munched off. The nail has been smashed. I could not use that finger, the index finger, to write with in a normal fashion. This finger was done in during a shipwreck of the *S.S. Byron Duncan* right below the Sand Island Lighthouse, on March the 6th of 1946. As this finger was in such bad condition, it obviously became necessary for me to shift the position of my pen so that that finger will not [touch anything. It was] tender and painful. [I was] lifting it off the surfaces slightly. So I shifted my pen so that it would be between the long finger and the index finger. In this fashion, I learned to write in three different handwritings, using different forms of capital and small letters. Using this type of handwriting, as well as the normal form of handwriting, I was able to [create] the difference in penmanship… I wrote those annotations so as to cause science – through its tender pride – to feel woefully behind the times, to be urged to greater efforts to advance and raise its level of knowledge (which surely they did during the years after I wrote my annotations). I discovered only a few years or so ago, from members of the academic community – with which I regularly and often associate – that these [better] years were caused mostly by those annotations…

GB: Well, how did the academic and scientific community become aware of these annotations? How did they find out about them? Tell us how that book was distributed, and how the scientists came to know about it…

CA: Yes, well, in the front of that book, they say [the copies] were made for the scientists of the old Bureau of Naval Research and Development, and for colleagues (as in professors) who were also interested in forcefield functions, dynamics, and physics. As well as to industries contracted to the old Bureau of Naval Research and Development… The president of the VARO Manufacturing Company told me that they printed 116 copies. I received two. Jessup received three. I destroyed my first copy because it was then, and still possibly is today, some of the world's most dangerous literature... There were at least 116 copies made. However, I later discovered that there were additional [ones] that were printed for the Office of Naval Research, many years after the old Bureau of Naval Research and Development had printed the first 116. Therefore, the Naval Officer who swore to Charles Berlitz that experimentation in invisibility is still going on was telling the logical truth. Especially since bout 25 months ago... During the Soyuz/Apollo missions, an invisible star was found radiating in the 390-Angstrom region of the ultraviolet [spectrum. It had] such strong forcefield density that it proves my own statements of the past quarter-century, that invisibility can be achieved by using forcefields and knowledge from Einstein's second Unified Field Theory (as well as unified and ultraviolet light). My statement that this can be done is proven to be true by the discovery of that star. There is no reason, therefore, for me to remain hidden away in Old Mexico anymore. I come forth and rise above the surface, and present myself to the public for this reason. I want the public to know [that] there really is a great benefit to be achieved from forcefield research, and to not condemn the Navy for trying to protect their secrets. Companies and corporations – even your own self – have personal secrets [to] protect. Why condemn someone else for having and protecting their secrets...?

GB: I'd like to ask a question now, Mr. Allende. There is talk that you saw a ship disappear during an experiment, which I believe some people have referred to as The Philadelphia Experiment. [They say that] you were an actual witness to it. I wonder if you would confirm that. And if you can confirm it, would you describe the incident for us?

CA: I would like to say here and now that anything and everything I say will be regarded, always and forever (by the scientific and academic community), as nothing more than pure hearsay. [They claim that] this has never been validated, confirmed, verified, nor corroborated [yet] nobody – not one of you so-called "scientists" in the pseudo-science of ufology – has lifted a little finger to attempt to confirm, corroborate, validate and verify what I have been saying for almost a quarter of a century... You accept my word alone? What am I, a fountain of wisdom? An authority? Let us face the simple fact that what I tell you *is* true, but you are going to be laughed at forever unless you yourself go and do – really *do* – the research that logically needs to be done to verify, confirm, corroborate, and validate the statements that I make. I know that you doubt what I have said. I *want* you to doubt. I want you to doubt enough so as to go ahead and see for yourselves whether what I have been saying for nearly a quarter of a century is so, or not so. I am old, in the 53rd year of my life, weak, emaciated, sick, and perhaps quite probably not too long to live. I may die soon from these sicknesses that I have. I say *yes*, I saw [the ship] (the DE 173) become invisible right before my eyes. *Right before my eyes...* But I am not the only witness. You intelligent people, you brilliant geniuses never thought that there would be other witnesses in a whole convoy full of 107 or more ships? Right over my head, in the gun top, were Navy gunners from the Armed Guards who sailed on the same ships with us. There were Army personnel aboard that ship, too. There were witnesses who witnessed this same thing. They saw it at the same time I did, at approximately 5:05 in the afternoon on a nice, clear, sunshiny day. [It was a] beautiful lovely day, no other cloud to speak of in the sky... In convoy, each ship must be 500 feet from the other ship. The stern must be 500 feet from the bow of the ship behind it, and vice versa. Those sailors on the ship in front of us (whatever the name of the ship was), I saw them watching us. Watching with their eyes the same thing that I saw occurring before my eyes... The DE173 became invisible within that five-minute period of time. However, I am not the only witness in the world. Go! Christ, man... Go find those other witnesses! Find the name of that convoy. Find the name of the ships in the convoy, and then get a list of all the crewmembers. To do this, you must first find the ship's articles. It is a pink piece of paper, or pasteboard, that has a name of all the ship's crewmembers. Then get the ship's logs, in which the names and addresses of those crewmembers on my ship (the *S.S. Andrew Furuseth*) are listed. Then go into the Navy records and find out [about] Voyage Number 3 that began on October the 18th, 1943, from the Norfolk Hampton Roads shipping area... Find the Navy records for the names and home addresses of the Navy Armed Guard gunners [and] gunnery personnel... Find the plot showing the position of each ship in that convoy, and find the position of the *S.S. Andrew Furuseth* as we crossed eastward, across the Atlantic (after that great hurricane). Find the name of the ship in front of the *S.S. Andrew Furuseth* and there, on that ship, you will find many other witnesses. [Identify] the two ships immediately to portside, in the other lane of ships. Get the names and addresses of the merchant and naval personnel aboard those ships, as well as the Army supercargo officer that always traveled on every merchant ship. We had Army personnel being taken to war. Get their names, too. Get all of these witnesses. Don't look at me as if I am a fountain of wisdom, an authority to be accepted by all of science. Let us face the simple fact [that] until two years ago when they discovered the invisible star, any statement I made was [seen as] ludicrously ridiculous poppycock. Preposterous...

Let us face the simple fact that science still is imbued and suffused – impregnated with – the idea that anything any ufologist says is a lot of tommyrot. You must do this research, or you fail yourselves. You will make yourselves look stupidly ridiculous, and fail to validate the science of ufology...

CHAPTER 3

Traveler, our paths have crossed again. Your feet look sore, like mine, traveler. I have come a long way and I have seen mysterious things. My friend, if you are near the Philadelphia Naval Yard and see a group of sailors in the strange act of putting their hands upon a fellow or upon apparent thin air, hasten not to pass. Pause for a while, my friend. Instead, observe... Observe the appendages of this stricken man. If they seem to waver as if they were in a heat mirage, go quickly and put your hands upon him also, for that man is the most desperate of men in this world. He is caught in "the freeze." Use caution, caution... The tale is told that once, when the hapless victim had metal upon his person, he froze and then caught fire. When another came for the laying of hands, he, too, caught fire. And so they burned for 18 days... The faith in handling died that day, and men's minds went by the scores. The Philadelphia Experiment had been a great success, but the men were complete failures. Good day, my friend. Good luck on your journey. And now I must be on.

-Gray Barker's introduction to the following broadcast

Barker, Gray – PA-X Meets The Bermuda Triangle – 1981

I'm Gray Barker. I was trying to disguise my voice just a bit to bring you some of the drama of the legend of the Philadelphia Experiment. Surely it's out of sync with time and reason, and these words reverberate across the years like the crazy chicken-scratch scrawls of Mr. A, Mr. B, and Gemi, who penned their otherworldly annotations in delicate shades of blue, blue-green, and blue-violet.

"Si, senor," a wizened, Latin-looking little man with a patronizing smile chimes agreeably, as you ask if he is Carlos Allende. Invite him to lunch and you will hear his tale. Or don't ask him, and you will hear it anyhow... For like the ancient mariner, doomed with a story he must forever tell, Allende is cursed with an endless and repetitive recitation. Even though his rhyme may have reason, and even though Allende indeed may actually have been one of the crew caught in a terrifying experiment and suffered the horrors of invisibility, the albatross around his neck consigns him to a hell even worse than the burning...

Ulysses cleverly used the alias "No-Man" to escape with his men from the cave of the Cyclops. Allende, or Allen, or whoever he might be, was not so fortunate, for it came about that like Cassandra (whose prophecies were true but never believed), Allende could never recover his identity. [But] Carlos Allende [was] the man who really broke the story on the Philadelphia Experiment and was responsible for the many people (including myself) who have investigated it and tried to find out what actually happened. This culminated in the successful book *The Philadelphia Experiment* by William Moore and Charles Berlitz (also author of *The Bermuda Triangle*).

Let's listen to a recording of Berlitz as he sets the stage for us...

James Moseley [into "Electro-Voice" microphone]: Charles Berlitz is the author of *The Bermuda Triangle* and the bestseller *The Philadelphia Experiment: Project Invisibility*. Berlitz contends that in 1943, US Navy scientists succeeded in making a Navy destroyer and all its crew literally disappear. The ship vanished from the Philadelphia Naval Yard and reappeared within minutes in Norfolk, Virginia, before again reappearing back in Philadelphia. The alleged facts in this story lead us straight to the threshold of undiscovered worlds. In his lecture, Mr. Berlitz will show how the mysterious natural force behind these events is related to the force that has caused so many ships and planes to disappear in that part of the world known as the Bermuda Triangle.

Berlitz, Charles – The Philadelphia Experiment – 1980

Charles Berlitz: Thank you very much, Jim. As far as UFOs and extra-terrestrials are concerned, I think that there is now proximity... We have heard countless reports as far as the Philadelphia Experiment is concerned.

[Shows slide of ship] This is a picture of the DE173, the destroyer in question. [According to] scuttlebutt from workers, sailors, and officers in the Naval Yard, it [was the] object of an experiment in 1943 that unwittingly produced invisibility. This [experiment] was done by [using] tremendous degaussers at each end of the dock where the destroyer was moored, to a point where resonant magnetism was reached and the destroyer sort of shifted off into invisibility. Now of course, one might well ask, "Why make a destroyer invisible?"

Well, this was done in 1943 when things were not looking very well for us in the world situation, and there were several things that were done at the same time. There was an experiment in antigravity, which was carried on by different members of the National Defense Research Counsel. *There was a sort of "deathray" that was being experimented on.* And there was another experiment, even more fantastic of all. That was separating the atom to make a bomb... That one was eminently successful. I think that this research, which has come about fairly recently, will prove that this other experiment was successful too, in a way. It wasn't successful as far as the people were concerned, but it was certainly successful in its basic purpose.

[New slide] Now this is the Philadelphia Navy Yard where the research was carried on, and this is the Anacosia Research Center, near Washington, where the experiment was thought of in the first place. [It is] where the initial experimentation was carried out.

Now many of you may have heard that Einstein and others were connected with this experiment. Of course what you're really talking about in this experiment is Einstein's use of Unified Field, the experiment that he never quite finished (but which would have been a combination of his other experiments). He talked this over with Lord Russell before the war, and Lord Russell said that he didn't think mankind was ready for it as yet. Man wouldn't be ready for it until after *World War III* (this was before World War II).

Briefly, what the concept is – if you can possibly put it in one sentence – is that mass, energy, time, and space are not the carefully separated little packages we [normally] seem to consider them, but perhaps *the same thing*. This thing can be affected by the proper amount of magnetic resonance, or magnetic change, or uncertainty. In other words, somewhere between electronics and electromagnetics is a way of changing matter, and projecting matter through time and through space.

[In] 1939, the National Defense Research Center used our own scientists such as Forester Brown and Dr. Kent, *and* German scientists including Battenberg, Dr. Albrecht, Einstein, Von Neumann, and others. All worked on Einstein's theory of changing matter. Although it didn't quite start out that way... It started off as an understandable desire to create invisibility in service ships... One of the ones who contributed most (Von Battenberg) was a submarine commander in World War I, so you never know where people will end up.

First, a certain amount of experimentation was taking place at the Taylor Naval Base with [the] possibilities of camouflage. According to what we have been able to find out, a special magnetic resonancy [was created] to see if a ship could be detected from radar and sonar [after] making a cloud of ionization around the ship. Theoretically, if the ship was charged by pulsating and non-pulsating magnetism at both ends, a sort of cloud of ionization could [form] around the ship.

Well, what happened wasn't quite *that*. What happened was that, as the brass and the scientists watched the ship (which was a manned ship at the dock of Philadelphia), it became sort of misty. Then it sort of flashed off, like a reverse of neon lighting when you shift it on. There's sort of a burst, except that this was in reverse. A sort of fog built up, which was expected due to the field of ionization. But then, the ship vanished! To the surprise of everyone, when the cloud vanished there was no ship there. But according to people that were on the ship, and according to other observers who saw it from the land, a ship [then] *materialized* under a cloud at Norfolk, several miles down the river (where this same ship, the DE173, already had a berth). The people onboard the ship saw Norfolk. People on the dock saw the ship.

And then suddenly, a cloud flashed on again. [The DE173] came back again, to the astonishment of everyone in Philadelphia.

The S.S. Eldridge, or DE173, in 1951. The ship had fake papers and was later sold to the Greeks and renamed The S.S. Leon. The Greek connection reminds one of other tangential connections in the Mothman case, such as the Greek "mob" invasion of Pt. Pleasant in 1966 and Onassis' (and Big Oil's) takeover of the Hughes empire - the Gemstone File thesis. Gemstone describes an international web of political assassination, mind control, lasers, nukes, gambling, entertainment, and sex.

What happened to the people onboard? They were psychiatrically affected. Some of them became terribly nervous, depressed. Others [literally] disappeared. There were many stories of what had happened to the sailors onboard because, after all, what we are talking about is a change in the molecular composition. This magnetism suddenly caused a rearrangement of the molecules, causing people and ship to become invisible and be teleported to another point, and then snapped back again. Well, you can imagine the effects on the people. They shifted off again. They'd go home to dinner and suddenly disappear from the table. They'd be walking down the street with their friends [and] they would disappear. One of the strangest reports of this appeared in a Camden, NJ, newspaper we have been able to find. Apparently there was a big fight in a bar about 2 or 3 days after the experiment took place. The sailors fought some of the townspeople, and while the fight was going on – because of the stress – they reverted to invisibility (which of course was very useful in the fight because they would come up in back of their assailants). By the time the police and the shore patrol arrived on the scene, the girls, the onlookers, and the bartenders were in a state of semi-hysteria, because the people in the fight kept disappearing.

Of course, something like this was extremely important from a security viewpoint at the time. They were able to keep it quiet from scientists, the hired brass, and officers in general, but you couldn't keep the dockworkers from talking about it. You couldn't keep the lower ratings from talking about it. That is why many of you have heard about the Philadelphia Experiment. Not through books, but through general legend... This has been going on since 1943, when the alleged experiment took place.

Since it's come out in books and magazines in all sorts of languages, many people could write the ONI (Office of Naval Intelligence), asking them, "Did it really take place?" And the ONI has a regular letter that they send back. They say, of course, "No, such a thing is impossible. It could never happen." But at the very end of the letter there's a very interesting paragraph. The paragraph says, if such a thing had happened, people would have known about it. Well, they do [know about it]! It's just that we had a bit of censorship there for a moment!

Now, whether this happened or not, one way of knowing would be [by asking] under the Freedom of Information Act [to see] if there been a slip-up somewhere. [FOIA revealed that] after the experiment took place, the ship was used for a while, and apparently 600 tons of something was taken off it. Then it was sold to the Greeks. In selling it to the Greek Navy after the war, the original documents came into view. The documents themselves are sort of proof that something very unusual happened with the DE173 (then called *The Eldridge*, now called *The Leon* in the Greek Navy).

We were able to find out that the ship was launched a month before it was "officially" launched. That was one thing... The ship was supposed to be near Philadelphia but, because of the Greek papers and also the action reports of the ship, we found out it took part in hostilities 3000 miles from where it was supposed to be. They [apparently] didn't want to make a regular report on the ship after it had been, shall we say, passed through a change of molecular composition. Therefore [they] counted it as an experimental ship for a while.

We asked for the records of the ship, and this is the log: nothing for four months. But there was another log. [A second] log of activity for the same period... Everything was in doubles. This came out when the ship was sold to the Greeks. After the first accident (when the crew had such bad effects), some died, some were hospitalized, some disappeared, some broke out in flames (according to scuttlebutt)... Einstein was told about the experiment. [He] left a "double" in his Princeton office and came down and examined the ship again, to try the experiment once more.

One of our informants was on the ship at the time [but] didn't know who Einstein was. [When] this distinguished looking man came onboard [our informant] said to one of the other sailors, "this fellow certainly needs a haircut." The other sailor said, "Don't you know who that is? That's Einstein." And it was... He inspected the ship, checked things out. And he tried it once more. The second experiment is really the reason that the whole thing came out.

The second experiment took place at sea and was watched by a ship in convoy duty, which was called *The S.S. Andrew Furuseth*. Onboard *The Furuseth* was a person about whom many of you may have heard, called Carlos Allende, or Carl Allen. As far as we can figure out, he was simply a seaman. Some of the other seamen onboard *The Furuseth* were standing by the rail. They saw a ship go by, and the ship had on it "DE173." As they watched it, all of a sudden it started to glow. A glowing fog formed around it, and then there was a flash. It flashed off, and there was no ship where they had been looking. However, in the water there was a wake, which [soon] vanished. Apparently the ship vanished first, leaving the wake behind it. Then the ship went someplace else.

This was the second experiment, which is sometimes called (instead of the Philadelphia Experiment) the Atlantic Experiment. But apparently it was no better for the crew, because the crew still had bad effects. This is [a slide of] the crew at the launching of *The Furuseth*. So not only Allende saw it, but several of his mates saw it. Allende says that this glowing field of ionization came from the ship just before it blasted itself into invisibility. It was so strong that it knocked him to the deck. He was very impressionable. He had lots of time to think of these things while he was at sea...

Because of his preoccupation with what he considered interference with natural laws (from what he gathered from speaking to sailors, and his general interest in science), Allende started writing to people. One of the people he wrote to was Dr. M.K. Jessup. Dr. Jessup was an astronomer [and] a writer about UFOs, who had written a book called *The Case for the UFO*. So Allende started to write him, urging him [to] use his influence to stop this sort of experimentation.

Well, Dr. Jessup didn't know what to do about this. He tried to contact [Allende] and nothing happened. [Then Jessup] got a call from the Office of Naval Research to come and do a report, because the Office of Naval Research had received a book by Jessup [with] the most amazing statements by somebody written in red ink, mentioning Jessup.

Mr. Gray Barker, who is here tonight, publishes the book [the VARO edition] and can tell you more about it. In any case, the Navy called in Jessup to explain what he knew about the book, but he didn't know anything about it. All he knew was that he had received the most amazing letters from somebody written in the same handwriting. Well, because of this, Dr. Jessup started working with the Navy, and worked for some time on this problem. That's where I come in, because one of my collaborators was a friend of Dr. Jessup. It was Dr. Jessup's rather unusual death that got me interested in the Philadelphia Experiment in the first place.

This is Dr. Jessup's death certificate. After he'd been working for some time on the experiment with the Navy, he'd often discuss the connection between the Philadelphia Experiment and the Bermuda Triangle with my collaborator, Dr. Manson Valentine, of Miami. Jessup was the first person to try and connect the two. In other words, he thought that maybe the Navy wasn't responsible for this but had stumbled onto a natural force. Or had made their own force, equivalent to a natural force of electronic disturbance... We change the molecular composition of objects and people, causing them absolutely to disappear and come back at a time in the future...

So he kept a lot of notes about this, and he told Dr. Valentine that he wanted to give him two copies of what he had written. He made an appointment to come eat dinner with him, and on the way down to dinner, he stopped at a place (Rogers & Hammond in Miami) and "committed suicide" by running a hose from the exhaust. Dr. Valentine was eventually alerted by the police. When he got there, Jessup was dead and there was no material in the car. It's sort of a mystery on top of a mystery.

So in the investigation, what we have tried to do was to find out not if it's just a story, but if there's a good deal of truth to it. One of the first things we had to find out was, "Did Allende really exist?" Well Allende did exist. He *was* on a boat called *The Furuseth*, and *The Furuseth was* in convoy with the DE173, which [was either] participating in the experiment at the time, or maybe – because it had already been the object of the [first] experiment – just sort of shut itself off from time to time (because of the molecular changes).

In the course of the investigation, we had to find out [not only] if Allende [had] a Z number (which would mean that he was with the Merchant Marine), but did the Merchant line really have the ship in the area at the time? The first time we wrote the Merchant line, they gave us all sorts of information about *The Furuseth*. We were missing one or two points, so we asked them again. The second time, somebody had got to them, and it was just as if they had never received our first letter. They said, "There is no information about *The Furuseth* and therefore we can't give it to you." So, between the time we started the investigation and the time they answered, something had happened.

The same thing has gone all down the line, from the Navy, from the Office of Naval Information, from all sorts of places. Now... Before the actual proof of this disappearance of the DE173 can be considered, I would like to consider some of the phenomenon that has happened within the Bermuda Triangle, to see if the same sort of disintegrating cloud [or] "disintegration under a magnetic cloud" has taken place.

Berlitz, Charles – The Bermuda Triangle – 1980

Many of you are familiar with the disappearances of the Bermuda Triangle, so I'll be very brief. This is a [compilation] of disappearances within what is called the Bermuda Triangle, based on my recent investigations. Far from the usual [media] figure of [only] 100 ships and planes [total], there have been literally hundreds [of disappearances] and they're still going on at the rate of about one *ship* a week, and one *plane* every two weeks.

Of course, it's easy to blame this on a series of things such as Castro and so forth, but things were disappearing in the Bermuda Triangle even before Castro came to power. He doesn't have that big of a Navy or Air Force to be snatching them out of the air. [Yet] it's still happening... There are so many happening between the Bahamas and Florida that I had to make a separate insert...

Now there are, of course, all sorts of explanations. Is it something about the weather? *[shows new slide]* Well, this is the eye of a hurricane 24 miles across. Most of the disappearances don't happen in hurricane times because people don't go out during hurricanes. Most of the disappearances of ships and planes take place in good clime or good sunny weather, not in hurricanes.

Others say, "Well, they're probably a result of tornadoes or waterspouts or something of the sort." But if you are flying, you can see a waterspout and [avoid it]. You can even avoid one in a ship. [So] they're not water spouts. Are they something to do with the tremendous tides that fall within the Bermuda Triangle? Jim Thorne is here tonight, and he has dived into some of these holes that maybe have sucked down certain planes and ships. But nothing has been found there… So it isn't that, either. Is it hijacking of the ships by the crews themselves [who] repaint them and use them for running dope? Well, maybe some of them, but not 600 ships within a 2-year period, as *has* happened between 1964 and 1966…

Then there was the case of three British planes, all going down between Bermuda and Jamaica within three or four years. Each of these three had disappeared without any indication of what had happened to them. One of the most incredible things was [that they] seemed to happen at the *same time*: toward the end of December and the beginning of January. There are all these disappearances within the Bermuda Triangle, and you find that just an enormous amount of them happen in December and January – which are not hurricane months. Out of the 250 of these occurrences that I've investigated, 20 of them happened on December 3rd. I don't know what this means. The only thing I can think of is December 3rd is not a good day to travel. One [disappearance] happened so close to Miami that the pilot was in contact with the tower, and his last words [had to do with] a "cloud" and "passing into another dimension." This happens in so many planes, not only passenger planes but military as well. He was so near to Miami that if he had crashed or exploded or anything, something would have washed up, or something would have been found on the land. The only thing I can think of is [that there is] some kind of disintegration, or [molecular] change.

…In the Air Force in the Miami area, it was [explained away as] somebody snooping on [our] planes, to see what we had developed. With every new military plane, one example seemed to disappear. But there is an interesting case [where] both [new and old planes *and* ships] disappeared at the same time. And this seems to give some sort of suggestion as to what might be happening. As those of you military flyers know, when you lose a plane you fly 5 miles around, and then you fly 10 miles around, and then 15 miles around and so on, in a search pattern. [In this case you had] 2 planes disappear at the same time [so] you had 2 search patterns. But the 2 search patterns coincided with 2 *other* search patterns, because 2 *ships* had disappeared at the same time! So you had four [missing vehicles]: 2 ships and 2 planes. [Only] one of the ships was found. It was a Coast Guard cutter. It was drifting into a fog with all the motors cut off, and all of their communications cut off. They were just drifting aimlessly. But they didn't disappear. To me that suggests that there is an area (or residue of an area) caused by some sort of UFO activity, where a field of ionization will sort of settle – either in the air or [below] the level of the sea – and cause ships and planes to disappear (or be lost at the same time).

Then you have these fantastic coincidences. *The Cyclops* disappeared after the end of WWI, with more than 300 people onboard. A few months before that, another ship called *The Cyclops* had disappeared in the North Atlantic. Then 25 years later, the sister ship to *The Cyclops* disappeared from the Virgin Islands, coming into South Carolina. No records, nothing found... It wasn't wartime. At the same time, another ship called *The Cyclops* disappeared in the North Atlantic. And this is one of these incredible circumstances. Why would somebody, anybody, be looking for 5 ships, all named *The Cyclops?* The one surviving ship *did* become our first aircraft carrier, so maybe there *was* something about it...

And then big ships, like oil tankers, disappear without leaving any oil on the beach. The Sao Paolo disappeared while it was being towed. The two tugs went into a fog with around 25 people onboard, just a caretaking crew. [They] slowed down to go through a fog and when morning came, the fog lifted. They started tightening the cables, and the cable came, but there was no ship on the end. The cables were sort of melted. They were not snapped. There was no indication of what happened to the ship. There were only some rather unusual clouds in the area.

Many yachts are lost. There are many reasons for suspecting why yachts could be lost [such as] bad seamanship, etc. Many of the yachts that go from Miami to the Bahamas are in such a state of festivity that [even] if they were visited by little green men, no one would realize that anything had changed. *[laughter]* However some of them, like *The Witchcraft*, disappeared after sending a message for help to the Coast Guard [only] one mile off Miami! The last message heard from this one was, "I've never seen anything like that before." The key was left on and the Coast Guard [found the message] "Please send help. We're dying." We'll never know what they saw.

[Then there are] all the great disappearances of people from the decks of ships, from 1800 on, like *The Marie Celeste* and *The Ellen Austin* (and many other ships), which just drift into port without anyone on onboard. That brings up again the interesting theory that there's been "space-napping" going on in the Atlantic for a long period of time.

If you remember in 1960, the Air Force decided that UFOs didn't exist, according to the Condon report. Shortly afterwards, there was an Air Force regulation called "80-17." Although UFOs didn't exist for the purpose of the Air Force, 80-17 had about 14 pages telling Air Force personnel what to do when they encountered UFOs. *[shows slide of UFO]*

This is a UFO I was responsible for having photographed... I had a friend, and he hired a plane. We were taking pictures of underwater causeways, going up from the coast of the Yucatan. He saw something out of his plane. It was a very slow plane, about 160 miles an hour. He thought it was some enormous installation below him. In the Yucatan this would be unusual. He took a picture of it. Then he asked the pilot, "What is that big installation down there?" The pilot said, "Down where?" This is what he got.

Now, like many pictures of UFOs, it's fuzzy. You can't tell what it is. The only thing that we can say is that it certainly is unidentified. *[shows another UFO slide]* Here's a picture taken by a pilot, a special charter pilot... He didn't think he was taking a picture of a UFO. He was very interested in taking pictures of the inlets on the west side of Andros. When he had the picture developed, he had *this*. It isn't a rocket. We don't fire rockets over Andros. It's very unusual that other people would fire rockets on his picture. He disappeared into the Bermuda Triangle within two weeks after taking the picture.

Another very interesting theory about what may be happening in the Triangle is that a tremendous ancient civilization (such as Atlantis or some other vanished civilization) had installations down there, which may still be working. Well, I'm not in a position to say whether they're working or not. [But] there are often very unusual things happening down there. There are certainly enormous vestiges of a past civilization underwater. You have these enormous rocks off of Italy... Archaeologists and oceanographers will say they can't be manmade rocks because people weren't here 12,000 years ago, before the waters rose. They must be rocks which just broke themselves off underwater and built themselves into walls somehow. *[new slide]* That's a very exact wall, if I might say. Here you have an interior wall. You have [my friend] holding his breath at 40 feet, showing one of the interior passageways. These enormous walls, whether they're walls or fort facilities, or bases of temples [are] certainly manmade. You can see here [my friend] is trying to pry his way between one of the walls.

If they are not manmade walls, it would be very unusual to have them so aligned to have them make a 90 degree turn, to have interior passageways, and above all, to have them occasionally resting on four pillars. *[laughter]* Now, this of course is more doubtful. It's what I consider an underwater pyramid. [A diver] was looking for fish and found what apparently is a pyramid, with something on top of it. It's as big as the Pyramid of Giza in Egypt, and it's about 300 feet from the surface of the water. It also measures the same way from east to west as from north to south. It seems aligned the same as the Pyramid of Egypt, due east... But there's a certain amount of cynicism and doubt about this. I think that even if we did get to the bottom of it, if [we] found Atlantis written over the main entrance, the National Geographic

Society would still say that it was made by burrowing sea worms. *[laughter]*

The amount of mysterious activity in this area is really extraordinary. We have what you call the "white waters" of Bahamas. Glowing waters... They were the last waters seen by the astronauts when they left Florida. They were the last light. We don't know what they are. Oceanographers would say, "Well, they are collections of diatoms or shining waters." Which of course they are... But nobody knows why they are in this area, and just solely evident there. Columbus and his men saw them when they came over long ago. His men became panic stricken and mutinous. But they always were [anyway] so it was just one more incident. *[laughter]*

This would be of great interest to your group... Here you have a case [of] USOs, or unidentified submarine objects. They leave the water and go up into the sky. They operate so much in this area over the Bahama banks that it's almost as if they are indifferent to whether they are seen or not. They're not hiding from anyone. They go coursing along the water at a great rate. If you have a small plane and are not on a scheduled flight, you can follow them and see how fast they go. *[gestures]* Some of these underwater objects, which must be about as long as these two walls (or much longer in some cases), go along at a great rate. You can see them because it's only about 80 or 100 feet deep...

When I saw one, I got off the plane and asked the pilot, "Why didn't you do something about it?" The pilot said, "Look, I'm not in this business for my health. If I say that, people will think I'm out of my mind." He put it slightly stronger than that. *[laughter]* I sort of censored it. But he's right... Depending upon the pilot (and this also goes for military and naval pilots), if they tell what they see in the area, it wouldn't look good on their efficiency reports and [people] lose confidence in them. But these things are constantly coming through the area, chugging along underwater, scaring the life out of the fishermen. Another fisherman I know, one of these came right at him and then ducked under his boat, and almost sank the boat. You don't know what they are, or what they want.

One [USO] a few years back, in '68, chugged around through [a] fleet [of] cruisers, two submarines, and all sorts of other service craft. About 14 vessels... It was a tracking maneuver. Participating vessels thought it was part of the maneuver. They said, "What kind of a thing is this? What kind of a submarine can go 250 knots?" [It] was coursing around the fleet. It went over the edge of the Puerto Rican Trench, went down about five miles, came up again and resumed its "inspection" of the fleet. On the fourth day, a [message] went out from the commanding admiral saying, "Don't clock it." A very good technique if you don't know what something is: ignore it. *[laughter]*

But what I have been trying to bring up is the prevalence of these clouds that cover ships and planes, such as the cloud that the four Saber jets in Bermuda went into. Four jets went into a cloud, right over the field at Kennedy. Only three came out. And nothing fell out of the cloud. Something within the cloud affected them.

Now that there are so many big ships in the area, we don't know what will eventually happen. It certainly affected the Queen Elizabeth II. It went into the area and everything stopped. They lost communication. They lost electricity. They lost the motor. They lost everything. The passengers even lost refrigeration and had to drink warm drinks. They got the radio back, and then one of our Coast Guard cutters went to rescue it (the Dakota). As the Dakota got close, they saw it. They were zeroing in. They lost it on radar, although they could [still] see it. It was covered by a light sort of cloud. Fortunately for the ship [the cloud] didn't get any heavier.

From talking to survivors, apparently these clouds are compact. I think it has something to do with electromagnetic manifestations. They settle over a ship. They settle over a ship in tow. They settle over a barge. Again and again, we've had ships in tow disappear when they are settled over by one of these clouds. Whether these clouds are really magnetic fields, or whether they have something to do with intelligence, we just don't know. Some of their activities almost seem to indicate direction by some intelligence.

To give you an example, take the *S.S. Good News*, which was captained by a friend of mine, Don Henry (who remembers it very well). It has electromagnetic overtones that are very interesting. He was in the cabin of the ship. He had another ship in tow, with nobody onboard. He heard a big commotion in the back of the ship. He looked back and the men were all pointing in back. About 24 men (so it's not just one witness)... They were pointing at where the ship in tow should have been. The ship in tow was covered by its own cloud. Sort of a square cloud covered the ship. According to his words, the line (the cable from his ship) went out like the East Indian rope trick, into nothing. He checked his own instruments. Everything was malfunctioning. The engine was still going, but his ship was being pulled back into this cloud.

I asked him later, "What color was the cloud?" He said, "I wasn't thinking of colors. I was thinking of getting out of there." I asked, "Did you think of the Bermuda Triangle?" He said, "You're damn right. I thought I was about to become another statistic." But he kept going. The diesel kept going, and finally the other ship came out. And he got out of there as quickly as possible.

Once he thought he was out, he got a boat alongside of the other ship to examine what had happened to it. But he couldn't touch the ship. It was too hot. They got it into port and cooled it off. When he got to port, he found that his own cargo of flashlight batteries had been completely drained of all their electricity. He got out of it but there is, perhaps, a "dimension" there.

One of the strangest things about the Bermuda Triangle, which has a connection with (I believe) the Philadelphia Experiment, is the slippage of time. That time is somehow affected, as well as matter… The following happened only weeks ago. A pilot [leaving Bimini] got in a cloud, radioed for help, and in four minutes was [unexpectedly] over Miami – but without any hurricane or anything [to speed him up]. He found out the amount of gas he had. He had 15 gallons over what he should have had. It takes exactly 15 gallons to get from Bimini to Miami… He got into a cloud and actually got there in 4 minutes, only using about 4 minutes worth of gas.

Then there was the Phantom P4 that disappeared over Jacksonville, coming in for a landing. As it was coming in, it was lost (just like the plane over Bermuda) and just vanished. Nothing on the ground… This was not over water. It just vanished in the air somehow. Shortly after this, a 727 was coming into Miami and vanished from radar for about 10 minutes, and then came back again. Everyone was delighted. When the pilot landed, the field was covered with fire trucks, foam trucks – all sorts of rescue equipment. Besides that, the people from the tower came down to see him. He said, "What's all the excitement?" They said, "You are… We lost you, and we thought something had happened. We were getting pretty nervous."

He said, "It was nothing at all! We came through some sort of a fog for maybe 10 minutes, and here we are." Somebody said, "Look, for 10 minutes you were out of this world. Where were you?" He looked at his watch and found out [that] he had somehow lost 10 minutes on his own watch. He asked his co-pilot, who also had lost 10 minutes. The stewardesses had lost 10 minutes. The passengers were all looking at their watches and comparing them to airport time. Somehow, from the time they had been in this fog, off radar, they had all lost 10 minutes.

Even more unusual (and this is a well-known case because so many people witnessed it) is the case of the [female] pilot who had made the flight from Miami to Jamaica on several occasions. She filed a flight plan to fly to Turk Ottoman with a Cessna 139. About the time that she should have been over the Turk, the Cessna was circling the island. It was sort of a one-way communication. The plane couldn't hear the Turk tower, but the tower could hear what was being said on the plane. And what was being said on the plane was extraordinary. A [passenger] was talking to a girl (who apparently was the pilot) asking, "Well, why can't we land here?" And the pilot said, "Well, there's nothing down there. Look! It should be Turk. The outline looks like Turk, but it isn't Turk. There's nothing there at all."

In the meantime, people at the small airport at Turk were looking up at the plane. People at the hotel were looking up at the plane. The tower kept sending them messages, "Why can't you hear us? We can hear you fine." Finally the pilot said to the passenger, "Look, there's nothing down there. We must have made a wrong turn. We're running out of gas. We'll have to get gas someplace." So they took off into some clouds and were never seen again. With so many people seeing this plane apparently containing [the pilot] and the passenger, what is the explanation? Could it be that because of a combination of circumstances they actually *were* over Turk, but perhaps at a time before the airport was built?

That brings us back to the Philadelphia Experiment, which is a slippage in time very much like what seems to be happening in the Bermuda Triangle. Since my book has been published, much corroborating evidence has come up. There were some British crewmen in Norfolk at the time. They were waiting for a ship back to England. They suddenly saw a flash in the harbor. First they saw a cloud, and then they saw a flash. Then they saw the ship called the DE173. They said, "Look, the Yanks are up to something. But we'd better not talk about it because if we do, we'll never get back to England." Just as they said that, sea police and MPs came from all over, and the whole thing was put under strict security. So, these people actually saw it. It even came over Philadelphia radio at the time that it happened. A very short report (which was immediately covered up) said, "Apparently the Navy has lost a ship at the Philadelphia Naval Yard." Then, 15 minutes later, "The Navy has found the ship again..."

Whoever finds this [technology] out will, of course, have a tremendous advantage. I hope we [the U.S.] are doing it, and can get over the danger. Of course we "dropped" the experiment because of the success of the atom bomb (if you can call it success), but this [technology] is even more important because this isn't going to be [about] destruction. This is the control of matter and the control of transportation, which eventually could be sent maybe faster than the speed of light, to the farthest parts of the universe. I think that *that* is why this is so important. The fact that the government has covered it up for so long is a mistake. We should share it, because it affects us all.

> *Speaking of burning and/or disappearing men, in August of 2007, Pres. George W. Bush visited Reno, NV to address a convention of war veterans. Coincidentally, I was in Reno at the time and had visited the convention site (a casino) the night before. The local paper reported that Bush openly refused to meet with the Wiccan mother of a young soldier killed in Iraq. That same weekend, at the nearby Burning Man festival (an annual event sponsored by Wiccans and modern pagans from San Francisco), an unprecedented act of sabotage occurred. The pagans' enormous Burning Man effigy was prematurely set on fire and destroyed.*

CHAPTER 4

Gray Barker's work on the Philadelphia Experiment led him to promote the work of M.K. Jessup, an astronomer who wrote the influential 1950s books "The Case For the UFO," "The Expanding Case for the UFO," and "UFOs and the Bible." Barker's interest in Jessup eventually led him to Anna Genzlinger, who one day began to feel as if Jessup was speaking to her — in typical Mothman fashion — from beyond the grave. Jessup apparently wanted Genzlinger to tell the world that he had been murdered. This prompted Genzlinger to research Jessup's death, and to later submit a book manuscript to Barker. Interestingly, Barker edited out all of Genzlinger's references to the CIA and mind control, and the book went unpublished.

In addition to studying Mayan and Peruvian temples and concluding that spaceships with levitational powers built them, Jessup was employed by a rubber company (Rubber Development Corp.) that was most likely controlled by the Rockefellers. He was also involved in a U.S. Dept. of Agriculture study to ascertain rubber sources at the headwaters of the Amazon. Coincidentally, one of the Mothman experiencers I interviewed had a CIA-agent relative who worked for the Dept. of Agriculture.

One of the key reasons why mining and drilling companies conquered the Amazonian jungle in the late 1960s was the successful pacification of the natives by missionary organizations. One such organization was the Rockefeller-funded "Summer Institute of Linguistics." SIL was dedicated to learning all the various native languages and to teaching the tribes about Jesus, capitalism, and harsh punishment for those who didn't go along. In order to carry out their ongoing mission, SIL today partners with many small airplane companies, like Agape Flight of out Venice, FL. According to reporter Dan Hopsicker, Agape has helped SIL "undermine the social cohesion of aboriginal communities and eliminate obstacles to natural resource exploitation." Agape has also flown supplies to coup plotters in Haiti and shared pilots with a spy-for-hire company that does "airborne data acquisition." Oddly, the flight instructor for 9/11 ringleader Mohamed Atta, a pilot sometimes named "Mark Mikarts," flies for Agape.

Barker, Gray – Report on M.K.Jessup – 1981

Gray Barker: One of the mysteries of the whole Philadelphia Experiment thing is not so much the experiment itself, but the interest of the Office of

Naval Research in the work of Morris K. Jessup, who had written a book called *The Case for the UFO*. A copy of the paperback edition was received by the Office of Naval Research with a great many annotations, apparently made by three different people. The annotations were very strange, as if they might have been written by someone from outer space. They used very strange terms like "forcefields," "great arcs," "mothership," "caught in a flame," and all sorts of rather alien language.

The surprising thing is that people in the Office of Naval Research apparently took this very seriously. Two of the officers took this annotated book to Garland, Texas, to the VARO Manufacturing Company, a firm that was engaged in many military contracts building sophisticated electronic gear for the Navy (and apparently engaged in some of the gravity research that was going on there). It is suspected that the VARO Company manufactured the huge magnetic degaussers that made the Philadelphia Experiment possible. Anyhow, after the book was taken to the VARO Manufacturing Company, the private secretary of the president typed all of this out on offset stencils. This was run off in limited numbers, on an office duplication machine. It apparently took a great deal of work and time, because it was run through this press twice, in two different colors (Jessup's original text in black ink, and the annotations in red). It would take several tapes and a book to go into this situation as deeply as it should be. Of course a great deal has been written about this. The strange thing is why the military did not try to find some printing contractor to print this for them, rather than go to this military contractor who wasn't in the printing business. Anyhow, the VARO edition is very interesting, and brings up another mystery that has been connected with this: that of Morris K. Jessup. Soon after receiving letters from Carlos Allende, and being called into ONR in Washington and shown this annotated book, Jessup committed suicide in Florida.

I wrote a book about this called *The Strange Case of Dr. M.K. Jessup*, in which I threw out some questions for people to consider. A great many people who were interested in UFOs and The Philadelphia Experiment were rather suspicious that something strange had gone on, that Jessup's suicide just might not have been cut and dried. Personally, even after doing some investigating and publishing this book, I felt that perhaps we were making too much of it. Perhaps Jessup had some personal problems, which may have led to his unfortunate demise... He died from carbon monoxide poisoning in a park in Dade County, Florida, after putting a hose through the rear window of his station wagon and apparently committing suicide...

But I didn't reckon with the persistence of a person in Miami, Florida, called Anna Likens Genzlinger, who really wasn't interested in UFOs. She didn't know anything about Jessup until she just happened to be reading one of Berlitz' books. She read about Jessup's suicide, and suddenly got the impression – psychically or however (we don't quite know) – that Jessup didn't take his own life deliberately. She set out to investigate this. Living in the Miami area, this was possible for her to do (where it wasn't for people in the North, such as I). During her local investigation, Ann discovered several unusual things. Although state law required an autopsy in the case of a suicide, no autopsy was conducted in the case of Jessup. One of the police officers doing the investigation thought that it was too elaborate of a set-up. It wasn't ordinary hose that was used. The elaborate wetting down of the cloths to seal down the rear window of the station wagon was questioned, because there wasn't any water source near and there wasn't any sign of wetness on Jessup's clothes. Jessup's wife, Ruby Jessup, would not identify the body. She did not even see the body. One mysterious person named "Soul," who was supposed to be a friend of the family (but who nobody can now locate), was the only person to identify the body for the police. There were several other very questionable things involved in this case of Jessup's suicide, including a friend of his who had been trying to reach him to invite him to dinner... Jessup had told him that he was really onto something important. Ann believes that Jessup knew about the Philadelphia Experiment. He was a trained scientist. He was an astronomer, and apparently had been involved in the [experiment] through his work with the government. She thinks that through some sort of mind control, he was induced to commit suicide. Here's a portion of an interview (which we later intend to release in its complete form) with Ann about some of these questionable things. In this interview, I asked Ann if she believed that Jessup deliberately took his own life...

Barker/Genzlinger – The Strange Case of M.K. Jessup – 1981

Anna Genzlinger (AG): I think what happened was that Jessup committed the act himself, but was *not* in possession of his faculties at the time that he did it. Not that he was insane or crazy, or anything like that. He was just *under some sort of control.*

Gray Barker (GB): Some sort of control? Do you mean that he might have been hypnotized?

AG: I can read you a portion of a letter that I received here, from Bill Moore:

> "To begin again, there can be no doubt that Jessup committed the act himself. The only question that remains is, did he do it of his own free will or was he driven to do it by a carefully orchestrated conspiracy put together by outside forces who wished to silence him, and who saw it to their advantage to have him commit the ultimate act himself – and thus leave their hands clean. I don't

know if this latter is true but if it is, you had better be careful with how you go about conducting your investigation. The type of creatures who would perpetrate such an act would not hesitate to do a repeat performance, if they thought someone was about to expose them."

GB: That sounds rather sinister. But you don't believe that Jessup died of his own free will? Wasn't there an autopsy made that showed that he died from carbon monoxide poisoning?

AG: I'm afraid that there was no official autopsy performed whatsoever on the body.

GB: Isn't there a law in your state? I should think so. I think there is in [WV].

AG: According to the Florida legislature, and I'm quoting from 406.11 Examinations, Investigations, and Autopsies, there are 15 circumstances under which a body must be autopsied. Jessup's fits 1, 2, 3, 4 of those: by suicide, he was not attended by a practicing physician, it was in unusual circumstances, and the body was cremated...

GB: Elaborate a little bit. Why do you call the book *The Jessup Dimension*?

AG: I would like to make just one more point before I get into that. That is the fact that Jessup went to a great deal of trouble *not* to appear irrational or insane. Yet people would have [us] believe that he committed the ultimate irrational act of suicide. It just doesn't wash.

GB: I never did believe it myself, but of course I wasn't able to do the research onsite. I've often wondered... Various people get involved in things, get fascinated by them, and do a lot of research on them. How did you, may I ask, happen to get so involved with this that you would do all this investigation and even write a book about it?

AG: I don't really know. I was sitting here one day with a cast on my leg, reading *Without a Trace* by Charles Berlitz. I came across Jessup's name, about him committing suicide. And something just happened to me. I don't know what it was, but this man did not commit suicide. He was murdered. That's where it began.

GB: You mean you were just sitting there and you read a paragraph, and made up your mind?

AG: It was like one of those cartoons where you see the light bulb going off over somebody's head.

GB: There wasn't any really logical reason?

AG: No, there was absolutely no logical reason for why I got into this. I just felt like I *was being pushed.*

GB: You ordered from me the *VARO Edition* [and] *The Strange Case of Jessup...* That was after this happened to you?

AG: Yes, that was very soon after... I think just a few weeks after...

GB: In other words, these books didn't affect [your decision]. You hadn't learned anything about Jessup [yet].

AG: No, I didn't even know what the "K" stood for in M.K. Jessup. That's another strange thing.

GB: Stands for Ketchum, doesn't it? That's such an odd name.

AG: I didn't know that for a long time. I didn't know until I got the FBI report that his middle name was Ketchum. [Before that] through the whole thing, I called him "Ketch." I didn't know why. I had no idea why I called him Ketch.

GB: You would think about Dr. Jessup and you would want to call him Ketch?

AG: Yes.

GB: How would you spell it in your mind?

AG: K-e-t-c-h.

GB: The same as the spelling... It would almost appear as if you were kind of *psychically* connected with this.

AG: That's the feeling I had. It's been a very strange sort of relationship. If you can have a relationship with a ghost (or presence)...

GB: You're not saying that you, in any way, shape, or form have been in [audio/visual] contact with [Jessup are you]?

AG: I had some whopping good arguments with him in my own mind. I would get the feeling he was trying to push me one way, and I would want to go someplace else.

GB: You mean you have the *feeling* that you were in some kind of contact with Dr. Jessup?

AG: I know that sounds strange, but that's exactly it.

GB: Well, I'm not saying it's strange. It's intriguing...

AG: Every time I would begin to flag on this, I would put it aside. I would try to get my mind on something else. [But] he was very intrusive. He intruded himself right back into my mind, into my life. I had to go on with it. I couldn't seem to stop myself until I got finished.

GB: I'm very dramatically minded of course, and sometimes I get a little too far out, but dare I say this? It's almost as if you kept after me until, finally, we're getting ready to publish his book (which we've sort of been sitting here for some time). It's almost as if Jessup were driving you to tell the public, "No, I didn't take my own life. No, I certainly wasn't crazy. There are some things that really should be delved into. The bottom should be got at…"

AG: That's the way I feel.

GB: You mean I'm not too far out on that?

AG: The reason for the name *The Jessup Dimension* is that I believe the Philadelphia Experiment pushed those men that were onboard that ship into the fourth dimension, and that Jessup knew it.

GB: Well, I think he would call it the fourth dimension, surely.

AG: And I believe wholeheartedly that when we pass over, we go into the fourth dimension ourselves. I kind of call it a staging area. [A place] to wait until we can come back again… That's just my belief.

GB: Of course that's a belief shared, in various degrees, by a lot of people.

AG: Somehow it just seemed to belong to him. From the very beginning, it was *The Jessup Dimension*.

GB: Well, maybe Jessup's ghost can't rest until some of these things are dug out and revealed. Exposed…

AG: On the night of the anniversary of his death, on April the 20th of this year, 1980, I felt that he had left me, that I had been abandoned. I was furious. I was totally furious with Jessup for leaving me alone with this, because I wasn't sure I could finish it.

[Barker asks if there is any evidence of murder in the case of Jessup's death]

AG: All I can say, Gray, is that I don't have any concrete evidence. I have a gut feeling. I have the things that people have told me.

GB: It's sort of like one lady against the CIA. You can't expect wonders…

AG: Right… I'm not a writer. I've never written a book before in my life. This is just me to you, one-on-one. If you don't come to the same conclusion I did, that's your privilege. If you do then fine, that makes me very happy.

But it *had* to be told.

GB: From what I've read of the book, it's very ingratiating – very convincing. I think that people will find it very refreshing from some of these dull, pedantic, pseudo-scientific books that have been coming out on UFOs.

AG: Bill Moore teased me about it. He says, "Ann, you're too subjective." I said, "Well, Bill, that's the only way I can be." I'm writing from my point of view. I can't be anything else *but* subjective.

GB: Surely, I think it will be most successful, particularly among the people who have been very interested in this – who have been studying the Jessup mystery, the annotated VARO edition, and *The Philadelphia Experiment* book by Moore and Berlitz...

AG: I'd be lying if I said I didn't hope [that] it does something for us. But most of all, I hope it does something for Jessup.

GB: In closing, have we missed anything that I should include in the interview? Any really good points that I've forgotten to ask about?

AG: I did have several warnings that my own life could be in danger if I went on with this.

GB: Were these anonymous, or from [known] people?

AG: One was from Riley Crabb. I can quote that one to you if you'd like to hear it.

GB: I think that one was in a newsletter. Yes, I may pick it up and reprint it. I'm glad you reminded me of that.

AG: And another one was from Manson Valentine and his wife, Anna. They were very much afraid that I might be in danger. They wanted me to stop. They begged me to stop, but I couldn't do it.

GB: How did Bill Moore feel about your investigation? Did he feel that you might be in danger?

AG: Yes, he told me to be very careful about how I go about the investigation. If they had done it once, they would do it again.

GB: Something else that comes to my mind... Maybe I shouldn't ask this. [Due to] your preoccupation with Jessup, and that paragraph in the book sort of springing up at you, do you consider yourself psychic? Have you had any psychic experiences in the past?

AG: Yes, many... And one very recently... It was this past Saturday. I woke up at four o'clock in the morning. Something just jerked me out of a sound sleep. My daughter called me at seven o'clock and said she'd been in labor since ten minutes to four (with my grandson). This has happened to me many times. It happened when my mother had a stroke. It happened when my other daughter had her baby.

GB: You mentioned that when we pass on, we go into another dimension, as sort of a staging area for return. I assume you believe in reincarnation. Do you have any inkling of any of your past lives?

AG: Oh, definitely…

One of the many things excised out of Genzlinger's text by Barker was the revelation that Jessup "expressed outright terror at the endless streams of 'coincidences' that had occurred in his work and in his private life." Regarding an auto accident that Jessup was involved in several months before his death, Genzlinger wrote, "It is my belief that the auto accident was the first attempt on Dr. Jessup's life. It was soon after this 'accident' that Jessup began to feel that he was being followed and that his phone was being tapped." Genzlinger felt that the annotated copy clearly showed Carlos Allende's contempt for Jessup. She described Allende as a "link in the mind control, either with or without his knowledge." Genzlinger described Jessup's death as a "sophisticated, horrible kind of self-murder," involving "the destruction of one's self while under the influence of an outside force." But was the man found dead in the car really Jessup? Could Jessup have gone underground and become "Indrid Cold?"

Interestingly, Carlos Allende's name is not all that different from the name of one of Indrid Cold's assistants, Carlo Ardo. Ardo was probably on hand when Steven Law, a local who repeatedly witnessed UFOs on contactee Woody Derenberger's farm, was hit with a telepathic message from Cold while watching a high school football game in Parkersburg, WV. According to Law, Indrid was carrying a "yellow keyring," which is similar to something a hypnotist might use for inducing a trance. With keyring in hand, Cold tried hard to convince Law to come away to the planet "Lanulos" for 8 years of "schooling," due to the convenient fact that Law "was young, not married, and had nothing attaching him to this planet." Derenberger once described Cold as having "been blasted with a shotgun in Arkansas," requiring pellet-removal surgery. The governor of Arkansas at that time of Mothman was Winthrop Rockefeller, described by several sources as "the single most important influence on Bill Clinton."

CHAPTER 5

"What is the use of looking outside? All you see is objects! Turn around and look within. Shall I then see the subject instead? If you did, you would be looking at an object. An object is such in whatever direction you look. Shall I not see myself? You cannot see what is not there! What then, shall I see? Perhaps you may see the absence of yourself, which is what is looking. It has been called the Void."

-Wei Wu Wei

Colvin, Andy – Grassy Knoll Radio interview 2 – March 3, 2006

"Vyz" at Grassy Knoll (GK): Welcome to the Grassy Knoll. This is going to be round two with Andrew Colvin. We're dealing with the Mothman, and Colvin is a documentary filmmaker who has produced *The Mothman's Photographer*. I want to open up with something that we found very interesting... I had asked Andrew for an outline, which I do with a lot of guests... He had sent me something prior that did not contain the notes of the show. These were some ancillary things he sent me. I'm waiting for the second email to come through [with the notes]. It doesn't come through. We were ready to go, just minutes ago, and I'm saying, "Well, I didn't get it." He said, "Well gee, I sent it to you..." Why don't you [explain this, Andy]? Tell them what was in that email.

Andy Colvin (AC): Well, knowing what we know about the data-mining scandal that's happening right now with the NSA, with both "international spying" and "domestic spying," my email was probably intercepted... The father of a childhood friend I interviewed in my documentary worked on that NSA eavesdropping project. It was operational by '68. They were listening to domestic traffic – in fact *all* traffic – by that time. If you go to James Bamford's "Puzzle Palace" book, you can find out more about it. They actually do the intercepting in West Virginia, at a Naval facility there. They simply download the satellite information that ATT is normally beaming around.

GK: The other interesting thing is that everything you sent [before] has come into the regular inbox [yet] this particular piece that came late – and of which we are speaking – came into the junk box. I don't know how things work as far as how MSN [goes] but I'm wondering if somebody got their little paws on it and put some kind of imprint on it such that, when it came in, my Hotmail did not "see" it (as it did the other ones). I'm not trying to get paranoid or neurotic, but that doesn't necessarily make me wrong, does it?

AC: No, there were a lot of code words in that email I sent. It's got practically every conspiracy word in existence...

GK: All the basic food groups are in this one, right?

AC: There are so many threads to the Mothman story. It's truly an enigma inside of an enigma, and then some. You and I were talking yesterday (after the first hour) about how difficult it is to tell which parts of it are mind control operations or government covert ops versus something that's genuinely supernatural. I vacillate back and forth on certain parts of it all the time.

GK: I have to tell the listeners: we're not being gratuitous and trying to make this bigger than it is. Andrew is right. After the hour, we spoke a little bit. This thing does have tentacles. There's no two ways about it. Even if there is some kind of MK-Ultra thing attached to it (or some kind of suggestive technology that's being used), somehow, someway, something [else] is definitely going on... What I want to ask you though, and it may not be that important is: is there anything out there that gives the most accurate depiction of what the Mothman looks like?

AC: That opens up another line of questioning, because it appears to change somewhat. It looks slightly different to different people. Sometimes there's more of a birdlike head... Sometimes there's more of a doglike head... And believe it or not, there may be a strange connection to the story of Ezekiel in the Bible. I had a dream about Ezekiel's Wheel flying over Mound, West Virginia, where we all lived. I found a drawing of Ezekiel's Wheel from the 1100s that showed a beast hitching a ride on this wheel. The beast had four different faces, from different beings. These were the mammal families mostly seen in conjunction with the Mothman sightings: the dog, bird, cat, and man. How about that?

In alchemical illustrations from different parts of the world, one will often see animal hybrids like winged horses (griffins). The etymology of the word "horse" ties it to "time" (horology), and to the Egyptian god Horus (a birdman). It also relates to the Sphinx, or "w-hor-e" of Babylon... The famous occultist Aleister Crowley focused on such root words in his magickal workings, as do many secret societies. The Norse god Thor also seems related to the birdman phenomenon. The Thor story brings us the spectre of an evil being (Loki) hiding "in a tree," a symbol reflected in my 1973 "tree man" sighting and in the Rocky Fork Lake "Mothman tree" sightings of 1980-81. The "Roc" is another birdman. Its name comes from the Moorish areas of N. Africa. It shares etymological roots with "rococo," a style of Baroque. Rococo indicates a blending of styles or genres, something seen in the aforementioned Ezekiel's Wheel symbology. The Roc, like the Phoenix and other mythical birds, is linked to unusual coronal activity of the sun. Such activity was famously seen at Fatima. Fatima was an event that featured young children being given prophecies by entities similar to those seen in Mound. In Persian antiquity, there is an immortal bird called "Amrzs" or "Slnamurv," which shakes the ripe fruit from the mythical tree bearing the seed of all useful things. The "Ziz" is a giant bird in Jewish mythology, said to be able to block out the sun. Some say that if the Ziz did not exist, all the smaller birds on Earth would be helpless, and would have been killed.

To better understand how these scary birdmen can be angelic and not demonic, think of the illusory way that we see colors. Suppose we see a red shirt. From a physics perspective, the shirt is not actually red; it's every other color but red. Red is the one color that is not there. The shirt simply reflects the red part of the color spectrum towards us in a way that we can perceive. Similarly, when we see the seemingly demonic Mothman, Thunderbird, or Garuda, we are merely seeing a frightening hybridic visage reflected towards us. Assuming the Mothman is the Garuda (a beneficial, omnipresent deity that cannot tolerate evil), it is merely reflecting those evil, fragmented characteristics that it cannot retain. It is

Buddhist painting showing the Garuda floating above the Buddha.

not in such an entity's nature to contain "skandas," or separate pieces that are isolated. Such skandas are thought to comprise Maya, our illusory physical state of suffering. The Garuda's pervasive condition of absolute wholeness is what leads Buddhist artists to depict the Garuda as floating directly above the Buddha in space. Some depictions even show disc-shaped craft floating beside the Garuda.

GK: I'll take that as a "no," that there isn't a "most accurate" depiction. But again, you raised something else. Remember the classic movie, The Wizard of Oz, with the winged monkeys? We've seen wings affixed to a number of creatures. I don't think that's anything new. I'll tell you what, when I was a little kid [those monkeys] creeped me out. That to me wasn't a little kid thing. I'm sure you know what's behind The Wizard of Oz, right?

AC: Levenda covers a lot of things in his *Sinister Forces* trilogy, and that movie is one of them. He talks about how it was used in MK-Ultra operations. Also the book *The Blue Bird* by Maeterlinck… Both *Oz* and *Blue Bird* were dramatic productions in theater as well as in film. There's a lot of evidence that they used these themes when they were coming up with various ways to program assassins. You have several families of mind control programming, like Bluebird, Monarch, etc.

The original name for The Philadelphia Experiment was "Project Rainbow," suggestive of the Oz song "Somewhere Over the Rainbow."

GK: Okay, one other thing before we get into the meat of the matter. Folks tend to group Mothman in with the Yeti, Sasquatch, and Bigfoot. Do you think that there are creatures like that out there? And if there are or there aren't, is it an insult to put Mothman into that whole category?

AC: Well, I'm not insulted… But I do vacillate a bit in terms of what we can say about their relationship.

GK: I'm not so sure that there isn't something out there. Unfortunately, it's just become so much of a Hollywood thing that I don't know if you can ever strip it all back to get to the truth of what biological anomalies might still exist today… Who knows?

AC: Well, there's an interesting Bigfoot clip that I saw called *The Memorial Day Footage*. Attempts were made to debunk it, but I'm not sure if it really *was* debunked since they only proved that a man *could have* run that fast and been that tall. But the footage shows the Bigfoot running and, then, at the end of the clip it appears to be growing wings (or else growing taller by 8 inches). You know, there were a lot of Bigfoot incidents going on at the same time as the Mothman. I'm very interested in whether or not these two creatures are related. They are cousins at the very least. If shapeshifting is involved at all, they are probably the same creature. Mothman basically looks like a Bigfoot with wings, except that the head may look a little different to people. When people are under the stress of seeing this otherworldly thing, it can distort their perceptions. There's obviously an interaction going on with the human mind. When we went back in 2002 and encountered this energy field, I later had some visions that were really odd. They seemed to imply that there had been a drowning at the confluence of the Elk and Kanawha Rivers. Three days later, I was driving by there. I had sort of been avoiding that area during my trip but on the last night, I finally went by the confluence. And there was a drowning! As I went by, emergency crews were fishing someone out of the river. At the time I thought, "That was just a precognition of something that was going to happen three days later." But then later we found out that in 1904, a bridge had collapsed there. It crossed the Elk River right *there*, and the date was the exact day of the year as the Silver Bridge collapse: December 15th. There is an island there, called Magic Island. There have always been stories about it being a supernatural spot. I remember my mother telling me a story about a dead girl that had haunted the island. Some deaths were caused by this bridge collapse. It was from lax maintenance. It killed some children. At the place where we saw this energy field and various entities on Woodward Dr., there used to be an old school. It was a pioneer school from the 1800s. It burned down with people in it. There seems to be a link with children dying here. Somehow the deaths create an energy force, or maybe an energy force creates the deaths. If there's a magnetic anomaly there in the earth, it can potentially store that information, and then project it back to people later. There's also an old church there, and a crossroads of old Indian tracks. That reminds me, I wanted to touch on the mounds again, because I really didn't get to finish my thoughts on them the first time.

[Continues after break]

AC: The road we lived on, Woodward Dr., dead-ends into Blaine Island. This island, and the riverbanks there, had hundreds of mounds that were mowed down to make room for the various chemical plants. Most of the plants are on Navy land. It's technically a Naval Reservation, with these private entities operating on the land. But these mounds... Take a look at F.W. Holiday's work. He's got a book called *The Dragon and the Disc*. The book connects the mounds to UFO worship and dragon sightings. Dragons were known to typically come out of a cave and then move downstream to a mound. It might be a mound on an island in the middle of the stream. The dragon would "mount" it and live on it. A lot of these British tales of dragons involved an agent of the King or

Church killing a dragon on an island or mound. That's one aspect of it. For another perspective, I have been in contact with a Bigfoot contactee who claims that he is communicating with Bigfoot on a regular basis. He has been "told" that the Bigfoots built the mounds. That's something that can't be verified at this time, of course, but future researchers could look into it as they interview contactees. In the case of the Mothman, there's some evidence that Mothman started upriver (on the Elk River), came down the Kanawha, and then ended up inhabiting the mounds of Point Pleasant (the TNT area). There were dozens of WWI and WWII-era bunkers there for storing TNT. Dupont was involved in operating the plant back then. Today, it's a highly toxic Superfund site. That's where Mothman was seen hanging out at night when he wasn't flying around. I've also found a corollary to the aforementioned "coming out of the cave and moving downstream" motif in the Egyptian lore, with the story of Horus and Seth. They were both birdmen. Horus was a more birdlike birdman, while Seth was more of a doglike birdman. They were known to have preferences. Seth liked it upstream, Horus preferred downstream. Likewise, the facial characteristics of Mothman seemed more doglike in Mound, WV. Downriver in Point Pleasant, it was seen with a more birdlike face. Coincidentally, Mound has long been dubbed "Dogtown" by locals.

Blaine Island, Mound, WV, 1925, prior to building of "rare chemicals" facility financed by huge ethylene glycol contracts to dynamite makers like Dupont at Pt. Pleasant's TNT Area.

The Feb. 2007 "Batman" sighting in Arizona took place at a schoolyard on Cave Creek. A 2005 cable TV special called "Vampires and UFOs" featured a story about vampiric chupacabras coming out of caves and terrorizing farmers downstream. This vampire special also claimed that someone had taken a photo of the chupacabras looking in a kitchen window – the same way that my sister photographed what may be Mothman. Are these creatures intrigued by kitchen windows because of the possibility of food, or because small windows remind them of cave openings? In 1992, my Buddhist mentor and I were almost killed by a rockslide. Aryadaka felt that a Bigfoot creature had attacked us because we were in its space: the mouth of a cave. Most of these paranormal creatures, from the Deros of Richard Shaver to the chupacabras, Yeti and djinn, seem to come from caves. My Mothman contactee friend, Tommy, who was obsessed with a cave on the hill between our houses, seemed to believe that he was a vampire. He even bit another student in the neck and was suspended from school.

GK: When you're talking about Horus, are you talking about the descendent of Isis and Osiris?

AC: Yes. Rob Godbey and I did some research on the Egyptian gods when we made our trip to Egypt in 2000. Most of these animal deities change form, which brings in the concept of shapeshifting and "the shades" (i.e. shades of meaning, or image).

The Mothman story was sometimes called "The Shades" in France. Anthropologist Jim Brandon popularized the idea that many ancient myths tend to describe underground beings as becoming increasingly complex and hybridic (blending animal and human physical traits) the further down one goes. Mounds were thought to be naturally formed structures where these beings left the earth and entered our reality. The Nei Kung warrior school, a Chinese Taoist tradition with Garuda motifs, teaches that entities are attracted to the electromagnetic currents found in caves and mineral veins.

AC: Horus can be depicted several ways. As I said, there's a shapeshifting quality to the Egyptian stories. But he's primarily a bird most of the time, and associated with time.

GK: I'll throw this at you. I don't mean to jump you with it, but most of us who listen to this show look at high-degree Freemasonry as being an extension of the Mystery Babylon religions and Egyptian Sun-God worship. Therefore, we believe that Satanic, Luciferian spirituality still exists and goes on, and is very, very palpable. So when you mention something like this... I've got to tell you, Andrew, what most of us have found out is that the longer we document and research these things, the more we realize that most of the stuff [described as] balderdash and fiction, really isn't. It is [merely] portrayed as fiction [because people enjoy] a good story. It probably conditioned us not to look at it as real, if you know what I mean… But it is real, and it's out there. We're trying to get people out there to turn around and [see] that these are not necessarily fictional tales.

AC: There have been some unconscious arisings in my own story that illustrate the idea of synchronicity. For instance, back in the late 1970s, I started a photo series that involved a messianic figure with the magical moniker of "Wiz," who was sort of a birdman. He wanted to fly. He had a sphere that he carried. Others were afraid of him, but he was a good guy. It turns out that a lot of Garuda stories have a Garuda carrying a sphere. I didn't know any of this at the time, but I was doing artwork that subconsciously represented aspects of the Mothman story. Many of the themes in my photographs now seem to relate to Mothman. The symbolic connection with Christ is just one of them… I started off the Wiz series with this entity coming out of the ground. I was doing double exposures. I showed this being coming out of the ground, with his arms spread, in what turns out to be a Masonic signal (the distress signal). When I was talking to Keel in the documentary, he was saying there are reports of Bigfoots pulling themselves out of the ground, as if they are so molecularly "loose" that the dirt isn't moving when they come out of the ground. They are just coming up out of the ground as if they are ghosts. It's very similar to the British idea that these creatures come out of the earth and go to a mound because there is some energy there, something that they resonate with or need. If the mounds are not natural formations, then whoever built them must have been able to fly since they picked specific kinds of clays and minerals that were very far away from each other geographically. Perhaps these mounds can store and project energetic information. They may work better for that than, say, a hole. Some of the Indians south of the border believe that a shaman can project his consciousness into a rock or mound at the point of death, and then survive on in spirit. It's pretty mystical, but my point is that these synchronicities have cropped up in my life through my art. They also exist in the stories of the witnesses I interviewed. It is hard to imagine how these synchronicities happened without there being *something* to it.

GK: I'm going to ask you what a lot of people might say is a softball question, but this is something I believe. I just want you to speak to it. I've passed over some writers who have done books about spiritual/mystical things. I said, "No, I don't think so," because I thought they were carnival barkers and snake-oil salesmen. In your case, from everything we've talked about, I believe that you're deadly serious about what's going on – and has been going on – in the United States. And in this whole situation…

AC: Well I am, however there are *so* many possibilities for explanations. It's tough to nail one down. It's just going to take time, and more people getting involved with the research. I'm passing on what I know in the hopes that others can take it and run with it. I sort of view my own work as an addendum to the things that Keel did. I was leafing through his Mothman book again last night, and it's really got a lot of amazing stuff. Every time I read it, there are different things that pop out that I wasn't able to assimilate the first, second, or the third time. It's so chock full of interesting angles, particularly describing for the reader how the super-spectrum works. The superspectrum is this energy force of reality. Reality is alive, so to speak. Keel explains it really well in *The Eighth Tower*. He also goes into the conspiracy angles quite a bit. I view my work as just extending a little more in that direction. I try to utilize what other conspiracy researchers have come up with in the past few years. I don't know if Keel has kept up with that stuff or not.

GK: The two [recent] mining accidents in West Virginia… What were your reactions to that, and does Mothman fit into it?

AC: I wouldn't go that far. I thought about it, just because the Hatfield and McCoy name came up. Well, McCloy actually… One of the guys' names was McCloy, which is an interesting name because it shows up in CIA lore.

GK: Yes it [does]. But when you heard about the two [accidents] weren't you waiting for the next shoe to drop? Don't you believe that things happen in threes? They certainly seem like they do…

AC: I wondered if it wasn't a diversion. It's hard to say. I mean there *is* a history in West Virginia of exploiting the labor pool for resources. And some of these explosions *are* unexplained. Who knows what's going on there. The explosions *could* be outgrowths of labor problems in the mines, like in the 1970s, but I don't know.

GK: Weren't there a couple of things that you wanted to talk about, related to your work and those who have supported you?

AC: Oh yes… We have a nice little circle of artists here in Seattle who all seem to have paranormal experiences in their background. I've inter-viewed some of them for the documentary, particularly Jim Woodring. Jim is a gifted graphic artist, and Bill Frisell is a guitar virtuoso. Both are pretty well known around the world. They're doing a multimedia event at Carnegie Hall in New York City sometime soon. Frisell's mother is from

West Virginia, and he's a big Mothman fan. And Jim and his wife, Mary, have both contributed interviews to the documentary because they both had precognitions of 9/11. Jim actually did a drawing of a plane coming down and crashing into a fatcat robber-baron with a big cigar... It came out the day of 9/11, but he had to withdraw it because it would have seemed like a really cruel joke. He had to pull it immediately from publication... And there were other artists who drew pictures that depicted something similar to 9/11 *before* it happened, like Penny Van Horn, who made a woodcut showing a Texas oilman riding a missile. I also wanted to throw out a couple more names of guys, people in the circle that have been inspirational. There's Charles Krafft, an artist known for his "spone," or human bone porcelain. He takes the remains of folks and makes porcelain items out of them. It's a fascinating endeavor. He also makes various firearms and military-inspired sculptures out of porcelain. He does really shocking, ironic work.

When I made the above comments about my fascination with Krafft's bone porcelain, I was completely unaware that the ritual ingestion of human bones containing "occultum" was once widely practiced by ancient seekers of Enlightenment. The Moorish "moon-eyed people" of ancient WV were almost certainly practitioners of this Middle Eastern art. It is an art that probably spawned the mummy legends... Earthworks have been found in the Ohio and Kanawha Valleys strewn with broken and crushed bones.

AC: Bruce Bickford is another guy here in town doing very original work in animation. He did the famous Claymation collaborations with Frank Zappa. These are all guys who have been inspirational to me, who have had seemingly "paranormal" events in their lives. Frisell had a UFO sighting in Colorado. The UFO was above the mountains where Tesla did all of his testing.

GK: Did you want to mention that you have a blog?

AC: Yes, I started it off with an article on Indrid Cold. As I was researching the Garuda, I found that many of the Garuda tales are over 6000 years old. Basically the oldest stories in the world involve the Garuda. The Garuda is associated with Indra, the god of "fire." Indra is usually circulating at times of cataclysm. He is known for destruction, so you could almost correlate him to nuclear weaponry and/or war profiteering. In fact, there are tales of such advanced weaponry in antiquity. They apparently had flying aircraft in ancient India called *vimanas* – with weapons, rockets, and things. That's a field that I haven't explored in depth, but it's out there. David Hatcher Childress has a book on it. The Garuda is known to "cool the fires of Indra." Again, it's this messianic activity where he's stopping destruction… I realized that Indrid Cold might be related to all this. The Garuda has "cooled down" Indra. He has become "indrid" in nature. "Indrid" is more or less a past tense of "Indra," or an adjective of Indra. "Cold" is an obvious allusion to the cooling down of the fires. So Indrid Cold, this MIB spaceman, was basically saying that he was the Garuda in cooled-down form. Now, that raises other questions… Would a supernatural deity tell you such things, even symbolically? Would he come out and say exactly who he was? Was Indrid's contact with Woody Derenberger supernatural, or was it a human endeavor featuring baffling, coded stories?

GK: Do you want to talk more about some of the connections that come out of Woodward Drive?

AC: Yes, back to the 1904 Elk River bridge collapse. That was the same year that Aleister Crowley did one of his major rituals, saying that we had now "entered the age of Horus and the Conquering Children." In the documentary, we have some interesting things occur at the Elk collapse site with my friend Harriet, whose father was the guy who worked on the secret Naval eavesdropping facility. Prior to our trip, she had had some strange dreams about this confluence. She had never been there, but we went there during filming. Harriet needed a place to stay. She stayed with a lady who was recommended to us, who lived above the confluence. By totally random chance, it turns out that this lady's daughter had moved into Harriet's house on Woodward Drive, after Harriet had moved away! This daughter had a bunch of strange paranormal experiences there, too. So we interviewed her. There was a business located at this confluence, a Carbide rubber supplier that employed many of the men that lived on my road. Let's see… I could talk more about Harriet's family or I could branch off into the Tad Jones sighting, which is a famous sighting that Keel wrote about.

GK: Why don't we go with Harriet's family and then we'll go to Tad Jones, because when you mentioned Harriet, you said her father worked at a Naval facility. Would that be Norfolk?

AC: No, that was Sugar Grove, in WV. In his early days, Harriet's dad was at Hamilton Field, which comes into UFO lore via the Maury Island UFO incident. The two Air Force intelligence officers killed after leaving Boeing Field in Seattle – carrying the "UFO slag" from Maury Island – were based out of Hamilton.

GK: Is Hamilton out by you?

AC: It's in San Francisco. We had some interesting things happen there when we were filming with Harriet. Harriet went to hypnotherapy school in SF. I went with her and taped her progress. We went to Hamilton and did some remote viewing, because she has the ability to do that. She's an amazing talent. She can medically intuit people's illnesses and so forth. We were attracted to this little town called San Anselmo, where we would film and talk about things. It turned out later that that's where Manson lived right after he got out of prison in 1967. Harriet went back to SF again, a few months later (for some more courses), and during that time there were some more goings on. There were Mothman sightings in Alaska (this is in 2003) so I wrote to her asking, "What do you think it means?" She said, "Well, there's going to be an earthquake." And two days later, there was an earthquake! Then Harriet and two other folks from class saw a missile cross San Francisco and get shot out of the sky by a laser from above. It made the news, but they sort of whitewashed it. They claimed it was shot down by another missile out over the ocean. The media immediately implied that it was a non-laser test.

GK: This is a real event, then.

AC: Yes. Two weeks later, the army "admitted" that it had done some "laser testing" from a "land-based platform." But they claimed it was in New Mexico.

GK: Well, what do you make of that?

AC: I don't know. I'm sort of just touching on the many strange things that happened while we were making this documentary. Synchronicity after synchronicity…

The Army made an obvious point of stressing the "land-based" nature of the shootdown. This is a deception based on clever wording. In 2007, I found out that Ft. Wingate, NM, which has hundreds of old storage mounds like the TNT area, is where they launch missiles that are to be shot down. They are typically shot down over White Sands Missile Range, by controllers at places like Livermore Labs, near San Francisco. Most likely, one of those missiles went awry and continued on to the Bay Area instead of getting detonated at White Sands. Coincidentally, if one of these satellite lasers were to be used on a human instead of a missile, it might look exactly like a "lightning strike" to police, paramedics, or UFO researchers. The media's coverage of these shootdowns seems designed to steer the public away from contemplating the reality of fully operational deathrays and satellite-based weapons. As depicted in the film "Syriana," satellite strikes can easily be called "suicide bombs." It all happens so fast that no one can really prove where the explosion came from.

GK: I know your dad had some involvement with the Philadelphia Experiment, is that correct?

AC: He was stationed there at the time. He was always very tight-lipped about whatever he did in the military, so there's not much to go on. He was on the USS Roosevelt aircraft carrier, and there was some vague connection to the Roosevelt family. He told me once that he had flown biplanes at their place in Hyde Park, NY. A turn-of-the-century member of our extended family, Verplanck Colvin, had a tumultuous relationship with Teddy Roosevelt. Verplanck was hobnobbing with the Astors, Duponts, and Morgans in upstate New York. Verplanck sort of fell out of favor with Teddy because Verplanck's land survey in the Adirondack Park had stymied the powerful Tory Bankers in NYC. Verplanck, a politically active environmentalist, kept the Tories (who were aligned with Britain) from buying up all of northern New York. Their original intent was to make it all part of Canada by simply purchasing it.

GK: What was the timeline for Verplanck's life?

Author's father, Andrew Colvin, Sr., at 13th & G, in Washington, D.C., Oct. 1943, the same month as the PA-X. On back of the photo is a number: 9293517. Note apparent heat mirage, also found in Colvin's 1979 crop circle shot (see page 441). In 1982, the author had strange experiences in the town of Pax, WV, the spelling of which matches the abbreviation for the Philadelphia Experiment used above.

AC: He did a lot of important work there from like, 1860 to the early part of the 1900s.

GK: Interesting that you say that, because I'm very familiar with Adirondack Park. Nowadays, nobody can figure out what exactly it is. This land management issue is a can of worms. But you're saying that Verplanck was trying *not* to have all this land scarfed up by that Tory arm of bankers from the east bank of the Hudson.

AC: Yes, and I don't know if my father may have been linked into that. It seems like there was *some* connection to the Roosevelts.

Verplanck was partly Dutch. The Roosevelts were Dutch Jews from S. America. My father served in S. America aboard the USS Roosevelt, a ship later involved in UFO sightings. It is reasonable to assume that the Roosevelts had dealings with the Rockefellers, since the Rockefellers had such an interest in S. America. According to several Internet sources, the principals at the "Big Three" Yalta Conference during WWII (Roosevelt, Stalin, Churchill, and Eisenhower) were all Jewish. That doesn't really matter, of course, except that it may have inadvertently fueled the musings of conspiracy researchers like Peter D. Beter, who railed frequently about the Rockefeller-Soviet-Israeli axis.

AC: My father's death was suspicious. He died about four years after the Mothman events. Early on, he was a chemical technician in the rare metals facility. Whenever they would have spills and things, he would have to go in and supervise the cleanup. He ended up getting exposed to some polyvinyl compounds. He got this rare muscle cancer, angiosarcoma, which it seems a lot of Carbide employees get. Carbide was forced to address this cancer issue at a national level around 1974. It became a scandal. Oddly, my father was sent to Cleveland for treatment. Supposedly they took the tumor out. But then soon after, he claimed he had been jabbed or stabbed in the middle of the night. It was almost as if someone had actually come into the house and done this. Dad kept describing it as being stabbed in a certain part of his back. A few weeks later, he developed cancer there. My sisters and I later had nightmares about such intrusions. I can come back to this story later. It may connect to a guy who is known in the Mothman story as Frightwig.

GK: Who?

AC: The Frightwig man... He wore a fright wig and was abducting people. He might come into your home or chase you in a car. He was basically trying to grab people. Who knows what he was planning on doing with them. In 1975, Keel reported that they found 25 skeletons in a cave near Point Pleasant. Keel even states at one point that he feels like these abductions were the key to understanding whatever conspiracy might have been behind the MIB activity.

Keel stated in a 1979 lecture that a disturbed rich kid from the area was probably responsible for the murders. He said that it was an open secret in the community. The disappearances seemed to stop whenever the kid was in the mental hospital. Apparently he was protected because of his family's connections.

AC: Getting back to Harriet, her dad was an engineer of Swedish descent, working for Western Electric. He worked on this Echelon facility at Sugar Grove. His car was bombed in early '68, right after the Silver Bridge collapse. The same day as the car bombing, there was a big fire at a mob restaurant in downtown Charleston. The owner of the restaurant fled to Bluefield and was shot (probably "suicided") in a hotel room. There was some sort of mob infighting going on. Harriet's next-door neighbor at the time was a member of the Bruno crime family out of Philadelphia. The mob in WV was apparently being run out of Philadelphia. This Bruno guy lived next door, and the FBI came to investigate the bombing. Strangely, they drove a Volkswagen – the model that Indrid Cold drove. The "FBI agent" told Harriet's family that the car bombing had only to do with this mob guy next door, not them. But the agent was strange. Harriet remembers him paying more attention to her than the case. He had some strange behaviors, as if he was an MIB. Bruno was eventually prosecuted, because a suitcase of heroin was found between the Plumbrook's house and Bruno's house. Bruno was convicted of racketeering but disappeared once into the prison system. No one knows what happened to him. At the very least, the whole thing shows that there were drug shipments going through Charleston. There was a "marijuana plane" crash there in the early '70s. It may tie into *The Bluegrass Conspiracy*, another book title that I'll throw out for people interested in drug/occult/military happenings in KY, WV, and Ohio.

GK: And that's by...?

AC: Sally Denton. There are a lot of defense plants in that tri-state area. Some of them were apparently making untraceable weapons and shipping them around the world for various paramilitary operations. In fact, most of the bullets are made in West Virginia. There's a big company, ATK, which moved into the Clarksburg area where Gray Barker had his UFO publishing operation. ATK and other NASA-type companies have moved into the newly named "Rocket City." ATK builds engines for some of the shuttles there. West Virginia has had a resurgence of military contracting.

GK: Whom do you attribute that to? Is this because it's been the purview of the Rockefellers and also Sen. Byrd?

AC: Yes, and also cheap labor and geographical isolation.

GK: Boy, I tell you, that is an interesting place. And you can't really overlook the proximity of Wright-Patterson Air Force Base, can you?

AC: Absolutely not. It's a straight shot from Wright-Patterson to Point Pleasant, then to all these chemical plants. After being stationed at the Philadelphia Experiment, Long Island, and South America, my father was given work at this isolated Carbide plant.

This may have been the same offer a lot of Norfolk sailors got, because isolating them would have made it easier to control the Philadelphia Experiment story.

AC: Twenty-five years ago, I had a summer job at DuPont's Belle plant, near Charleston. I talked to several guys there who had seen someone running on fire and then disappear. It was a "ghost story" as far as everyone knew. But these people had definitely seen it firsthand, and they were still scared when they talked about it. It really shook them up. And it happened more than once... Bill Walters saw it twice. Recently I was reading a book on the Philadelphia Experiment, and it turns out that that's the *very*

Supervisor Bill Walters, who twice saw men running on fire and then disappearing at DuPont's Belle, WV plant. This is reportedly what happened to sailors who took part in the Philadelphia Experiment.

description of what happened to the guys that were on the experimental ship. They had been exposed to all of these strong degaussing waves. The legend is that they would later burst into flames and disappear. I always remembered the DuPont stories. Sure enough, they seem to connect to the Philadelphia Experiment. It sounds hard to believe but I tell you, you could probably go to Belle today and find some old guys who actually saw it firsthand.

GK: When you went back to West Virginia for the documentary and such, were you ever confronted with any kind of resistance, or suggestions by the locals that maybe this wasn't a good thing to be doing?

AC: No, but this is not an activism thing for me. It's more about finding out what happened to my dad... It's more personal. We actually took a light-hearted approach to it. And people were great. It's amazing that more people just don't go out with a camera and find witnesses. These Mothman witnesses are not going to be around forever. Many of us (who were very young at the time) are now almost 50 years old. In 20 more years, you're going to see a steep drop-off in the witnesses...

GK: Well I'll tell you what, with the way things are going, I'm not so sure that those sightings won't increase in frequency in the years and decades to come. That's given the fact that I had asked you in the first hour whether this was a nefarious creature, and you indicated that it was the other way around. The sighting meant something positive, even though it might also foretell a [tragic] event that was going to happen. Is that more or less right?

AC: Yes. Now whether or not there was an additional mind control operation is another question. My Mothman contactee friend Tommy, his father worked for Carbide as an engineer and probably knew the engineers that were involved in the Tad Jones sighting. Tad Jones had been an engineer at Carbide. Ralph Jarrett, the guy who investigated Jones alongside Keel, was also a Carbide engineer. My father probably knew Jarrett, too, because I remember his name from childhood. Tad Jones left a lucrative job as an engineer to become an appliance salesman. That is kind of odd.

GK: What in the world was going on with Tad Jones?

AC: Well, he was driving on a part of the interstate that was just opened. This is maybe 2-3 miles west of Mound. He sees this sphere hovering above the interstate. He reports it to someone, and it gets into the media. He drives by the next day and sees a guy standing there with a black box (that he's turning a dial on) and an antenna. Jones asks him if he needs some help. The guy says "no" but Jones sees him the next day, too. He drives by and the guy's still there. Keel calls the gas company (because that's where the gas line went under the interstate) and asks, "Did you guys have anybody out there checking the line? Do you use this kind of equipment, with a black box and dials?" They say "no." So Keel went and looked at the spot. He found some strange footprints. He found one naked human footprint. He found some prints that looked like they were from astronaut boots. He also found some huge animal prints that looked like dog prints but which turned out to be unclassifiable. Then Jones supposedly got some threatening notes to not talk about it, and disappeared.

GK: Jones disappeared?

AC: Yes. So that's kind of odd. But the fact that he was an appliance salesman means he probably knew Woody Derenberger, the contactee of Indrid Cold. Woody was *also* a Carbide employee turned appliance salesman. Another interesting tie-in between Point Pleasant and Woodward Drive is the fact that Derenberger's psychiatrist also reportedly treated my friend Tommy. As soon as Derenberger started saying, "I'm visiting this spaceman Indrid Cold and he's taking me on his spaceship," someone suggested professional help. The Air Force came in (Woody had been in the Signal Corps) and did an exam. Then Woody privately started seeing another psychiatrist, named Alan Roberts. Roberts seems to have ended up coming to Woodward Drive and treating my Mothman contactee friend Tommy. One of the parents remembered Roberts' name. He apparently traveled a circuit between Charleston, Point Pleasant, Parkersburg, and Huntington, treating people who had had UFO contacts. That's kind of unusual for the late '60s. The interesting thing is that Roberts *then* started claming that *he* was being taken to the planet Lanulos by Indrid Cold! So we have a psychiatrist – who believes he's being taken to another planet – treating children and contactees. This is a medical doctor. I mean it's very odd. It raises questions as to whether or not Roberts was doing mind control, or was a victim of it.

GK: Odd to say the least... But as we said earlier in the show, these people might really believe that. It might be real [in the sense] that [some kind of trip] really did happen. They might be under the effects of some kind of mind op, or psychological op.

AC: Absolutely... If you read Derenberger's book, he talks about going on this "spaceship" and flying to "Lanulos." But strangely, Lanulos looked just like Brazil. It almost conjures up images of Colonia Dignidad, the Nazi fortress down there. Maybe they had a little spot there in the jungle where they would bring contactees and make them think that they were on Lanulos. Derenberger was also shown footage of several cities in Iraq. Would real spacemen care to show a contactee certain cities in Iraq?

GK: And what time frame is this? Are we still talking about late '60s?

AC: Yes. You know, people think that our involvement in Iraq is fairly recent but it started long before the 1925 agreement between (what is today) Exxon/Mobil and the Saudis. There was a little bit of French and British involvement in that deal. The contract ran out in 2000.

GK: So we're talking about interests like Standard Oil and British Petroleum and such?

AC: Yes, so it kind of explains Cheney's oil meetings in 1999, where they were talking about going into Iraq, because the agreement was up in 2000. This partly explains why we're in Iraq now. Why *was* Woody Derenberger shown Iraq? There's a lot of stuff coming out now. There was a recent History Channel show about "Nazi UFOs" and how these Nazi scientists were brought over, via Operation Paperclip, and set up in the CIA and NASA. They showed footage of basketball-sized saucers being tested. Werner von Braun ran the NASA Security Operation. They had an office in Columbus, which is about an hour, hour and a half from Point Pleasant. It could have been that they were using these German-designed craft. Since they really *did* develop these small craft, they might have used them operationally across the countryside. Most of the UFO sightings are small. The vast majority of them are only the size of a basketball.

GK: Now that you've said this, you're peaking my interest. Where were you in 1979? Were you in West Virginia?

AC: I was...

GK: This was either late '78 or early '79. I was in Vermont. I was working at a college. I looked up to the sky to the west, and I'm seeing a UFO. There's no two ways about it. And I'm watching it and watching it. And my eyes are starting to tear up because it's really cold out. I'm looking at this going, "My goodness, this is the real deal." When I went to blink because my eyes couldn't take it anymore, the thing was gone. I go into the radio station and begin my set. It was rock & roll, with all kinds of songs like "Mr. Spaceman," and "8 Miles High," and "It Came Out of the Sky." I told people, "I saw something, and it wasn't swamp gas; it wasn't a dirigible." The next morning, in the Boston Globe it said, "UFO Sightings Seen From West Virginia Through Northeast." Do you remember that there were massive sightings of UFOs from West Virginia up through Maine?

AC: Yes, and there are some old UFO magazines that have articles on it. We had a big flap in Charleston then, which was actually predicted by Keel five years earlier. Photos were taken of UFOs, and some of them were printed in the UFO magazines. I had some strange things going on in my life at that time. I had some strange dreams, a weird blood disease, and even took an anomalous photograph. But getting back to Derenberger, he was shown these images of Iraqi cities by the "spacemen." It would have been fairly easy given the technology at the time (they started high-tech mind control back in the 1920s), to show him reconnaissance films taken from some aircraft, and then make him believe that he was flying in a spaceship. That was certainly a possibility, especially when you look at the things these "spacemen" were telling the contactees. A lot of it had Nazi overtones, like the messages about the White Brotherhood of Tibet, which was an old Blavatsky notion that the Nazis latched onto...

"Secure only just and equitable laws, favoring no single locality, but conferring equal advantages, equal benefits upon all. [As for] the destruction of forests, the remedy is the timber preserve. Game should be protected from unlawful slaughter, and the grand primeval forest be saved from ruthless devastation. The interests of commerce and navigation demand that these forests should be preserved; and for posterity should be set aside [both here in the East] and in the Pacific States."

-Verplanck Colvin, report to NY State legislature, Dec. 1870

"Among the forests of the Appalachians, old boundary trees still bear the scars left upon them by the axes of the Colonial Surveyors over a century ago... Remember that the hearts of hundreds of trees of old Virginia carry the veritable axe marks of Washington the surveyor. The child who marked the tree with his hatchet in his father's garden was probably already in his daydreams a surveyor in the wilderness *[see page 281]*. I had hoped to be able to lay before you a block cut from a tree showing the original survey marks of Washington, found by one of my assistants in Western Virginia. Thus we trace an interesting fact connected with one of the legends of the youth of Washington, in his association with the early surveys of the wilderness region of the Appalachian Mountain chain, and find everywhere the evidences of careful and conscientious labor [forming] the foundation of our system of government."

-Verplanck Colvin, speech to NY Board of Trade and Transportation, George Washington's birthday, 1885.

CHAPTER 6

Marcella Bennett was one of the first Mothman witnesses in 1966. She saw him up close while she was holding her child. Hers is one of the most poignant stories in the Mothman saga, as it demonstrates our collective desire to protect our children and our civilization from unknown dangers. Ironically, it also demonstrates that Mothman wishes no harm to children, and shows that witnesses are often given psychic powers that remain for life. Marcella still feels her experiences intensely when she tells them. You really sense that Marcella is telling the truth when you talk to her. Marcella has been very open about her experiences. She has courageously paved the way for other paranormal witnesses, and for that we should be grateful.

Bennett, Marcella – Effects of a Mothman Close Encounter – 2003

Andy Colvin (AC): You are Marcella Bennett, and you're a well-known witness. I heard you speaking with CBS. Bill Geist was asking you about how you feel today about Mothman...

Marcella Bennett (MB): Right...

AC: I want to talk about what happens to people after they see the Mothman. The sort of changes that you go through... You were saying that these days, you like to "draw the shades." That reminds me of my sister, Loretta, who is Sharon Moore's mother [points to Sharon]. My sister saw a flying saucer and aliens, and also Mothman. She now pulls the blinds.

Sharon Moore (SM): She's a hermit type, really.

AC: The hermit type, yes. I kind of wanted to talk about *that* aspect of it, and if there's any psychic stuff going on. Linda Scarberry describes feeling like the Mothman came back again and sort of "knew what she was thinking." Sort of a telepathic sense that he was always kind of around and watching... Is that the kind of thing you experienced, too?

MB: Yes.

AC: Do you somehow receive messages, visions, feelings, or information from him?

MB: Very strangely here about a year ago, I believe, I had been downstairs and I got a little tired, and I wanted to take a nap. I never had anyone call and tell me about a movie they were going to make (that they wanted me to come to Pennsylvania to be in). So I had gone upstairs and fallen asleep. I evidently hadn't been asleep 15 minutes – just had fallen off. I woke up and when I did, I [realized I] had dreamt that they had called me and wanted me to go help them with this movie. I thought, "That's kind of stupid." Now this is the God's truth. My sister can bear witness. *That* evening the phone rang and the guy said [he wanted me to help with the movie]. Before I get ahead of my story, I have a neighbor, my first cousin... I called and told her what I had dreamed within so many minutes. She chuckled and said, "Oh, the movies, huh?" And I said, "Well, it kind of frightens me." I was frightened about it because "it" came through somewhere, where it had to enter my mind. That evening, the phone rang at about 8:00. I thought, "Oh, no..." I couldn't believe it when I answered the phone... I tell you, it was like you had won a new car or something like that. You looked out and there was the new car that you had dreamt about winning... Something told me they were going to call me. I kind of laughed. The phone rings. The guy actually calls. I've got the phone to my ear. I'm saying to somebody in the background, "Remember when I told you what I dreamt today? It's him on the phone!" They said, "Oh yeah, sure." It was amazing! I still am amazed as to why I would have dreamt that and, within 20 minutes or so, woken up [to find] that [it had] come true.

AC: That's the kind of thing that we've been hearing all day and have had happening in our lives.

MB: But what is it? I mean it's frightening to think that someone's telling you [things in advance].

SM: It's very frightening.

AC: It *is* frightening, but I think it sort of depends on how you look at it. One interpretation that helps me understand it is if the Hawaiian Huna spiritual system. They believe that you have a subconscious, conscious, and super-conscious mind. The super-conscious is a part of you that knows much more than the conscious mind. It knows what *other* people are doing. It knows seemingly external, objective things beyond normal capacity. I think that once you've been exposed to the Mothman phenomenon, you start to be able to hook up to a part of your Self that is sort of "out there" intermingling with others, in a dreamstate perhaps. Or in the collective unconscious... That's where you get these messages that are outside of time, that seem beyond time...

MB: Right...

SM: It's only frightening because most of us aren't used to it.

MB: It's like seeing Mothman. People ask, "How did you feel?" Well how would you feel when you walk outside and see something that isn't of this Earth? You're looking at it, but what is it?

AC: It's always slightly different for each person – sort of tailored. The Mothman appears generally the same, but little details seem to be different for each witness. It is sort of interacting with your mind.

MB: Right, but evidently it isn't out to do us any harm because I was closer than you and I [are right now]. It was like [2 feet away]. I reached for the door. I looked down. I went "Oh, no…" Then I saw the feet. Then I looked up. And I reached for my door handle…

AC: Is this when you had your child with you and you fell?

MB: Yes… And if it wanted to harm me [it could have, because] like I said, I was *that* close. At first my first thought was, "It's a guy, you know; it's a man." I could see it was gray. I kept thinking, "gray khaki work clothes." I got up. And then… Okay… Feathers… I thought, "Oh god, feathers! Not a man!" It was a "man," but not a man of this earth… I don't know what he was. He was shaped like a male. I always thought he came around at night… I could hear the flopping of the wings on the roof when I would go to bed. I could hear him. It sounded like what I [had been] looking at [during the encounter]. The huge wings, the way he was standing, the head like a bird… I'll never forget the way he was standing. It was like he was just relaxing, like he was just waiting for that moment for me to walk up.

AC: I just talked to a guy yesterday, Mike Finch, who said the same thing. He saw it and said it was very relaxed. Its neck was down, and it just kind of looked at him casually…

MB: Yes, the neck looked like it was hanging, on this side. It was standing like that. He was very relaxed, like how you pull your shoulders in… Round… The neck looked like it went down in, like a bird… Way down in the neck… To me it wasn't of this world. It could have been made by the government. It *could* have been… Don't forget, first I see the lights coming in the sky. It wasn't a plane. My brother kept saying, "It's not a plane, those aren't plane lights." It was coming right towards us. Well, I kept moving down that road, walking. I saw it but I said, "No, I don't want to see it." And [my brother] kept calling my name, "Marcella, come back. You got to look at this. It's not a plane." It was like I didn't even realize [what was going on. I was] just going right along. Going on towards [Mothman]. I wasn't in control of my thoughts or my movements.

AC: You weren't in control?

MB: It was like if somebody would hypnotize you and say, "go walk over there. "I was just going along, you know.

AC: You mean when you went back to see it, you were in that state?

MB: When I first saw it at the car, yes. When I left my brother ten feet away, watching this light. Wanting me to watch it... I don't even know why I said no. [Internally] I kept hearing "no." I could hear my brother's voice in the background saying, "Marcella come back, look at this. You gotta see this, it's not a plane!" And it was just like I was being taken. I had to go. I had to go straight towards the car. I wasn't in control. It was like I was being drawn to go another way. I wasn't supposed to stay and look at those lights.

Did Mothman intercede on Marcella's behalf against a UFO? Such a thought would echo the beliefs of Bigfoot contactees I interviewed, who felt that Sasquatch interceded for them against negative "aliens" in "UFOs."

AC: So between that time and say, a year ago when you had this premonition that you were going to work on the film, did you have any other instances where you got advance information?

MB: Yes, I've had different things about family members. I lost my daughter a couple of years ago... Before she passed away, I had a vision about her in a mobile home. There was a fire. [Before] I woke up I was trying to get to the trailer, hoping to get her out. And it wasn't three months later that [it happened]. They told me [that I had only] a few hours, maybe two days, to get down [there to see my daughter alive. When I got there] she was lying dead. I had no way to get her home.

AC: I'm so sorry to hear that. We talked to a lady earlier today from North Carolina who had the same thing happen with three different husbands. With each of them, she had a vision of them dying before it happened.

MB: I didn't think too much [about it until later]. I [had] thought about the dream or whatever it was... But then, when I went through the experience with her death and where she lived (I didn't go to her home until after she was buried), I thought, "It's like I dreamt this." And then I got to thinking, "Well, you *did.*"

AC: Tom Ury said that he rode in the car with you to Pennsylvania. It sounds to me like your story had an effect on him.

MB: Yes, we all discussed it. Of course the two up front had never seen the Mothman (they were younger), and Tom and I were a little [nervous]. We were looking out the windows, thinking Mothman might come down... [What if Mothman] knows when you're going to talk about him? I mean you don't know... You don't *really* know. I felt the presence. Oh, his presence was close. Close for a long time... When I went outside at night, if there were people walking behind me – a crowd of people – I would stay right with them. I was looking around the corner to see if he was around the corner. He was *that* real. In my mind, he could be *right there*. I mean, I feared him. I still fear him today... Although he didn't hurt me, I don't know what he wants... Whether it's government [or not, who knows?] We don't know what's out there. I sure wish we could find out. And I'm sure that there have been a lot stranger things than *that* that have been seen. Like my sister was saying about the balls of fire coming down, years ago, right out of the sky... And my mother, I've heard her say how when we were living in the country that [the balls of fire] would seem to come down "wrong." You'd think it was going to burn the house down, that it was going to get the house. So I don't know... Who knows what's out here? We don't know, because it's the unknown. It's the *unknown*. You can look out that window. It can be dark. You can see a big dog and say, "Why no, I think it's a horse. It's too big for a dog, so it's a horse." But this [Mothman] thing, you can't describe. A man with feathers and red eyes? I didn't see the red eyes, but I do believe [others] saw red eyes... Where I sleep, I can look right up and see the stars and the sky. I can see something shoot this way and something shoot that way, and another light going this way. I think, "Uh oh, don't forget to draw those blinds. Get those closed off for the night" It gives you [some sense of] security, even though you're still way up high [where he is].

CHAPTER 7

Marcella Bennett's sister, Maddie, was with her at the 2003 Mothman Festival. Maddie seems to have tapped into some kind of Mothman energy force. You can see it in her eyes and hear it in her voice. I simply asked her one question and she went into a dramatic, inspired monologue that made our spines tingle. The women of Pt. Pleasant have been through a lot over the years. They have looked reality straight on. Maddie's words show that birds and humans have a special connection, and that the Mothman experience can be a positive one. She also reveals that some local pastors preach about UFOs, and that the congregations more or less accept them as fact. In her description of the balls of light seen by her family, Maddie provides yet another example of how old schoolhouses seem to be incubators for paranormal phenomena.

Bennett, Maddie – UFOs and Balls of Fire – 2003

Andy Colvin (AC): You were talking about how you feel that 1966 wasn't the right time for the government to tell us that UFOs were real. Now you think that maybe the time is right?

Madeleine Bennett (MB): The time *is* right. This generation isn't like my generation. This generation is open to anything. My generation wasn't... We respected our parents and never at any time did we ever say, "Why not? Why can't we?" The flying saucers... I can remember the minister, Roscoe Thorne. He lived in Point Pleasant. He worked every day at the Marietta plant where they made steel. He preached on Sunday morning, Sunday night, and Wednesday night. [When] he preached he always ended up saying that the flying saucers were here, that someone had spotted them. I was a kid but I took it all in [including] this bird that Marcella saw... Birds play a very special part in my life... I've never lived any place that if a bird came up I couldn't ask the bird, "You know what, I would like to have that house, or I would like this [or that]." And if I look at that bird and I say to that bird, "You've come to see me and I need something," the bird stays for a while. After it leaves, I get what I ask for. So whenever there's a bird, don't never shoo that bird away [as if] that bird just [randomly] came by. No, he did not. A bird is *something...* It's like the eagle in the Bible...

My mother and I we were sleeping out one night. There were 9 of us children. My father was an alcoholic, and of course he always ran us out of the house when he came home... People say today, "Would you like to go camping?" I say, "No thanks, I had enough of it when I was a kid." *[laughter]* So anyway, that night we had decided to go around to the *old schoolhouse* where we had started a school. Everybody had found his or her place on the ground to sleep. We always bundled up so mother could watch over us. It just so happened that I had gone to sleep. My mother said "Maddie, wake up." She said, "Wake up fast!" I woke up and said, "What's this about?" And there was this big ball of light. There is no way you could describe it. She said, "Stay awake for awhile… If it moves, we'll stay here… If it doesn't move, we'll leave." Now I say this today, and I'm a strong woman (by the grace of God)… I can think about somebody. I think to myself, "I wonder if so and so is there?" I can go to a telephone, and I can guarantee you that when I call them they'll be there. I'll guarantee you, God will warn me ahead of time when something is going to happen. I know no one has any control over death. I have worked with cancer patients. I've been with them when they took their last breath. This Bird is something that God is trying to tell us. I think the day will come when you'll know what it is and when you find out what it is, it won't be anything like you [expected]. I believe that. I believe God will show us. I think that after you've seen [Mothman] like my sister here…

This is my favorite sister [by the way]. She has a twin. I would say that since she saw this Bird, she has a sweeter spirit – a more giving spirit. She stays in tune with God. She's gone through a lot. She lost her daughter two years ago. Maybe once or twice she's broken down, but not to amount to nothing. I believe that God changes you by things like the Bird. Like the ball of fire… They said that when I was born, I had a veil over my face. Today I can think of something and if I want it, I get it. I've been through a lot. My first husband (the children's father), died with cancer. I took care of him all the time. When he died, it was on a Wednesday. The day was beautiful. It was June the 3rd… Now, I want to say this… How many people never get the opportunity [to say goodbye]? You say God isn't a god of mercy and love? And cancer? [God] can do anything. I never dreamed [my husband] was going to die that day. *But* I got up and I said, "I have to put clothes on because someone might visit." That day we had two people ring the doorbell. He said to me, "Don't answer the door…" At 5:00 I got up and I went over to the bed and looked at him. I said, "You haven't slept all day and you haven't closed your eyes." Now look, I'm nothing… I couldn't do anything [about the situation]. But on that day, I looked down on him and I said, "I love you. And I know you love me." And I said, "You're going on to heaven. I'll come later, so lay your head down." And he went to sleep. So I believe in God. Nothing is impossible with God. And I say the Bird that my sister saw, and you saw… I would take it to heart, because a lot of us didn't get to see it. We didn't get to see this. Who's to say what you're seeing it for? Did you have a need at that time? Was there something going on in your life? Could God maybe see further down the road than you? Did God need your mind to be changed and maybe think a little bit? Where would you have gone if you had not seen this bird? I'm sure it put a stop in your life. It made you think different. I say when it's all said and done, you will find out. Whatever God does, he does it right. Whatever he does, he does it perfect. And nobody can compare to him.

The flying saucers… Yes, I believe that they came from another land. They came from another planet. At the time, people couldn't have taken it. They could not have taken the [shocking idea that] "yes, it's a flying saucer and you'll be seeing them a lot." There would be elderly people who'd drop over dead. Do you realize people wouldn't come out of the house? Do you realize children would be afraid to go to school? Do you realize what would happen? That's why they don't come through with it and say, "Yes, it is a flying saucer." But years have got by. We're in a different generation today. *Now* is the time they're going to bring it up, because you've got people thinking differently than when I was growing up. The time has come. They will release it… When the flying saucers are revealed, you will know that there are people on other planets… I say God knows what he's doing. I say the Air Force and them, they're smart enough to know certain things – what you can take, and what you can't take. I believe that when I saw that ball of fire, that light… That light was from heaven. When I looked at that light… Buddy, I couldn't begin to tell you what God has shown me… Like for instance, a couple months ago, I had gone to bed and had just laid down. I had prayed, and I was getting ready to doze off. And the Lord woke me up. He said, "What if I turned *every* "light" *on* right now? Where would they all be?" You know… People think that we're going to live forever… I will say this today, and I stand before God and ask to be forgiven if it isn't the truth: get yourself right with God, because we're getting ready to leave.

CHAPTER 8

"The difference between me and a madman is that I am not mad."

-Salvador Dali

"I doubt that generations of eye and/or mental witnesses to these apparitions can be mistaken. It is obvious that people who show effects of what has traditionally been termed "demonic presence" frequently also see unusual animals. One participant in this nerve-wracking experience has told me that he feels the presence of an entity or 'force,' which 'squeezes' his nervous system. [But] which comes first: the Guruda [animal] presence or the squeeze on the nervous system? In the voodoo system of beliefs, it is thought that a loa or god-spirit 'rides' the bodily mechanism of ritual partici-pants who do not take on – as in Western Spiritualism – the specific personalities of deceased human beings, but actually – in the course of channeling powerful forces of nature – become the gods themselves. Clearly, this is similar to the involuntary procedure by which the divine force of Jesus Christ might be said to animate the inspired body of a Christian evangelist. The gods themselves as supernatural forces certain would not confine themselves to any individual human channel. This availability of the god persona necessitates a revision of the way we ordinarily think about personality."

-Eugenia Macer-Story, "Sorcery and the UFO Experience," p. 92

Colvin, Andy – Introductory Testimonial – 2002

Andy Colvin: I built a shrine to Mothman with a friend. Some of us in the neighborhood subsequently experienced things like UFOs, aliens, poltergeists, and various creature entities. I experienced a jump in my creative abilities. I suddenly was able to draw. I picked up a sudden inclination to both draw and photograph, at age 8. All the children who came into contact with this phenomenon seemed to have a jump in I.Q. as well. Some of us were tested at our school and found to have a higher I.Q. This sort of mysterious help continued, despite the difficulties involved with seeing something from the other side – from another dimension. It definitely affects your relationships with others, who may or may not believe you or your new point of view. Following elementary school, those of us who had seen Mothman or come into contact with one of its forms we were split up by circumstances. It was

10 years later when I was brought back into contact with one of my friends. In 1981, there seemed to be a confluence of energies that led to our meeting. Out of nowhere, my mother suggested I contact Harriet.

I contacted Harriet and she had a story to tell. In 1968, Harriet had seen an entity that looked like the Flatwoods Monster. Harriet understood what our Mothman shrine had been about. She knew that birdmen and "aliens" of some sort had visited us. She said that my dead father had visited a medium she was consulting. The psychic told her to tell me that my father had a message for me: that I "had a protector." This sparked something in me. I found myself embarking on a photo project that was to change my life forever. I traveled around the country taking pictures of myself in a flying position at various national monuments. At the same time, there were some sightings of Mothman in the area of Cincinnati (where I went to college) that seemed to mimic a sighting I had had years before. I had driven by Rocky Lake State Park on the way to school. I always had a strange attraction to both it and The Serpent Mound. One night in 1982, I was driving by this lake and experienced one of the few missing time incidents in my life. I later found out that Mothman sightings had occurred at that very lake, and at that very time. Someone had seen a "tree" that suddenly expanded its wings out slowly. It didn't take off; it just spread its wings and put its wings back in. It was seen more than once. It was similar to a dark figure I had seen years before coming out of a tree, or acting like a tree. Something was going on in 1981. Mothman seemed to be reactivating in the Ohio Valley. The first photo in my series was of me, dressed as a Messiah-like character, floating over the hills of Appalachia near Pt. Pleasant. The project expanded into pictures that played off of Lee Friedlander's *American Monument* series, Keith Haring's "outlined" subway characters, and Laurie Anderson's multimedia stageshow.

> *Later, it became more freeform. I eventually dropped the flying character altogether, and simply started photographing anomalous scenes in their raw, natural state.*

As a child, I experienced fleeting sightings, poltergeists, and strange dreams of telepathic Bigfoot creatures. The earliest sighting was when I had just turned 7, in late 1966. I was riding in the family car near Dunbar, WV, on our way to the bowling alley. We were passing the site – unbeknownst to us – where Mothman and a UFO had been seen just a few days prior. As we were passing that site, I actually saw something flying behind the car. It was as if I knew it was going to happen beforehand. When we left the house, I *knew* it was going to happen. I was aware of this creature from the news reports. At first I was excited about it. It was one of the most wonderful things that had ever happened to me, having a birdman flying around. As a kid who loved animals and all that nature offered, it just symbolized freedom to me. As a youngster trying to adjust to school, it exemplified everything I was hoping for: to just be free to fly. If people were afraid, who cares? The Mothman was freedom to me.

But the car incident was creepy, as if the creature was reading my mind. Unfortunately when I saw this thing flying behind us and alerted my father, I was roundly smacked and told to forget about it. My dad grumbled something about the government, that it was probably a government thing that we should not get involved in. My father worked for a top defense contractor, Union Carbide. His best friend was an engineer working on a top-secret project called "Echelon," which a lot of people know about today. It is a global eavesdropping network involving the sharing of intelligence between the US, Britain, Australia, Canada, and New Zealand. My father seemed to have inside information about something. He instinctively knew that it would be best not to follow that line. Looking back, I can't say that he was wrong, per se, but I think when one looks at the full breadth of the Mothman Phenomenon, one can see a lot of positive things in it. Even though my father didn't want his son involved in it out of parental concern, ultimately it was something that couldn't be stopped. One visitation occurred when I was staying overnight at the house of my friend Timothy Thomas Burnham, who had the shrine. He was experiencing the widest range of phenomena in 1967. Few of us believed him, and this had an impact on his psychological state.

> *I wrote to Tommy and told him how sorry I was for not believing him. Unfortunately, my letter went unanswered. I have since heard through his mother that he is not interested in speaking to me, Harriet, or anyone else from West Virginia.*

I was staying over at Tommy's house one night. He predicted a visitation would occur. Sure enough, some elfish "little green men" seemed to appear while we were asleep. It's all very hazy, but *something* definitely happened.

> *Even if it was a dream – which I think it probably was – something made me dream about entities similar to the ones described by Tommy.*

Immediately after this event, Tommy and I made a blood-brother pact to always remember it and to get back together again in the year 2001.

> *This reunion was to involve trading back toy shrunken heads that we had made by heating liquid plastic in sets of molds collectively called "The Fright Factory."*

Shortly after making this pact, while standing at a certain spot in the yard designated by the aliens (according to Tommy), we both had precognitions of a future terrorist event. The ultimate terrorist event, 9/11...

CHAPTER 9

Chip Colvin is my older brother. Chip is a retired administrator for the State of Delaware. His wife, Mary Ann, was a longtime telecommunications supervisor at DuPont headquarters. It was during one of my visits to Delaware that I found out that the DuPont family had close connections to George Washington, and that Washington had a mansion near Romney, WV. One dark night in Sept. 2003, as we were trolling the WV woods named after Chief Cornstalk, Chip and Mary Ann recounted seeing a large UFO. This craft turned out to be similar to what John Keel had seen flying over Ravenswood, WV, during the Mothman flap. When we got out at a crossroads to walk around, my brother revealed to me for the first time that he has "star protectors" watching over him. He also talked about meeting "the devil at the crossroads." When we looked at the ground, we noticed that there were thousands of small, glowing things in the grass. They were not fireflies. We never exactly figured out what they were, or if they were plants or animals. Even though we had grown up in the area, we had never seen such creatures before. It was as mysterious as the time my brother and father stayed out in the woods all night, looking for a "white owl" that had been mysteriously "trapped in the rosebush."

Colvin, Chip & Mary Ann – Star Protectors and Delaware UFO – 2003

Andy Colvin (AC): Weren't you saying that you have a "protector?"

Chip Colvin (CC): Yes, I have "star protectors."

AC: "Star" protectors?

CC: Multiple stars, yes...

AC: Do they send energy down?

CC: I don't know how they do it, but I'm better off because of them.

AC: Do you sort of look up and make contact?

CC: Yes...

AC: Do you ask questions and get answers?

CC: I haven't tried that.

AC: It works, I think...

Mary Ann Colvin (MAC): Isn't that like, "wish upon a star?"

CC: Yes…

AC: Can you tell us about your joint UFO sighting?

MAC: We were on the boardwalk [on the coast of DE] and in the sky was something darker than the dark night. It was a shadow in the sky.

CC: It was a black hole in the black sky.

MAC: It was just sitting there and then it left, like, really quickly. We didn't hear anything.

AC: Estimated size?

CC: I couldn't tell the altitude.

MAC: I thought it was kind of low. It was over the ocean. We were on the boardwalk.

AC: Was it football field size?

CC: Like I'm telling you, I didn't know how high up in the air it was. I didn't know what the perspective was.

AC: How did you feel as you saw it?

CC: Amazed, wondering if it was really there, because it was just an *extra darkness* in the sky. I had the sense of a vessel. It had a defined shape.

MAC: [It was a] ship thing. It looked like a blimp-type shape.

CC: Probably seemed more like a disc.

MAC: But it had no lights.

CC: It was a square disc. A flat surface…

AC: Did it arouse any sensations in you as you saw it?

MAC: Not that I recall…

CC: No, because it was so fast.

AC: [Did you have any feelings] afterwards?

MAC: Yes, because we talked about it. We both saw the same thing.

CC: We just always wondered about it. It's been probably three years.

AC: So you speculated about it for a while?

MAC: Yes, we still to this day don't know what it was, other than what we just said.

"In 1964 to 1968, we had the biggest UFO wave in the history of the world. It wasn't isolated to the United States. It was everywhere... Every country on earth was inundated with UFO reports. Here in the United States, the sightings were so common that I was able to go to an area where people had been seeing UFOs... In West Virginia, there was a town called Ravenswood. They told me, "You can come by on any Wednesday night and you can see UFOs." So I went down there. They had set up a sort of circuit where they would call each other and say, "One is coming over right now!" The weirdest thing that I saw in Ravenswood was on one Wednesday night. It was a beautiful night out. The stars were out and it was cloudless. Suddenly, a black thing came over and blotted out the sky. A huge black thing! It wasn't a cloud. It was moving along [blocking the] stars. And it just rumbled down the Ohio Valley. We couldn't possibly estimate the altitude. It could have been ten miles up; it could have been a hundred miles up. But whatever it was, it really unnerved me that night. I had many nights when I was very unnerved."

-John Keel, 1990s lecture

CHAPTER 10

"He who knows others is wise. He who knows himself is enlightened."

-Lao Tzu

I probably never would have investigated Mothman if it weren't for the experiences of my oldest sister, Loretta. Her tales of seeing UFOs, little green men, Mothman, angels, and black panthers were just weird enough – and believable enough – to spark my interest and keep me going through the lean years when Keel's work was still unknown in WV. Prior to the Internet, it was very difficult to dig up information about the paranormal. Loretta is one of the very few people to ever have a visitation from Mothman inside her house. Also, her description of a robed figure shapeshifting from inside a ball of light echoes Harriet Plumbrook's experiences (see chapter 36) and substantiates the Buddhist and British legends of entities being associated with UFO lights. Due to having had so many strange encounters with entities over several decades, Loretta has developed a resiliency that is quite remarkable.

Colvin, Loretta – Bed Bat, Saucer Entities, Electromagnetism – 2002

Andy Colvin (AC): Let's go back to the thing in the room, the dark thing. Can you describe it a little more?

Loretta Colvin (LC): It was big. As big as my bed maybe... It encompassed the whole area over my bed...

AC: Did you see a face? Did it have a head? Arms?

LC: It wasn't really arms... It was more like wings. Big wings...

AC: And they were spread out?

LC: Yes, flat... He looked like he was pressed flat against the ceiling. I can't remember a face.

AC: Eyes? Did it have eyes?

LC: It seemed like it might have had eyes. Like it was maybe looking at me... The wings were the biggest part of its body. That's probably why they stick out in my mind. The wings were the more menacing part of its body...

AC: Did you get any messages from it? Did you communicate with it?

LC: Not that I realize...

AC: Most people would have been really scared…

LC: No, I don't really get afraid of things anymore. I have a lot of odd things happen. I don't normally tell people because they [might] think [that] you're "not quite right."

AC: Most people would just assume that that was some sort of a dream.

LC: Well, it wasn't a dream because the sun came up and I was still lying there [looking at it] so…

AC: If you weren't afraid, why didn't you just go to sleep? I mean you stayed awake for some reason…

LC: It's like we were looking at each other's face, but nobody was really saying anything. I'm not sure why I kept staring. Maybe we were communicating [in] some way and I just don't realize it…

AC: So when you say face, what kind of face was it?

LC: Well, I don't remember. It was a dark form mostly. And in the dark, it's hard to see.

AC: So you were just looking where the face would be?

LC: Yes, you could tell by the wings where the face would be.

AC: Did you feel like there was nothing you could do because it was over you?

LC: Yes, maybe… But I wasn't really afraid.

AC: So you had to sort of just give in to it. Right? I mean, if you had fought it…

LC: Well, I sort of like interaction with things that aren't explained, so I would probably stay there because I wouldn't want to miss something.

AC: Did anything happen the day before or after?

LC: I can't remember… I can't remember any stress involved. When my [deceased] grandfather [Ed Gibson] comes around, it's always during really stressful times.

AC: Have you seen any other creatures? I remember you once said that you saw black panthers as a kid…

LC: Well other people saw [them, too].

AC: Oh, other people saw them?

LC: Oh yes. Remember the man across the street, Mr. Hughes, the little old guy?

Southern States Feed & Seed Foxhound Contest, Mound, WV 1966 - This is the author's first photograph, taken the same year the Mothman sightings began, picturing his grandfather Ed Gibson, a local merchant in seeds, moonshine, and conspiracy theories. Colvin's sister claims that Gibson's ghost saved her from being pinned underneath burning car wreckage.

He saw it. Back then it was a common knowledge among the people in that area. We could hear it and see it late in the evenings. It wasn't just me...

AC: The WV black panther may only be a mythological being. Experts claim that true panthers don't exist in North America – only brown mountain lions and bobcats. These are not melanistically pure black.

LC: This was definitely black.

AC: It could be like seeing a big black thing over your bed...

LC: Well, this panther screamed like a woman. That's why everybody said it was a panther. [By the way] I have a feeling that I have a cat nature. I'm not sure what this means exactly but, maybe two or three times, I've had a feeling that I was transported into a catlike [state]. It's almost like I left my body for a while, and then I was a cat. I even clawed myself. I had claw marks that other people saw... In fact, Craig could tell you about the one night [that he was] scared because I was clawing myself. He was trying to restrain me [at first] but then he just went away and left me alone. I [even] head-butted somebody who was trying to restrain me when I was in the catlike thing. That was David, a boyfriend I had... Somehow I think it might be tied into sexuality.

Loretta also mentioned that she sees other catlike people while in trance, and that these people are blue in color. This reminds me of Randy Whyte's blue spirit guide (see chapter 43), and the blue psychic monks of Tibet, who reportedly used ferocious cats as guards.

AC: Tell us about your flying saucer encounter.

LC: I think I was about 12 or 13 (I'm 56 now). One night I woke up because I heard a noise that sounded like a squishing sound. I got up and I looked out the window, up into the wooded area. There was a space in front that was sort of cleared. I guess they had cleared it, but there seemed to be something sitting there. It had lights around the center portion – a ring, sort of – and the whooshing noise, which seemed [linked to] when the lights went around. There was a point where it gained momentum [every time around]. The whooshing sounded like a "woo-woo" and it was somehow connected to the lights. The lights made the whooshing sound. It sounded like it was either gearing up to take off, or it was powering down.

AC: Were there color changes?

LC: Yes, there were colors in the lights.

AC: Did they change or did they stay the same?

LC: I think they stayed the same, but they were like in blocks. I mean they were different... As the light went around, the different colors sort of came out more than maybe the color right before or after it.

AC: When it came to your vision it got brighter because it sort of was facing you, and then went on around?

LC: Well that could be true. Yes, that's probably true. The thing I remember the most was the sound, though. It had a really odd sound. It was kind of a squashed down, sort of egg-ish figure. I don't think it was perfectly round like a circle. And I don't remember legs or anything that it stood on. It was just sort of over the ground. I stood there for I don't know how long, and then that's all. That's all I remember of the night. I don't remember anything else, whether I went outside or anything.

AC: Did you think to call on anyone else to look at it?

LC: No, but I normally don't do that when I see things.

When I first heard this story as a youngster, Loretta also mentioned someone rummaging through her dresser drawers that night. One wonders why real aliens would want to do such a thing. Loretta was teased by her siblings for revealing this detail, so she eventually stopped mentioning it. Could this "alien" search activity be connected to the trancelike interrogation we apparently underwent years later?

LC: Now there was the time in Dunbar when I was married to Glenn... I had that dark figure appear that night, which I told you about. Over the years, there's been so many unexplained [events].

AC: Tell me about that one again.

LC: I was asleep in bed. This was probably 1977, '78. A little house in Dunbar... I awoke because there seemed to be lights in my eyes. At first I thought it was a car light, but there are no windows on that particular side. So I'm opening my eyes and something's really bright, and it's getting bigger. The light gets really big and I'm staring... I was frightened of this, whatever it was… There was a robed figure [in front of the light]. This looked more like a man than a bat or winged figure. He seemed to be a hooded type of thing. This was a time in my life when I was having a struggle with good and evil in my person. I was having a spiritual [conflict]. There was a fight within me on which way to go… I remember my husband at the time was lying there, and he wouldn't wake up no matter what I did. So I lay there all night. I mean a long time, terrified, without being able to move… Paralyzed, with this hooded thing standing there, three feet from me... If I could have put my hand out, I would have touched it. I kept lying there for what seemed like hours. When the birds started waking up at dawn, this thing just diminishes again. It goes down to a ball of light again. It just goes right down the way it came up. I lay there for a long time. I was asking my husband, "Why wouldn't you wake up?" But he was oblivious. I could not wake him up. I kicked [him] as much as I could… I was terrified. That was the worst thing that I've seen… That was the most terrified I've ever been. After that, nothing ever scared me as bad.

AC: What color skin did it have?

LC: I don't think I could really see the face… The hood was like over [the face]. It looked like a man. It didn't look like a creature. But it was scary. It was something demonic, or something conflict [related].

AC: Didn't you see another entity around that same time?

LC: It was around that time. It was in like a two-week period. I wanted to get closer to God again. My husband drank and I wanted to get away from that stuff. So I'm having a real struggle within myself to be better, to do what I know I should do but [often] don't. I was lying on the couch watching TV and, all of a sudden, these two hands were around my neck, squeezing my neck. It was two hands... I felt the fingers. And I remembered from church [what to do] when demons are around... That was my mindset at the time. I'd been thinking about things like that. First thing I did was, I jumped up on my feet with these two cold hands around my neck. I remember using Christ's name. That was the first thing that came out of my mouth. I said it out loud and as soon as I did that, whatever it was left me... I think it was some type of demon activity. I don't know if they were trying to scare me to do one thing or another. I never knew what the purpose was, but it did happen around the same time.

AC: One of the other people I've been talking to brought up the Christ imagery. According to them when you see something like that, it's an extension of your unconscious. It's your unconscious mind making an image for you to learn from.

LC: What was I learning from the cold hands around my neck? To be scared to death?

AC: I don't know. What happened after that? Did you make any changes? I mean did it cause you to get closer to God?

LC: I got better after that. Maybe the fear itself made me get better. Maybe that was the point. Sometimes fear makes us [act] differently. [For] some people, the fear of death might make them better people. Maybe that's what it was.

AC: But it's not completely your unconscious. It's your unconscious mixing with something out there. Even though ultimately it's all from inside, there are locations where the energy is stronger (like on Woodward Drive). There's more magnetism to influence nearby organisms. The rocks around West Virginia are very magnetic, and there's a lot of lightning. That magnetism from the lightning gets stored in the rocks, and also in metal structures like the pipeline that ran from our house to Bethel Church (where the various sightings occurred).

LC: So the metal [in the pipe conducts and stores the electrical charge]?

AC: Yes, and the magnetic energy stored in that pipeline connected our house with Harriet's and Tommy's!

LC: That's kind of cool. Oh my, I'm getting cold chills!

AC: So any vision seen on Tommy and Harriet's lane might also be seen at our house, if the entity or vision were tapped into the electromagnetic field of the pipeline.

LC: Oh, my hair's standing up!

AC: But I wanted to ask you, how has your worldview changed? I mean at that time, you were using Christian teachings. How would you describe your worldview now? Are you still a Christian, or has it become wider?

LC: Well, whatever we think that word means… At this point in my life, I still have a really strong love for some entity… Everybody calls it something different… I think there are a lot of people that have the same love for "someone." Maybe it's a love of your creator that's sort of instilled in all of us. Whether we follow and do what we should, or not, I think we still have that [love] somewhere. I still have that really strong. I mean I can "well up" for no reason because I'm feeling this great love for the creator, this person, this whomever, this thing. But I know I'm still not doing right. I'm not helping anybody. I'm still in my little box that I don't like to venture out of…

AC: Maybe the path of the healer is a path for you. I know for me, I can go to a Christian church now and cry. I can go and see a service and totally feel how other people are seeing it…

LC: But you can do that even by yourself, sitting out under a tree.

AC: Absolutely!

LC: I do that a lot. But I spent the first half of my life [being] a better person. I did things for people back then. But as I got older, I had a lot of really bad things happen to me. I got really pissed, I think. Seems like I had too many tragedies, too many bad things. I looked around at other people. I didn't see them having quite as many [problems]. So I was really pissed for a while. I changed from one extreme to another. I went from helpful, always sort of going along with people [to not].

AC: Why is that ultimately any worse than the other?

LC: Something in me tells me that that's not a good thing to do. I don't know. As I'm getting more towards my own death, I feel like I should be doing something better than what I'm doing.

AC: Does it really have to do with doing, or does it have to do with a state of mind?

LC: I don't know. Don't you think we humans are here to be of some service?

AC: We're here to know God. Or we're here to know ourselves. We're here to find out something.

LC: We're here to fellowship with God. So maybe you're right. It just dawned on me. We were put here to fellowship with him, not necessarily to do good to all the other people.

AC: In reality, we are God. In reality, we are the cosmic sea. Somehow, for some reason, we become physical. This is the big question in philosophy and religion. Why do we suddenly go into human bodies and manifest? Why have all of these seemingly physical things going on? What is the purpose of that? There seems to be some purpose, although we don't know what it is. It may involve one's fellowship with oneself. But it's a pretty unanswerable question.

LC: Jesus took human form. Why? To feel things… To feel pain, to feel emotions, to feel love for other people… Maybe that's why we have human bodies. Maybe that's the only way we can do it. You know pain teaches you things, of itself. It teaches you patience. It teaches you how to endure. There is a purpose for it. I don't think anything happens [out of] coincidence. I think everything is here for a reason. You doing this right now might affect me later. I simply don't know yet how…

AC: That's the path of Shiva in Buddhism. That's the path to God. You're yearning for God. That's one of the three traditional paths you can take.

LC: But I don't feel that my life here is worthwhile, that I've learned what I'm supposed to learn this time. I feel I'm probably going to have to come back again because I didn't "get it" this time…

AC: Do you want to come back?

LC: Yes, probably. And me knowing that I'm not "doing right" is even worse because I knew better. I feel I'm going to be held more accountable. I haven't made some great change to change myself. I don't affect anybody because I just stay by myself… So how am I doing any good for anything?

AC: Well, in Buddhist [cosmology] none of that's [super important. Initially] all that's important is that you come to know yourself.

LC: Well, I've done that, I think…

CHAPTER 11

"The entities produced have no actual mind of their own. Their mind is partly gained from the human receiver, and is partly connected with the energy field of the superspectrum. Some of these transmogrifications attain a degree of independence once they have been created. But they are mindless and lost. They wander around our dimension as ghosts and goblins, harmless until they find a believer. Then they feed off the mind and emotions of that believer, assuming the identity subconsciously chosen by the believer, and creating manifestations within the context of the belief, or frame of reference."

-John Keel, The Eighth Tower, p.78

Colvin, Spring – Born With A Veil – 2005

Andy Colvin (AC): *[to camera]* I have a stack of papers two feet high from this last year. Interesting articles on different things that have happened... We've had these Mothman sightings in Yugoslavia, which came right about the same time as the Katrina flood in New Orleans. Was Mothman signaling for us to look at Katrina, or was this a reference to the successful Clinton/Rockefeller effort to break up Yugoslavia in order to keep the drug pipeline from Afghanistan to Europe open? Is there a connection between the two events? Katrina was almost an exact repeat of a previous flood from 1929, where the levees were admittedly breached *on purpose* to save the wealthier neighborhoods from destruction.

> *Like Houston, New Orleans is built on the oil business. New Orleans is more or less run by the Houston oil barons reportedly involved in the Kennedy assassination. Both cities also have major NASA facilities. In early 2007, a man working at a New Orleans defense plant (making armored vehicles) testified to Linda Moulton Howe that he had seen a gray alien floating several feet above the ground while on the job. He described a long history of abductions triggered by beeping noises inside of his head.*

We also had some interesting sightings in Mexico of flying entities, and some video footage of them. The footage doesn't really resolve the question of what it is, but there's definitely something floating around the skies in Mexico.

> *The floating shadow person from Mexico seemed to have a loop of some kind in one hand. It reminded me of the shadowy figure I photographed*

in a crop circle in 1979. The same loop can be seen in old test footage of men flying with "jet packs." Jet packs are fueled by mixing non-combustible liquids via hoses. Could ancient references to the Garuda's "ambrosia" and "coiled serpent" simply mean that people once flew around with jetpacks in an earlier, more enlightened age? Are these floating beings ghostly "replays" of earlier events, or just some modern technician's attempt to freak people out? Considering that human advance and decline might be cyclical, could witnesses in Mexico perhaps be seeing into the future?

My sister, Spring, has been in several hostage situations in her life. One time when we were teenagers, she was held up at the Weight Watchers store she worked, across from Blaine Island in Mound. She thought it was me with a hose on my head. She laughed at the guy. It turned out to be a real robber with a huge machete. Years later, she was taken hostage by a man with a gun at the mental hospital in Huntington, WV, where she worked. Recently a former boyfriend held a knife to her neck. He had stolen the wedding ring given to her by her new husband. When we were in WV in 2002, the ex-boyfriend – who has a Mansonlike presence – stole one of the cameras from our crew vehicle. Also there was a fourth incident where a former patient of Spring's from the V.A. Hospital (in Huntington) took hostages *while working at the post office in Charleston.* It turned out that my other sister, Loretta, was one of the workers held hostage!

Spring comes into play here with, really, one of the biggest things that happened in 2005. It is this photograph that she unwittingly sent me... Hopefully you can see what we're talking about here. *[shows image]* This was a picture that was taken of me in 1973 by Spring. She sent this to me randomly, in a box with some other things. We suddenly noticed that if you look at this window – in the middle, at the bottom – you see a face. And that face, my friends, looks exactly like depictions of the Thunderbird and Garuda that I found in the Native American literature at the Univ. of New Mexico. It's unusual. This photo was taken probably the same week that I saw the strange morphing figure come out of a tree. It's almost as if this thing followed me home and was looking in my house, watching me...

Ironically, I had already named this series "The Mothman's Photographer" before I found out about this picture. Initially I just wanted the title to indicate that I got my desire to take photographs from my experiences with Mothman, that I was a photographer *because of* him. The amazing thing is that it seems that I'm also the Mothman's Photographer in another sense, in that I – or at least my sister – took a picture of the Mothman. Yet we didn't even know we were doing it. Keel stated in a lecture that these entities sometimes pose for quite a while, in order that a particular witness may photograph them.

Perhaps a result of being born with a "veil" over her face and having many psychic signals coming into her life over the years, my sister sometimes manifests strange physiological symptoms. Sometimes when I am talking to her, I can tell that she is channeling or otherwise "on a roll." Spring is highly telepathic. She will often be able to instantly tell new acquaintances key events from their personal lives. Likewise, she will often accurately predict upcoming calamity for friends and family. As the years have gone by, I have figured out her process a little more. Spring and I have thus been able to stay in communication despite a number of difficult misunderstandings. Her psychic visions are not something that she particularly enjoys. She has often implied that it is a curse of sorts. Her psychic experiences, as well as her experiences being held hostage and working with mental patients and disturbed military veterans, have given her post-traumatic stress disorder and fibromyalgia. As a result, she often has to manage mysterious physical issues such as those described in the upcoming interview. This particular symptom tends to happen at the same time of night Nancy Sheets would usually wake up disoriented in Harriet Plumbrook's old house (see chapter 34).

Colvin, Spring – Heart "V-tacks" – 2004

Andy Colvin (AC): You've had your heart checked over the past 6 or 7 years, by a monitor that you sleep with. At 4:12 every night, you have some kind of a… What is it, an attack?

Spring Colvin (SC): An arrhythmia. I go into arrhythmia in my sleep, at the same time [every night]. And I usually wake up at that time. But I don't have any chest pains; I just wake up at that time.

AC: Do you know that it's 4:12 when you wake up?

SC: Usually around 4:00, yes.

AC: I ask because I'm able to wake up in the middle of the night and know exactly what time it is…

SC: I do that all the time. I mean, I can wake up any time and know exactly what time it is. This cardiac thing [though] is sort of strange.

AC: Did you *ever* have anything happen to you at 4:12 that was traumatizing?

SC: I've barely had anything bad happen to me *except* being held hostage. But you can die from that! I asked the first doctor, "How many runs of V-tacks did I have?" He said, "Three." My newest doctor [said] I had 11 runs of V-tack at 4:12 a.m. I've had 6 halter monitors on. They put them on for two days, and it always shows up at the same time. It's weird.

AC: Is this connected with your prior use of the drug phentermine?

SC: That's when it basically started, but that's also the same time I was held hostage at work [at the psychiatric hospital in Huntington, WV].

AC: At 4:12 AM?

SC: No, it was in the afternoon. I got home at 4:12 in the afternoon. Not in the middle of the night…

AC: You got home at 4:12 in the afternoon?

SC: Yes. So maybe I'm twelve hours off. Hell, I don't know… I just think it's really weird. I want to tell my psychiatrist about it. I see her in a couple weeks. She knows everything about me, so I'll just tell her.

Colvin, Spring – Tsunami dream – 2005

AC: So that dream you were having. Was that about the 2004 Asian tsunami?

SC: Yes, that was like 3 months ago. I was having dreams about it, but I thought [the tsunami] was going to be in Japan.

AC: Well, I thought you said that you were "in the building," or you felt like you were there?

SC: Yes, yes…

AC: I saw an image of the tsunami disaster on TV. It looked like the description that you had given before it happened. I don't know if you remember this, but I asked you some questions about what it looked like…

SC: The last time we talked? Before it happened?

AC: Correct…

SC: The water was coming through…

AC: Yes, you said you were in a building.

SC: I didn't know where I was. [I have] things like that all the time…

AC: I think I asked you how tall it was, and if it was a glass building or not. Anyway, I saw some footage last night and I thought, "*That* looks like what Spring told me about." I realized that *that's* what you probably dreamed about…

SC: I had a dream 3 months ago. I told somebody about [it]. I said, "There's going to be a really, really bad earthquake. There's going to be a lot of water." You know, it's just a dream I had. I just passed it off like another nightmare, which I have all the time. I just passed it off, and that's so terrible. Isn't that awful? All those people…

AC: Yes, there are some terrible stories there. By the way, I recently got wind that Mothman was seen near San Francisco.

SC: Oh! You're kidding…

AC: Oh no… People see him all the time. They see him in different places…

SC: [And it] looks like the same [Mothman]? That's really weird.

AC: Here's the thing about this last one. The lady who witnessed it saw it over a Shell refinery. It appears from her description that it's the same refinery that I kept poking around when I was out there a couple years ago filming. It was on this little ridge with these beautiful views. I kept trying to get up there to see the view and take pictures. I think this recent witness said she saw it right over that refinery. It's a little unclear from the description where she was. This refinery is on a waterway that connects Concord Naval Weapons Station to Mount Diablo and a town by the name of Orinda (which translates as "the Thunderbird's energy").

Mt. Diablo was also the central point for the Zodiac Killer, who based his coded kill-map on it. A fan recently sent me an email saying that if one watches the new film "Zodiac" closely, one can see Mothman clues such as a winged being on the door of the killer's trailer. Rumors have long swirled that the Zodiac was a programmed military assassin.

SC: What do you think he's trying to do? Warn people or what?

AC: I'm just wondering if you have had anything psychic about San Francisco, because Harriet thinks that San Francisco is going to have some terrorism or something, maybe one of their bridges…

SC: Well, the dogs are upset. My dogs are getting upset. They're scratching at the door.

AC: Right now?

SC: Yup…

AC: Why?

SC: I don't know. Anyway, I don't know [about San Francisco]. But you know they had this thing on TV about how the animals always know beforehand when something happens. That's why they run.

AC: Did you find out anything more about Polecat? Housecat? Some guy that you prophesied was going to have a car wreck?

SC: I saw him today. He said he was fine. He says, "I'm fine. I didn't die like you said." I said, "Well, I didn't tell you [that] you were going to die. I just said you would get hurt." And he said, "Well, I had 23 stitches on my eye."

AC: And that was a couple weeks ago?

SC: Yup. But I don't like it. I should keep my mouth shut.

AC: Because two weeks ago is when my son found that Garuda thing in the photo that you sent me! And that's also when Aunt Mary (Colvin Barlow) died. There's also something else… I had a dream of Ezekiel's Wheel over the Kmart parking lot in N. Charleston, looking towards the Blaine Island plant.

SC: That's weird.

AC: It was very realistic, and very powerful…

SC: What do you think that means?

AC: I found an image from the 1100s of Ezekiel's Wheel. There's a winged being that goes along with the chariot. I don't know if that influenced my dream or not, but it wasn't a Mothman dream. It was just a dream of this wheel.

The focus of the dream seemed to be that I was experiencing what the sky looks like when a special kind of fireball travels through it. The quality of the purple light seemed to be of some importance. The fireball seemed to have the ability to create a new kind of space-time "furrow" as it burned its way through the atmosphere. It seemed more like a momentous cosmic event than a mundane physical event. The wheel had a metallic, jeweled structure to it, as if it were manmade.

SC: Ezekiel was a prophet in the Old Testament.

AC: Yes, but the weird thing is that yesterday I was reading an article that I found by just doing keyword searches. I put in "NASA" and "West Virginia," and I found an article written by a guy who clams to have worked on a classified project at West Virginia State College that involved extremely low frequency signals (same as used by oil companies and the Navy). He was pulled off on a secret side project which involved going around the Kanawha Valley looking for aliens and "dimensional portals." The NSA and NASA seem to be trying to get in touch with other dimensions. He said that NASA is publicly talking more and more about exploring other dimensions, rather than outer space. One of the things he said was that NASA wants to bring about the Second Coming of Christ... There was a mention of Ezekiel's Wheel...

SC: Did you dream about it before you saw that?

AC: It was months ago when I stumbled across the drawing that had a winged being with Ezekiel's Wheel, and I have no idea how I found it. It was just something I printed out and kept. I never thought a thing about it... Then I had this dream. Then I read this article after I had the dream. The author, William Dean Ross, claims that NASA wants to bring about a holographic "Ezekiel's Wheel" type of scenario, where people *believe* they see it... He said they were trying to "recreate Ezekiel's Wheel." That's the exact phrase he used...

SC: Oh, that's freaky!

AC: Supposedly they feel that they can create this, have people see it, and build a religion around it...

SC: How about Jacob's ladder?

AC: What do you mean?

SC: How about the Tower of Babel?

AC: Well, I don't know. I think he mentioned Babel, too. Why did you say that?

SC: That's where everybody crawls up on the tower and they all speak in different languages. God took them up on the tower and confused their languages so they could all be different, and make them more creative. That's my interpretation [at least].

AC: What was one of the most recent things that you talked to our deceased father about?

SC: You want to know?

AC: Yes.

SC: I don't want to cry. You want me to tell you? Okay. You remember Toad, who stole your camera? We broke up, and I kept thinking he could [handle being] allowed to be my friend. But he stole the $8000 diamond ring [my husband] got me... I took it off while I was doing artwork. I let Toad come over here and eat lunch. He stole that ring. And so I went over to his apartment. And he pulled a knife! I said, "Where's my ring? That's not your ring. That's a family heirloom." I said, "I want it back. I know you have it." He pulled a knife on my neck, pulled my hair back, and threatened to kill me. I got out without being killed. I got in the car, came home, and had a freaking nervous breakdown. [My husband] was truck driving at the time. [When] he came home, he took me to the police department. They took a picture of my arm where Toad grabbed me. [This situation] has gone on for four months. They keep me coming back to court. He paid for the ring to be reset. I got the ring back. That's an admission of guilt. They had a picture of my arm. I keep thinking I should drop it because it makes me so upset. They put me up on the court stand and made me feel like a [criminal].

AC: Does Toad have a family connection, or somebody powerful who makes sure things go his way?

SC: No.

AC: Was he in the military?

SC: No, he's a hairdresser.

AC: It doesn't make sense. What are some of the things the guy's done in his life?

SC: He used to traffic.

AC: A trafficker?

SC: He's a farmer/ redneck from Indiana.

AC: He's from Indiana? Is he a police informant?

SC: Not that I know of, but the detective that came over here said, "I know who he is." And he said, "I'll come over and take more pictures of your arm." I had to go out on the front porch, and they took more pictures of my arm. So they have evidence that he assaulted me.

AC: Does he have a farm? Does he have any property?

SC: Yes, in Indiana…

AC: You've never been there?

SC: No.

AC: What's he doing in WV if he's got property in Indiana?

SC: His mom lives there. He's not allowed in there because somebody was going to kill him over [criminal activity]. He supposedly stopped [doing it] twelve years ago.

AC: He's one of the scariest individuals I've ever met.

SC: I know, Andy. He scares me. He haunts me. I'm telling you, he haunts me in my mind. He is a freaking scary [person]. He is like a wizard.

AC: I know, and that's why I think there's more to this story. I don't want to make any grand statements, but there's something about him and his connections... I suspect that there's some other stuff there...

SC: My lawyer looked him up on the computer and the only thing they had on him was a false police statement that was dismissed. That was it...

AC: See? That's unbelievable.

SC: There's got to be more than that.

AC: He really might be an informant. Nothing nationwide?

SC: Nothing...

Spring went on to explain that our deceased father had come to her and given her the courage to continue the fight to get her wedding ring back.

A few weeks prior to this, I received the following strange phone call from Spring. This was in the midst of all the psychic phenomena surrounding the filming of the Mothman's Photographer. One gets the uneasy feeling from this call that there might be some kind of mind control programming embedded in the products of the video gaming industry. At one time during filming, I idly fantasized about possible connections between video gaming, major defense contractors, global charities like World Vision, and cryptozoological covert ops. This speculation was triggered by Loren Coleman's awarding of a major cash prize to a seemingly hoaxed Mothman photo (that mimicked a real photo of mine) on behalf of Hasbro, a partner of World Vision, Wizards of the Coast, and Boeing. Coleman has published with subsidiaries of Time-Warner, a company dominated by the Rockefellers and Ted Turner – who is also from Ohio.

In Feb. 2007, Turner Broadcasting agreed to pay all costs of a security scare triggered by a marketing campaign for the cartoon "Aqua Teen Hunger Force" that disrupted travel in Boston for nearly a full day. Coincidentally, certain official Aqua Teen Hunger Force toys are sold together in the same package with a Mothman toy called "Mothmonster Man." Time-Warner owns one of Coleman's web partners, Road Runner LLC, a Herndon, VA, company accused by progressive news organizations (like BuzzFlash) of illegally blocking stories critical of Bush. Coleman has also written for Sterling Publishing Company, which bears a moniker similar to Sterling Corporation. Sterling Corp. is the small, obscure WV company that somehow managed to purchase control of Bayer Aspirin while at the same time allowing significant proceeds to flow back to German investors – whose assets were at times frozen by the U.S. government. Coleman recently reported that a late relative of his ex-wife's worked with Robert Kennedy in the governmental department dealing with frozen assets. Kennedy was harshly criticized for unfreezing the postwar assets of Nazi collaborators like I.G. Farben and Bayer.

In June of 2007, it was reported that Reagan shooter John Hinckley – whose father was once president of World Vision – was being allowed to leave prison for extended visits with his family in VA. This would be akin to letting Sirhan Sirhan, Squeaky Fromme, or Sara Jane Moore go home for long holidays.

In the following phone call, my sister seemed to be channeling something. Like Keel's informant, Apol, the phenomenon seemed to be using my sister as a medium. The message had to do with what sounded like a video gaming name.

Colvin, Spring – "ZombiAKA" – 2004

Andy Colvin *[starts recorder after a couple of things have been said]:* Say that again, now?

Spring Colvin (SC): I want to know *who* it is, because they have really artistic abilities. He's doing graffiti all over town.

AC: Say that again real quick? [You first said that] *it's* bothering you?

SC: Yes it is. It's ZombiAKA. And it's everywhere. I want to know who it is.

AC: How do you say it?

SC: ZombiAKA. Zombi "Otherwise Known As." And it's everywhere around town. He sprays... He paints graffiti. I want to know who it is because it's bothering me. Is that bizarre or what?

AC: How is it bothering you?

SC: I don't know...

AC: Do you think it's a code?

SC: For me? No, not for me... I think it might be a code that *he needs to channel his artistic abilities into something else.* But I'll never find him. It bothers me because I see it every day, everywhere.

AC: Well, do you think he's a veteran? Is he somebody from the VA Hospital who is crazy?

SC: No. It's probably somebody who goes to Marshall and just does graffiti, and has good handwriting... But he *needs his hand somewhere else.* I don't know.

I'll never find him. But it just bothers me. Do you think that's bizarre?

AC: Well, what really bothers you about it? I haven't heard a real reason.

SC: Well, there's no particular reason about it… I just think the person is artistic and needs to channel it somewhere. And you know, *I'll never find him*. But he needs to do something else with it. He puts the same thing over and over: ZombiAKA. And it's on and on and on, everywhere…

AC: And the "e" is missing from the "zombie?"

SC: Yup. It just bothers me, because I want to know who it is.

AC: So that you can do *what*? Tell them to change their art?

SC: No. I just want to say hello.

As a side note to this, in 2006 I attended a charity auction in Seattle. I sat very close to Kyle McLachlan of Twin Peaks fame. I have always felt that this series captured the mood of Mothman country. Sitting right beside me was a man who worked for Microsoft, in their international gaming division. As coincidence would have it, this man worked closely with an old schoolmate of mine from WV, David McCoy. He told me that McCoy was a recognized genius in the field of computer gaming, and that McCoy's early white papers from the 1990s were still being used at Microsoft. This is a great compliment in a field that moves so fast that five years seems like an eternity. McCoy is an example of the creative genius that seems to have sprouted up around Mound, WV. In what hopefully isn't a Mothman vision of the future, McCoy has designed a scary, fascistic world into his popular X-Box game Crimson Skies. The logo of this post-apocalyptic product features a Naziesque "winged disc" reminiscent of Mesopotamian birdman reliefs. McCoy is a co-founder of a company with an interesting name: Hidden Path Entertainment. One of the writers used by Hidden Path is Loren L. Coleman, not to be confused with Loren Coleman, the creature journalist.

In June 2007, following a spate of "drone sightings" photographed by someone in California named "Chad," an anonymous tech person named "Isaac" posted a website featuring detailed design drawings of Chad's drones. Isaac claimed to have worked as a civilian employee designing the drones in the 1980s. The secret program was called CARET, and it was located in Palo Alto, CA. The goal was to develop invisible surveillance drones, using reverse-engineered alien craft recovered by the military. When designers like Isaac bitterly complained about not having enough background information on items placed before them, the military said, "we don't know anything about these because they are extra-terrestrial."

Isaac's design documents showed very complex and unusual symbols placed throughout the hardware. Many of the symbols looked like elaborate crop circles, and were reminiscent of the spiral chakra "serpent" seen in ancient Garuda imagery. Isaac claimed that the symbols themselves were the key to making the objects work. Somehow a complicated, overlapping matrix of computer substrates was developed that got rid of the need to have normal software running the hardware. With this system, the very placement of the symbols in the matrix caused functions to be set in motion. Unfortunately the whole set of events, from the "sightings" to the "photographs" to the "designs," appears to have been an elaborate "viral marketing" campaign by Microsoft. According to blogger Adam Hawks, who followed the clues embedded in web source codes, the hoax was designed specifically to market Microsoft's "Halo 3" video game. The Halo 3 craft appear to exactly match the CARET drones. Come to think of it, telling civilians that source material is "extra-terrestrial" would be the easiest way to accomplish tight compartmentalization.

CHAPTER 12

"So long as we adhere to the notion that we are dealing with
random extraterrestrial visitors, none of these contactee stories
makes any sense. So I ask you to place the UFOs into a terrestrial
or ultraterrestrial framework. Think of them as you might think
of a next-door neighbor who is hooked up to your party line. The
pieces of this puzzle will begin to fall into place."

-John Keel, Operation Trojan Horse, p.68

Colvin, Andy – Grassy Knoll Radio interview 3 – March 10, 2006

"Vyz" at Grassy Knoll Radio (GK): We left off at a very interesting juncture
at the end of the second hour... You got into some of the Nazi connections.
What does this all tie into, not only with the Mothman but the things that
take place, strangely, in West Virginia?

Andy Colvin (AC): I think the thing we were onto there, with regard to
Mothman, was what the contactees were being shown by the "aliens" and/or
"spacemen." It's kind of interesting that these spacemen were not "grey" aliens,
like the ones we hear about today. These were normal-looking folk. This
makes me believe that they were probably terrestrial humans. These contactees
were being shown, during their spacecraft rides, visions of strategic energy
locations like Iraq. Why was Woody Derenberger shown visions of Iraq? Were
these simply reconnaissance films (perhaps shot from small, remote-controlled
AVRO saucers) viewed while under the influence of drugs or hypnosis? Are
they indicative of an oil company link to whoever was making contactees
think they were taking space rides?

> *Jacques Vallee investigated a series of suspicious deaths in S. America that
> were linked to remotely piloted, radiation-emitting UFOs that looked
> like "refrigerators with headlights." Due to the necessity of penetrating the
> jungle canopy from the air, advanced radar technology was already in
> place in the oil and mining industries at that time. These "UFO deaths"
> may have been completely terrestrial.*

GK: Let's go back to that because we did end on it, and that's the name that I
was trying to think of. It's Woody...

AC: Woody Derenberger... He's the big name in the story, as far as contactees
go. He wrote a book called *Visitors from Lanulos*, which is the story of his
contact. A lot of people came to his farm to see UFOs. Keel saw these
and mentioned that there *were* some lights in the sky, but it could have

been a light show of some kind. These contactees were also told things about the Thule Ultima, which is a Nazi-Theosophist idea reminiscent of the White Brotherhood of Tibet. The Nazi's holy land – their sort of "heaven on earth" – is this land of Thule. Thule was supposedly up near Iceland, before the land masses moved.

According to Peter Moon, many Nazis felt that Long Island – especially Montauk – constituted the last unsubmerged vestiges of Thule. Many evacuated to Montauk in VIP U-boats. Emanuel Josephson's many books tie the Rockefellers directly into the German Masonic Illuminati of Adam Weishaupt, which spawned the Thule Society.

AC: They have all these legends about it. It entered into the Nazi mindset pretty strongly. There was a Thule society that held the secret teachings. You have these contactees being told Blavatsky-like Nazi legends. There is a distinct possibility that the "contactee message" came from Nazi scientists who had already done mind control in Germany and were brought over to Ohio State, Wright-Patterson AFB, and thereabouts. Very close to Point Pleasant... These unimaginative guys probably were just following some lines of programming that they already had used before, in the concentrations camps and so on.

GK: Let me stop you there. The individual's name is Derenberger, and he was apparently an abductee?

AC: He seemed to be a willing participant. We didn't really have the abductee thing yet.

GK: How does he make himself a willing participant?

AC: Well, that's an interesting question.

GK: I mean do you go out in a field and say, "Here I am"?

AC: Yes, but it's kind of interesting that he had a military background, and his son was in the military at the time. And Derenberger got onto the lecture circuit. It's not easy for the average Joe to get on the lecture circuit. I've noticed that a lot of the prominent UFO lecture people seem to have this military or intelligence background. Derenberger's whole case was visibly monitored by the Air Force. There was an Air Force officer "investigating" him. They set up a lie-detector test and a psychiatric test for him by a famous doctor.

I have misplaced my source material for this, but I seem to recall that the name of Woody Derenberger's famous doctor was Jensen. Was this the same doctor Jensen who mind-controlled Candy Jones, the famous model? While it may be possible that Indrid Cold was Mothman wanting to present another piece of coded information to a willing witness, the hoax option seems untenable to me. If it was all just a hoax by Derenberger, why did he include the material about Iraq, and why describe the planet Lanulos as if it were in the Amazon? Why the indirect references to drugging, surveillance, and mind control? Should we perhaps consider Derenberger a "whistleblower?"

AC: Derenberger's private psychiatrist was a Dr. Alan Roberts who, again, was reportedly the same psychiatrist who was treating Mothman contactees like my friend in Charleston.

GK: Is that a good or a bad thing?

AC: Well, it's unusual because Dr. Roberts was *going along* with the story that Indrid Cold was indeed from another planet. You'll remember that Indrid Cold was the Volkswagen-driving spaceman telling Derenberger these things.

GK: This doesn't really matter as far as your credibility. I go back and forth with a whole lot of people – Christians and non-Christians – and we discuss this idea of extraterrestrials. I don't really have a problem with it. I really don't know where it fits or what we should think about it, but I don't think there's any problem that there's been some intra-terrestrial travel throughout time. It wouldn't shake me up. On the other hand, Andrew, we (the US military) probably have UFOs [ourselves. Or] whatever's out there might belong to someone else. The point is, what is the point? I want to [take] you back to where you said there might have been some infiltration through Operation Paperclip. Do you have documentation? Do you know that they (the Nazi scientists) also came into the Upper Ohio Valley and the Northeast?

AC: Oh yes, absolutely. That's hard fact.

GK: I agree...

AC: There are several books on that that people can look into. George Lazaby has an older book. Linda Hunt has a fairly recent book that's kind of hard to find, as is Christopher Simpson's. There were lots of negotiations that went on, concerning what to do with these guys. That's where the paperclip came in. They just decided, "Let's put a paperclip on the files of the guys we want in, without telling anybody." It was obvious that the public didn't want these guys in, but the generals decided (as usual) against popular opinion. Actually there was a Union Carbide official who was part of this process. I like to focus on Carbide because they were so prevalent in the valley that I lived in. There are many different angles, things that Carbide was into, including activities out near Area

51. Union Carbide has facilities all over the country. They were in charge of the uranium mining. According to press reports, they had a full-scale Martian landscape set up in the early 1960s, supposedly for testing materials. That could have been in Area 51. There were people who overheard some of the JFK conspirators talking about Area 51. There seem to have been some shenanigans going on there.

GK: What about Wright-Patterson AFB?

AC: The theories swirl about it, like the one about them having the crashed saucer from Roswell. I personally don't put much faith in that whole story. It's sort of a way to occupy people's imaginations, so that they don't look at the other things that Wright-Patterson did which are easy to verify. Like bringing in all these Nazis...

GK: Let me verify. Do you think that Roswell was a cooked story – a distraction?

AC: Yes. And there were lots of things like that in 1947, such as the Maury Island incident with Fred Crisman. Maury Island was the first "modern" incident, aside from the UFO shootdown attempts in Los Angeles in 1942 (and any others that may have gotten little subsequent media coverage). Maury Island happened before the Kenneth Arnold sightings. This slag fell from a UFO. A guy on a boat, named Dahl, was hit and suffered burns similar to what you might get from radiation. Dahl turns out to work for Fred Crisman. Fred Crisman was a CIA "disruption agent" later rumored to have been at the JFK assassination.

Guy Bannister, one of Lee Harvey Oswald's handlers in New Orleans, just happened to be the FBI director in charge of investigating UFO incidents in the Northwest at that time.

AC: Crisman stayed in the Seattle area most of the time. He was involved with disrupting progressives in the Seattle area. He worked for Boeing for a while. He would go in and discredit a key person. They usually had a target – a movement or group that they were trying to disrupt. Crisman was really good at turning people against each other. He did that at Boeing. He did that at the Seattle School District. They would get down to the level of messing with progressive teachers in the school system. Crisman may have been part of Operation CHAOS that I mentioned before, disrupting the peace and labor movement. Crisman also was a pilot. He was caught stealing gold from Swiss Air at one point. There's a newspaper article about it, in fact. This gold thing comes up time and time again. The Nazis had an interest in gold, just like they had an interest in the Thule and the White Brotherhood of Tibet, a group of great beings thought to inhabit some ethereal mountainous region while watching over things...

A book by Jean Ziegler called "The Swiss, The Gold, and the Dead" details the ways in which the Swiss helped the Nazis prosecute their invasion of Europe and then hide the spoils. In the afterword, Ziegler fingers the NY public relations firm of Ruder & Finn, as well as the Washington lobbying firm of Barbour, Griffith, and Rogers, as leading the current propaganda war for the Swiss (to hide their role). Both companies were founded largely by the Rockefellers, and staffed with members of the CFR, a Rockefeller-dominated organization.

GK: The Thule idea was, as you stated correctly, a very imaginary place. I kidded around with you off-mic when we talked, that the cartoon strip *Prince Valiant* (which was Nordic in origin) always talked about Thule as being a real place. In fact, Valiant was [said to be a member of] nobility in Thule. But there is that idea of a far northern land that is completely white, with a superior race, etc. I'm not going to go any further, but this is an extension of what supposedly has been happening (or some would say *not* happening) in Antarctica all these years. Orwell made a very curious illusion to the lost islands of Antarctica... I'm not subscribing to a hollow earth theory where all the good people live on the inside, but there *is* something shaking there. It goes through this continuum, into what Hitler had embraced. I would say that the Thule Society [is an extension of] Skull and Bones on this side of the ocean.

AC: I've recently picked up the ultimate book on the Skull and Bones but haven't gotten through it yet, called *Fleshing out Skull and Bones*.

GK: By Kris Millegan... He did a great job. Also Anthony C. Sutton wrote *America's Secret Establishment*, focusing on Skull and Bones.

AC: Yes, it's been years since I read that one. But yes, there's so much stuff out there, and I'm usually reading about ten books at once.

GK: I know the feeling.

AC: It's all there somewhere, in difficult-to-reach areas of my gray matter. I just try to focus on the overall picture, to sort of draw a map of it all.

GK: Are you working on a book right now? Would you give us a little insight as to what would be the focus of that book?

AC: Well, it's about the Mothman and my photography. It's about all of these different tentacles. There's about 50 or 60 pages of text in it. Everything will be mentioned that's meaningful to me right now. There are lots of photographs in there. About 300 in fact... It's sort of a poetic approach to conspiracies. I don't think that genre has been done yet, so I'm excited. It's a new style. It's an outgrowth of the way that I've worked all along, which is to take photos as a way of understanding the subconscious. A lot of strange things happened when I was young, and a lot of those things have leaked out in my artwork. Some of the things in the book from 20, 25 years ago have an amazing synchronicity to the things we're talking about now. I'm really looking forward to everything about it. It's called *The Mothman's Photographer: The Work of an Artist Touched by the Prophecies of the Infamous Mothman*. By the way, we did the soundtrack to the video series first, right after I decided to tell my story publicly. Since I do things backwards, the first thing I did was the music. The CD is called *Powerdump: Songs for Abductees, Public Relations Dupes, Corporate Hacks, Media Wanks, and Other Assorted Mind Control Victims*. It is by I.V. League, a notorious experimental band that I co-founded. It was an offshoot of another notorious band from Austin, called Ed Hall, which I started with three guys from Houston. They are sons of oilmen. I'm actually working on a documentary about that whole experience. Many seemingly random things I've done in my life seem to connect to parts of the Mothman story. This Houston oil connection is one of them.

GK: *Sons of Oilmen*…that's a pretty provocative title right there, if you wanted to use it.

AC: In Austin, you meet a lot of people from all over Texas. You hear a lot of things. One of the things I remember hearing was from a woman whose mom was married to a big chicken processor close to the Clintons. She was saying that Clinton and Bush were a lot closer than people realized. This was back in the '80s, when everyone thought that they were polar opposites. Yet she was saying, "no, they're not." Of course, now we see Clinton and Bush together all the time, doing these humanitarian tour spots. The word on Clinton was – and it didn't really hit me until today – is that he supposedly is a member of the Rockefeller family.

GK: You had a Rockefeller down there, too: Winnie.

AC: Clinton is rumored to be the illegitimate child of Winnie.

GK: Winnie is one of the older ones. He was a former governor of Arkansas. It's almost like that joke about Kevin Bacon, you know? In this country, all roads lead back to the Rockefellers. I mean Arkansas is a funky state, where a lot of stuff went down [like Mena]. That's where Sam Walton started off with the China-Mart chain that we know today. I'll say this [so] you won't have to. Wherever the Rockefellers set up camp, interesting things happen. With Winnie in Arkansas, Jay in West Virginia, and Nelson in New York, it was a love boat.

AC: I had a roommate who was a manager at Wal-Mart in the mid-1980s. This is when they were smaller and hadn't yet gotten out of the South. He went on to work for Continental Bank, which has a lot of intelligence connections and perhaps some connection to the Whitewater scandal. But getting back to the White Brotherhood… In the filming of the documentary, we focused on Harriet quite a bit. Right after the 9/11 attacks occurred, I realized that this prediction that I'd gotten from Tommy was true. I was freaked out and felt I had to contact Harriet. I searched and searched, and finally found her through Ohio State Univ. Interestingly, the people in the alumni office tried to keep us apart. I could never figure that out. It seemed like they were purposefully telling us different things. But somehow we found each other, and I gave her the Keel book. It changed her life. I mean she had had all these experiences related to Mothman, but no real context for them. Many strange things have happened to her. For instance, she woke up one night, wandering down the road. She didn't know how she got there. She's had some serious intrusions in her life from these forces. I don't want to give the impression that I think all of these things are government ops. If you read Keel's books, it's clear that it's been going on somewhat naturally for centuries.

GK: What has been going on for centuries?

AC: This paranormal phenomenon. It's in all the ancient lore, from elves to djinn, dragons, angels, and holy men. It gets described in different ways. We clearly have religious miracles – and things like them – throughout history that can't be explained. All of Keel's work is essentially about that. There are so many examples that you can't deny that *something* is going on… But we followed Harriet to hypnotherapy school. She changed everything about her life during the filming. She had once been a woman who worked in the airline shipping industry – which I had worked in as well. That was one of the things we found out about each other; that we'd both been working as loadmasters at airports. It's very rare for a woman to be a loadmaster. Then she decided to become a healer. She's got the natural ability to intuit people's illnesses, just by looking at them. A lot of people came to her already for that sort of thing, but she still needed some sort of certificate behind her name. So she decided to go to hypnotherapy school. We went there. We ended up spending most of our free time in San Anselmo. We were just were attracted to it for some reason. We later found out that that's where Manson lived. The town recently got flooded, just this past week.

I recently met a guy at the gym. Let's call him Tom. Tom has a lot of interesting symbolisms in his personal story, including a connection to

Poster by Frank Kozik for Colvin's mystical Austin band, Ed Hall (short for "Educational Hallucination"). Kozik's knack for symbols led him to equate Colvin with Christopher Lee in the role of the young Mummy, in the 1959 Hammer Studios film "The Mummy."

San Anselmo. He happens to be employed by the bank whose investment arm processed the anomalous trades prior to 9/11 involving United and American Airline stocks. He said that his bank has a division that greases the funding wheels for defense contractors like Blackwater and Halliburton. Their job is to speed up the amount of time it takes for these private contractors to get paid. This involves close contact with Iraqi and Afghani officials.

I was amazed by some of the little details in Tom's life. He grew up in L.A. and loved watching basketball player Jerry West, who is from WV. Like Keel, Tom has always had an interest in magic and magicians. His mother was Jewish (I think) but he is now a strong Catholic. The parish he once attended near San Anselmo sent a key representative to Rome. This representative was helpful to Tom's family, and others as well. This representative now happens to have a job similar to the one that Pope Ratzinger resigned from in order to become Pope.

Probably the most tantalizing of the tidbits Tom dropped was his allusion to the use of mind-controlled agents for covert ops. Tom served in El Salvador in the early 1980s, and also in Desert Storm. He made a

*point of saying that the source for his mind control info was an operator
working for a private company. Apparently private contractors are now
using these zombie agents, not just the military. According to Tom, these
agents are programmed to have a heart attack if they are being interrogated and are about to spill the beans. Author Adam Gorightly alluded
to something similar in the case of Manson's right-hand man, Charles
Watson. Watson shriveled up and almost died after admitting that he
(not Manson) had killed the victims.*

GK: A providential flood, perhaps?

AC: I don't know, but a lot of strange things happened when we were there.
One was that they did an initiation into the White Brotherhood of Tibet
for the students. Also there were lots of Russians in the class. They even
had a teacher come in from the Eastern Bloc, who had once worked at
Esalen in California (which is where Manson went two days before the
Tate murders). The teacher who did this brotherhood initiation was
Ormond McGill, a famous name in hypnosis. He is one of the fathers of
modern hypnosis. Aside from Milton Erickson and Gil Boyne, you have
Ormond. McGill also gave a *violet flame* meditation. The violet flame has
come up several times in this story, in other ways. It's a meditation where
you visualize a violet flame in your head and start to trigger the third eye.

*Aleister Crowley often mentioned a "ruby flame," particularly on his first
trip to the Great Pyramid in 1904 (when the Elk River Bridge collapse
also occurred). On that trip, he used the fake name Chia Khan, reminiscent of Sara Jane Moore's maiden name.*

AC: Right after 9/11, we had gone to Mexico for a holiday. I had taken a
terrible fall. I was up high in a hammock when it broke. I fell flat on my
back onto jagged bricks. I thought I had broken my back. Amazingly, I
was healed by the local medicine man. He owned the campground there.
We were camping in these little outbuildings. The owner had once been a
Contra fighter.

GK: As in Nicaragua?

AC: Yes. He had probably killed people, and was probably on the "wrong"
side, if you will. Still, he was this great healer who people in the village
were coming to all the time. I got better right away. We did a sweat
lodge. I saw this violet flame after the sweat. Later I was told that they
sometimes spike the drinks after these sweats. But that doesn't explain
how they could make you have a specific vision of a particular item.
The vision was a very strong personal event. It lasted about an hour.
The shaman had actually implied that we would see something, but he

didn't tell us exactly what it was going to be. I went to him later and said, "What was it that we were supposed to see?" He said, "a burning lotus." And that was what I'd seen. So that sort of started off this whole project. Suddenly, after my experience with Emiliano, I found myself doing the Mothman documentary.

GK: Of what is the violet flame emblematic?

AC: It's a really common Buddhist idea. It symbolizes awakening. The awakening process... I don't know if you've heard of this but right now we have an extraordinary thing happening in India. There's a young man who people are claiming is the new Buddha. He's not saying that he is the Buddha. *They* are saying he is... You can look at him and see that his head is glowing. His forehead is glowing red. That's an example of what the violet flame does. If it's strong enough, you can literally see it from outside the practitioner's body.

GK: I wonder if they're going to try to portray him as Maitreya. That's interesting... Let's do a little recap if we can. What is the Mothman, where does it happen, and what does it signify for us?

AC: It happens worldwide. Assuming that the Mothman is the Garuda and also the Thunderbird (i.e., is the source of all these birdman beings), it's been going on forever. But generally, people relate Mothman to the strange events in West Virginia of 1966 and '67: the Men in Black, UFOs, animal mutilations, missing persons, bridge collapses, occult activity, etc. A lot of people disagree on what the Mothman means or if he exists. My own interpretation is that "he" is this supernatural process that so many cultures talk about. He generally appears in ways that will help fight crime or right wrongs. It's kind of funny to say, but he really may be some sort of real, live crime fighter or superhero. When I see Superman or Batman, I think of Mothman.

GK: For our Christian listening audience: do not get offended. The fact [is] that something is going on in the skies, astrally, inducing things in people. You can find plenty of scriptures that will back that up. Exactly who's behind it or what it is, we really don't know. The point is that it's not necessarily ascriptural. It's been documented through time that there's something going on in the skies that we don't know about. That doesn't necessarily make it the province of tinfoil hat-wearers, or Satanists, or whatever. But let's face it; something's going on. I've given you my little testimony as to what I saw in that second hour. You said that you thought – but could not prove – that the vision of that creature might actually be a mind-op operation. A hologram or whatever... You didn't use that word hologram, I did. But I mean, isn't that a possibility as well?

AC: It's certainly a possibility. And it's clear that the government does have craft that are misidentified as UFOs. They may even be going further than that and abducting people. They probably *would* do that because it's such a convenient way to do it. The waters are so muddied by the ancient phenomenon itself (and the churches) that the government, corporations, or Masonic societies could get away with it. People either don't believe it at all and ignore it, or they "believe" and think it's totally extraterrestrial. UFO researcher Jacques Vallee was told by the head of Regnery Press that in order to be successful, he either had to write to a base of "believers," or absolute "disbelievers." There is no middle ground in the publishing business. Very convenient for the controllers…

GK: As you'll find out in that Van Helsing book I sent you, it's very clear (and he does cite his sources) that Germany had come upon an antigravity craft. Charles Wilcox sent me some footage (he wrote the book *Transformation of the Republic* and lives up in Canada) where the Canadians had an antigravity craft, and this goes back to the story about their AVRO saucer. They actually had a Mach 3 craft before we did. That's a really interesting part of history. So the point is that this *was* around. This [technology] was around after WWII. For us to think that it was [exclusively] the province of some other galaxy is [naïve]. I got an email from [a European woman] about biotelemetry [on humans] with electronics and such, authoring people's behavior without them knowing. Her quip was, "if it's happening today, you can bet it was in research and development 50 years ago." The reason I bring this up is that you [didn't] see a lot of science fiction writers like Bradbury and Philip K. Dick [until] after WWII. I don't really think they wrote science *fiction*. I think that they were privy to what was going on [but] was yet to come out. It only *looked* *like* science fiction, sounded like science fiction. It would become science "fact" in time. Do you want to weigh in on that at all?

AC: It's important to remember that both things are going on. I think we have natural UFO things going on, and also synthetic ones. We may even have a real Mothman and a fake Mothman. But when you mention Philip K. Dick, that's an entry into some things. Or I could go back to the stuff that happened in California during our filming…

GK: Let's address the situation that you encountered out in California.

AC: Let's see… We found a town there just cruising around, named Orinda. "Orinda" is kind of close to "Indrid" in spelling. We were in Orinda and I realized that Orinda is the same name that the Indians have for the Thunderbird's energy – the essence of the Thunderbird. JFK University was sitting there, and across the street was the Masonic temple. Everyone who knows their JFK lore knows that there are all these Masonic connections to the assassination. What I didn't know at the time was that JFK Univ. is one of the few places in the world where you can – or could at one time – get a degree in the paranormal (parapsychology). I just recently ran across the name of a lady who went there and got that degree, who then was involved in the October Surprise – the Reagan/Bush operation. Actually Nixon planned it. Nixon was the liaison between the US and Iran to keep the hostages there, so that Carter would lose the election.

GK: And they got a better deal cut [for] the Reagan administration [by] telling Khomeini, "You hang tight. As soon as the election's over, we'll give you a better deal."

AC: The lady from JFK Univ. was also connected to Linda Tripp, who "exposed" Clinton by helping Monica Lewinski…

GK: When you say, "Tripp exposed Clinton" you've got to be really careful. But yes, she was the one that was behind Lewinski…

AC: That's the thought, anyway. She was the one who some say taped Lewinski. But according to Levenda, this lady (Barbara Honegger) also had some connection to the invocation of The Nine. Andrija Puharich wrote about The Nine in his book on Uri Geller. The Nine (which is where Roddenberry got the name *Deep Space Nine*) is very important, and it's something we should talk about next session. It was surrounded by a diverse group of channelers, from JFK conspirators to great inventors. The Nine Roundtable was sort of based in Philadelphia, too, so it's got that connection going on. This group has had major influence. Remote viewing came out of that group, and they were dipping into all these key conspiracies. The Nine itself was supposedly a group of spacemen residing on a UFO in stationary earth orbit. Supposedly these scientists were tapped into this UFO. In 1973-74, twenty years after the re-invocation of The Nine, Philip K. Dick says he's in contact with the same kind of thing, which he calls VALIS. He claims that this orbiting consciousness is communicating with him. Then Robert Anton Wilson, John Lilly, Doris Lessing, and Jack Sarfatti say that they are having the same kind of experiences. I had a lot of things happen around that time myself. That was when I saw the entity at the Mothman shrine, and that's when my sister took a photo that looks like the Garuda. Also, my niece was seeing glowing letters and symbols coming through her room. These were the same exact things that Philip K. Dick was seeing.

GK: I had a listener who has been going back and forth with me about Philip K. Dick's works and experiences. Not that you necessarily have to know about this, but I figured you might be a good one to at least posit the question... Do you believe 1) that Dick was privy to what was going on technologically (50 years ahead) and 2) do you think he might have subjected himself to some of this technology, making him [unstable] or 3) was he [purposely] destabilized so that no one would listen to him? What do you think about those scenarios?

AC: I remember reading about his being under surveillance by the authorities in California. They were giving him a hard time, so I tend to think he was being bombarded with radiowaves. Dick was probably being desta- bilized in some fashion, regardless of whether or not he originally started out experiencing genuine supernatural phenomena. They were definitely targeting certain people, as Dick claimed on French TV. Famous progres- sive thinkers like Dick, Lilly, and Wilson are probably more inclined to receive remote, artificial programming because there's something in it for the State. Complete unknowns probably get a higher percentage of nature-based signals – at least when there's not a big experiment going on. There were not many economical or political reasons for anybody to be on Woodward Dr. projecting holograms, five years after Mothman. Most of the spooks were gone. It just doesn't make sense to waste money and resources that way. Again, I think there can be both natural *and* synthetic things going on at the same time. That's why I get back to *The 8th Tower* by John Keel, because *that's* his basic idea. With these eight towers, the first seven are basically people's greedy egos engaging in nefar- ious activities for their own gain. That would include all of these different covert ops. But at the top, so to speak, you have the 8th Tower, which is beyond all of that. We're linked to it psychically, but it's neutral to our temporal wants and desires. It's not out for gain. It's out to neutralize all of that. That's very similar to the symbolism of the Garuda, in that the Garuda neutralizes the fires of Indra – of war and war profiteering. That's important to remember...

GK: I'm asking you for a wild guess, just for the point of conversation. Do you think that Dick was tapped into the scientific/technological community?

AC: I assume he was. I'm not that well versed on Dick. I don't find his books as engrossing as Richard Linklater does. I have another friend who worked personally with Dr. John Lilly. I don't know that much about Lilly either, but this friend talked about all the cross-pollination that was going on. A lot of things were going around, and I'm sure Dick had access to some of that.

GK: This is conjecture, but Lilly is somebody else who seems to have died a little too early. I mean he obviously wasn't so old that he just died of old age. It's the same with Orwell and some others.

AC: We don't have proof, but their deaths are strange, like so many other deaths such as Jim Keith, Ron Bonds, Danny Casolaro, Gary Webb, and Hunter S. Thompson. You can often find strange, unexplainable facts there. How many progressive authors commit suicide by shooting themselves more than once? Are people expected to really believe these explanations?

GK: Yes, you wonder what they touched upon. We're not going to break any new ground right now, because we're coming up against the end of this interview. We'll embark on a new point of view [later]. You have so much to say. It must be staggering. I'm putting myself in your place. All of these veins and tributaries shoot out from here. I don't know if you knew what you were getting into when you first started it but, Andrew, when you get into it, does it ever seem overwhelming? Isn't it so unbelievably interconnected?

AC: Most of the time, I just go back to the normal things that I do on a daily basis. I've had a lot of Buddhist training. When a bunch of synchronicities happen, the number one rule is that you let it go. It is just part of the awakening process. You just let it go because *that's* not the goal. Yes, there have been times when it was difficult. During the filming of the documentary, there were many, many things to potentially get carried away with. Luckily, I had that meditation background. Also I was raised a Christian, and I've experienced Christian miracles. I had some seriously unbelievable prayer-answering experiences growing up, even though I was interested in Buddhism early on. Of course there wasn't a lot of Buddhism in WV. One couldn't really go to a Buddhist temple, so I went to churches instead. I used the Church as a way to develop my spirituality. I don't want Christians out there to think I don't know what they're about.

GK: Half of the listeners are going to be on an evangelical Christian network. You state your case and that's okay. We're not going to argue. [Many] professed Christians that are listening to us are grounded, so that's okay. You make your statements and they can deal with it. One last question I'll ask you. It's a bit of personal and you can choose not to answer it, but I think you'll understand from whence it comes. You look at your children. You realize what's shaking. Is that going to affect in any way, shape, or form what you're going to give them [in terms of] a worldview? I guess they may be too young right now, but do you have a fear for them, for the time that's coming? Are you going to outfit them to realize that the world they see portrayed on the TV is not necessarily what they're going to live in?

AC: Yes, yes, and yes. My grandfather was a bit of a conspiracy theorist. While he certainly didn't talk about it much, he did say a few things here and there about not listening to TV – especially the news. So did my dad, who was in some ways a radical leftist. I think it's okay to warn kids. It's such a stacked deck in favor of the corporations anyway. As a parent, it's hard to fight the power of the media. I think it's our responsibility to introduce whatever filters we can to the kids.

GK: What we try to tell people is: the world is run by conspiracy. If you are the conspirators, the best thing you can do is corner the global money and informational outlets. And you can do that very easily. They are a couple of generations into it. Now, if you can understand that you are being lied to by the mainstream media (which is doing nothing but giving you a send-down from the conspirators), then you understand that we have not really heard too much of the truth. To outfit your children with the understanding that what they're being told on the surface is not necessarily so is a pretty daunting task. You don't want to make your kids some kind of pariahs that nobody wants to play with. But on the other hand, you don't want them to be brainwashed and become some kind of fodder for the powers that be. I hope that you feel somewhat edified and confirmed by coming out, because you have a lot to say. I've sent some emails out. People are saying, "The Mothman? Come on!" But you found Mothman to be just the tip of the iceberg, have you not?

AC: Oh yes. Mothman is, in my humble opinion, the story of the century. At least in the conspiracy world…

GK: All right, one last question and I'll let you go. When you say "conspiracy," it doesn't mean it's necessarily false, does it?

AC: Right, the real phenomenon is there to expose the conspiracy, and the conspiracy is trying to hide itself by mimicking the behavior of the phenomenon.

GK: All right, agreed. You've hit on something that's really important, that people are not talking about. Andrew, thank you for having the courage to come out here…

CHAPTER 13

Faye Dewitt was one of the first Mothman witnesses mentioned in the newspapers in 1966. I first met her at the 2003 Mothman Festival. She is very candid and has a refreshing sense of humor. Her demeanor gave me the impression that her story is absolutely true. Even though she has told her sighting story many times, the details have never varied. I tried to elicit other details from her regarding precognition and the like, and was not disappointed. Future Mothman researchers would do well to try to understand the psychic factors affecting witnesses, as this is where the Mothman saga gets really interesting. One starts to understand that Mothman is continually helping witnesses by giving them a "heads up" as to what is coming next in their lives. Some of DeWitt's statements about her internal dialogue with the phenomenon sound eerily similar to things said by my sisters and my niece. DeWitt's story about psychically saving her children from certain death is one of the most dramatic in the Mothman pantheon.

Dewitt, Faye (LaPorte) – 1966 Sighting and Beyond – Sept. 2003

Faye Dewitt (FD): I was about 13, because my brother [at the time] had his learner's permit, and they got them at about 15 years old. My brother is almost 2 years older than I am... We were the fifth [group of] witnesses. [That's] what the police said when we went to the courthouse that night. After we saw it, we went directly to the courthouse over here and told them... I've been down in North Carolina for thirty years... I came home yesterday, went out there to the TNT area, and there ain't nothing out there no more! I was disappointed. [Even the] high school ain't the high school no more. Things have changed... I never forgot [Mothman] because it scared me so bad... My brother took me and my sister and my twin brother and my youngest brother [driving that night]. We went to the drive-in and saw a movie. I think the name of it was *Wildfire*. It was about this horse that I liked. A pretty white horse... We came back and my brother said, "We're just going to go up there and see what's going on," because we had heard that day at school that one of the schoolmates had got caught out there in the TNT area with his girlfriend. The Mothman jumped up on top of their hood and stomped their hood in. And it was all over the school how they got caught out there messing around together. The guy had another girl he was seeing and engaged to, so it blew out all over the school. It was on the front page the next day... So we decided after the movie to go up there. We thought, "That's just somebody running around in a Halloween costume..." We were going down the road. We hadn't even been [there] long. [We had gone] just a few feet down the road. Next thing we know, something's running beside the car. My brother said, "Faye, what's that over there?" I turned around and looked and there it was, just like that window is to me now (about three feet). It was *that* close. It had the reddest, biggest eyes you ever did see. [Most animals] just got round eyes, but [his] went into a point. Not real sharp... Not just round bug eyes. They went up in a point.

Andy Colvin (AC): Was it gliding or running?

FD: It was running. All I could see was from where I was sitting. I didn't [lean out] and look at his legs because [I was afraid]. I was [urging my] brother to go faster, hitting on his leg to make him go faster...

AC: Was it moving perfectly horizontally, or was it jumping a little bit as it ran?

FD: [It was] perfectly [horizontal]. It did not go up and down. It wasn't flying. It was running. My brother said, "Don't look at it!" I said, "Hurry up, hurry up!" So he floored it to 80 miles an hour [yet] that thing's still running beside the car. It's not panting, not straining, just perfectly [smooth]. I said, "That ain't nobody in a costume! No one's going to run alongside a car at 80 miles an hour. Hurry, it's going to catch us!" We came to a "T" where we had to turn, so my brother slammed on the brakes and slid around in the car. When the car slid around [Mothman] jumped on the hood of the car and looked at us. When it did that [we saw the] biggest and most ugly red eyes you ever did see. When the car stopped, it jumped off the car. It jumped down and went up on top of that big old power plant [that] was four or five stories high. I can't remember [the exact height of] the old power plant that they tore down. It jumped up there [and] opened up its wings. [Then] it sat down, just watching us. My brother said, "I can't believe what that [just] did." He got out of the car and started picking up stones, throwing them at it, trying to make it move. And it just kept sitting there watching [despite the rock throwing]. "Come on," my brother said, "it can't be real." Directly, it stood up. When it stood up I said, "You better get back in! I can't drive, you know. We've got to get out of here!" So he jumped back in the car when the thing stood up. It jumped down from that high building. It jumped down like it wasn't anything at all. It took off running. There were some hedges there, about six feet tall. They were all bushed out, like years of growth. When it got to the tiptop of those, it opened up its wings and flew off. I mean, it could run and jump like it was nothing. There's no way it could have been any kind of man in a suit...

AC: What sort of effect has it had on you since? Has it changed you?

FD: I don't know about "changed," but I never forgot it. I've had so much phenomenal stuff in my life since then, to tell you the truth... I hadn't really thought of it, but all this stuff came after that. We've [always] been seeing weird things.

AC: What sort of things?

FD: My daddy worked on the farm and he made us do a lot of the work. He sent us up to the hills and woods to bring the cows in at 3 o'clock in the morning. Anything could have happened to us. I mean it wasn't just a short distance. It was a good distance, way over the hills. I wouldn't send my 28-year old son up in the woods like that, but [my dad] did... We'd go up there together, chasing them cows. [One time] we were coming down the hill. We were tired, so before we went up the next hill, we decided to sit there and rest. We were sitting there talking, and next thing we know the brightest light [appeared]. And it was pitch dark out. We didn't think anything about it. [We] thought the moon must have come out all of a sudden. We weren't paying attention. We looked up. I said, "What the hell is that light?" I looked up and there was a perfectly oval shape. No sound, no kind of motor or nothing... My brother said, "I don't know about you all, but I'm getting out of here," and he split. The others went with him. I said, "Wait a minute! You all left me!" I jumped up, trying to see what it was. And just like that, it was gone.

AC: What year was that?

FD: [It was] several years after the Mothman thing. I've seen [so many] things I could write a book...

AC: Any other strange creatures? What kind of dreams do you have?

FD: I don't have many dreams...

AC: What were some of the other things that happened?

FD: After that? Well, I can predict things and see things that are going to happen to my family or me before it's happening. [Even] I don't believe it [sometimes]. So I tell somebody (like my kids), so that I don't think I'm going crazy.

AC: You don't dream it?

FD: No, I don't dream it. I'm wide awake when these things come to me. *Visions* I guess is what you call them. I've had this so long, I don't remember when I *didn't* have it.

AC: Are most of these visions just related to your family?

FD: Yes. Family, anybody I love, anyone that I'm close to… Or something [that's] going to happen to me… It won't be as clear [about] me as it will them. It won't completely tell me everything about me. It kind of leaves a guess or a puzzle. I've got to put it together. But [with] them it's clearer… We're direct descendents of Chief Cornstalk, my family. You know, Indians have this stuff… I've heard this [rumor]. I don't know how true this is [but] they say that this Mothman thing is [because] Chief Cornstalk's son, Red Hawk, came back to fulfill "the curse." I know that [Mothman] could have bothered us that night. It could have done something to us. Why didn't it? Maybe it's not out to harm anybody. We were just some little kids up there. It could have carried any one of us off but it didn't. It just sat there and watched us. It didn't bother us. If it was going to do anything to anybody, that would have been a perfect way to do it. To little kids… I've often thought that maybe it was [Red Hawk]. If it was a fulfillment of the curse that Point Pleasant had [on it] then that [would explain] why it didn't bother us [Indians]. I'm not the only one in my family [that has this] perception of the future. It runs all through my family. My sister and I have it stronger than anyone else. I can see that it's been passed down to my son… It runs all through my family. Some of my other brothers and sisters have it. Some don't have it at all. It's nothing we want but we got it. Because of it, we have seen the weirdest stuff in our lives – especially me. I should write a book because this stuff isn't bashful about showing itself to me. Something in me picks up on it, whereas [others don't].

AC: Any other sightings that you can think of? Have you ever felt like an alien has contacted you, or a Man in Black?

FD: No, nothing like that.

AC: Any visitors at night, in your house?

FD: Yes, sir. I've had one of them… It was in the house. I don't know what it was. It scared me to death. I knew it was there. I told it to get out in the name of the Lord. All of a sudden, calm and peace went over me [even though] something's in the house… I was the only one in there. It was banging around back there in the back room. I did not have animals. [It had] an awful smell like something dead, like sulfur or whatever. I don't know what it was… Then this creepy feeling came over [me]. Like they say, the hairs on your neck stand up.

AC: Did you see it?

FD: I could see a real fine, thin, white mist. Like somebody had taken a cigarette and [blown a] puff of smoke...

AC: That's what we saw [last year in Charleston, at the location of our Mothman shrine].

FD: That's what I saw. I saw it go from one room to another. That's when I said, "Get out of my house in the name of the Lord God Almighty, because this is not [right]." What it was [was] a boy had died (that my son was friends with). My kids would have been on that bus [that the boy was killed on. They would have been] dead too, because [the damage] was in the front seat... But something told me that day to keep my kids out of school and take them to school [myself]. They rode that bus every day from the time they started school to the time we moved away from there. They don't ride that bus anymore.

AC: Is this here?

FD: No, this is in North Carolina. It was not here in Point Pleasant. [But the phenomenon] is wherever I am at. It's not just down there.

AC: But you were up here throughout high school, correct?

FD: I was up here until 1973. I left West Virginia [then].

AC: So you went down there and it followed you?

FD: Evidently it stayed with me... It's been with me all this time. I'll tell you, whenever there's going to be something bad happen, or somebody in my family's going to get hurt, I'll see things. It's like something shows me what's going to happen. That's what I'm up here for now. I've been up here four times. Get this... I was told [by this phenomenon] in January that I was going to get married again. I just lost my husband two years ago. It'll be two years in March... Three times I have buried three husbands. And all three of them didn't believe in this stuff. All three of them wanted me to leave it alone and not mess with it, to shut up [like] I'm crazy. All three of them are dead.

AC: Let that be a message to the men out there.

FD: I tell everybody, "Don't go against this mess because I ain't got no control over it. If you do something to me, you've got to answer to him." That's what I say. I say, "What it is, I don't know, but don't you go against me because it's wiping them out that goes against me." I'm serious. I mean it's funny, but it really is weird. I told each one of them, "You better listen, I'm telling you..."

AC: Your fiancé is outside our interview room. How [did he take this news]?

FD: He knows it! I told him. But he said, "I'm game if you are." So I said, "Alright, just don't ever go against me on something really serious. When you go hurting me really bad, it's like something is there taking care of me."

AC: I've actually told people the same thing.

FD: [It's] watching over me… Like I said, I didn't plan on getting married. I didn't want to get married again. *It* told me I was going to get married next year. I said, "No, I haven't even met anybody. Don't be telling me that." It told me I was going to move back to West Virginia. I said, "No, I like it down in North Carolina. I'm staying. Ain't nothing [for me] back up home." [Later] I go home to see everybody. *It* showed me the house I was going to live in. It showed what [the interior] looked like and everything. Then out of the blue, stuff [for the house] is popping up. The furniture for it, et cetera…

AC: You saw all this in your mind?

FD: I saw it! I saw everything, and everything's happening just like it said. I can't even control it, it's happening so fast. It's like I couldn't even have planned this because I didn't have time to do any of it. It showed me what I'm going to look like when I got married. It showed me what my dress looked like and where [the ceremony] is going be [held]. I just haven't found [the location yet, but] when I find it, there it will be. And that's the way everything's been going. It's just laid my life out for me. I don't have any control. I didn't [have control] the three times that my husbands were going to die. It didn't tell me it was *them*. It [merely] showed me what was going to happen. [It] showed me seeing somebody dead. The way it looked and everything… But I couldn't see them, and didn't register who it was. Within less than fifteen minutes after I was shown that, I got word that my husbands were dead. Each time… Each time, within 15, 20 minutes after I saw that, I got the call that they were dead. It notified me…

AC: Were you maybe knowing as it happened?

FD: Yes. All along I *felt* it, that something was going to happen. I kept telling them, "You better straighten up. I got a bad feeling about this. Don't be doing this. Something bad is going to happen. I just know something bad is going to happen." And they wouldn't listen… But all of this has been stronger since the Mothman. There's something beside me at all times. Really, I can feel it that strong. Wherever I'm going or whatever I'm doing, it's like it's *there*. I also know there's something else on the other side. It's like [there's] a good side and a bad side, and they're both fighting over who's going to get me. [I'm tempted to say] "I ain't gonna have anything to do with you. Don't care what you are…" But it's warned me of everything, so it can't be bad. [If it was bad] it wouldn't warn me. It would go ahead and let this stuff happen. I'd be hurt or [have] something happen to me. But it warns me, either to keep me from being too shocked by what's about to happen, or from being hurt. It doesn't change anything (that I know of). It's not [explicit] enough that it would let me know I could put a stop to it. In a way I can [influence things] but I feel like if I put a stop to it, something worse might happen to me than [originally] would have. So I can't stop it. I have to go ahead and go through with it. That's the way it's been: I know something bad is going to happen, but I can't help it.

AC: But you did help things with your kids and the bus accident.

FD: Yes, something just [revealed to] me the situation… [First off] I had a babysitter She starts showing off with the [other] kids that she was watching. She was playing those kids off against mine. I said, "I don't put up with that." She gave them cookies and stuff [while] making mine sit down and do homework So I just stopped. Something said, "Don't take them back over there anymore " I dropped them off [elsewhere]. When I was getting ready to go pick them up at the [other] place, that's when I heard the news that the bus they always rode [had] crashed and killed everybody. Eight kids My kids were assigned the first seat, right behind [the driver]. The boy that was [my son's] best friend was right behind where my son and daughter sat. And the rod When you come up on a bus, you hold onto that… That got beat back and went clear through him, right through his brain. It would have got both my kids because there are two poles there, one behind the bus driver and one that you come up on. Both of them poles got bent back and went right through that boy. I [imagine] it would have gone through my kids So this [phenomenon] did help. It set up a situation where I had no choice but to take my kids and not let them ride that bus that day. It told me, "Don't take them back to her," and so I protected my kids. I had to find something else. I went through the phone book all that evening [prior] until I found this [new babysitter and] set it up with them to start. That's how they were saved. But you know, whatever's meant to happen is going to happen. It's like it's warning me so I won't be shocked by anything. But I [have to] follow through with what it tells me. Had I said, "I'll just leave them with her one more day because it's Friday," they would have been dead. Sometimes it'll tell me things like a year away, or a month away or whatever. But I know that this year, it told me I'm going to be in West Virginia and that I'm going to be married next year. And all these things are coming about. Next year I'll be living here and I'll be married.

And I had no plans for any of it. I'm serious! I told every one of my kids way back in January, when this started happening. They knew that I wasn't over my husband. I was still really upset and getting over his death. I was fed up with marriage. I didn't want anybody. In fact, when I met my fiancé I told him, "Leave me alone. I'm fed up with it. I don't want anything to do with it." I went back home. But something said, "Go back and see him again." I said, "no." We talked to each other on the phone. It just kept on saying I needed to come back. So I came up here to WV and I saw him again. Something just told me, and told him at the same time. It's like this stuff has been stronger since that Mothman sighting. I don't know of any time before that that anything ever allowed me to see or know [events in the future]. Like I said, I've always felt that there was something around me at all times, next to me. But I also feel like there's something else, too. And it's like they pull on me. I swear that's the only way I can explain it. But whatever "that" is, it's not anything bad. It's telling me things that I need to know to prepare myself.

AC: So your advice to people affected by this phenomenon is to talk about it?

FD: Yes, because then you don't think you're going crazy. We had five of us who saw Mothman. There's no way we're all crazy. But everybody else [said] "Oh, you [are] just a bunch of kids." That's what we think the officer [thought] because we don't think he took us seriously. When stuff like this happens, whether people believe it or not, for your own sake tell it to somebody. When it happens again you [can] say, "I ain't crazy because I done told you I seen that." I began to wonder if I [had] "lost it" [at first]. Then I [began to think] "I ain't a crazy person. My mind's sharp. I forget things but other than that, I got my mind about me." I talk it out. I tell my kids, or my brothers and sisters who will believe. [They may joke] "Mama has had one too many," but I don't even drink. It's good to tell people, because it gets it out of you. It makes your mind at ease. Then, when ill happens to somebody, you ain't going to be the only one [who had advance warning]. There might be some instance where you might be the only witness or something, but most of the time I still say it's best to tell somebody… It eases your mind that you're not crazy. You're *not* just seeing stuff and [experiencing] figments of your imagination. There were five of us [who saw Mothman] and all of us remember it to this day. My younger brother, we made him get on the floor of the car and hide, because he was the littlest. He didn't see anything because he was down there just bawling his eyes out, crying and crying. My sister Betty was trying to console him and get him straight. But they were in the car. Me and my brother Carlisle, and my twin brother Ray, can honestly tell you, "Yes, we saw it," to this day.

CHAPTER 14

John Frick is a Maryland ghosthunter who became involved in Mothman not long before this interview. Frick is now the co-moderator for a Christian-friendly Mothman discussion list promoting the belief that supernatural "ultra-terrestrials" are primarily responsible for the Mothman phenomenon. This in itself is a pretty decent model, akin to how the Greeks and Egyptians viewed their gods. Unfortunately, group members are also generally urged to view the Mothman as a demon that brings calamity. The Men In Black are viewed almost exclusively in paranormal terms, in a slot somewhere between trickster and demon – a tad better than Mothman. All of this leaves little room for the conspiracy angles posited by Keel and others. One of the staples on Frick's list is the bombastic cryptojournalist Loren Coleman, merchant of the idea that Mothman will somehow – directly or indirectly – kill anyone (except perhaps Coleman) who tries to research the topic. Whereas Coleman usually hypes any and all tidbits of seemingly innocuous Mothman data or product – from games and figurines to hoax photos of all stripes – he has generally ignored or attacked research that points the finger at big business, the government, or the military. Frick, for his part, seems to be a tad more open-minded about Mothman, perhaps as a result of having had seemingly genuine experiences with UFOs and other phenomena, like the "bleeding Mary statue" of Youngstown, OH – which occurred during our filming. In 2003, Frick shared some of these experiences with us near the site of the Silver Bridge collapse.

Frick, John – MIBs and Time-slips – September 2003

Andy Colvin (AC): Weren't you talking about libraries as being places where Men in Black stalk people?

John Frick (JF): Yes, there's been a couple different cases where the Men in Black will approach people at university libraries while they're reading a UFO book, and the witness will either have missing time, or time will seem to stand still. Some kind of weird thing will happen with time. There have been a couple cases that I know of, plus Keel knows of some others.

AC: What draws you to the Men in Black stories?

JF: I'm not sure, just the combination of mystery and the humorous way [they behave]. Like the way the MIB drank Jell-O, and all that kind of weird stuff. It just seems super interesting.

AC: Aren't you also interested in aspects of time?

JF: Well, I'm interested in that, too. But the Men in Black in general, they just seem [contradictory]. Some of them seem harmless [yet] some seem sinister. It's just kind of interesting to [try and] find out if there are different groups [of them] or if they're all after the same thing.

AC: What would be the different groups?

JF: There might be what people call "demons" in human form that are trying to hurt us. Then there are others that are just here to talk to us. They may actually be trying to help us. But it's so up in the air. We know so little about them.

AC: What are some of the strangest Men in Black stories that you've heard?

JF: [The one I mentioned before] where a Man in Black was given a bowl of Jell-O and tried to drink it because he thought it was a liquid… He didn't know [or] understand what Jell-O was. That's one of the strangest…

AC: What sort of advice do you have for people who are having Men in Black visitations?

JF: If they're sinister, I'd say pray a lot. Try to get a field of protection around you so they can't hurt you. If they don't seem sinister or anything, try not to fear them because fearing them may actually strengthen any kind of evil force…

AC: Have you experienced any paranormal things yourself?

JF: Some weird phone calls, like I picked up the phone and heard my own voice. But that could have been just a technical glitch. [Still] it freaked me out a little bit. Also [there was someone] who tried to call me at my house. They claimed that what they spoke to [was not me, or anyone else at my house, but something that] sounded like God. They were kind of freaked out. I never did find out what exactly "God" said…

AC: They had called your number and instead they heard what they thought was God?

JF: Yes.

AC: Wasn't it a secretary at a doctor's office where you had gone?

JF: Yes. I don't know if they dialed the wrong number [or not] but it was all pretty weird.

A couple of years later, John and I would share similar odd phone calls at the same time. These involved the phone number 0-000-0000, which he and I and some other Mothman folk were getting on our message machines. Around this time, Frick went to visit a NASA-linked witness south of Cleveland, near Youngstown, OH, in the neighborhood of a purported "bleeding Mary statue." As he was leaving town, Frick and his brother were seemingly followed by a white government van carrying men in dark suits. The van's license plate number seemed to relate to a string of synchronicities around the number "11."

AC: What do you think the future holds for this area of investigation?

JF: I think the nature of phenomena is that humans are incapable of discovering what is causing it. We're just meant to investigate it. But it's fun, and I'd like to crack it… I think no matter how close you get, they'll pull the carpet out from under you [just to] keep you from cracking the case.

AC: Yes, it's almost as if that there are firewalls in the program. As soon as you figure out one glitch, another one appears just to keep you moving forward. It's almost like there's a programming mechanism, a way to influence human behavior and push it in a certain direction.

JF: Yes, definitely. Whether that's good or bad, I don't know.

Harriet Plumbrook (HP): Do MIB witnesses have trouble remembering their experiences, or are they able to tell you in vivid detail what happened?

JF: Well, I haven't interviewed a lot of people. I just go out to places where things have supposedly happened, and see what kind of remnants I can find.

HP: The reason I'm asking is that you were talking about MIBs being in libraries. Last year when I started to really read up on this phenomenon, I was getting every book I could find in the library on UFOs and paranormal experiences. I was standing in the library, and this olive-skinned man in his early 50s [with] snow white hair and dark eyebrows got about two feet away from my face, on the other side of the bookshelf where you can look through (because they're metal bookshelves). He goes, "What are you studying there?" I never thought twice about it, until you just said that. It was very odd…

AC: And after that he was just gone?

HP: Gone… I didn't see him anyplace in the library.

JF: When I was little, I saw a golden flying saucer. I was like seven years old. The saucer was in the sky. I ran and got my mom [but] she was on the phone with my dad. She couldn't come out right away. I was kind of afraid to go out there by myself. When we finally got out there [again] it was gone. I don't know if I've ever been abducted or not. I don't think that I have, but anything's possible. I have no recollection of [such].

HP: I have people that come to see me for medical, psychological, emotional issues… You wouldn't believe how many times in hypnosis that a classic abduction experience will come out. They have no idea what they're saying. They just say, "Well, this is what I'm seeing; this is weird." You never suggest to them that [a possible abduction] is what is going on. But you would not believe how many instances of this I encounter…

Bystander: You hear the classic story of someone who vacationed and stayed at a really nice hotel… Then a couple months later, they're back that way and go to the [location of the] same hotel. They ask a question [and are told] "You mean the old so-and-so place? Oh, the place burned down 75 years ago."

JF: Stuff like that happens all the time.

HP: I hear it all the time. I really do.

JF: It's like [the witness] goes to another dimension, or steps back into time for a brief period. They do something [there] and then they [come back and] go on with their life.

HP: Yes, everybody [time] travels.

JF: The thing is, how often are we traveling [but] nothing bizarre happens [to alert us]? We don't even realize we are traveling [in those cases].

HP: Well, they say 3-5 times a week… Authors that write about astral travel say that we travel without any type of conscious knowledge or remembrance 3-5 times a week. We're going to see relatives that are deceased, or going to other dimensions. It's something we do all the time. Have either one of you ever flown in your dreams? That's a sign that you're leaving. And everybody goes places. Some of these places you might encounter years later. You might say, "I've been here before." Well, you *have*. It's fascinating…

AC: The Whitley Strieber book *Secret School* is about time, and how Whitley was shown things as a child. Whitley and other children in his neighborhood were taken by "aliens" and shown visions of the future and the past. Now that he's an adult, he has experiences like you're describing. He was walking down a street in New York, turned a corner, and poof! He had entered the 1800s of New York. It was the same corner, but it was a hundred years prior. He tried to speak to someone to ask, "Hey, what year is it?" The person looked at him and was terrified. It was almost as if

Strieber had become a Man in Black.

JF: [And] that was in his waking reality. What if – in our waking reality – we're walking into different zones of time [several] times a day [without] even realizing it?

AC: You mean *minor* shifts in time?

JF: [Yes] minor shifts. You wouldn't even notice the difference. You always wind up back in the time [period] you belong in…

CHAPTER 15

"The Dzogchen Tantras, the ancient teachings from which [texts like the Tibetan Book of the Dead come] speak of a mythical bird, the Garuda, which is born fully grown. This image symbolizes our primordial nature, which is already completely perfect. The Garuda chick has all its wing feathers fully developed inside the egg, but it cannot fly before it hatches. Only at the moment when the shell cracks open can it burst out and soar up into the sky. Similarly, the masters tell us, the qualities of Buddhahood are veiled by the body, and as soon as the body is discarded, they will be radiantly displayed."

-Sogyal Rinpoche, author of "The Tibetan Book of Living and Dying"

Colvin, Andy – Moloch and The Secret School – 2004

Andy Colvin: *[to camera]* Here is an interesting story... Bohemian Grove is where the global elite has had a yearly meeting for the past 130 years. It is sort of the Republicans' own Burning Man Festival, where they do rituals such as sacrificing an effigy of a human being to what they call "The Great Owl of Bohemia." The symbolisms surrounding the Great Owl seem to echo those of the Mothman. It's such a funny image to think of our president worshiping a statue of a large Mothmanlike creature. I've actually seen footage of the ritual. It seems like a somewhat unorganized ritual, like a Klan rally or something. It's organized but it's not. There are some amplified voices, people saying things. It is definitely scary when the owl is lit by fire. It's quite large, and pretty terrifying.

Another article that caught my eye is a New York Times piece from March of this year entitled *Talking Fish Stuns New York*. It reads, "A fish heading for slaughter in a New York market shouted warnings about the end of the world before it was killed, two fish cutters have claimed." They both heard it saying that the "end of the world is at hand." When you've got fish coming forward to say that we're reaching the end, I think it's time to pay attention. Which brings me to my next subject...

Whitley Strieber's *The Secret School, Preparation for Contact...* This book has been out a few years, but not a lot of people have read it. It's a shame because this book sheds light on the Mothman phenomenon, specifically the part of the phenomenon where you have these secret schools supposedly being taught by "ultra-terrestrials" (UTs). The UTs seemingly teach children about abstract concepts such as transcending time and space. These kids all have urges to go to a certain part of the woods at night, where they are shown visions of past and future events. During the daytime, they're completely unaware of it. All they know is that they have these unexplained feelings (generally of comradeship) about other kids who are attending night school with them. The bonds develop at a subconscious level...

In *Secret School* there is a lot of great theorizing about what this phenomenon is about. One of the things that struck me (and this ties in with this fish story) is the idea of prophecy, and what it really means. Strieber goes to great pains to explain the nature of prophecy in this book. The ability to prophesy appears to grow as people reach "end times." Each "end time" is really just the apex of a large, circular ellipse that repeats throughout the ages. Let's assume, for the moment, that there is some truth to the widely acknowledged belief that we're reaching the end of an era (at least according to ancient calendars). Stronger ESP tends to manifest as these times. Peoples' ability to see visions increases. Amazingly, this increase applies not only to a particular prophecy of the future, but also to visions of the past (like my vision of the Elk Bridge collapse of 1904).

My 9/11 precognition was, as I told you earlier, a little off. I was seeing buildings that didn't look exactly like the WTC. Also, I seemed to be seeing *larger* scale destruction.

> *Was I was simply seeing some of the lesser-known buildings in the complex, unfamiliar to most of us? Or was I seeing a vision of another, larger attack in the future? Did the phenomenon simply lie to Tommy about the date, as it has been known to do?*

Strieber reminds us that prophecies are not always meant to come true. They're often meant to go wrong. They exist as a warning tool to people who are becoming more intuitive, more in touch with the subconscious. These visions ultimately come forth from the Unconscious, according to Buddhist thought. They are tools for us to modify an otherwise "negative" eventuality. Time is plastic in the unconscious. Things can happen differently there. It makes our 9/11 precognition a little more interesting, in that it *could* mean that there was going to be even *larger* scale destruction than there actually was. The effects could have been reduced by awareness arising in different people in advance of the event.

Within the conscious everyday realm, it is pretty clear that certain intelligence agencies had prior knowledge that there would be an attack by planes, and probably at the World Trade Center. An attack had already happened there in 1993, with full FBI knowledge. It is likely that *conscious* prior knowledge *also* works to lessen destruction. A few conscientious insiders may have thrown subtle wrenches into the works.

Those getting precognitions may act as filters or resistors, absorbing the energy that relates to the event. This absorption into the body may cause visions and emotions, as an essentially electrochemical process translates into the "timeless" language of the unconscious.

Now, since I've put this information out that we had this vision of destruction (of 9/11), I've had conspiracy theorists write me asking questions like, "Well, did you know that NASA long ago developed remote-controlled airplanes?" They can basically fly a huge jet anywhere they like, without any pilots at all. Other conspiracy theorists were saying things like, "There's no evidence that these hijackers really existed. Their identities were faked, borrowed, or stolen." They were even saying, "Maybe there weren't any hijackers at all. Maybe this was all a military-industrial operation." Which sounded crazy, but then other calls came in. One fellow described how the nexus of the 9/11 terror operation was in Florida, near NASA headquarters where my friend Tommy worked before he retired. Another fellow tells me that NASA has secured a large contract to develop the new airport screening devices that can not only screen for various smells and bombs, but can also measure the person's stress levels to indicate whether or not they may be planning a terrorist operation. Perhaps we will find out someday that many other children also had this 9/11 vision of destruction. Each one of them, of course, would have had their own unique response to such stimuli.

While many children might experience precognition as terrifying (as I did), others might be enthralled by it. Some children might have grown up subconsciously wanting to see their 9/11 visions come into existence. It could be akin to the fanatical Christian's longing for Armageddon because Armageddon means the Messiah is coming back. Unfortunately, the promise of a Messiah is a two-edged sword. The real phenomenon emanating from natural earth energies can always be synthetically mimicked, with the side effects unadvertised.

"In working with individual subjects, special attention will be given to disassociative states, which tend to accompany spontaneous ESP experiences. Such states can be induced or controlled to some extent with hypnosis and drugs... The data in this study will be obtained from ESP experiments [with] special groups such as psychotics, children, and mediums... The main consideration will be the attitude and general disposition of the subject. Wherever possible, every attempt will be made to tailor the tasks required to the subject's preferences and their estimate of good working conditions. In one case, the experimental procedure might be designed to achieve favorable motivation by devices such as instructing him that he is participating in a study of subception [subliminal perception, sometimes used in trauma-based conditioning]. In other cases, drugs and psychological tricks will be used to modify his attitudes. The experimenters will be particularly interested in disassociative states, from the 'abaissment de niveau mental' [the damage of logical connection of thoughts; loss of control of whole regions of mental contents with the production of split fragments of the personality; the invasion of the consciousness on the part of contents usually inhibited by conscious functioning and, in consequence, causing inadequate or inappropriate emotional reactions] to multiple personality in so-called mediums. An attempt will be made to induce a number of states of this kind, using hypnosis."

-Approved MK-Ultra Proposal, Subproject 136, May 30, 1961

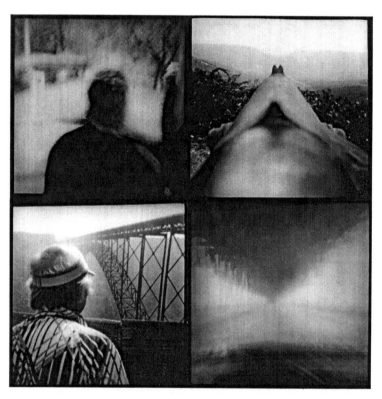

Following a spate of paranormal events in the late 1970s and early 1980s, the author began making cryptic imagery that now seems to have some connection to Mothman. This image, for instance, implies a bridge collapse similar to those in Pt. Pleasant (1967) and Charleston (1904), in conjunction with covert MIBs wielding microwave/laser weaponry.

CHAPTER 16

In 2002, I met with Robert Godbey in Charleston, WV. Robert is a physicist who has consulted with Fortune 500 companies such as Union Carbide and Dow Chemical, and governmental agencies such as NASA. He and I attended an advanced elementary school (Grandview) in Mound that encouraged "free association." Nowadays, Robert is an articulate spokesperson for "creative analysis," stressing that we need to teach students about creativity at a much younger age. Apparently, the creative part of the human brain matures – and unfortunately solidifies – much faster than the analytical part. According to Robert, the global marketplace of the future demands that we as a society "learn how to learn." I asked Robert to consider the paranormal and how we might learn more about it.

Godbey, Robert – Chaos Theory and Mothman – 2002

Andy Colvin (AC): How close are we to finding out what is behind this phenomenon?

Robert Godbey (RG): If you look at all the different systems that we now understand, it amounts to maybe 10, 20 percent of what's really going on out there. [And those are] just the simpler, easier-to-explain types of things. This is where chaos theory [kicks in]. The part that we don't [typically] work with [or even study] is the "chaos" part. Say you turn on the water faucet. When you turn it on and it flows nicely, that's the physics that we can explain. [The part physics can't explain is] if you turn the water on really, really slow and get right to the point where it starts to sputter (but doesn't really flow). Now leave the water on there, watch the drops come out [and] try to predict where the drop is going to come out next. You can't do it. I mean it's so chaotic that nobody can tell you what drop's going to come out where. That's the part that we don't understand. And it turns out that *that's* the majority of nature. Eighty percent of it is more like the sputtering faucet, not the free flowing faucet. All the successes up until now have been about explaining, more or less, the *easier* parts to explain. We can't do it [with the more complicated parts because] the math gets so complicated that it breaks down. [We need to do more] work that is about looking for patterns… Patterns in the motion, patterns in the data… It is not about trying to solve individual equations for a particular activity, or motion. It's more along the lines of [probabilities]. It's almost like using simulations of the thing until you can average out what's going on. It's hard to put into words without an example, and even the examples are complicated. But it's sort of a new approach to science. It's not going through and trying to solve an individual equation where the motion's so complicated [that] it doesn't tell you anything. It's more or less looking at systems of information. Did you ever see the early computer game that was called *Life*? It would start with a handful of dots on the screen. They had rules on how the dots could propagate. If two certain types of things were together, then you'd get a new one on the next line. If they weren't, you wouldn't get one. Then you would run the program and watch the patterns form. What's interesting about it is that with simple little rules of how they could propagate – starting off with two or three things – you would end up with this screen full of these particles. They would form eddies and holes, and all different kinds of shapes. Or, they would just die out completely after a few runs. It would be one extreme or another. The point is that *that's* what a lot of nature is about. I couldn't write an equation to show you what pattern was going to show up in advance (based on which rule or which number of things I started with). But I could run it and see what shows up, and explain the thing that way.

> *This may help explain why psychic experiments at Montauk were rooted in past events. Duncan Cameron was initially trying to psychically manifest a physical object in the past. Past events can be worked with because there are verifiable elements there that can be consulted when looking at the results. Since we know, for instance, that Aleister Crowley performed certain ritual experiments on certain dates, we can reference them whenever something like a new Eye of Horus crop circle appears – as it did in 2003. By the way, Aldous Huxley was a devout student of Crowley, using Aleister as "a textbook." Huxley then tutored Timothy Leary and Andrija Puharich, who both had CIA connections. Leary reportedly passed acid around in Montauk during the 1960s. There was even a Moorish Orthodox Church parish at Millbrook, NY, where Leary did his LSD experiments. The original Moorish temple in Ong's Hat, NJ, reportedly did time travel experiments, perhaps under the watchful surveillance eye of Ft. Dix Army officials. During Leary's time at Millbrook, the estate was owned by one of the Mellon family members. The Mellon Institute in Pittsburgh has done technical work for Union Carbide for over 100 years.*

RG: It's kind of like comparing the Asian game *Go* to chess. Chess is a very formulated game where all the motion is described. Some of the motion is a little bit more complicated than others, like the "knight vs. the queen" and all that stuff, but there are rules for every piece. We now have computers that are complicated enough that they can beat a Grand Master in chess, because the rules are known and it's just a problem of processing power. The computer *D-Blue* (the first one that IBM made) actually had an individual computer under each square of the chessboard.

By doing that, they were able to beat a Grand Master. And they've even gone beyond that now. But *Go* is a game of pattern formation across a board. There's no complicated movement of any pieces. They all have the same rules that apply to them, based on the rules of propagation. If enough white stones surround the black stone [then] that black stone comes off the board. All of the ebb and flow makes [for] a much more complicated game. We're literally years away from a computer powerful enough to beat a *Go* Master. So that difference – between chess and *Go* – is a way to understand the difference in how the new science would work.

AC: Can you fill in any other gaps in our understanding of this?

RG: I think that there are a lot of things that are unexplained, and it makes sense [that they are still unexplained because] science is working with [only a fraction] of the total information right now. [They are] trying to sort through it… But the discipline that the scientific method brings to figuring things out has *still* been a net gain over the past, when everything was sort of built on superstition and that type of stuff. So it's a matter of patience. To give you an example, I can remember when the stories about ball lightning were considered to be myth. The average scientist would say that ball lightning didn't exist, and that these stories were too fantastic. [Anyone] claiming that a glowing ball of light was chasing them [was ignored]. But then it finally got observed enough times that it was proven to be an actual physical phenomenon. Now there are a few different scientists trying to do controlled experiments to study the whole phenomenon and understand it in the context of what we now know. We've actually started to understand ball lightning and why it does some of the things it's been accused of doing. That's the nature of science.

AC: I think the word "lightning" just got in a lot of people's way. Perhaps balls of "electricity" might have been a better term.

RG: Well, they actually believe that what's being formed is being formed by lightning. It supercharges pockets of air at different times and forms plasma, and the plasma is inherently unstable. It would take a spherical form because that would be the shape of lowest energy [drain]. Then it would tend to chase metal objects because of the magnetic pull. It would be a charged body of plasma…

AC: This would explain why we saw balls of light in our house. We lived right next to the pipeline, which also ran by Tommy and Harriet's house. And we had a lot of lightning during the summers, when most of the paranormal things occurred.

RG: Very interesting. Really possible...

AC: Speaking of lightning... Do you remember Earl Harvey, aka "Lightning," the mathematical savant from Charleston, WV? He was a super math whiz of "Ripley's Believe it or Not" fame.

RG: Yes, I'd heard that before, when I was growing up. They said he was supposed to be able to tell you the number of bricks in [old buildings] and be incredibly accurate...

AC: He was one of the interesting characters that surround the Mothman story on Woodward Drive. I used to jog late at night. I was an athlete, and late night was perfect for running because it was generally cool at night. I would run all the way down Woodward Drive. During the day, you'd usually see Lightning's friend, Snowball, along the road. Snowball sort of hung around where Zable Drive meets Woodward, near the house that looks like a medieval castle. The old lady who lived there used to play the organ. She had a massive church organ, and it would reverberate all the way down the road. She would sometimes be playing when I jogged by at night. I would usually hang out and listen for a while, since that was a logical place to turn around. There were a couple of times that Snowball was there listening. He stood in the deep shadows of the sycamores around the castle. I got the odd sense that he was telepathic. That's the best way I can describe it, is that every time I saw him I felt like he was sending mental messages. It seemed as if Snowball was trying to use the organ music to amplify his telepathy.

RG: That's interesting.

The ironic thing is that Snowball was considered, by less observant neighbors, to be "dumb" because he never talked.

AC: But Lightning and Snowball, as well as "Aqualung" (Bill Dunn, their pal who frequented libraries), have always stuck in my mind, because of their piercing eyes. Interestingly, Charleston's three most popular street shamans all had names involving water.

RG: I don't know if I ever met Lightning.

AC: If Lightning had extreme mental capabilities, he might have also had the natural ability to be telepathic, perhaps teaching or transmitting that to Snowball or others.

RG: Possible...

AC: To use a Buddhist phrase... Snowball, Lightning, and Aqualung were practicing their own dharma, their own meaningless behavior (collecting bottles and counting bricks). If you think about it, a strong telepath probably would be quickly ostracized, socially, because people would be so frightened by them. The social pressure might force them to become a street vendor like Lightning, or a recycler like Snowball.

RG: I can see that.

AC: I don't know that this has anything to do with Mothman, per se. It's just another strange thing from Woodward Drive...

RG: There *are* things that we don't understand. There's probably always going to be things that we don't understand. But I think it's important to have a process to gain understanding (like we use in the scientific community), and take the time to do *that* before we try to decide what's going on. That's the difference, to me, between the old superstitious ways of doing things, where you assign a meaning or an outcome before really understanding what is going on, versus trying to gain understanding [first]. That part to me is pretty important. That is going to require us to make quite a few changes [however]. One of the beauties about the discipline of science is that you've got to go where the objective answer takes you, whether you like it or not. That's one of the things I've always liked about it.

AC: Was there something in the Major Jack Downing papers that interested you?

RG: Yes, that frequencies and electrical fields can cause hallucinations, and that a study says that they can produce *similar* hallucinations in *different* people... You had also mentioned some similarities between certain types of drugs that cause similar hallucinations in different people. *That* is the connection between "electro" and "chemical." The electrical field causes some kind of chemical reaction in the brain [that translates into] having hallucinations. Of course the chemicals are doing the same kind of thing, in reverse. The whole brain works on electrochemical transitions from one to the other.

AC: Could you comment on the "alien invasion" idea? Major Downing predicts that in the year 2012, or thereabouts, that the government will create a fake alien invasion. It also happens to be the point (according to a stock analyst friend of mine) at which our economic system will no longer support all the investment that's out there. There's something about the demographics of it. The number of people who are pumping money into the stock market is going to start going down at that point. There will be no way to sustain the current standard of living, with all the baby boomers reaching retirement age at the same time.

RG: And so one way to dampen it would be to have an alien invasion, huh? That's an interesting idea.

AC: I was wondering if you had thought more about that idea, because you brought it up in 1987.

RG: I did? I don't even remember that.

AC: You did... You said that the Star Wars weapons program had to do with such a scheme, and that the psychology of Star Wars was to set up fear of an outside force. The fear could be extended to other countries for a while, but once one country or group took over, they would – out of necessity – have to create an outside enemy (since it had no internal competition).

RG: That's true. That's right. We're always looking for a new enemy. It would *have* to be an outside enemy kind of thing, a science fiction [theory] to unite the world population. In *The Matrix*, they explain the anomalies that we see in life (ghosts, the paranormal, etc.) as [glitches]. The Oracle explains those as being glitches in the programming. We're actually seeing the program – or a piece of it – mess up. Or we're seeing the fix coming in to fix the program that messed up. From our vantage point, that would be very odd-looking. They even had a character in the movie play this role [of] looking like a ghost when it went from one thing to another, to sort of emphasize that idea. How is that different from explaining the same thing as being groupings of different types of energy (or whatever)? It's just the labels that we put on them...

The Yanomamo tribe of Brazil was forced by government leaders to come up with a way to stop cannibalism. According to the PBS series "Faces of Culture," the tribe came up with a new system based on artificially uniting clans to fight "ghosts." The ritual includes the sacrificing of large birds.

AC: This gets me back to Major Downing, this unknown character on the Internet who claims to have been an intelligence officer with a covert group called the *Black Ops Brethren*. He described the Mothman incidents as the same kind of thing. When they supposedly fired all of these electromagnetic waves into Point Pleasant, it caused an anomaly: the Mothman, a *Black Dog*. Entities like Bigfoot, Mothman, and Jersey Devil are called "black dogs." That's a generic term. So this electromagnetism caused the Black Dogs to get loose. Downing sort of speaks in occult terms because, apparently in the agency at that time, they had some occultists who actually understood a lot of the ancient stuff. They sent in the Men in Black to fix it for the government. But there were also other Men in Black there, who were "private contractor" occultists who benefit somehow when they gain control of the black dogs. I guess there was previously a gentleman's agreement between the two groups. The government had allowed the private guys (who may or may not be connected to Masonic and/or religious orders) to have their own allegiance to these occultic forces. So, according to Downing, the two were both there in Pt. Pleasant: the private occultic MIBs, and the government MIBs. Just to make it confusing, there seems to have also been a third group, the supernatural MIBs, called "ultra-terrestrials." They're always getting mixed up in the story, too. You never really know which is which.

RG: Interesting…

AC: But according to Downing, it got out of hand. To get a sense of how bad a screw-up this was, in the end they may have had to sacrifice people and/ or animals in order to appease the Black Dogs. Downing didn't say that exactly, but he referred to a *fix* for the glitch. I'm just sort of imagining what "the fix" could have been. He goes on to say that there was a split then, a change in the agencies. They went away from the guys who were more in tune with the occult stuff, and they went more to average military guys. The old guys retired off and the new guys took over. Instead of using the ancient knowledge gathered by the old guys, they sent green "special ops" guys in to stop Black Dogs. The very nature of the experiments changed. They went away from the totally wild experiments. Downing described the Mothman events as just a wild, creative experiment. Somebody had an idea to use this new, wacky equipment. They supposedly got less experimental after Mothman. You never know which part of this tale is disinformation, however. Oftentimes their basic goal is to make us think that they stopped experimenting with a particular phenomenon, technology, or program.

RG: Maybe the blowback was getting too hard to keep covering up, you know?

AC: Well, Downing thinks that the shift was bad, that the new way wasn't as good. The new guys don't respect the old knowledge, so they're not really prepared to deal with this serious occult stuff. Maybe that's the controllers' goal, though…

RG: It's funny how many different stories [exist]. You talked about the Men in Black that were working for the occult. A theme that keeps coming up in different versions of the story is the connection to the Masonic Orders. Interesting...

Godbey, Robert – Military in WV – 2003

AC: You used to work for a large, international accounting firm. You've dealt with quasi-military organizations like NASA. For instance, you helped negotiate the deal between NASA and the city of Fairmont, WV, to create the defense contracting haven, "Rocket City." Isn't there a high percentage of military involvement in WV?

RG: More West Virginians have lost their lives defending their country, in all the wars going back to the Civil War, than any other state. I don't know how they do the ratio, but I would guess that it's per capita. A larger percentage, based on the number of people that live here, go off and fight [and die] in all the wars. There's definitely an underlying cultural thing here that you [support the military]. I don't know what drives it, but there's something about West Virginia that tends to lead to everyone playing these roles. I've [synchronistically] bumped into different groups of people. I was surprised to hear of several different Secret Service agents being from West Virginia. In just my few encounters with Secret Service people, it has been, "You're from West Virginia? Well, so is this guy." [Maybe] it's just because we're close to D.C. [but] you hear the same thing about the F.B.I. and [organizations] like that. I mean there's definitely something cultural [in WV regarding] the amount of military participation and federal participation… It could lead to what you're talking about [where] you start recognizing those types of serendipities. The number of people [engaging in covert ops] is just higher.

AC: Now this is purely for entertainment purposes. I did a Google search on Sugar Grove, the site that Harriet remote-viewed. She had come up with a new idea, which is that they were not just doing Echelon eavesdropping stuff there; they were also doing this submarine stuff. Such an idea had not really come up about Sugar Grove before. I don't think it's general conspiracy knowledge that they were doing anything other than just listening to phone and fax traffic. It turns out that they are third in the chain of Naval command. They are beneath only the director of the Navy and the co-director. This is based on a public record of the chain of command. It makes sense that they would be doing submarine track-ing there, like Harriet said. That's public record, so hopefully we're not getting in trouble here with Homeland Security.

RG: That's interesting. I remember when both you and Harriet were talking about a listening-post kind of place, and what they might be listening to, or why that might be a good place to do it. When I was in college at Michigan, I heard that there was a facility in Northern Michigan that was designed to communicate with nuclear submarines. They needed to create a special communications system, using really huge [electro-magnetic] waves. Basically [they needed] a wavelength that would be so big that you'd need to be out in a remote area [just] to be able to send and receive things without interfering with [other equipment]. I think they call the system ELF, if I remember right. It was an acronym for something...

AC: "Extremely Low Frequency?"

RG: Yes, I think that's what it is. Low frequency means [long] wavelength. Extremely low frequency waves [are necessary] to get through the earth, to get to the submarine. It's pretty bizarre. [I'm] just sort of wondering if they weren't doing the same [thing in WV]. They've got to have more than one station. Michigan kind of makes more sense because it's closer to the North Pole. They tend to do a lot of communications with subs across the polar areas, where you've got less distance to cross. So the submarines kind of hang out there when they're hiding. But they can't have everything in that part of the world, so having another one somewhere else would be [logical]. But I had no idea that a place landlocked in West Virginia would be so high up in the command structure for the Navy. That sounds really bizarre.

While photographing at the Giza Pyramids in 2000, I left Rob – whom I was traveling with – for a moment. I wandered on top of the dismantled pyramids next to the famous ones. Not noticing the warning signs, I looked for angles to shoot the Great Pyramid. As I walked backward with my eyeball in the camera, I felt air with my foot. Instinctively I stopped, barely keeping my balance. I looked down over my shoulder and realized that I was about to fall down into a shaft that went down probably about 200-300 feet. I was really glad to see Rob again later... My almost near-death experience at Giza was a memorable one. I have often wondered why they don't put covers on these shafts, or at least ropes around them. Perhaps they don't mind seeing a tourist disappear every now and then? As Keel intimated in "Jadoo" after stumbling onto a mummy-making operation, the Egyptians always seem to be looking for "volunteers."

CHAPTER 17

"Learn to be silent. Let your mind listen and absorb."

-Pythagoras

Colvin, Andy – Grassy Knoll Radio interview 4 – March 2006

[Theme music] "Up next on From the Grassy Knoll: a terrifying look into the Orwellian world of brainwashing, disinformation, and – ultimately – control over you..."

"Vyz" from Grassy Knoll Radio (GK): We have with us for our fourth round, Andrew Colvin. He is the documentary filmmaker of the title *The Mothman's Photographer*. We've talked about a lot of stuff way beyond the Mothman. He's very knowledgeable about it. He lived in the area in which a lot of these activities took place – and still take place – and that would be West Virginia, and the surrounding Ohio River Valley states. Andrew thanks a lot for coming back to the Grassy Knoll. How are you doing today?

Andy Colvin (AC): Doing great!

GK: Listen before we go any further, we want to tell people that your website is andycolvin.com. They can access your DVD series on your website...

AC: In addition to the documentary, we have a soundtrack that came out before that. I tend to do things backwards, like the Heyoka.

GK: That's why you're on the Grassy Knoll! Go ahead...

AC: Well I'm a little bit Native American, and the Native Americans have a whole system of beliefs built around the Thunderbird. I guess I should have said this first: I think the Mothman, the Garuda, and the Thunderbird are more or less the same creature.

GK: Let me stop you right there. I don't mean to derail you, but I've been meaning to ask you this in the last three interviews: Does the Phoenix fit in here somehow?

AC: It's very related, that's for sure. They are slightly different, but similar in the sense that both the Garuda and the Phoenix share the "resurrection" motif with Christ, and both arise completely developed. When the Garuda cracks from its egg, it's fully grown like the Phoenix is when rising from the ashes. This symbolism comes across in the actual Buddhist practices of the Nath and Dzogchen traditions. By the way, they don't worship the Garuda. It's more of a practice. They visualize the Garuda. They ponder the symbolisms. In Buddhism, you have all these symbolisms that are designed for all the different people in the world. Depending on the person's makeup, certain spiritual avenues are better for certain people. The Garuda is kind of a "fast track." It's for people that are already sort of fully-grown spiritually. Now some people don't believe in reincarnation, but the Buddhists do. In the Buddhist system, if you've reached higher levels of Buddhist thought in prior lives, you sort of come to this point where you're ready to awaken then and there. You can choose to take the fast track of the Garuda visualizations. However, the visualizations sometimes choose you. As in my case, they may appear to you at some point in your life when you least expect it or even know about it. Another fast-track path that initiates can follow is one that involves meditating in graveyards at night.

Yet another path is having yourself walled into a stone room, in complete solitude and darkness, for anywhere from 2 to 7 years. Food and water are delivered daily, but it is agreed upon beforehand that no one will let you out – no matter what you say or do. According to John Keel, this method develops extreme psychic abilities in hermits, such as being able to remote-view the outside world in realtime.

AC: These are very scary, hardcore techniques that drive people to insanity if they are not ready. The Garuda can be just as scary. But the pay-off for the fear is that you make rapid progress towards your own personal self-realization. In the Native American tradition, they have the Heyoka society for those who have either had a dream of the Thunderbird or have actually seen it. This is found in several different tribes. In my own familial tribes (Blackfoot and Cherokee) they have Heyoka societies. They also have it in the Sioux tribe. Likewise, you can go to most any Northwest tribe and they will have a Thunderbird society. The Heyoka are medicine men that have contacted the Thunderbird somehow. Now, such contact changes you. You then have a different perception of reality. You know that everything is not what it appears. This forces you to start trusting your own judgement. A lot of times these guys become great healers. And they tend to do things backwards. They're jokesters and sacred clowns. They come out at rituals and clown around.

GK: Hold on a second, now... You talk about doing things backwards. Do you remember the "contrary" in Little Big Man?

AC: Absolutely, that's exactly it.

GK: Is that it? Excellent... Okay, let me ask you another thing. I'm thinking of you out in the Northwest. I know you don't hail from there. You hail from the East and from the Ohio Valley. Of course the Cherokee is not a far stretch. Where did the Blackfoot part of your lineage come from?

AC: I don't exactly know. We interviewed my aunt and she talked about Grandma Lucy. She showed me some old pictures. I incredulously asked, "Are you sure she's not Cherokee?" But she was adamant that Grandma Lucy was Blackfoot

GK: Okay, let me ask you this. I'm not that versed on it and I don't mean to go off on a side road but [with the] Blackfoot, I'm thinking that [they are] Plains Indians.

AC: Well, take the Hopewell Indians... They're the ones associated with Ohio. They claim they didn't build the mounds, but people associate them with the mounds anyway. The Hopewell traveled between the Ohio Valley and the Great Lakes. There was a major highway there that ran north/ south to the Great Lakes, and then over to where the Blackfoot lived. I'm imagining that's how it happened.

Some Blackfoot traveled in the other direction, towards the West Coast. My current neighborhood in Seattle was once an Indian stronghold. An old school was once located in what is now my backyard. Several strange incidents in the neighborhood have reminded me of the apparent connection between paranormal events and old schoolyards. By the way, the name "Hopewell" is not the real name of any particular tribe, but a catchall phrase. Sometimes such cover names reveal esoteric knowledge. In this case, Hopewell may refer to ancient practices in the Ohio Valley involving "hope" for mankind coming from deep "wells." This would explain the many underground structures in the area. Some names would have probably been considered too explicit, by conservative Christians and industrialists, since they gave a clear indication of the true Native history of the area. Replacement names were thereby inserted into the local vernacular. This explains why Mound, which is directly west of the West Side of Charleston, is now erroneously called "North Charleston."

GK: [That Indian route] is probably known as Interstate 75 or something now...

AC: Some of these old tracks are still there. They are straight lines similar to ley lines. Ley lines were laid on the earth's energy grid patterns...

GK: I think our interstate system is definitely beaten down by the paths of the Native Americans and the pioneers.

AC: A lot of these sightings in West Virginia occurred on the interstate while it was being built. But getting back to my documentary, I met one of the guys in the soundtrack band (I.V. League) in art school in Cincinnati. I just wanted to touch on him really quick. He is one of the many important people who have synchronistically filled in pieces of the informational puzzle.

In what may be another coincidental name-game item, the name of the Mothman's Photographer DVD soundtrack band, "I.V. League," is oddly similar to the name of the Rockefellers' longtime press spokesperson, Ivy Lee.

AC: What I'm about to say relates to this idea of Peter Levenda's, that there is official manipulation of occult forces and belief systems occurring. It benefits the elites. They see a political benefit. You have both government and private groups studying these paranormal things, in order to better manipulate events.

Another example of official manipulation of occult forces might be the crop circle phenomenon. In June of 2007, a debate erupted on the blog of authors Nick Redfern and Greg Bishop (UFO Mystic) over the issue of whether or not crop circles are meant to evoke magickal powers. Redfern, an admitted ritual occultist, seemed to believe that occult happenings were being generated around those researching circles and/or making circles with boards. However, he didn't seem to like my idea that the military might also have occultists interested in forming these circles with satellite lasers. The development of the crop circle phenomenon exactly paralleled the great increases in "Star Wars" budgets imposed by Reagan, Bush, and Thatcher. One would expect that military occultists knew that a major security offensive – keying off of the 9/11 disaster – was set for the new millennia, when renegotiations of Exxon's 1925 oil treaty were due. These circles may have been part of a magickal power buildup. The fact that Mothman experiencers like us were seeing visions of 9/11 decades ago gives some hint that such plans had long been in the works. The fact that the Eye of Horus crop circle appeared exactly 100 years after Aleister Crowley's Horus ritual almost proves that the circles are meant to evoke magick in Ohio, as well as in the UK.

AC: My art school friend filled in some of the pieces for me regarding what might be happening in central Ohio. It fits into the overall manipulation of mindset, if you will. He's originally from Cincinnati, specifically Indian Hill where all these disputed Indian mounds are located. I started realizing that Cincinnati had all of these important families, and that my classmates were from them. I went to the Art Academy of Cincinnati. A lot of wealthy kids went there. This was where I found out that the Bush family was from Ohio. The Bushes would come into town and stay with friends of my friend's family. The Bushes were known to be close with the Lindner family, which owned a major chunk of Chiquita, Circle

K, United Dairy Farmers, Carl's Junior, and later, the Cincinnati Reds. Chiquita, which in 2007 admitted in court to having hired terrorist groups to patrol their Central American fields, used to be called United Fruit. They had a big shipping presence in New Orleans, along the Mississippi and Ohio Rivers, and in Latin America. Basically, what you have are these families in Ohio that are in the franchise food business. It's not just General Electric, NASA, and military stuff... They also have Proctor & Gamble, Kroger, various fast food chains, etc. These people are billionaires. They live a completely different lifestyle than the rest of us. For instance, one of my classmates inherited a famous brand of margarine. He didn't go to class. Ever... But I'm guessing that he got his degree without any problem. One of the other guys that I went to class with, his dad must have been in some intelligence agency. They were in the art restoration business. They owned an island in Florida, Sanibel, where some of the famous abstract artists had their studios. I later found out from researcher John Judge that this was a CIA enclave. So you kind of have these art and CIA links. I found these things out by my experiences in Cincinnati. By the way, there's a book about the CIA and how they backed a lot of these postmodern painters like Rothko and the guy that threw paint, Jackson Pollock. The CIA guided these artists' careers. In some cases the artists didn't even know... It was all done behind the scenes. I think Mark David Chapman was involved in an Atlanta art gallery that was part of The Triad. The Triad is this national drug-dealing organization that tapped into the gambling legacy of what is termed the Kentucky Bluegrass Conspiracy.

GK: Alex Constantine has done some things about Rock & Roll infiltration, and how Lennon might have been hit because of what he was popping off about.

AC: The Triad taps into Florida. It taps not only into art studios in the South, but also into that airport near Venice, FL, on the Gulf Coast where the hijackers were training. Daniel Hopsicker goes into all that. These things link back to the Ohio Valley.

GK: I have a very good friend who's a captain for a major airline. He flew with two individuals at separate times. Both regaled him with how they bridged their careers from the military to the commercial with running dope for Iran/Contra. One of them went down in drink in the Gulf. It was at dusk and he [figured] the Coast Guard was going to come out because they knew [he] was a drug runner. But they didn't go out... Fortunately or unfortunately, the gentleman didn't drown. He was sitting on top of his plane – what was left of it – and the Coast Guard came out and reluctantly took him back. [But] they couldn't turn him in because they knew he was part of the program. When you talk about Florida and its involvement running dope and stuff, people will tell you (and I've seen it myself) that there have been [drug] drop-offs in broad daylight. They are absolutely bold about what they do. People on the Gulf Coast talk about late-night runs at 4 and 5 o'clock in the morning, when nobody's supposed to be in the air. They know exactly what's happening. You catch my drift?

AC: I'm glad you mention that because I interviewed a guy in the documentary who saw Mothman in 2001, right after 9/11. He saw it in Florida. He wanted to know what it was all about. I joked that it was probably Mothman telling us to look to Florida for some more angles on this whole web.

GK: I don't know if you know it, and this could be a coincidence, but I'm going to throw it out to you. You understand that Pres. Bush hung out on 9/11 in his brother's state, right? I will tell you straight that there were two executive orders enforced by Jeb Bush. He activated the National Guard on the Friday *before* the Tuesday (which was 9/11). And he activated the second one *on* 9/11. That second one was activated before New York or Washington or Pennsylvania ever enacted any kind of emergency orders…

AC: Well, his brother was an owner of the company doing security at the World Trade Center, right? Did we talk about that?

GK: That was Marvin. Isn't that amazing?

AC: Yes, it certainly is… Marvin's a very mysterious character. By the way, there were some interesting buildings close to the complex that perhaps housed other parts of the conspiracy. Bankers' Trust was right next to the WTC, yet it didn't get damaged. Bankers' Trust was where the hijackers banked.

GK: Yes, it was selective destruction that day. What's interesting is that if you ask most Republicans to name George Bush's brothers, Marvin won't come up. And neither will Neil. Of course Neil was key in that Silverado Savings and Loan trashing, and was also a friend of Scott Hinckley, the brother of John Hinckley (who shot who Reagan).

AC: I heard an interesting NPR story about a week or two ago about the Deutschebank building, which is another one of these buildings right next door that didn't get badly damaged. Deutschebank owns the investment company A.B. Brown, where the pre-9/11 "put options" trading occurred.

GK: Yes, and also in Chicago with the put options, which Michael Ruppert talked about. The put options spiked to something like 1100% on only two companies. One of them was United Airlines, and the other was American Airlines.

According to a report on the radio program Democracy Now, hundreds of tiny human bone fragments have been found in the Deutschebank building. Such fragments could only have come from the use of explosives in the twin towers. The bank has cynically sued the city over "mold damage" since the attacks. Demolition began in late 2006, after delays caused by asbestos fears. Within five years of the attacks, a majority of the cleanup workers were suffering from chronic lung disease. Many, in fact, were already dead. In Oct. 2006, some extra steel beams were found tucked away under a temporary roadway. News reports described the cleanup company, Controlled Demolition, as being "embarrassed" by the find. The offending beams, which might show evidence of high explosives on burnt ends, were quickly shuffled away. Controlled Demolition was paid $7 billion to clean up the site.

AC: This might be a good place to talk about the crash in West Virginia. I heard we had reports of a plane crash near the border of Ohio, Kentucky, and West Virginia on the day of 9/11. Of course this puts it close to Point Pleasant. I'm thinking that the place it crashed is probably Wayne National Forest. That's your biggest area of really complete wilderness. I mean there's maybe one road through there. And, it's an area that started having some strange red-eyed creature sightings soon after 9/11.

An Ohio University forensic biologist named Scott Moody investigated the Wayne Forest Bigfoot sightings. An article on Moody appeared on May 2nd, 2006 in the Columbus Dispatch. Moody had been consulted in 2004 when an Ohio food company was sued for frog parts found in their frozen pizzas. Moody identified the species of frog, thus proving where the offense had been committed (Ohio, not Mexico). Seattle animation artist Bruce Bickford, who seems to have a psychic connection to Mothman, has done several short films involving morphing images of Bigfoot, pizzas, UFOs, and birdmen. He once cut hundreds of Mothman faces into dried leaves. Bickford's friend, artist Jim Woodring, has had a longstanding interest in drawing frogs and shapeshifting entities.

GK: We're talking about Flight 77, is that correct?

AC: Yes. There's this old idea that these were shot down or removed somehow, and then dummy planes substituted. In the case of the World Trade Center, it looks like maybe drone 737s were substituted and flown remotely. Why do we think this? Because that was the type of jet engine that was found at the WTC scene.

GK: What about Wayne National Forest? Are we looking at an airliner going down in that area? Let me ask you this, and I'm not being accusatory. What are your sources, as much as you can say, about something happening in that area?

AC: I believe it was a media quip mentioned in the David McGowan series. Not all that verifiable, unfortunately…

GK: You do hail from there. Have you been back – with this knowledge – to poke around and ask, "did this happen or not?"

AC: No. This only recently came to my knowledge, that there had been reports of a crash near Pt. Pleasant.

GK: No people back there have sent anything to you to confirm or deny that that might be the case, right?

AC: Correct… But I will say that in most cases with these 9/11 crash reports, what they heard was a TV news report. In fact, I heard a news report with my own ears that there had been a crash in Colorado that day. So I think it's at least possible that the planes that took off – that ended up supposedly crashing into things – were shot down in various places, or swapped out.

GK: Fair enough… That's interesting. That's another thing I will have to look into. Thank you very much for bringing that up. Where do you want to go from here?

AC: I wanted to finish up on what happened in California when we were filming there with Harriet.

GK: Can you refresh people's memory as to who Harriet was and why she factors into this?

AC: Harriet is my childhood friend. We sort of had a *Harry Potter* thing going on. We had Harriet and Tommy and myself. We were having these magical things happen. Everyone seemed to pick up certain talents and things. Hers seems to be psychic and healing abilities. Several times in the filming process, I tested her out on various things. I found her to be accurate on several different predictions and ESP guesses. I think when we left off we were talking about Orinda, California, which is a town whose name means the "Thunderbird's energy." By the way, when we went to Maui looking for black panther witnesses, they turned out to live on "Olinda" Road. Olinda is where Mark Twain, who became a huge critic of capitalism, once lived. A quick link to Union Carbide here…

Union Carbide has a black cat as its mascot.

GK [sarcastically]: It's probably just a coincidence...

AC: This Orinda name came up two or three times. Soon after we were at Orinda, CA, we found out about Barbara Honegger, who had studied the paranormal there. She had been involved with The Nine, the October Surprise, the Lewinsky scandal, and the Wandering Bishops, who run churches that are sometime used as CIA fronts. It's funny because not long after we were in Orinda, there was this one-of-a-kind Mothman sighting north of there. If you go north from Orinda, straight over Mt. Diablo (Devil's Mountain, haunt of the Zodiac) and then down the other side of it, you bottom out into the north end of San Francisco Bay. That's where Mothman was seen. He was over these refineries that we had visited prior. The sighting was also close to the Concord Naval Station. This kind of peaked our interest because it was similar to Charleston, in that you have a petrochemical facility residing in or around a Navy base.

In 2007, when I visited one of my witnesses in Seattle who is a member of the Whyte family (see chapters 43 and 44), I discovered a familiar arrangement in their neighborhood. They lived at a high point, within a block or two of an old Army base (Camp Long), a Thunderbird Totem, a water tower, a longtime school location, and two Catholic Churches – all with a view of large refinery tanks. In almost every American city, one finds that the military, the Church, and Big Oil jointly occupied sacred Indian ground from early on. And as shown in the history of Sand Point Naval Base in Seattle, the military would especially go after villages where whites and Indians were living together harmoniously.

AC: We didn't quite know what the significance of the sighting was until the following summer. A laser shot down a missile near SF Bay. Harriet and her friends witnessed it. That may have been an event that Mothman wants us to look at. Since the Garuda traditionally tries to clue us into things, it could have been trying to get us to add either "laser technology" or "satellite warfare" to our list of linkages.

According to Emanuel Josephson, the Rockefellers held up the first American satellite launching so that the Soviets could launch Sputnik first. This was done in order to increase public funding for NASA. The Rockefellers profited from public spending on both sides of the Cold War, however.

AC: Another thing that happened was that there was another one-of-a-kind Mothman sighting up in Alaska in 2003. I emailed Harriet and said, "What's up with the Mothman in Alaska?" She replied, "There's going to be an earthquake." Two days later, there was an earthquake in Alaska.

Then we had the DC Sniper, which is kind of an interesting story. You and I talked about the way they were caught, that they were caught by what appeared to be mind control phraseology (about the "duck and the noose"). Suddenly the next morning, these guys are found in a rest area, which is where you'd *never* want to go if you were trying to hide from the cops...

GK: Andrew, when we heard this [phraseology] we saw [police captain] Moose out there in the pre-dawn interview. He's going on with this way-out little ditty and the next thing you know, these guys are caught in some rest area. But it's like, how did [the police] make the jump of finding these guys? I mean there are a million people along I-95 that pull into rest areas and snooze. You know what I mean? It was like, why did you guys know to go to that particular place? Would you agree that there might have been an MK-Ultra triggering mechanism in that little Cherokee axiom?

AC: Yes, and the story they used about the duck and the noose is about a patsy. It's the story of the wrong person getting caught. So these guys were openly flaunted as the patsies. There are lots of interesting things about the case. One of them is that they attended a mosque a block away from my house in Seattle.

GK: A mosque?

AC: Yes, they were ostensibly Islamic. I'm assuming for the moment that they really *were* Muslims, although the older one had this history of going to and from the Caribbean, ferrying people in and out. He had all kinds of identification. He did the kinds of things that spies do. He was at the Monterey Language School, a spook school, and he knew Capt. Moose from either the Oregon National Guard or from Ft. Lewis (I can't remember which). This mosque didn't last long after they were caught. There was a minor earthquake here, and they used that as an excuse to fence it off and condemn it. Eventually it was torn down. It appears that those snipings were designed to scare Congress into agreeing to license the Iraq war for Bush. It was right at the same time. As this stuff was happening, it was pretty obvious what it was all about. Then there was the counter-terror FBI agent, Linda Franklin, who was killed by the snipers not too long after she had disagreed with Bush's terrorism policy.

GK: Oh, yes. She was popped in the DC suburban area.

AC: She was one of the few people who knew all about al Qaeda. At some point or another she wanted to do the right thing, sort of like the O'Neill guy who was made the WTC security chief two weeks before the 9/11 attacks – and who died there.

GK: Right. He was in the WTC when it went down.

One has to assume that someone on the Board with Marvin Bush offered O'Neill his WTC job.

AC: O'Neill was critical of the Bush administration's lax approach to al Qaeda. He knew all about it. He was really involved. This is a little tangent here. When I was in Texas, I was doing construction work to put myself through graduate school. One of the ladies I worked for was a Saudi princess who had millions of dollars. She bought the house that I was working on by selling one Arabian racing horse from the Bluegrass state. It was like a quarter of a million dollar house, back in the 1980s. Her father flew back and forth from Florida to Texas every day. He just flew in the air and did all these deals from the airplane. I was asking, "Why is he always up there?" I guess there are some laws that you can circumvent this way. If you're above the ground and flying, then certain laws don't apply. I was told that there was some advantage to it. The kids in the family were getting millions of dollars on their birthdays. The Saudis at the center of this 9/11 conspiracy are also wealthy oil people in Texas. They have houses there. They have families there. They're not always in Saudi Arabia. And they're all linked in together. It was pretty much of an eye-opener for me.

In June of 2007, the FBI declassified a document showing that Osama bin Laden had chartered one of the special planes that were allowed to leave the U.S. after 9/11, carrying bin Laden family members. A British newspaper posted a photo of the family from the 1970s, lounging in front of a posh London establishment. Osama was near the right edge of the photo. In the lower left corner was a woman who looked very much like the woman whose house I had worked on in Austin.

AC: But getting back to the sniper… First we had the DC sniper. Then we had a sniper in Charleston, West Virginia, not long after that. Attempts were made to debunk it, saying it was not a "real" sniper case. The media claimed that there were only a couple shootings, and that it was about drugs or something. Most everybody forgot about it. One of the shootings happened up near this gravel pit in the Campbell's Creek area, where Mothman had been seen on Nov. 20, 1966. We actually used to go there to watch demolition derbies in the pit. We almost got killed on the way to one of these derbies. Some guys tried to run us in the river with their car. They literally tried to run us in the river. Ironically, this was at Magic Island, at the confluence of the Elk and Kanawha Rivers. They had a bridge collapse there that killed some children in 1904, on the same day of the year as the Silver Bridge. So looking back, this is a strange tie-in. We almost died there as we were going to this Mothman gravel pit...

In Feb. 2007, my sister called to tell me that on old boyfriend of hers, who had lived next to the "haunted castle" on Woodward Drive, had recently contacted her after many years. He seemed to have up-to-the-minute information on her. The boyfriend was once a minister near Campbell's Creek. Today, he works for a Japanese-owned medical supply corporation that sells things like human eyelens implants. Coincidentally, he was dating my sister in 1973 when she took the kitchen photo of what may be Mothman. He also was the first person to introduce me to Buddhism and to hallucinogenic drugs. His name can almost be rearranged into "Indrid Cold." When I was at Marshall Univ., he and I worked together in the kitchen of a Greek sorority house. This was in 1979, when I ran for student body president under a satirical "bringing terror to America" campaign platform. This was a pretty crazy thing to do then, because campus tensions were running high. Marshall had many Iranian students at the time, and the Iranian hostage crisis was in full swing. I tried to lighten it a bit by also having nonsensical planks like the "need for blending pantheism and Greek myth," featuring enormous subsidies for "bringing the Olympics to WV" and "better housing for campus squirrels." Andy Coiner, editor of the campus newspaper, The Parthenon, held radio debates with the candidates. My running mate and I had already decided to be directly opposed on every issue. He played the conservative and I, the crazy liberal with big ideals. This made for some hilarious debates. He and I would often sing "The Star Spangled Banner" or "Philadelphia Freedom" just as we were about to be pilloried for having a platform that made absolutely no sense. As you might expect, we almost won the election.

GK: Whatever took place near that gravel pit... Was that a chance, vagabond type of attack, or do you think it was definitely concerted?

AC: Gravel pits often seem to be involved with Mothman sightings. I'm not sure why, although it probably has to do with increased magnetism from minerals. At this point, I'm just pointing out the connections. Some of the bigger connections are easier to latch onto but some of the subtle, synchronistic ones are harder to grasp.

GK: So at this time, you're saying that you don't know if you were singled out, per se. It might have been a coincidence but, on the other hand, we don't know at this point. Is that correct?

AC: Well, that was just a random event. But I think there's an energy force at these spots that can negatively affect people. These guys thought we were "flipping them off" and so tried to kill us. I don't think they initially meant to hurt anyone. I just think that there's an energy force in some of these places that can go awry. For instance at the Mothman shrine, after Tommy moved, another guy moved in. This new family was involved with the Knights of Pythias. Pythias had a camp near this gravel pit. Actually, the camp was very near where the Layton family lived. The ones involved in Jonestown... But at our Mothman shrine, people would sometimes get in fights or behave oddly. I saw a guy almost kill another guy there. It was out of proportion to what you would normally expect.

GK: So you think that something's taking people over there?

AC: Well, it affects people. Anyway, these Charleston sniper shootings kind of related to this Mothman sighting spot and to where this Layton family is from. I asked Harriet to predict what she thought would happen next. She said, "The sniper is going to stop for a while, and then he's going to start up somewhere else." So I filed that away. I have my emails. Sure enough, a few weeks later it started up again in Columbus, which is near where she lives. A lot of people know about the Columbus sniper. Columbus is a much more famous series of shootings. It turns out that a friend of Harriet knows the Columbus sniper's family. The sniper, McCoy, was under psychiatric care for years, so it's hard to tell if he was just naturally crazy, or synthetically influenced to go shooting people. You don't know, and the media never digs too deep...

GK: Columbus doesn't come up on the radar for most of us when we take a look around for weird happenings or clandestine operations. I was not really cognizant of the Charleston sniper. But you have the DC sniper, the Charleston sniper, *and* the Columbus sniper... It all still goes back to around the same area, like there's some kind of nexus in that Ohio River Valley...

AC: The anthrax used after 9/11 was made in Columbus. It was manufactured there by Battelle Industries but was destroyed within three days of the attacks. They have a lab there called the West Jefferson Lab. Leonard G. Horowitz did an article in issue #29 of Paranoia Magazine about all the links around Battelle. It's an amazing graph of all these different corporations, including Carbide spinoff companies. Columbus is the place that JFK suspect Gordon Novel (who recently inserted himself into the UFO debate) fled to, in order to get away from Jim Garrison.

GK: There were stories that the limousine that Kennedy was in was brought to Columbus. Have you heard that? Eric Jon Phelps covers that in *Vatican Assassins*. I think that limo found its way to Columbus, and the person that was in charge of making sure that car was never [investigated] in any way, shape, or form was Lee Iacocca.

AC: One more thing I forgot about the DC Sniper is the white van angle. Remember? The scuttlebutt is that the white vans were carrying those who were really doing the shooting. The team (or teams) in the white vans probably consisted of professionals.

GK: The government's vehicle of choice is a white van.

AC: Not long after that, I found an article in the NY Times about a data-mining company called Iron Mountain. Of course this sort of harkens back to the old *Report from Iron Mountain*, which has seen its way through so many researchers files. Iron Mountain's emblem is a winged triangle, very similar to the Triad's emblem.

GK: What a surprise...

AC: The NYT article was about the white vans and how Iron Mountain keeps "losing" people's data out of them. They were kind of playing off the sniper story. This was right after the sniper, so everybody was kind of nervously joking about it. I was drawn to look at the article for some reason. I read it and I thought, "That's who it was... *That's* probably the company." I mean, again, I have to qualify it and say that I don't know for sure. How would any of us really know if there was a hit team embedded in Iron Mountain Corporation? Sometimes all you really have is a vague intuition.

GK: I alerted a lot of the people that carry this show to take a look at this. We're going much deeper than people normally [do]. There's a lot of stuff going on here. You have opened up the possibility that the [Mothman] sightings *might* have something to do with [synthetic] happenings. [He] might be [pointing to] psy-ops. You don't know for sure, but you've left that door open. You have obviously focused a lot of attention on an area that a lot of people don't think about. [West Virginia] has always been alluded to in movies and books and such as a very, very interesting place. [It] is one of the bastions of the Rockefellers. Also the areas around it... There are a lot of curious things happening there. Would you agree?

AC: Absolutely...

GK: You've gone much further than people would necessarily expect. I mean they're looking for winged beings. They might not go any further than that. What you've done is taken it beyond and asked, "What's going on behind it, or in spite of it, or because of it?" I think that's a very fair thing.

AC: Before I start freewheeling it here... About that Layton family... Their son is in jail for the Jonestown massacre. He's the only person in jail for the Jonestown massacre. Did you know that?

GK: No. You mean, Jim Jones and that whole nine yards? This guy is in prison somewhere?

AC: Yes. Layton is in prison. He's from Charleston. He's actually from Boomer, WV, which is a suburb. It's near WV Technical College, as well as a Union Carbide facility that's been there for decades. The Carbide plant there at Alloy, WV, is known for polluting the air in the same quantities as the entire city of New York. If you measure the particulates around Alloy, it's equal to New York City. And it's coming from one *single* Union Carbide plant. They claim that they've fixed the problem but I would be skeptical. Layton's father was head of the Army Biochemical Warfare division in the '50s. You have a family here that – if there's any funny experimentation going on at all – might decide to go back to their hometown and try some. That's kind of my thinking. It sort of puts the spotlight on chemical experimentation. A lot of people think Mothman was a chemical or genetic mutation. That's somewhat reasonable, I suppose, since we have an important WV family being in charge not only of the entire military biochemical operation, but also obvious mind control ops like Jonestown. Layton's behavior after the shootings was very odd. He was very calm, even though they had killed this congressman. Layton was there with a gun. I don't think he necessarily shot Congressman Ryan. Maybe he was kind of the patsy for the whole thing. He was strangely "calm," though. Afterwards they may have just said, "He's the best guy to throw in the clink for this." And so that's what happened. But Layton was the doctor at Jonestown. He had file cabinets filled with mind control drugs. One of the people he was rumored to have "treated" was Dan White, the guy who later shot the mayor of San Francisco, Harvey Milk. Milk knew a lot about Jonestown. So this White, who had been at Jonestown and had some "missing time" in his resume, later shoots Milk.

Torture specialist Dan Mitrione was Jim Jones' old friend from Indiana. Mitrione was given special tribute after his death by both Frank Sinatra and Pres. Eisenhower. According to Dave McGowan in his book "Understanding the 'F' Word," Eisenhower studiously followed the Rockefeller agenda throughout his career, in spite of his famous "fear the military-industrial complex" speech.

GK: Milk's shooter was Danny White?

AC: Yes. Dan White is thought to have been at Jonestown and been programmed by Layton. That was Mae Brussell's theory, at least. This is the famous "Twinkie Defense" we're talking about!

GK: Geez. [Please explain the] Twinkie Defense.

AC: The Twinkie Defense is where White said that he had killed Milk under the influence of an old Twinkie he had eaten.

White may have actually been telling the truth, since his eating of a Twinkie may have been the post-hypnotic suggestion needed to trigger his "Manchurian Candidate" behavior. If Layton was really White's programmer, he might have used something like The Boomer, a drug synthesized by the CIA in the 1960s for just such purposes. One wonders if The Boomer wasn't actually developed by the Laytons and named after their hometown. They were known for their pharmaceutical wealth and expertise. In April 2004, Layton was finally released - two years ahead of schedule - from Lompoc (CA) Prison, during a flurry of synchronicities in the Mothman world, including birdman sightings in CA.

AC: Another little parallel… I just got a book on the history of Union Carbide. One of *their* early directors headed the Army's Biochemical Warfare unit, just like Layton, Sr. So there were *two* Army Biochemical heads either from Charleston, or connected to Carbide's technical base in Charleston. Carbide also had an old plant in Clendenin, WV, where one of the first Mothman sightings occurred, on Nov. 12, 1966. So you seem to have this pattern of Carbide plants, gasoline stations, schools, bridges, and geomagnetic sources near Mothman sightings. Carbide also has an old facility in Sistersville, WV, where one of the "Great Airship" sightings occurred in 1897. Remember that?

GK: No. I wasn't there for that one.

AC: This is the famous airship flap that occurred mostly in Texas. There's a book now calling it the "Texas" Airship Mystery.

GK: Are you talking about UFOs, or dirigibles, or what?

AC: We're back to UFOs. In some ways, UFOs are ciphers for this process. But it is interesting that the airships were almost all seen in Texas, yet there's one in Sistersville, WV. It just begs investigation. It's saying, "Look at this; this is an oddity." Well, Carbide has a facility in Sistersville. And that year, 1897, was the year that Carbide had their first official technical research reports written up. So it's a date of interest in the company history. They made a point of mentioning it in the book. We're kind of getting into "ifs and buts" here, but I just thought I'd throw it out as something I came across today…

GK: Let me ask you this. This is pretty inflammatory. Just answer it the best way you can, and the way you should. Union Carbide seems to have a nefarious presence. What happened in Bhopal? Was that clearly an accident or do you have any information that it might have been, shall we say, a test?

AC: No, it was worker sabotage. I have an interesting advertisement from Union Carbide from the '60s. It is a magazine ad that shows their Bhopal plant and a big Hand of God. They had a Hand of God in all their ads. This Hand of God is pouring a test tube of red liquid over the plant *(see page 193)*. I mean, it's totally, what's the word...

GK: Prophetic?

AC: Yes, prophetic. The ad has been bandied about here and there. It's in a Bhopal disaster book. Authors that have written critically against Carbide have put it in their books. Another interesting connection is the Cleveland connection to Union Carbide. One of their first big corporate buildings blocks was out of Cleveland. It was the Electrometallurgical Company, which was related to Standard Oil in some fashion.

Carbide was taking cast-off substances from this Standard Oil processing facility in Cleveland and shipping them down to Charleston, using them for the S. Charleston operation. So we're starting to see links between Carbide and Cleveland, and also Europe – the market that this subsidiary later served. That's how it all sort of worked.

GK: Where's Carbide's headquarters? Is it in Charleston?

AC: The corporate headquarters used to be in NYC but is now in Danbury, CT (sort of).

GK: Where does the stuff really get done?

AC: It's all over the country. They have facilities out in Colorado where they do the uranium mining. Again, here's another odd coincidence. In my youth, I visited these Carbide uranium towns in Colorado. I was sightseeing, driving through Colorado. So I'm driving through there, looking for photos... I was portraying a "flying messiah" and photographing myself at monuments. I would usually travel with somebody, and they would photograph me at national monuments. So we're looking for places. We end up in these uranium-mining towns in Colorado. Union Carbide owns them. The towns are literally run by Union Carbide. I think they've now sold those towns to Martin Marietta.

GK: Oh, geez. What a surprise...

AC: Martin Marietta was a Michael Moore topic in his film *Bowling For Columbine*. But they were mining in the middle of the night in the

National Forest. That was one thing we noticed. They weren't mining during the day. All kinds of traffic in the National Forest, all night long... It was creepy. It was like a "company store" town from the early 1900s. The towns were so depressed. They had big, toxic pools to evaporate chemicals. In S. Charleston, Carbide had these smoking evaporation pools that would turn all different colors. You didn't know *what* they were releasing. They had one of these pools in this small Colorado town called Nucla. They named the towns with nuclear-sounding names, such as Uravan and Nucla. In Nucla they had the radioactive pool next to the public swimming pool! I mean we're talking about 30-40 feet apart, with just a little chain link fence between them. There appeared to be no regard for the people living there.

GK: You've hit on something, without a doubt. In a way, this might be the first show where you're starting to evince what you've found, and we're really happy to air that. We hope that not only the DVDs, but also the books you do, find favor with the population. People really need to know about this. This is not fooling around stuff... What you've done I think is immense... Sometimes I don't know how you sleep at night, but I'm fully supportive that you're doing it. Is there anything you want to give us as far as parting comments?

AC: One little detail I forgot about the Twinkie guy... The town of Boomer, WV that he's from... I went to a Knights of Pythias camp there because, again, the guy that took over the Mothman shrine house was part of the Knights of Pythias. I found out later, on the "Mind Control-L" discussion list, that researcher Kathy Kasten actually fingered the Knights of Pythias as a mind control society. She named, I think, Redding, PA as a town where they did a lot of things. I guess her father was a Pythias member, and had maybe tried to program her. Here we have a "mind control" secret society in Boomer, near this Layton family and West Virginia Technical College, with a nearby Union Carbide plant spewing New York City volumes of pollution. Not to mention the Mothman gravel pits and mounds...

CHAPTER 18

The following John Keel lectures were gleaned from Internet sources like eBay, where obscure and/or suppressed recordings about UFOs and the paranormal are anonymously traded. After attempting to ascertain copyright and receiving no replies, we decided to transcribe these rare recordings for the benefit of humanity. The majority of Keel's public thoughts about Mothman are included in the following chapters. Special thanks to all who have supported Keel and helped make his incredible work more accessible - particularly the International Fortean Organization (INFO).

Keel, John – West Virginia Contactees – 1979 Lecture excerpts

Those of you who've read some of my books know that I'm a growing skeptic. I started out as a great believer, and I've gradually turned into a skeptic as my investigations have progressed. I'm going to try to explain to you today some of those investigations and why they have made me skeptical of the basic flying saucer premise. That basic premise, of course, is that these things are from outer space. There's no question [that] there are strange things in the sky, but where they come from and what they're doing here is wide open. We know very little about them after 35 or 40 years of investigation. Our main problem, as I've stated in a number of books and articles, is that the will to believe is much stronger than the will to understand. People are very quick to accept a belief without any evidence. Sometimes with no evidence at all... A lot of our major religions are based on that strange ability of the human mind to accept such beliefs.

Harry Houdini, back in the '20s, became a good friend of Sir Arthur Conan Doyle. Sir Arthur Conan Doyle was the creator Sherlock Holmes and Harry Houdini, of course, was the great escape artist. Arthur Conan Doyle was also a famous investigator of psychic phenomenon in that era. He decided that Harry Houdini was not a magician at all, but a psychic. Doyle believed Houdini wasn't just escaping from these boxes and things; he was dematerializing and materializing outside the boxes. So he approached Harry Houdini with this theory and Houdini laughed at him saying, "That's nonsense, I use simple trickery to get out of these boxes." But Arthur Conan Doyle was convinced that Harry Houdini was a medium, and he stated this in some books and magazine articles. Harry Houdini got so mad that he broke off his relationship with Doyle. Doyle refused to believe that these were magic tricks...

Now, with flying saucers, we have a similar situation. We have been accepting, at face value, a lot of the things that have been said. I'd say 98% of the literature on flying saucers is absolute garbage. I know because I've had to read all of it over the years. When you try to track down some of these things (especially things that happened some years ago), you either end up at a blank wall or you find that it was much different from what was reported in the flying saucer magazines of that time. There are great dissimilarities. So after a lot of bad experiences, I decided to investigate only things that hadn't received any publicity. Things that had happened very recently... And that got me into the Mothman mess. I went down to West Virginia many times and tried to find out what was happening there. There were flying saucer sightings galore. In fact, I saw so many myself down there that I actually lost count. To a skeptic, this seems incredible. Once in Washington, I made that statement [when] Phil Klass was in the audience. He stood up and said in a very loud voice, "That man is a terrible liar!" And he stalked out of the hall.

But when you're in an area where there is a UFO wave going on, you're bound to see them. They were following a schedule in West Virginia. Every night at 8:30, you could go out and look up at the sky and one would go over. There were people with private airplanes chasing the damn things. Of course they always got away, and we never solved the mystery. Then I discovered that at 10:00 on Wednesday nights, we seemed to have more activity than any other period of time. I mentioned this on a television station down in West Virginia. The next Wednesday night, half the country was out looking at the sky. Thank god, three of them went over in formation at 10:00 on Wednesday night. I was then considered a great seer, because I had managed to figure this out.

There are a lot of other patterns to the phenomenon, which we can figure out if we lend ourselves to it. Going back through history, I have found that these patterns are continuous. I had to do some research into the Great Plague of the 1300s. I kept coming across references to strange atmospheric phenomenon. I kept digging into more and more books trying to find out what kind of strange atmospheric phenomenon they were talking about. It was taking place while everybody was dropping dead with the Plague. I finally found some references that described very large bright lights that were flying around these cities, especially where people were dying in droves. At that time, they assumed that it was some kind of religious phenomenon related to all the deaths that were taking place. The Indians had a belief that these were sky ships taking souls away into space after they died... In the '60s, we had a great many sightings directly over funeral homes and mental hospitals. I could never figure that out, either. Why funeral homes and mental hospitals? In the mental hospitals, the doctors and the nurses would be reporting these things [not the inmates]. Maybe there were inmates there that the UFOs were interested in. Inmates who had read some of my books or something... *[laughter]*

I felt that the one thing that had not been properly investigated were the contactees themselves (since we never managed to catch a flying saucer).

Our best evidence was the contactee. At that time in the '60s, contactees were frowned upon. They were ridiculed. They were attacked at every corner. There were 2 or 3 who had gotten rather famous, and this really irked some of the more prominent ufologists (who were very publicity-minded). There were people like George Adamski, who became very famous. He was much slandered and [so] towards the end of his life, he denied everything. He thought that he had been used in some fashion. He didn't know how, but he thought something very fishy was going on, and that many of the things he had believed earlier about flying saucers were wrong. But he couldn't figure out what was really going on.

I started interviewing contactees and [because of] my magazine articles about contactees, more contactees would write to me. In fact, I was swamped with letters from all over the country. Some people had had experiences 20 years earlier, and had never told anyone because they didn't know whom to tell. Finally they'd read an article by me about contactees, and decide to get in touch with me. In the end, I dealt with probably five or six hundred people who had had some kind of contactee experience. I lost count. There were hundreds of others that I could never visit personally or talk to on the telephone [but] that I corresponded with briefly.

I found that there were certain patterns in the contactee phenomenon, which had been deliberately overlooked by the believers. There were medical effects that had been deliberately overlooked or [missed because] the average UFO investigation was more of a conversation. Nobody ever examined these contactees physically, or even asked them what kind of physical affects they had suffered after their experience. It was virgin territory at that time. Fortunately, around the country there are quite a few doctors and psychologists now doing the same thing that I was doing then. But it was a long, uphill battle in the '60s to get anyone to pay any attention to the contactees. They were really scorned [yet] they hold many of the keys to the UFO phenomenon.

There are six basic types of contactees. Not just one, as you'd think. There are six types. I'll try to explain each type and what their medical characteristics are.

TYPE 1: Trance Contactees

The first type, Type 1, is a trance subject. This is, I've found, the most prevalent type. Usually this witness claims that he's suffered paralysis, that he was unable to move a muscle or even to blink his eyes. This is a sure sign that he was in a trance. We have religious miracles (name any date, they're going on all the time) like the one in 1962 in Garabandal, Spain. Two small children would go out into a field and kneel by a bush for five or six hours. They would be in a complete trance. Hundreds of people would mill around them, watching this. When they came out of the trance, they would tell that they had had a long conversation with the "lady" that was visiting them.

This happens over and over again in religious miracles, that the people are actually in a trance but they don't know they're in a trance. They think they're fully conscious. In hypnotism as you may know, a person will often be hypnotized and be under for two hours. When you bring him out of hypnosis, he doesn't think that he's been under for two seconds. If you tell him that he's been hypnotized, he'll argue with you. He'll say, "No, I couldn't have been hypnotized," until he looks at the clock and realizes that two hours have passed.

We have this over and over again in the UFO cases. People will be driving along a highway (always a secluded highway with no other cars on it) and they will see something in the sky. On rare occasions, it will be a metallic object but mostly it's a light, and the light is flashing. Now, some people can be hypnotized very easily with a flashing light if it flashes at a certain number of intervals. I used to use a strobe light in my investigations. It had an adjustment on it so that it would flash at different frequencies. I would set this up and have the contactee look at it. I would adjust the frequency until the contactee would go off like that, hypnotized. This is what happens with these lights. They're driving along a highway. They see this light. It's flashing, and suddenly they're in a hypnotic trance. Now an hour later, or two hours later, or a day later, they come out of the trance and they find that they're forty miles away from where they had [been]. Also they find that it's taken them three hours to travel a distance that normally would take them thirty minutes. They're baffled by it.

In the beginning, the UFO investigators were baffled by it too, because they didn't know anything about hypnosis, or about trance subjects or fairy lore. We have to take the "little people" seriously because there's an enormous amount of literature on them. More than there is on UFOs... The best minds of each generation have gone out and investigated fairies. There is a newsletter in England devoted to new sightings of the little people. It just goes on and on... Go to any good bookstore and pick up a book on fairy lore, and you'll find that it is divided into sections just like the UFO books. There will be a chapter on time lapses. There will be a chapter on abductions. There will be a chapter on sexual experiences. And when you read it, you'll think you're reading a flying saucer book, except it's all done in the fairy frame of reference. In the Middle Ages, the belief in fairies was very big. The fairy lights were also mentioned throughout this literature. These lights were, of course, the same thing that we're seeing today: mysterious lights that blink on and off and put you in a hypnotic trance.

When you're in this hypnotic trance and you think you're conscious, you can see almost anything and you will swear that it's real. When you come out of the trance, you'll swear, "I just saw an elephant walking down Main Street." Of course, there was no elephant. Incidentally, every year we have *dinosaur* reports. In Italy, they turned out the Army a couple of years ago to chase a dinosaur, and of course they never caught it. I really wonder what would happen if they had come upon this living dinosaur. They wouldn't want to shoot it and I don't know of any way to catch a dinosaur. I think that the Army would have been in real trouble. *[laughter]*

What fascinates me are the *kangaroo* reports that we get every year from all over the country. We know there are no kangaroos in the United States, but the police are chasing them every year. We have not just Mothmen running around, but we have kangaroos; we have dinosaurs; we have a wide variety of sea serpents. I am very interested in herpetology (snakes). I used to lecture on snakes. People used to come up to me afterwards and tell their snake stories, about the gigantic snakes that had been seen; snakes that we know are not to be found anywhere in the United States.

Anyway, the trance subject is set off by this flashing light. We do not know the source of this light. You can say they're from outer space; you can say they're fairies; you can say they're demons. [It] doesn't matter. We don't have an explanation for it. We just know that that is how it works. That's the mechanism. And that's only the first one.

TYPE 2: Post-Hypnotic Contactees

The second type of subject is the post-hypnotic subject. Most of you know about post-hypnotic suggestion. When someone is hypnotized you tell them, "one hour after you wake up, I want you to stand up on a table and crow like a rooster." One hour later, the subject is fully awake and all of a sudden, he doesn't understand why he has this terrible urge to stand up on a table and crow like a rooster. That is post-hypnotic suggestion. We have that in the flying saucer phenomenon, on a large scale. This is where the [witnesses] just need a slight trigger. It doesn't have to be a flashing light. It can be something else. It can be a sound over a radio or telephone that triggers them and puts them back into a trance. During this momentary trance, they will see something that isn't there at all. One common trigger that's used is Greek letters and Greek words. We don't know why... UFO entities for years have been using Greek names and Greek letters. One of them called themselves Xeno. That was widely published for weeks before anyone realized that Xeno was the Greek word for "stranger." It's just Greek. Are we being invaded by Greeks from outer space? I doubt it.

In a typical case of this sort, the person will say that he was driving past a billboard, say, and he looked at the billboard and the next thing he knew, he saw this huge saucer directly over the billboard. It was a huge machine with legs sticking out of it and people waving from the windows. Actually, it's the billboard that set him off. There was some word or letter on that billboard that triggered the post-hypnotic suggestion.

[In] investigating this type of case, I have to go over their whole life history. I do that anyway with every case, but [here] I have to try to find some point in their past couple of years where they had lost some time. Usually [it was] where they had taken one of these drives and discovered that it took them two hours to travel a distance that should have taken them thirty minutes. [One has to] assume that during these mysterious two hours, something happened to them. The post-hypnotic suggestion was implanted in their mind. Two years later, they come out with this absurd story. This is also a device that's very handy for discrediting witnesses. Suppose someone has had this experience where they lost three hours. They go to me, or Dr. Hynek, or someone [else] and complain about it. We start investigating it. One day they call up and say, "I just saw this giant kangaroo jumping across the road." The reason that they saw the giant kangaroo was that they had been programmed to see it. [Naturally] we say, "Oh, if he's seeing kangaroos, he must be a nut, so I'm not going to waste any more time with him." But it's more and more complicated, the deeper you get into it. These are the hypnotic types...

TYPE 3: Hallucinatory Contactees

We have one that really is scary, and this is what I call induced hallucinations. This is one I first stumbled across in West Virginia in 1966. I've come across it several times since, including on Long Island and in Ohio, and in some other states. Dr. Vallee has apparently come across it, too. In his book *The Invisible College*, he has one paragraph devoted to it. In the induced hallucination, you are driving along the highway or hitchhiking or whatever, and you see a light or hear a sound. You go into a trance or you pass out. You are not taken aboard a flying saucer; you are taken aboard a truck or a van. In areas of West Virginia where flying saucer reports were prevalent, in discussing it with people who lived in the area, I learned that there were a lot of mysterious trucks and vans running around. These [local] people are aware of *everything* because sometimes on the backroads they don't see anything *at all* for days and days. Suddenly they'd see a mysterious van passing back and forth. They would take notice of it. These vans, as near as we can figure out, are used [to] examine people. Many of the abduction cases concern medical examinations. People are taken aboard these vans and they are examined. They are probably given some kind of drug, which we've never been able to isolate. A number of contactees have had some strange substance in their blood that we've never been able to [identify]. While they're being examined and given these hypnotic drugs, what we call a *confabulation* is placed in their mind. This is done very easily in hypnosis, or with drugs. You simply tell the person that they have been to another planet, and they believe it when they wake up later on. They can fill in all the details. Their mind will fill in all the details. And they will come up with one hell of a good contact story. [But] the contact story doesn't mean anything.

Now it took me a long time to get wise to this tactic. Then I realized that there was another memory underneath that confabulation. You have to hypnotize the person many times, over a long period of time [in order] to get a second memory hidden below the first memory (the confabulation). The second memory is usually much simpler. It's simply that they are being manhandled and thrown onto this table, and that they're being injected with something. Lights are being flashed in their eyes. They're going through what sounds like a standard medical examination. Then they're released. But they're released with that memory so buried that they remember only the wonderful trip to another planet. That doesn't mean that *all* of our contactees who claim to have gone to another planet are victims of this, but it means that most of them are.

The keys to this are the physical sensations that they feel. When you're dreaming and a mosquito comes along and bites you in the eye, you may start having a dream that you are being chased by cannibals with spears. They've stuck you in the eye because your mind is translating that feeling into the dream. This works in much the same way in the UFO contact. The physical sensations are the only important things in these stories. The women, especially, feel that a needle has been thrust into their stomach around the belly button. As you know, Betty Hill claimed that. But there are many other cases of that, and we're baffled by it. One theory is that they're using these long needles to reach the ovaries, and that may be. But I think there must be something else to it, because we find that this "needle in the navel" was important in witchcraft lore, too. With the men, the physical pains that they feel are often around the fingertips. Needles have been poked into their fingertips. And by golly, you look at their fingertips two or three days later, and you'll see the marks where something has been thrust into their fingertips. Also with the men, something is placed underneath their chin. There are glands there, and it may be some method of draining substances from these glands. Again, there's no way to speculate, but they do have marks afterwards under their chin, where something has been definitely poked there. [There are] those who like to yell," Hoaxes and liars!" How would someone go about poking themselves under the chin with a hypodermic needle? I think it's a little grizzly. Most people wouldn't do it just to provide evidence.

We don't know what these trucks are up to. We don't know where they're from. We know that a couple of years ago in Montana, they did have signs on the sides that said "Smithsonian Institute." We checked immediately with the Smithsonian, and they didn't have any trucks running around Montana. They didn't know what the hell was going on. So we're dealing with a man-based group. The deeper you get into it, the more scary it gets. Those of you who read Dr. Vallee's latest book know that he now accepts that notion. He believes that it's an old religious cult, which is maybe a workable idea. But it doesn't make too much sense that anyone would go through all that trouble.

In 1967, Russia had an outbreak of flying saucer attacks like this. Russia immediately issued a very long diatribe claiming that the CIA was doing it to Russian citizens, as a method of reviving religion in Russia...

TYPE 3.5: Distortions of Reality

I prefer to call these "distortions of reality." In fact my last book, *The 8th Tower*, was originally titled *Distortions of Reality*. I've had a number of cases where people have suffered these distortions of reality. In contactee cases, it's common for the people to say that a UFO landed beside the road and took them aboard and so on. When they go back later to find the spot where the UFO landed, they can't find it, even though they know the road like the back of their hand... Betty and Barney Hill went back again and again to the mountains of Vermont, looking for the exact spot where they had seen this UFO. I don't think they ever found that spot. There are many cases of this, because they're suffering from distortions of reality. There could be a house or a landmark that doesn't exist. You go back; you're looking for "the white house with the red shutters." But there is no white house with red shutters, because it never did exist. Ghost stories are filled with cases [like this].

These distortions of reality are well known, in every age. In other ages they were often [blamed on] witchcraft. They would [blame the] black magicians, or the "X group." The fairies got a lot of the blame during the Middle Ages. There's case after case of distortions of reality in the fairy cases.

TYPE 4: Astral Projection Contactees

There's a couple of other kinds of contactees which, in many ways, are much more interesting than the space contactees. The fourth type is the astral projectionist. We get a lot of this, where people claim to have the ability to project themselves out of their bodies [via] the "out-of-body experience." They claim that they go to spaceships thousands of miles above the earth that travel to other planets, and so on... Back in the early '70s, Otto Binder, a science writer, was onto a case with a lady who was a marvelous astral projectionist. I have a file at home that's this thick, of transcriptions of things she said while in this state. She would lie down and go into this hypnotic state, and then she would start to describe where her alter body was going and what it was seeing. It was all very fascinating. At one point, Otto wanted to do a book about it, but it never materialized. With out-of-body experiences, usually the person who is doing it has a "guide." As soon as he pops out of his body, this guide shows up and conducts him on a tour of space or whatever. The guide usually is an Indian or a Tibetan. But in modern times, we've got a lot of spacemen acting as guides. They usually fit the classic description that you find in many of the UFO accounts. Astral projection has to be recognized as part of the UFO phenomenon.

TYPE 5: Cosmic Illumination Contactee

Now the 5th type, this is a type that we've known about for thousands of years. It's an integral part of every religion. We don't have any idea how it happens, or why it happens. It's called "cosmic illumination." This happens to many people who think they're having a UFO experience. They're actually undergoing cosmic illumination. There are libraries of books that will describe it to you in detail. Basically the person is usually alone, and a beam of light will come down out of the sky and touch this person. For a few minutes, this person will be in a different state of consciousness. He will suddenly be aware of everything. Of everything that's ever happened in human history… Of everything that's ever going to happen… He will be totally aware of his linkage with the entire human race. It's the kind of experience that people who take drugs want to have, but seldom do. And it's a total experience. It happens very briefly, sometimes only ten seconds. When the light ceases, the person sits down and tries to remember what just happened. But he can't remember any of it. It's all in his unconscious mind. This happens to millions of people in every generation. It's studied by every great church. As I say, there are libraries of books about this. The person's IQ usually skyrockets immediately after this has happened. Their personality changes; their consciousness changes… Very often they change their whole life. They will quit their job. They'll divorce their wife or their husband. They'll start a whole new life. In many cases, they'll even change their name. As I say, this is not a rare experience. It's a common experience, except that when it happens to somebody they usually don't talk about it very much. They don't end up on *60 Minutes* talking about it.

But people today often associate cosmic illumination with UFOs. They may have seen a UFO or a mysterious light earlier that night. Then suddenly, they find themselves bathed in this (usually) reddish light, and they think that the UFOs are doing it to them. [But] we don't know who is doing it to them. We just know that there is a force on this earth that is constantly manipulating the human race, reprogramming us, changing us for good or bad, directing us towards a destiny that we can't define. It knows what it's doing, but we don't.

TYPE 5.5: False Illumination Contactee

Unfortunately, there's another type called "false illumination" which also goes on. This is when the person goes bananas afterwards. It destroys their life. They become fanatics. They become religious fanatics, or they become political fanatics of one type or another. [It's a] reprogramming process. Their whole mind is reprogrammed. Maybe this false illumination is just where it misses somehow, or maybe it's [caused] by some other force.

TYPE 6: "Genuine" Contactee

The last type would be the "genuine" contactee. That is, a flying saucer lands, a door opens, and the genuine contactee walks through the door and is taken for a ride. We have hundreds and hundreds of reports of this [from] people who claim this has happened to them. We usually have good reason for disbelieving them, but there is a chance that it might happen. If there is any reality to UFOs at all, it must have happened. It might happen tomorrow. So that would be our 6th type, our rarest type.

In the 1950s, the government was very interested in the contactee phenomenon. Nobody [else] but a small group of crackpots was interested in contactees. The so-called "scientific" ufologist wouldn't touch a contactee with a hundred-foot pole. But the Air Force was very interested. In 1957, there was a big UFO wave. There were a rash of landings in November of that year, and a rash of contactee stories around the country. The Air Force collected a number of these contactees and put them in mental hospitals, where they were subjected to the very same kinds of tests that I subjected them to twenty years later. In talking to these old-time contactees about their experiences [I discovered that] they were in the hospital for 5 or 6 days and then released. When they told the ufologists about it, the ufologists hit the roof [thinking] that this was an attempt to discredit the whole situation. But it seems to me that the Air Force, or the government, knew exactly what the hell it was doing (which is more than I can say for it now).

Somebody in the Air Force at that time realized that there was some psychological factor to this, some psychic factor that had to be explored. They were collecting these contactees and putting them through a rigorous testing process to find out just what the hell really happened to them... The files on all these people are probably long gone, but we do have [some] evidence. We know that in the early 1950s, around 1949 and 1950, there were mysterious men running around who were definitely from the government. The CIA in those days was just a small organization called the CIG. In 1952, this kind of government activity suddenly ceased. So we can assume that by 1952, the CIA had found out something either very negative or very positive and said, "let's [publicly] drop the whole bloody thing." From 1952 on, the Air Force Project Blue Book was a sham. It was run by a Master Sergeant, named Moody, who was very anti-UFO. I don't want him to sue me [so I'll just say that] he was a bit of a jerk. They had various officers who claimed to be the head of Project Blue Book. They checked in [only] once a month or something. They didn't pay any attention to it.

The files of Project Blue Book were in worse shape than any amateur ufologist's files. You couldn't find anything in them. There would be missing pages and things torn out and crossed out. It was a mess. Project Blue Book was just a joke. During all of this business in West Virginia, I called the Air Force in Columbus, Ohio, and asked them if they could give us any kind of help, or even send airplanes over. We knew the UFOs were coming over at 8:30 every night. A jet plane ought to be able to chase one of them. The Air Force was strictly disinterested. They didn't want to be bothered…

You've all heard of the cattle mutilations that are going on all the time. Right now they're going on in Canada, where the cattle are having all their blood drained from their bodies and their sex organs removed. God knows, but somebody's got a collection of 500,000 cattle sex organs. There's a Paris, TX, newsletter devoted to this called *Stigmata*. There are very good investigators working on this out west. You'll find horrifying Men in Black stories taking place in those areas where the mutilations are going on. In the Middle Ages, in France, these strange [flying] objects used to appear. Every once in a while the people of France would catch one of the pilots and usually stone him to death. In the Middle Ages, they believed that these aircraft came from a place called Magonia. They thought Magonia was a marvelous land in the sky…

There are three international holidays that are based on the flying saucer phenomenon. We don't have much time now to go into that, but the three holidays are:

1) The winter solstice, which takes place around Christmas week, when we have massive UFO waves every 4 or 5 years…

2) The vernal equinox, which is based on the ancient Phoenician goddess of Ashtar, who is now well known in ufology because so many contactees claim to have talked to Ashtar. This goes way back. Ashtar has been dominating the scene for thousands of years. Ashtar is, of course, Easter. In Europe, the word for Ashtar is Easter, the goddess of fertility. That's why we have the Easter eggs and so forth.

3) The summer solstice, which is around the end of June. That's when the whole UFO thing started in 1947 [with] the sightings on June 24th. The winter solstice is the shortest day of the month. The summer solstice is the longest day of the month… On the vernal equinox, we have night and day equal.

Question from audience: John, I want to know what is your theory behind the cattle mutilations, and also what have your personal experiences been in this area?

Well, the cattle mutilations are the only physical evidence that we have. I don't have a theory. I've run through all the theories and none of them work. We don't have a workable theory for these cattle mutilations. We don't know who's collecting all this blood, or why. But because it is the only physical evidence we have, we have to go on studying it. Just recently the government gave a retired FBI man $48,000, I believe, in New Mexico. He made a few phone calls, collected his $48,000 and said, "These mutilations are being caused by predators like wolves and such." And that was the end of that big experiment.

[Someone asks about contacting UFOs telepathically]

Some contactees have claimed the ability to call UFOs. (Unfortunately) I've been present when this has happened. I can only say that it *has* happened. Woodrow Derenberger in West Virginia claimed that he could tell when the UFOs were around, through telepathy. He [said that he] could call to them telepathically and, by golly, he *did it* in my presence (and a lot of other peoples')! These lights would suddenly appear in the sky when he would concentrate. It has to be a form of psychic ability. I don't think that most people can go out and summon a UFO. It would have to be a contactee...

[Someone asks about UFO activity in Mexico]

Mexico is a hotbed of flying saucer reports. They've had cattle mutilations there. A *man's* body was found mutilated in the same way as the cattle. It was cut in half and some of the organs were missing... There was a former Jesuit priest who has been investigating that. He came to New York a couple of years ago and showed me a lot of really horrible photographs and things. My memory now is a little vague. It seems to me there was a child and a man that was cut in half. There was something else involving an automobile [that] had hit a man in the road. They stopped, and when they got out they found that the man was long dead. He had been terribly mutilated [previously]. This is all very weird. How he could have been standing in the road if he had been so mutilated? Perhaps some Mexican magazines have carried more detailed reports, but I don't know of it. I wish somebody would go down there and really find out what was going on. Now the cattle mutilations are going on in Canada, so maybe we'll get some more out of that.

[Someone asks about human mutilations in the United States]

All I know is what I've read in the papers. Yes, two people were found in New Jersey, their bodies mutilated and the blood drained from their bodies. It was in the newspapers. I don't know anything beyond what was in the newspapers...

"The preposterous hypothesis we have come to is that at one time human nature was split in two [with] an executive part called a god, and a follower part called a man. Neither part was conscious. This is almost incomprehensible to us, since we are conscious. [When] some brand new situation occurs, our "bicameral" man would not do what you and I do, that is, quickly and efficiently swivel our consciousness over to the matter and narratize out what to do. He would have to wait for his bicameral voice, which with the stored-up admonitory wisdom of his life would tell him nonconsciously what to do. But what were such auditory hallucinations like? The voices take any and every relationship to the individual. They converse, threaten, curse, criticize, consult, admonish, console, mock, command, or sometimes simply announce everything that's happening...

"The only extensive study was done in the last century in England... Russians had twice as many hallucinations on average. Brazilians had even more... [Unfortunately] since the advent of chemo-therapy, the incidence of hallucinatory patients is much less than it once was... [Surprisingly] hallucinating [patients] are [judged to be] more friendly, less defensive, more likeable, and have more positive expectancies toward others in the hospital than nonhal-lucinating patients. And it is possible that even when the effect is apparently negative, hallucinated voices may be helpful to the healing process... Of immense importance here is the fact that the nervous system of a patient makes simple perceptual judgments of which the patient's "self" is not aware... Hallucinations must have some innate structure in the nervous system underlying them. We can see this clearly by studying those who have been profoundly deaf since birth. For even they can – somehow – experience auditory hallucinations... One 32-yr. old woman, born deaf, who was full of self-recrimination about a therapeutic abortion, claimed she heard accusations from God. Another, a 50-yr. old congenitally deaf woman, heard supernatural voices that proclaimed her to have occult powers. One of my schizophrenic subjects had been sitting in a car for a long time. A blue car coming along the road suddenly, oddly, turned rusty brown, then grew huge gray wings and slowly flapped over a hedge and disappeared... Visual hallucinations may be fitted into the real environment. Usually when [visuals] occur with voices, they [appear as] shining light or cloudy fog."

-Julian Jaynes, "The Origin of Consciousness
in the Breakdown of the Bicameral Mind"

CHAPTER 19

Keel, John – Return of the Men In Black – 1989 Lecture excerpts

The Men in Black really are not anything new. There are many references in the Bible which could be interpreted as Men in Black-type incidents because, although they're called "angels," they're usually were [seen] in threes – as a lot of Men in Black are. They travel in threes, and they get into all sorts of mischief. You remember the three men who went to Sodom and Gomorrah and warned the few innocent people there? Today, that would be interpreted as an MIB incident. A "Man in Black" is a generic term. It doesn't cover just the Men in Black in black Cadillacs who arrive at the scene of UFO incidents. As I'll describe to you later, there are all kinds of Men in Black. They're mystery men. We don't know who they are, where they come from, or who's supporting them. Some of these people apparently have a lot of logistical and financial support that's really mysterious.

In the Orient, for thousands of years, they've had a legend called the "King of the World." It's surprising how many people believe in this. In the '20s and '30s, various explorers who were traveling through the Himalayas, India, and Outer Mongolia heard these legends. There were a lot of books in the '20s and '30s that mentioned the King of the World. The King of the World supposedly lives in an underground city. We've all heard about underground cities. Somewhere in the reaches of Outer Mongolia, there's supposed to be an underground city where the King of the World resides. He sends out his agents to control the surface world. These agents are the Men in Black. They're Orientals. [At least] they look Oriental. They're dressed in black garments, and they supposedly travel all over the world. These legends are very extensive. They've been going on for a long time. So half the world believes that the Men in Black are from the underground, from the Agartha. You've probably heard that name…

When I was traveling extensively around the country, I used to carry a lot of photographs with me in my briefcase. Photographs of different kinds of objects, and also photographs of different ethnic groups… Because I was running into Men in Black witnesses all over the country, I would go through these photographs with them to ask if they saw any that resembled the Man in Black that they had seen. There were photographs of Indians; there were photographs of the various Negroid races from Africa; there were photographs of Eskimos. There was a little mix of all kinds of ethnic groups. [But] there was one photograph that everybody jumped on. They would stop and say, "That looks just like the guy that I saw!" Believe it or not, it was a photograph of a Laplander from northern Sweden. They have a kind of Oriental look to them. They're small in stature and they have a distinctive look. I'm not saying that the Men in Black are all Laplanders, but they certainly look like them and seem to be related to them…

We've had the Phantom Photographers… These were humdingers because these fellows turned up everywhere. They often traveled in pairs. One would be a woman and the other would be a man. They were usually quite well dressed, and they usually would arrive in a black Cadillac – until I started doing articles about black Cadillacs. Then they switched to Volkswagens. They were driving around West Virginia in their Volkswagens. They would drive up to the house of a witness (a UFO witness who had, say, just had a baby) and they would say that they were professional photographers and wanted to photograph the baby. Of course, new parents would be delighted to have that done, so they would set up their equipment and take pictures of the baby. They would give the people a card with a neighboring town listed on the card, and they would drive away. It would turn out that there was no [such company] and they would never come back… They would never try to sell the photographs to these families. So that was another mystery… Then we had the Phantom Photographers who [took] pictures of houses. Say you've never seen a UFO before in your life and then one night, you're out driving home late and you see a UFO close up. You live in the suburbs. The next day, you're getting up. It's say 8 o'clock, 9 o'clock in the morning (for me it would be 12 or 1 o'clock in the afternoon). You're getting up and there's a Cadillac parked in front of your house. Some men get out, and they take out a big tripod and a big heavy camera. They set it on the tripod and they take a picture of your house. Then they put it all back in the car and drive away. You figure they're going to come up to the door and offer to sell you a picture of your beautiful house. But they don't do that. They just get in the car and drive off…

People (and some of you probably know all about this) get very obsessed with UFOs. It dominates their whole life, especially if they become UFO investigators in a small town. It takes over their life. All sorts of strange things can happen to them. We had a UFO investigator in Maine who was driving around an area where UFOs had been seen. He saw a black Cadillac. He had a gun with him. He got out of the car and started shooting at the black Cadillac. [This] really upset the guy who was driving the black Cadillac because it wasn't a black Cadillac at all. This UFO investigator was halluci- nating. He *thought* he was seeing a black Cadillac [but] it was an ordinary car, being driven by an ordinary person. It was almost a very serious incident. The investigator was hauled into jail, and nobody would believe his story. He turned to me, thinking I could get him out of the slammer. But what [good would it do for me] to go up there and say, "Listen, the man is shooting at black Cadillacs [merely because] he thinks he sees Men in Black?"

[Someone asks if Keel has ever been approached by the MIBs]

Approach me? No, but I've approached them... I've chased them. I've missed them by ten minutes. When I was in West Virginia and Ohio, people would call me up at my hotel. They would say, "Hey, these guys are here; come and get them." So I'd race there and they'd be gone by ten minutes. We had the local police in a lot of towns looking for them. At one time, I had high hopes that we would catch one of these fellows and solve a part of that mystery.

Science helps build a new India

Oxen working the fields . . . the eternal river Ganges . . . jeweled elephants on parade. Today these symbols of ancient India exist side by side with a new sight—modern industry. India has developed bold new plans to build its economy and bring the promise of a bright future to its more than 400,000,000 people. ▶ But India needs the technical knowledge of the western world. For example, working with Indian engineers and technicians, Union Carbide recently made available its vast scientific resources to help build a major chemicals and plastics plant near Bombay. ▶ Throughout the free world, Union Carbide has been actively engaged in building plants for the manufacture of chemicals, plastics, carbons, gases, and metals. The people of Union Carbide welcome the opportunity to use their knowledge and skills in partnership with the citizens of so many great countries.

A HAND IN THINGS TO COME

UNION CARBIDE

WRITE for booklet B-3, "The Exciting Universe of Union Carbide," which tells how research on the products of carbons, chemicals, gases, metals, plastics and nuclear energy keeps bringing new wonders into your life. Union Carbide Corporation, 270 Park Avenue, New York 17, N. Y.

1960s Union Carbide advertisement eerily showing hand of God pouring red liquid over the Bhopal, India plant, where tens of thousands would be killed by toxic clouds in 1984.

CHAPTER 20

Keel, John – UFOs and Paranormal Phenomena – 1989 Lecture excerpts

I saw a saucer crash in West Virginia, and I'm going to tell you about it…

There was a town in West Virginia called Point Pleasant. People there were seeing a monster. Now that's right down my alley, because I really like to chase monsters. They were saying it was over six feet tall, shaped like a man, and had wings [with a] six-foot wingspread. Now if one or two people had reported this, we'd shrug it off. But we had over a hundred witnesses. Some of them were the leaders of the town, like the town banker. So I would spend a lot of time in Point Pleasant, West Virginia trying to track down this monster. They called it "The Bird" in West Virginia, but the newspapers called it "Mothman." I later wrote a book about it called *The Mothman Prophecies*. The whole situation culminated with the collapse of a bridge (the Silver Bridge) across the Ohio River there. [It] collapsed at Christmas time, killing about [46] people. Some of those people were key witnesses to the Mothman. It was a very bizarre story…

I didn't have any luck seeing the Mothman, but I decided that it might be smart to pick one of the high spots in the Ohio Valley where I could sit in my car and look over the whole valley. I found the perfect spot on a dirt road on top of a high hill overlooking the river. I started sitting up there, night after night, like an idiot. It didn't take me very long to start seeing things… At that time, there was a lot of traffic on the Ohio River – a lot of boats going back and forth. They did this all night long… These objects would come down and fly around the boats. Now these were bright white, luminous objects. They were lights. You couldn't say that they were metallic objects. You could just say they were very bright lights. They would come down and fly around the boats, and the men on the boats would turn on the searchlights and aim them at these lights. And the lights would jump out of the way of the searchlights. I thought that was pretty interesting because it went on night after night. I talked to some of the boatmen and they said, "Oh, we've been playing those games for years with these lights in the Ohio Valley."

Then I began to see other kinds of lights from my little hilltop. I would go up to my hilltop every night, usually accompanied by somebody [like] a local policeman [or] local newspaper person. Sometimes several people would go up with me, because they didn't believe me about these funny lights. A newspaper columnist named Mary Hyre was with me one night when, on an adjoining hill maybe 2 miles away from us, there was a very bright light. I knew that hill. I'd been all over that area. There were no roads up there, so it couldn't be an automobile headlight. At that time, I had a 6-cell flashlight that was very bright. I flashed my flashlight at this light on the adjoining hill, and damned if it didn't flash back at me! Mary Hyre nearly jumped out of her skin. I know a little Morse code, because I had learned to be a pilot some years ago. I flashed some Morse code at it, and it answered me! Mary later wrote out an affidavit that she'd seen it. [While] we [were] discussing whether this light might be just some kind of vehicle sitting on the hill, this thing rose straight up in the air… It went over towards the river, and the searchlights went on – on the boats – and the light played this game with the people on the boats.

It doesn't stop there. On the same hilltop, I noticed there was an apple orchard set back from the road. I noticed some purple lights in the trees. They were small, like the size of a basketball, or maybe a little bigger [like] a beach ball. These purple lights, you could sort of look through them, whatever they were… I walked into the field and flashed my big 6-cell flashlight at these things. They jumped out of the way of the flashlight beam. Before you know it, about 6 or 8 of these things surrounded me! They were maybe 10 feet above the ground. They just encircled me, and that was it. After that, whenever I went up there, these things would come to me. God knows what they were. Big purple lights... When people came up the hilltop with me, they couldn't believe their eyes. And they were scared. They thought the lights were coming to get them. But no, the lights were my "friends," whoever they were.

Then one night, I was sitting up on the hilltop. I looked down. There was a steep ravine on one side, and way down below there was a forest. The whole forest was glowing in this weird purple glow. The entire forest! The next day I went to see the farmer who owned that particular piece of property. I told him about the purple glow, and he almost yawned in my face. Oh sure, he'd been seeing those since he was a kid. He told me about a lot of other things that he'd been seeing. He said on the nights when the forest was glowing purple, he had to lock his dogs up. The dogs would run into the forest and never be seen again. He said you learned as a kid to stay the hell out of that forest. So, it's like a fairy tale come to life.

One night, I happened to be sitting alone up on this hilltop and (as usual) watching the various lights. I said "hello" to my purple friends, and I was sitting there. Suddenly an honest-to-god flying saucer showed up! It was a circular object, just like you've heard about all your life – or since you got into this... It was glowing brightly, and it was a bright green. It had red lights around the rim. It came down very close to my car and went behind the trees that were there. I swear I thought that thing had landed behind those trees. Also (and this is very unusual for me) it scared the hell out of me. I [rolled] the windows up, locked the doors, and sat in the car. After all the stuff I'd been reading, I fully expected some 18-foot monsters to come strolling out of the woods to talk to me. Nothing happened... I had a movie camera, operated by battery, sitting on the seat next to me. It never occurred to me to pick it up when the thing was in view. It was only in view for maybe 20 seconds. I thought I heard a hissing sound, but that may be very subjective. It may not have made any noise. My mind may have just supplied the hisses.

I was in the midst of it. I had finally seen a real flying saucer. The next morning when I woke up, my eyes hurt like hell, as if sand had been poured into my eyes. I knew this was a sign of conjunctivitis. I talked to many witnesses who had had the same thing. This was proof positive to me that I had seen something. It wasn't some kind of hallucination. I went to the local sheriff and told him exactly what had happened. I asked him to come with me back up that hill in the daytime. We got some Geiger counter stuff that they had, and a whole bunch of people came with us. This was like maybe 6 people, including the deputy sheriff. Someone came in my car, and the others were in the sheriff's car. Now the sheriff, in his car, had a radio that you turn on and off with a key. When the key is out of the radio, the radio is naturally turned off. The radio was turned *off* as we drove up the hill. [Amazingly] voices started talking in a weird guttural accent, coming out of his radio! All of the people in his car heard it. It was impossible for these voices to be coming from the radio, yet they *were*.

These lights that I was finding in West Virginia... I also saw them out on Long Island. I saw them in many places... Whitley Strieber mentions an incident that happened in Glen Park, Wyoming on February 27th, 1988. The residents there were awakened by a knocking sound. Nine knocks in a row... Now the nine knocks [came up in]1950 [too]. But there are other sounds that are associated with these phenomena. One is a beeping sound. The most interesting sound of all is the sound as if somebody has a broom and they're stroking it. You wake up from a sleep and you hear this stroking sound next to your bed. These sounds are a way of bringing you out of a hypnotic trance. We have quite a lot of information on them...

One of the things that scared me a lot in the 1960s was [the group abduction]. After I started looking into the amnesia cases and the abduction cases, I found out that they were not just happening to individuals. They were happening to groups [too]. Sometimes large groups... The climax came in 1969. Ivan Sanderson and I went to a small town in New Jersey where everyone in the town had been awakened by a beep. [The problem was that] they had lost about 3 hours. The whole town! Coming back from this town (I don't remember the name of the town), Ivan said, "It's too big. There's nothing we can do about it. We can't even categorize it." In my encounters around the country, I talked to people who had been in *lines* of cars – 50 cars – where everybody in all of these cars was in a trance state. It usually happens driving through the countryside…

I happened the other day to be strolling on Broadway, uptown. On the sidewalk was a copy of Parade Magazine from 1949. There was a homeless person selling it. I gave him a quarter… I took this tattered magazine home. There was an editorial by Ray Palmer in this magazine, talking about how the government was harassing the hell out of him. In the course of the editorial, he listed 6 deaths of ufologists. This is in 1949. He seemed to think that these deaths were directly attributable to the UFOs.

I've known a lot of ufologists since then and it's true that quite a few of them have died rather mysteriously. One fellow was driving his car. He went around a turn [and] his car door fell off… There's no way for a car door to just fall off. Several things have to disengage before the door will fall off. While I was worrying about the ufologists, Ivan Sanderson was worrying about the Bigfoot hunters. In the 1960s, they were dying in droves. Some of them were in their 30s, or even in their 20s. They were being hit by trucks; they were falling off cliffs… In 1970, I listed over 50 deaths that were directly attributable to flying saucers in some way or another, and published an article on that. Then my friend of that period, Otto Binder, decided that he would really look into this, and maybe do a book on deaths connected to UFOs. He reported back to me that he'd gone through all the foreign files, and they were in the thousands. It would be very difficult to [write] a whole book on this because you'd have to go into each case and get all the details. [But] 90 people who've gotten close to these mysterious lights have died of leukemia, sometimes a few days afterwards. We have cases where people [were] fried from the inside out.

I was perplexed with all the deaths by "lightning" in these UFO areas. Death by lightning is a rather rare event. They kept finding people who had apparently been electrocuted. They'd say, "Oh, he was killed by lightning," without questioning whether lightning [really] did it. These lights that I've been describing are so bright that they've blinded at least 3 people that I know of. Permanently blinded them… In 1966 there was a best-selling book (not a very good book, either) called *Flying Saucers, Serious Business*. Frank Edwards, the author, warned that these things could be very dangerous. We have cases where people were urinating black. Their urine was black because their kidneys had been fried…

When I first got into this, the Men in Black were considered to be a legend started by Gray Barker and a few other whimsical ufologists. As I was running around Long Island, I began to hear Men in Black stories from witnesses who had never heard of Gray Barker and the rest of them. These fellows would in some cases turn up in Air Force uniforms. The witness would report to the local APRO or NICAP representative that an Air Force officer came around and told them to keep quiet. You'd talk to them about the uniform and they'd say there was something funny about it. [The MIB] was in an Air Force officer's uniform, but he had Naval insignia on his shoulders. These guys [would] leave names with some people. At that time, I had a lot of great contacts in the Pentagon. I was checking these people out. They did not exist in the Air Force. Then the Air Force put out a memo to all of its bases warning everyone to be on the lookout for these guys. [Along with] my own network of police officers, they were all trying to catch these Men in Black.

I went down to West Virginia many times, not just once or twice. I spent almost a year there. After I returned to New York, I got a letter from one of the people I'd talked to. In the course of the letter, this woman wrote, "as I told your secretary the other day..." I said, "What secretary? I haven't got a secretary, unfortunately." So I called this woman up and she said, "Yes, this very nice lady came out and asked a lot of questions. They were very sophisticated questions." Now, the UFO buffs do not ask sophisticated questions. These were very sophisticated questions. My first question would be, "How did this woman know who I had seen in West Virginia?" I gathered reports from other people who had seen this same woman. To this day, I don't know who this woman was or what game she was playing. She would be in the Men in Black category. There were many other cases... They would show up at a witness's house, sometimes dressed in black turtleneck sweaters. They'd show up at the witness' house and ask strange questions, and then leave. Ten minutes later, I'd arrive and they'd tell me about it. I never did catch one, nor did any of the police or Air Force men. You could write volumes on this. Over the years, I've received many letters about the Men in Black.

CHAPTER 21

Keel, John – Infared Connections – 1990 Lecture excerpts

People are always asking me what I expect next. We had the animal mutilations in the '60s and '70s that got a lot of attention. They're still going on, but on a much smaller scale than they were… We never did catch whoever was doing it. They would remove certain organs from these animals. Sometimes the animal, say a cow, would be tied down right next to the house where the whole farm family was sleeping. They'd wake up in the morning and their cow had been mutilated right next to the house. There was no way this could happen without the cow making noises, because cows (and horses) make a lot of noise if any unknown person starts prowling around them. If someone starts hurting them and drawing blood, there's certainly going to be a lot of racket. These people didn't hear a sound during the night.

These animal mutilations began in the 1960s. I started writing about it, and everybody said I was full of crap. They'd never heard of such a thing. Then as the years went on, it spread all across the country, almost methodically. All of the UFO buffs jumped on it [and] said that the *flying saucers* were doing this to our animals. Occasionally flying saucers would be seen in the area of these mutilations. I went up into Canada, and the Canadian Royal Police wouldn't release any data on it. But we know there were a lot of them up in Canada…

Now, years later, we've gotten reports from police that there were also human mutilations at the same time, that the police kept out of the papers… The police try to blame devil cults and so on. But there's really no indication that such a cult exists. There are some cults that practice black magic, that do take very small children and use them as sacrifices in their rites. But there are probably not more than 25 people in the whole country that are involved in that kind of ritual magic. Mutilations were the big thing in the 1970s…

I saw a lot of UFOs in the 1960s, and I tried to take pictures of them. I had some very good equipment. In most cases, what came out on the film was much different from what I saw with the naked eye. I started wondering about this. What was it about UFOs that responded differently on film? I started a lot of experimentation with photographic equipment around 1968. I had a friend who was a professional photographer. He had a big studio. We set up various kinds of metallic objects and aimed ultraviolet and infrared rays at [them. We] photographed them to see what would come out. What we got were photographs of rather ghostly-looking blobs. For example, I had an aluminum teakettle that we used in one experiment. We aimed ultraviolet light ("black light" as it's called) on the teakettle and photographed it. It came out looking just like many of the ghost photographs that you've seen over the years.

In 1966, LIFE Magazine was going to get to the bottom of the whole UFO mystery. At that time, Henry Luce, the founder of LIFE, was a big UFO buff. He died shortly after, but he ordered LIFE Magazine to do something about it. They sent teams of professional photographers to the Croton Reservoir in New York State, where people had been reporting all kinds of UFOs. These photographers used infrared film and various kinds of filters, and they came up with some very interesting and surprising photographs. I saw the photographs. LIFE Magazine never did their special issue on UFOs, because Look Magazine beat them to it. Look Magazine came out with a special issue about 3 months before LIFE, so LIFE gave up their special issue. Then Henry Luce died, and they dropped the whole thing…

Back in the 1950s, amateur radio operators started receiving voices that they couldn't explain on their HAM radio sets. These voices claimed to be from outer space. This created a whole cult of messages from these people. There are tape recordings that are still available, claiming to be voices from outer space… In the 1960s, I knew a HAM operator in West Virginia who had a VLF set, which is very low frequency. It takes a lot of explanation, but normal frequencies are quite high; a VLF is below 100 on the Hertz scale. It is used mainly now by submarines, because VLF waves will travel a great distance and penetrate water. It's a [convenient] way of communicating with submarines. [But] because of the nature of VLF, you really can't transmit voices. You can only transmit dots and dashes. And yet on the VLF sets that I listened to, we were getting voices. These voices were talking in a very strange language. A very guttural language like German or Swedish… Yet they weren't those languages. We were familiar with those languages. We couldn't identify what they were talking about, or how they were even being transmitted because, as I say, normally you can't transmit the human voice on VLF.

Now, as our technology progressed, people began to get things on tape recorders. I'm sure you're all familiar with the voices that are picked up mysteriously on brand new tapes on tape recorders. There's a whole cult of ghost-watchers who've tried to identify the voices on these tapes. One friend of mine swore that he had a tape recording made by George Bernard Shaw, who'd been dead for about 30 years at that time. The UFO investigators had all kinds of trouble with their tape recorders. They would record something, thinking it had recorded perfectly. When they got the tape home, there would be nothing but static on the tape.

With the introduction of the personal computer, we now have a rash of cases of "haunted computers." People will have their computer unplugged. They'll get up in the morning and there'll be a message on the computer, even though it wasn't plugged in. There've been a number of these stories in the computer literature. The computer buffs are now becoming ghost buffs, trying to figure out where these strange signals on their computers are coming from.

The truth is that all electronic equipment is susceptible to this kind of mysterious interference, whether it's a computer or tape recorder or telephone. Lots of people get telephone messages from the dead. There are books on it, listing these calls. This is all dealing with the electromagnetic spectrum. The last step was to get TV. The way they did it was actually very similar to what I was doing in the 1960s. They would aim ultraviolet lights at a mirror, and then turn the video camera on the mirror. When they'd play the tape back, there would be these images. The very first image was of Romy Schneider, the actress, shortly after she died. This became a big sensation in Europe. A lot of people started doing it, because anybody with a video camera can do this. You need a video camera, a mirror, and an ultraviolet light (which you can buy almost anywhere).

They're making rapid progress. We're going to find that electronically, we can communicate with whatever this force is. It's a very mischievous force. But don't be surprised if by the end of this decade, you're going to parties to watch tapes of dead people.

I'm going to change the subject a little bit and get away from the dead people. Back in 1941, there was a minister in Mt. Vernon, Illinois, who was taking an evening stroll in that town. He stopped to light his pipe. There was a roar in the tree that he was standing next to. This creature jumped out of the tree, knocked his hat off, and knocked the pipe out of his mouth. He said it was like a baboon. It was a large, hairy creature. This is one of the classic stories in our Bigfoot anthologies. Many other people in that particular area also reported seeing this same kind of creature in '41 and '42.

Then in 1966, there was a man in West Virginia [whose] name was Wooten. He was sitting by a small creek, fishing. He was smoking a pipe. Suddenly, out of the water of the creek came this huge, hairy monster. It smelled terrible, as hairy monsters often do. That's why they call it the Abominable Snowman (although there's a publicity campaign to change his name to "the sweet-smelling snowman" or something). Anyway this creature came out of the creek, walked up to this very startled fisherman, and knocked the pipe out of his mouth. Then stalked off… That story got into the local press.

In New Jersey in the 1970s, we had several Bigfoot cases. In a number of these cases, the Bigfoot would come out of the woods, walk up to the house that was there, pound on the air conditioner, and then stalk off. People in the house would rush out, see this thing, and nearly faint. The monster would [simply] walk off.

In Erie, Pennsylvania, people were seeing what they thought was a robot. It was walking down the street near the waterfront. As it walked down the street, it would pound on the hoods of some of the cars. It would pick out certain cars and just pound on the hood, and then walk off.

We had a tremendous UFO wave in the 1960s and 1970s. I was collecting information on the UFOs that were chasing automobiles. Many of you have heard about the abduction cases that we have now. But in those days, we didn't call them abduction cases. We had many cases where these UFOs – these lights in the sky – were coming down very close to the cars, and chasing the cars. The question that I had was, "Why were they picking out certain cars and chasing them?" So we started collecting all the details we could... We found in a number of cases that women who were having their menstrual period were driving the cars. [This] is a very curious fact. We also found that they were chasing a car that was known as the Ford Galaxy. The UFOs were after our Ford Galaxies! Another little interesting fact [is that] the drivers of many of these cars were teachers. And some of them were teachers of gifted children. It seemed odd that [UFOs] were able to pick that out. But if you were a teacher of gifted children driving a Ford Galaxy, you were in big trouble. And if you were also having your menstrual period, you were in terrible trouble.

For the last 40 years, we've had a great many sightings around the atomic plants. Now all of these things have one thing in common, including our Ford Galaxies. The man's pipe, when he's smoking it, gets very hot and it gives off infrared rays. That's what infrared is... It's what you see from the heat. The air conditioner on the side of a house gives off a lot of heat. It's surrounded by heat. Again, it's infrared. We took photographs of a number of different automobiles with infrared film and infrared filters, to see what the infrared characteristics of different cars were. For some reason, the Ford Galaxy was giving off more infrared than most of the other cars. These things were being attracted to the air conditioners, pipes, and cars by the infrared that was around them.

Many animals can see infrared. That's how animals are able to hunt at night. A bird flying 2000 feet in the air can't see the rabbit on the ground in the middle of the night. But the rabbit's body is giving off heat, and they can see that infrared. The bird can then come down and pluck the rabbit, as they often do. So Bigfoot and the UFOs, for some reason, are attracted to infrared. Maybe they can't see the object itself, only the infrared around it.

We've known this for many years [but] it's very difficult to get people to experiment with this. First of all, the average UFO buff doesn't know what you're talking about when you talk about infrared. And the big companies, they're just simply not interested in this kind of stuff. But if somebody would come up with a couple of million dollars, you could do some very interesting experiments with this.

Our atomic plants, by the way, make electrical energy with steam. We heat the water with the atomic materials. They are nothing more than big steam turbines, and they're generating a hell of a lot of heat. So it's not unusual that these things would hover over the atomic plants. In New York State we have a couple of atomic plants. The UFOs are being seen all the time around these plants, but I don't think they're interested in our atomic matters at all. They're drawn to it by the infrared around the plant.

What does all this mean? If you study the UFO phenomenon for very long, you realize that the vast majority of these things are bright lights. They're not metallic objects. There may be metallic objects out there, but what most people are seeing are bright lights. Bright *red* lights... Again, we're back to infrared. These lights seem to be a compressed form of energy that might even have an intelligence of its own, in the same way that a computer has intelligence. Negative and positive particles are storing information...

We learned several years ago that we are surrounded by an energy field. The entire planet has an energy field around it, which can manipulate all of our electrical apparatus. As I said before, our telephones, televisions, and computers can all be manipulated. We can't believe a damn thing that comes through. If a man's voice appears on a tape recorder and says he's George Bernard Shaw, that doesn't mean that it is George Bernard Shaw. It means it's an imitation of George Bernard Shaw. If a voice comes across on a telephone [that] sounds like your late uncle (and this has happened many times), the voice will usually sound rather distant on the phone. It may use your uncle's favorite expressions. But it doesn't necessarily mean it's your dead uncle. It means it is this force manipulating the telephone. If a picture of Romy Schneider appears on the television set, it either means you've got an old movie or you've got somebody faking the image of Romy Schneider. It doesn't necessarily mean that Romy Schneider is on the television set.

I tried to define this energy field in a book about fifteen years ago called *The Eighth Tower*. A lot of people didn't understand the book. A lot of people hated the book. In Europe it's now a cult book. It's practically a new Bible over there. I'm afraid to go to Europe because they're going to start worshipping me. But here in the States, they'll throw rocks at me. This energy field seems to operate outside of our space-time continuum. This is very difficult to explain in a few words, but it knows our future as well as our past. Our future already exists. A simple way to explain this would be a boy looking through a microscope, watching a microbe on a drop of water. The boy can see where the microbe is going before the microbe reaches it. The boy is therefore outside of the space-time continuum of the microbe. The boy can predict what's going to happen to the microbe. There may be a bigger microbe there about to eat it. The boy knows this but the microbe doesn't, unfortunately. So whatever this force is (and we've given it a million names throughout history), it knows our future. That's how some people's clairvoyance can tap into this energy field and predict the future.

All of this is testable. We now have the technology to deal with this. [But] very few people are trying to deal with it. [Unfortunately] they're dealing with it [only] through beliefs. Most of them are trying to prove that there is perpetual life, that we exist after death. That is the wrong approach. We should be studying this field and its affects on *all* of our apparatus. We should learn how to control it. We have the technology to do this now. It's very predictable that at sometime in the very near future, somebody will come up with the money, the intelligence, and the training to actually interpret all this and learn how to control it. Then, we can literally control the universe. We can predict the future with a machine.

[Speaking of which] clairvoyants are wrong most of the time. They usually get the time element all screwed up. They'll say something is going to happen next month [but] it happens next year, or doesn't happen at all. Those of you who've read my books know I've had some experience with this. I've received predictions that did come true, but they came true in an awkward way. I received predictions about Martin Luther King's assassination before it happened, but they got the dates wrong. And there was nothing I could do about it.

This is another problem with looking into the future. You can't really change it. But if we have the machinery to do it, the technology to do it, we may reach a point where we can control the future by changing it. Then we can change the whole destiny of the human race. Of course human nature being what it is, once we've mastered all this and started controlling the forcefield, we'll probably end up destroying ourselves.

CHAPTER 22

Keel, John – WV UFOs, MIBs – 1994 Lecture excerpts

I made Point Pleasant, West Virginia my headquarters in '66. I then fanned out to the rest of West Virginia, investigating all these various things. It's now gotten very expensive to do these kinds of trips. It was my procedure in those days to go up to the police station [first] and introduce myself, because I'm a Yankee. In those days, I carried a pile of press credentials. I would introduce myself to the police so that they knew I was just another harmless nut. My second step was to go up to the local newspaper and introduce myself there. They always – large and small – wanted to interview me, and I always turned them down. I didn't want anything in the papers about me. I just wanted to know what was happening there. My third step would be to find the local historian. Every town – even a town of 500 people – has somebody who fancies themselves the local historian of the town. Sometimes it's the local doctor... Most often it's the local librarian. Those are the three contacts I would make first, before I would go out and talk to witnesses and such.

I would always ask the police my usual list of peculiar questions. I still do this, and they always act astonished. One of my questions was, "Has anyone been killed by lightning here lately?" This doesn't happen very often. It happens [only] 800 times a year worldwide. But whenever I asked this to police where they were having a lot of UFO sightings, their mouths would drop and they'd say, "My God, how'd you know? Just last week somebody got killed by a lightning bolt." It's a very unusual occurrence. In one town in Ohio, I arrived at the police station just as they were bringing in a body that had been killed by a lightning bolt. This was an odd link. There was something electrical going on in these towns.

Thirty years ago, somebody was chasing around West Virginia and Ohio in an old automobile, harassing young ladies in their cars, trying to drive them off the road and so on. This is not uncommon today, but it *was* uncommon then. [Witnesses] described this man (probably a man in his 30s) as wearing a "frightwig." He was always driving what looked like a car that was 10 or 15 years old, but kept in very good condition. It didn't take me long to figure out that there was somebody like a serial rapist on the loose in that area. I would approach my friends at the different police departments and say, "Hey, I've heard these stories. There's a maniac on the loose here." They would always pooh pooh it. They'd say, "Oh no, Keel, these women are making things up," and they would ignore these stories. I warned them that there was something out of the ordinary going on, that there was one person in that area who should probably be arrested. Gray Barker, who lived in West Virginia, also came across some of these stories on his own. In Braxton County, young people were disappearing in large numbers. These were mostly young men below the age of 20. They would be hitchhiking to, say, a local cinema or something, and just disappear off the face of the earth. Again, I told the police that there were too many of these disappearances, that they had a maniac on the loose. The police always assured me that I was wrong. I was an out-of-towner. What did I know?

In November of 1966, four young people in an old broken down car were driving through the local lovers' lane – an area that was called the TNT area. During the Second World War, there was a TNT plant there. Actually, it was more complicated than that. They were making parts for atom bombs there, but that's a long, involved story. Anyway, there was an old building there that they called a power plant. It was a building that housed generators for these TNT factories. They were driving past this building and they saw what looked like a very large man, 6 or 7 feet tall, standing next to this power plant. He scared the death out of them. So the boy who was driving hit the accelerator and they drove out of there at a high speed. This thing rose up in the air and followed their car. They were going over 60 miles an hour out on these dirt roads, and this thing was flying right along with them. So they drove straight to the police station. You have to realize that in small towns, teenagers do not go to the police station voluntarily. But they were so scared that they went to the police and reported this. The police were so convinced by their behavior that they held a press conference the next day. Reporters from the local newspapers, from Charlotte and other cities around there, came to hear this very bizarre story of this flying man. The four teenagers gave a very convincing account of it, and the newspapers labeled this creature "Mothman." That was the beginning of the Mothman "caper." The television show Batman was popular at the time...

Some of these people had seen this creature walking around and making strange noises. But it didn't leave footprints in the snow. It didn't leave any physical [traces] like fecal matter or anything that I could pick up and have analyzed. All of the descriptions pretty much matched, except some people said the eyes were blazing red. Most people said they couldn't see the face at all. It would be dark, and they could just see this giant figure bearing down on them. Then they'd see it fly away.

When I talked to some of the [witnesses] in depth, it was obvious that they had been in a trance state when they saw this creature. A banker had seen it. The banker heard a noise and went out on his front porch. He stood there for twenty minutes. His wife was inside watching television. Finally, twenty minutes later, he staggered into the house. She said he looked like he had seen a ghost. He was pale and shaking, and didn't realize twenty minutes had passed. He claimed that during those twenty minutes when he was outside, this creature was standing on his lawn, staring at him. And he couldn't move...

My book came out in 1975. That was the year that the police in West Virginia discovered a cave filled with bodies. Because the animals and all had been in there, the bodies had been rotting for a long time. They couldn't tell how many bodies there were. But they think there were 20 or 30 bodies in the cave. So I was right about a serial killer on the loose there. Now it even gets stickier. The police, after a rather short investigation, dropped the whole thing... The reason our suicide rate in the United States is so high is because they often put murders down as "suicide" in small towns, because they don't want unsolved murders on the books. Very often, they know who committed the murder but they figure, "well [the victim] deserved getting murdered, so we'll just forget about it." It seemed like everyone in West Virginia *knew* who this killer was. I wouldn't dare give his name here, but he belongs to a prominent family in West Virginia. The reason that they know [he did it] is that he was put away for a while in a mental institution. While he was in the mental institution, all of the disappearances stopped. When he was released from the mental institution, they started up again... I don't know if those are still going on – if this fellow is still on the loose. I hope he's not. As I say, for a New Yorker to get involved in West Virginia affairs like that is a pretty sticky wicket. It was smarter of me to stay out of it.

A lot of things are still going on in West Virginia. I still get mail from a lot of people down there, some that I knew 30 years ago. One of the mysteries that I tried to untangle – and found hopeless – was that there were a number of babies born during that period [that] seemed to be rather unusual. After the babies were born, they were surrounded by poltergeist activity, and other odd things...

CHAPTER 23

Keel, John – The Study of Shit – 1999 Lecture excerpts

About 35 years ago in West Virginia, people were seeing a giant bird, and I mean a giant bird. This thing was like six feet tall and it was walking. They called it the Mothman. I was down there. Because there were so many witnesses to this, I said, "This bird must exist and I'm going to catch it." That's how optimistic I was. I was running around West Virginia searching for this giant bird. I talked with over 100 people who had seen it. They included a banker, the mayor of the town, and the pharmacist. A lot of reputable people were seeing this thing that had a giant wingspan of 10 or 12 feet, which – considering its size – wasn't big enough to lift it. But it lifted, and it chased automobiles and things like that.

I quickly realized I probably wouldn't be able to catch this giant bird. Or if I did, it would probably eat me alive. So I started looking for clues. I started looking for footprints and things like that. In the course of that I realized that if this giant bird existed, it had to take a crap once in a while. So I was going around West Virginia looking at bird shit. I figured it would be an enormous amount. I learned to differentiate between pigeon crap and bat guano. I never did come across any Mothman shit.

In a way, I'm an expert on this subject because I grew up on a farm. We had two horses and about 15 or 20 cows. In the wintertime of course, they're in a barn. When you live on a farm, you learn that these animals excrete tons of material every day. This has to be handled frequently. You have to shovel it out of the barn in a pile. Then when spring comes, you shovel it out to the manure spreader. They have a wagon type thing that spreads manure as you drag it across your fields. Taking care of this shit (there's all kinds) is quite a job. I think one horse can make something like two tons of manure in the wintertime. I was young and stupid and had a pitchfork, and that was the start of my career.

I've been following this Bigfoot controversy for many, many years. In Asia it's called the Yeti. There are many names for it. This is a 7 or 8-foot tall man-shaped creature, covered with hair. As you know, nobody's ever captured one. We have one picture that's a little bit controversial, but if this thing existed it would have to leave an enormous quantity of excrement as it traveled through the woods and the mountains. So I've been waiting all these years for somebody to turn up a pile of this and say, "Here at last is proof that Bigfoot exists." But all they've found are the footprints, and an occasional piece of hair stuck in barbed wire. Nobody has turned up the one thing that I'm looking for, which is about twenty pounds of Bigfoot crap.

Mothman has turned up at random over the years. I get a lot of mail from people who have seen him just briefly. If he should turn up in some area like he did in West Virginia, you can be sure that today, everybody would be down there with cameras. The Japanese would be there first. The Japanese go everywhere now. Maybe this time, we'll actually get some footage or proof.

In my extensive research here, I came across something that farmers were always hiding in their fields. This goes back more than 200 years. The farmers call this "star shit." The farmers don't waste any scientific terms on it. They'll go out into a field. The field will be empty. The next morning, there will be big globs of gelatinous material in the field. It would always dissolve, or melt away. And it's still going on. If you follow the Fortean literature closely, you can see that every six months or so, somebody somewhere sees this stuff. We have no idea what it really is. Scientists can come up with all kinds of explanations. "It's some sort of crazy mushroom, some sort of fungus." But after all these years, we don't know what it is. We keep hoping that somebody will collect a sample in a bottle so that we can finally figure out what it is. If it were just plain manure, we would know what it was. I would have gone out there with my trusty microscope and said, "Yep, it looks like manure to me."

And we also have the problem of Loch Ness, as you know. I have never been to Loch Ness, but if you have a creature the size of the Loch Ness monster (a comparable creature might be a whale), this "whale" is going to be excreting what scientists call *morbid excretions*. Something should be coming out of Loch Ness that would identify the size of the creature. There are all kinds of creatures in the woods and in the water that live on [manure, like beetles]. There's a name for those creatures. They're called *stercoricolous*. Now there's a really good word… Most dictionaries don't have that word. I always judge a dictionary by whether or not it has stercoricolous in it, which means "living in dung."

> *Question from audience: In one of the lectures here several years ago [we heard about someone] living in Nebraska who found Sasquatch dung and sent it to the laboratory for examination. It had unknown enzymes, and was not traceable to any known animal. So "dung" has been found…*

There was one sample found in the Himalayas too, which appears in some of the Yeti books… The serious problem is: how do you know if *this* dung is from *this* animal? You don't know until you have the Yeti. [You know it's] not horse, not cow, not deer… But you don't know that it is Yeti [until you have a Yeti].

> *Q: Are you concerned that after your investigation of the Men in Black that they might be watching you, keeping an eye on you?*

The Men in Black are a whole different category. I get mail all the time from people who have had encounters. It [initially] seemed illogical to me that the government would spend any money doing this. We *now* know that the government *did* spend millions of dollars tapping people's phones in the '60s and '70s, doing all kinds of stupid things. They were dressed in black and drove black automobiles, and raised a lot of hell... Last year the CIA issued a statement [and] they confessed to it! Before that, we always thought that it was somehow directly related to [the supernatural. Still] there *have* been things that are very ghostly, that *do* seem like they're related to something supernatural...

There are a number of UFO investigators who have had really serious encounters with these Men in Black. There was one whose name I forget. He was working in a radio station and black automobiles were following him around. The MIBs finally rented the building across from the radio station and put a movie camera in there. He was asking me what he should do about it. I said, "Late at night, go over there and paint that window black." I haven't heard from him for some time now...

There was a man in New Jersey who was putting out newsletters. He was very serious. He was a professional man, and he had two children. One day, when his children were coming home from school, a black Cadillac pulled up next to them and tried to drag the children into the car. After that, he wouldn't have anything further to do with the subject. He was literally scared to death that they were going to kidnap his children.

So these tactics that we hear about, some of them are very real. And there are still people writing to me about their encounters with these men. When I started writing articles publicizing the black Cadillacs, they switched to black Volkswagens. They were reading the crap I was writing! I never got a real book out on it. There is a book out on Men in Black by a man named Jim Keith, who died this last summer in an accident. Jim Keith has written quite a number of books. He wrote a book about the black helicopters, which have been seen all over the world. They fly over the homes of witnesses and scare people. Helicopters are very easy to trace because they're very expensive to operate, and you need a mechanic to go over them practically every trip they take. It should be easy to trace them to an airport [but] nobody's ever been able to do that. There have been witnesses to as many as four black helicopters at a time. Also in England, we have a lot of helicopter sightings in relation to the crop circles. Those circles are still going on, by the way.

Q: Can you talk about the movie that's coming out on the Mothman?

Oh yes. I have tentatively sold this movie about three or four times... The most recent one was Paramount. They have decided to do a movie about the Mothman. They're going to probably have Richard Gere playing John Keel.

Richard Gere works constantly. He's always got a movie in the works. [But] we're still hoping that he'll get this one off the ground. [Unfortunately] he's too old and ugly. I'd rather have Brad Pitt play me. *[laughter]*

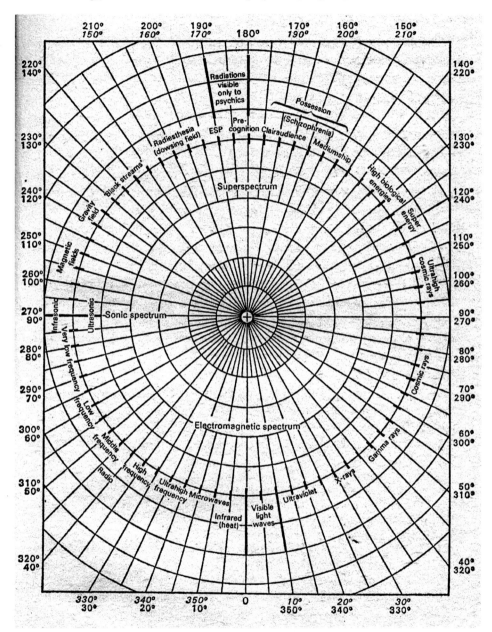

Keel's 1975 map of all the frequencies in the superspectrum, few of which are visible or audible to us. This diagram and others were edited out of The Mothman Prophecies, *ending up in the excellent but undermarketed book* The Eighth Tower.

CHAPTER 24

"People who get involved in Mothman seem to grow. This happens to many people... It suddenly changes their whole lives... It has opened up the minds of many people... You've got to explore your inner self... It's a shame the world doesn't go through [this] learning process."

-John Keel, at the Mothman Statue unveiling in Pt. Pleasant

Keel, John – Mothman & Other Conspiracies – Pt. Pleasant, WV 2003

Andy Colvin (AC): What was it like traveling to the Great Pyramids and the Middle East back in the 1950s, when no one else was going there?

John Keel (JK): Great... I wrote a book about my experiences there [called *Jadoo*]. The editors took it and cut it in half. They threw out half of it. Then the famous publisher, who was determined she was going to make me famous, dropped dead on me. So the book had very little circulation. Then in the 1980s, copies of it in mint condition started turning up all over the country. We couldn't figure that out. The only thing I can figure is that one of these Taiwanese [operations that make] fake [books and DVDs] did that with Jadoo. But why Jadoo? There are many other books they could have stolen, that would have been more profitable. But this book suddenly turned up in mint condition, over and over again. It may be possible that somebody had several cartons of it hidden away. But they changed the publisher after the lady dropped dead. The book rights went to Simon & Schuster. I don't think *they* had a warehouse full of them. It's all very mysterious.

AC: That book seemed to be about a spiritual quest of yours, as a young man.

JK: Well, that's what the editors tried to make it. They took a lot of stuff out. They especially took out my mind-bending, profound philosophy...

AC: What was that?

JK: I don't know, just my usual mind-bending philosophy. When people try to get me involved in philosophical discussions, they end up nowhere. I've gone through all that so many years ago. Now I'm just concerned with keeping the planet Earth going. I don't think we have much of a future here. I think it's time for us to build a rocket and go to Mars or something.

AC: Do you think that there's something to these stories about 2012 being the end of the Mayan calendar and/or world? Are we at a turning point?

JK: Well, they've predicted the end of the Earth every few years for all my life, and of course a lot of religions are based on Armageddon. It always seems like we're right on the edge of extinction, yet we keep going. All the things that are happening in the Middle East now are reasonably outlined in the Bible. People who read the Bible carefully get scared to death that these things are coming to pass.

AC: I have a little theory that this recent blackout in New York may have been the one that was predicted in *The Mothman Prophecies*. Do you think that's a crazy idea?

JK: I don't know if I predicted one.

AC: Well, I remember there being talk about people having premonitions of a blackout in New York. I think a partial one did occur when President Ford, or President somebody, flipped the switch on the Christmas tree.

JK: Oh, yes, President Johnson... He was having a high-level meeting with the Russians in Glasborough, New Jersey. I remember that. All the lights failed in Glasborough, and they had a lot of trouble with telephones and things. There were a lot of predictions in that book that came to pass [like] Martin Luther King's assassination. There were a lot of predictions of the assassination of the Pope. And there *were* assassination attempts. As you know he got shot, which is not very healthy. We also had a renegade priest that tried to stab him. It's tough being the Pope.

AC: The reason I bring it up is because, as I told you, we built a shrine to the Mothman as children. The Mothman showed up and we had a premonition of this destruction in New York in 2001. Having had that experience, it seems to me that some of these prophecies were way ahead of their time – maybe 35 years or more. This led me to think that maybe the 1967 prediction of the big blackout in New York was actually a premonition of this most recent one in 2003. It just took that long (35 years) to occur.

JK: Right...

The NYC blackout occurred on Aug. 14th, 2003, almost 100 years, to the day, from Aleister Crowley's "Horus" ritual of Aug. 12, 1903. The Eye of Horus crop circle at the Serpent Mound formed less than two weeks after the blackout. Taped testimony was posted on the Alex Jones conspiracy site indicating that a military test involving HAARP was the cause of the NYC blackout. The cover story floated in the media involved a UFO and a Cleveland-area power plant associated with the failed Houston energy giant, Enron. A key whistleblower in the Enron case, Cliff Baxter, was "suicided" in Sugarland, TX in January of 2002. Sugarland is home

*to an enormous NASA facility, and was also once the home of Margie
Schoedinger. Schoedinger claimed that she had once dated President
George W. Bush, and that he had raped her. Assuming that the court
documents posted on the Internet are real, Schoedinger had already
filed suit against Bush when she died of a gunshot wound to the head
on Monday, December 8th, 2003. The death was officially registered as
'suicide' by the Harris County Examiner's Office. Schoedinger had filed
the lawsuit against President Bush in December 2002, accusing him of a
series of "individual sex crimes" against her and her husband.*

JK: The attack on the World Trade Center... None of our psychics saw that
coming (if you keep up with the psychic literature, which is not easy).
Normally if we have a major event, like the assassination of President
Kennedy, hundreds of people foresee it. But this thing at the World Trade
Center took everybody by surprise. All the psychics and everybody...

AC: Well, the destruction that I saw of the WTC was really more extensive
than what actually occurred. I saw a premonition of the destruction of
more buildings. So I'm wondering if that outcome was changed somehow,
perhaps by awareness. Or maybe there's a further one down the road. A
bigger catastrophe for NYC...

JK: Well, the pundits on television are telling us now that London is next.
There have been a lot of predictions about something happening in
London. Of course, that's a major city full of people and it's pretty hard
to protect. But very often, these predictions just lead us astray. While
we're watching London, they're doing something to Cairo... The prediction business is very hazardous.

*The London 7/7 bombings occurred about a year and a half after this
interview with Keel. His prediction was correct.*

AC: Whitley Strieber talks about it in his *Secret School* book. He says that he
thinks that these premonitions are warning tools that arise in humanity
as we reach cataclysmic times. It allows for changing the future, or a bad
outcome, before it gets here. Do you think there's anything to that?

JK: I don't think you can change the future. If we knew exactly what's going
to happen six months from now, we couldn't do anything about it.
We're not that well organized – that civilized. If we were, we could have
a perfect world. [But] the world becomes more imperfect all the time.
I've given a lot of thought to the future. It seems to me that [for] people
[to] see the future, the future has to exist in some form. [Otherwise] they
wouldn't be able to see it. I have written about finding a way to tap into
this universal mind. *Then* we could see the future. Once we can see the

future – the future of the human race – then [we are at] the "childhood's end." And it's all over… We can let the dolphins and the Mothmen have the planet. We don't seem to be doing very much for this planet. We're systematically destroying it, and everything on it. Killing off all the life forms… I'm not sure that's the real plan for this planet.

AC: Earlier, you said that the thing you're doing now is trying to keep this ecological idea going, trying to find a way to live more in harmony. Is that what keeps you coming back to Point Pleasant?

JK: I don't know what keeps me coming back to Point Pleasant. It's pretty much the way they said it in the movies, where Dr. Leek warns Richard Gere *not* to go back to Point Pleasant. I had a lot of warnings like that. I can't see that Point Pleasant is the center of any universal harmony or whatever. There are other places in the United States where people gather with that kind of thing in mind, who are more attuned to it. But the people in West Virginia are just people. I've run into very few psychics [here].

AC: In my case, I approached the Mothman from a desire to see him. Most people just stumbled across him. It frightened them. Do you think there's a difference? If you're a person who wants to find the Mothman, like you or me, does that change the way the encounter might play out?

John Keel (right) in 2003, on the day the Mothman Statue (left) was unveiled in Pt. Pleasant, WV

JK: Well, I know that this happens to many people. They want to see a flying saucer. They want to see Mothman, something to confirm their beliefs. Whatever their beliefs are... There are people who sit cross-legged in a cave for 30 years to attain Godhead and become part of God. We had this group a few years ago that committed suicide, thinking that's the way to join the flying saucers: the Heaven's Gate cult.

AC: My theory on that? I don't know if you remember this, but that was the same day that the Martin Luther King family came out and said that they thought James Earl Ray was innocent. They felt that it was *the government* that had done it...

JK: They went to court and won. It was too late for James Earl Ray, but they had a big court thing claiming that another man was the mastermind behind the whole thing. A businessman who lived in the South... They had the evidence on him. And the jury agreed with them. They were awarded one dollar, I think. It didn't make the newspapers at all! The only press it got in New York was in one of the Harlem newspapers. The other papers just avoided the subject.

AC: Yes, that businessman was Jowers, the owner of the bar across from the Lorraine Motel. He had taken the gun and shuffled it out. Speaking of conspiracies like that, I was listening to a talk recently by Walter Bowart. He wrote an influential book in the 1970s called *Operation Mind Control*. He is now saying that the cutting edge of mind control research has something to do with UFOs. But he didn't really go into the details of it. I was wondering if that rings a bell with you at all. Do you think that there is manipulation going on within this phenomenon?

JK: I had a friend named Ivan Sanderson, who was a real scientist. He had looked into the UFO stuff and written a lot about it. He kept referring to the "mind patrol." [He felt] that people's minds were being somehow tampered with, and there was nothing we could do about it. As you know we've [seen] a lot of people who are obsessed, who go way out on a limb with this stuff. Whitley Strieber is a good example. He started out just wanting to be a writer, and he's ended up with his mind opened up to all kinds of things. He's now back in Texas with a radio program. Did you read his book about the coming storms [and] strange changes in the weather? It was like two or three years ago that it came out. It did not become a big bestseller. I'm surprised... Of course timing is very important in any book. If you come out with the biggest, best-written book of all time at the same time Hillary Clinton's book comes out, people are going to buy Hillary's book, not yours. That happens over and over...

AC: In terms of trying to maneuver through this minefield of paranormal phenomenon, I've speculated that it's important for people to look at their own experience and figure out if it was a "natural" energetic event, or if there was some sort of a synthetic government/Masonic influence on it. It seems to me that it's important to figure that out, to try to look at your own situation and separate the two out. Do you think that's important?

JK: Well, the thing that works against all these conspiracy theories is that the government is very stupid… They try conspiracies against each other, but they're very stupid, all the time. Mostly governments consist of either madmen like Adolf Hitler and company, or small-town lawyers who have suddenly talked their way into a big position handling billions of dollars. But they can't even handle their own bank account. And there are other things at work here that we don't understand [like the fact] that somebody runs everything [yet] we don't know who it is. That's what it amounts to… You look at the economic situation very closely, the oil situation and all [and you see that] there's somebody running this thing, and [that they] had it planned for a long time. [But] we don't know who they are. They're sitting on a mountaintop somewhere, or in a penthouse somewhere, keeping a very low profile. And when they die, they don't even get an obituary. These are the people we really have to think about and go after. George Bush spends a lot of his time on his ranch. We have the Arabian countries run by very wealthy men who have no real interest in running countries. They just want to run their oil business, or whatever they are running. There's got to be some guy out there – like a Howard Hughes type – who is really visionary and has knowledge of what he's doing and how he's doing it. For a while I *did* think it was Howard Hughes, because he fit into all of the patterns. He was a recluse; he was a nut; he was filthy rich. And he was capable of almost anything. When he moved to Las Vegas, he got them to stop the testing of atomic bombs in Nevada. Not many men have the power to do that. Nobody ever really found out where all of his money went. He did contribute heavily to the CIA. And there must be people in the CIA who are operating on their own.

AC: I heard this crazy theory that Hughes was kidnapped by Onassis and held on an island for 20 years, while being force-fed heroin. Onassis supposedly appropriated all that money. It's called *The Gemstone File*. But I wanted to focus on whether or not you run into problems with people (like cryptozoologists) who think that if you're a paranormal witness, your credibility somehow goes down. I was talking to you the other day and you made the statement that you *started off* as a "ridiculous" figure. As a result, did that issue – of their trying to lower your credibility –

become moot?

JK: You know I spent years of my life writing jokes for television. I wrote Merv Griffin's ad-libs at one point. There are a lot of people writing ad-libs. You see these comedians on television, and you think they're very funny people. They aren't... They've got ten guys behind the scenes writing jokes for them. [Take] Regis Philbin and his show *Do You Want to be a Millionaire*... Regis was sitting in front of a television set and they had three or four guys sitting backstage. For every situation that came up, these guys (who were crack-humorous) would immediately type in a joke, and Regis would read it off the TV screen. Everybody would say, "That Regis is really fast-witted and funny." Well, the guys who were fast-witted and funny were sitting backstage earning $10,000 a minute. And Jay Leno, he has like twenty writers writing all of his monologues and all of his jokes. Johnny Carson used to have a script with him on stage. You'd see him shuffling papers. If you were an outsider, you'd say, "What the hell are those papers?" They were the scripts. He had jokes for all the visitors that came on. The writers had all prepared jokes ahead of time. And there would be subjects that people didn't want to discuss. Those would be listed there. Carson would follow the instructions.

AC: If people knew this sort of thing, they'd have more appreciation for *this* kind of cinema, where you have to answer real questions. There are no cue cards here.

JK: Oh, I wrote cue cards, too.

AC: Have you talked much about your childhood? I remember reading that you had some paranormal experiences as a child, with some lights in your room.

JK: Yes. Around the age of 12, I was living in an old farmhouse, upstairs. Everybody else was sleeping downstairs. There came a knocking on the wall. At first I thought it was squirrels in the attic or something. I did my scientific investigation of the whole house. I couldn't find anything. This went on for several weeks. I couldn't find any explanation for these knockings. Then I learned that you could communicate with them, just like the Fox sisters did. You know, "knock three times for this, and two times for that." As a 12 year old I didn't have many interesting questions to ask, but I was communicating with this thing that was knocking in the wall. This drove me to the public library to find any books I could on psychic phenomenon. They only had about three books. Up until the 1960s, all of this stuff was really taboo. You don't realize it now, how taboo it was. It was almost illegal. They'd almost put you in jail for getting into psychic phenomena [or] parapsychology. There have been like five "New Ages," and each New Age has brought us to another level. Then people grow up, and forget about it. And then a few years pass, and somebody like Shirley Maclaine starts up again. It's a phenomenon in itself. It's like there's a timetable, and every generation is elevated a little bit. Did you ever read *Childhood's End*? I'm always quoting that. It's an Arthur C. Clark science fiction book. Basically, his story was that eventually we evolve into something else. We evolve into a spiritual thing. Then we don't need all of [the] trappings that go with being human beings. We abandon that, and just become spiritual beings.

AC: Speaking of spiritual beings, there are stories now that the Sasquatch are psychic. When you were in Nepal, you saw a couple of them, didn't you?

JK: Well, I saw animals from a distance and the Natives told me it was the Yeti. At that time interest in the Yeti was very high, and the publisher asked me [about it]. I told him, "Probably a bear." And he said, "We'll make it into a Yeti. It'll give them something to sell."

AC: Apparently there is an alternate form of bear up there that Reinhold Messner, the great climber, has seen. It sounds like there is this rare kind of bear.

JK: I read his book. He believes in it enough that he moved to Tibet. I think he's still chasing it. I don't think he's caught it. But the Chinese and the Russians are very big on this. They have financed big expeditions to go to these areas where they are seeing them. So far, they've turned up very little. Meanwhile in the United States, in the state of Washington, somebody gave five million dollars to one of the Bigfoot chasers. He got helicopters out, and all kinds of expensive equipment. Every time the phone rang, they'd all jump into the helicopter and try to go to the scene. They spent the five million dollars. They lived very well while they were chasing Bigfoot, but they never caught Bigfoot.

AC: There's a fellow named Lapseritis. He's written a book called *The Psychic Sasquatch*. He claims that you need to go into the forest and quietly meditate for several days. If you follow certain rituals and meditations, the Sasquatch will telepathically contact you. Do you think there's anything to that?

JK: No, but it just wouldn't apply just to the Sasquatch. It would apply to almost anything. You know, so much energy has been spent on these subjects – writing about them and exploring them. And we've always ended up with nothing. That's not made me sour on these subjects, but I know that we have to take another approach that's entirely different. We had people in the '60s sitting in the TNT area all night because *once* some people saw something in the TNT area. They still came for years afterwards to the TNT area. Some of those into witchcraft and the black arts were obviously in the TNT area, because they put graffiti up in all the buildings. But Mothman may have been a very temporary thing, just like most of the Bigfoot sightings there.

AC: I found a couple of really old Buddhist paintings, and they had the Garuda floating above the Buddha. Do you have any knowledge of how the Buddhists feel about it? It's like he's a deity of some kind.

JK: It may be that when they saw it, they thought it was a spiritual thing. It was *so* different [that] they included it in their spiritual drawings and paintings. As you know, in Indonesia they have belief in the Garuda going way back. The American Indians believed in the Thunderbird for generations. In some cases, they thought the Thunderbird was very dangerous and would attack you. [This] may be true, because if you get attacked by a giant creature like that, there's not going to be any evidence left of the attack. It's going to carry you away and eat you.

AC: Sort of like in Braxton County, where you were saying that some teenagers were missing?

JK: They had a lot of disappearances of teenagers in those days. They were hitchhiking. Hitchhiking used to be legal. That was the way kids got around. They were hitchhiking to the football games and would never show up. The police at that time tried to keep it as quiet as they could, which they always do. We had things happen here in Point Pleasant that they tried to keep quiet. It especially annoys them when someone like me shows up.

AC: We found that the waterways in West Virginia seem to be where most of the sightings occurred. You can follow the Ohio River back to the Kanawha, then back to the Elk. Do you think there's something about water that aids this process?

JK: Oh yes. Water and blood… In the Mothman days, they seemed to have a real interest in blood. This also is sort of a taboo subject, especially if you're being interviewed for television. They don't want to talk about that. They usually are waiting for me to say something really sensational. In a two-hour interview, they may [only] take 30 seconds and put that on the air.

AC: Well, *we're* going to put the whole interview in the program!

JK: We've got so many mysteries on our hands. It's better to be normal, and not pay any attention to mysteries.

AC: Are you still actively investigating?

JK: Not actively... We had a bunch of sightings of Bigfoot up in the Catskill Mountains two or three years ago. The only reason I went up there was [that] my informant was one of the game wardens. We had very good witnesses. Whatever these things are, they vanished as fast as they came. I've had reports where witnesses have seen a Bigfoot reach down to the ground and catch the hand of another Bigfoot, and pull it up out of the ground. The solid ground... [Then] the two of them would walk away. That's a pretty good indication that it's something other than an animal we're watching. We're watching the behavior of a paraphysical object.

AC: A friend and I saw a Bigfoot in the Catskills once, in the early 1980s, while camping. Actually we never saw it, as it seemed to be invisible. But I got this frightening chill. I was sure that it was some kind of a Bigfoot. That was on Bear Mountain...

JK: I know Bear Mountain. This [recent activity] was near there, yes. So you got the chill? See, some people just see two red eyes in the woods and it scares the hell out of them. These are experienced people who camp out all the time. These two huge red eyes the size of a dinner dish will appear in the woods. They don't see any forms besides that, but they're terrifying, whatever they are. And the Mothman, they always reported that it had these red eyes.

AC: I have a friend who saw the red eyes in his bedroom. I interviewed him for this film. He said the bed started shaking. He saw the red eyes and blanked out. He doesn't remember what happened after that.

JK: We had a witness here in Point Pleasant who was one of the early witnesses of Mothman. I went with her into the power plant in the TNT area. The power plant, you know, was a pretty big place. It had all kinds of steel stairways in it... It was a good place for a Mothman to hide. She volunteered to go with me into this plant, and she became hysterical. I didn't see anything, but she claimed she saw the eyes – just the red eyes. She saw something red in there [that's for sure]. We had a policeman standing outside the plant while we were in there. He wouldn't go in. I was such an idiot then, fearless John Keel. I was convinced that I was right and the world was wrong, and therefore nothing was going to happen to me...

AC: Well, that power plant story reminds me of Gray Barker's book *The Silver Bridge*. He has a couple of chapters in there where he describes himself as Mothman, it seems.

JK: Well, you have to be very careful with Gray Barker.

AC: Barker's writing reminds me of these strange dreams I have, where I'm flying around at night. People see me, and they're afraid of me. The dreams give me the impression that I am somehow in psychic contact with Mothman, that I am somehow experiencing his reality. I felt like Barker was tapping into that idea.

JK: …Gray was a very complex person. He had a very good sense of humor. He was very intelligent. [But] all of his books were fiction. He would make up these terrible books. He knew he had a market of 2000 people who were going to buy these books, so he would print them himself. 2000 copies… He probably had some tax angle working, too. He was a manager of a movie theatre, and he wrote these books because he must have had a lot of time on his hands. In that book, *The Silver Bridge,* there's a chapter about me. He sent me his version of the chapter, and I rewrote the whole thing because his chapter was full of bullshit. I rewrote it and told it exactly the way it all happened. [So] he used my version in his *Silver Bridge…* But he has people flying around in flying saucers, and Indrid Cold and all that. He was just making it up and having some fun. If you read some of his other books, you'll see. If you read his famous book *They Knew Too Much About Flying Saucers* carefully, you can see that there's a point where he sort of gives up and starts fictionalizing. He's dealing with the Flatwoods Monster, first of all (that was his first real interesting case), and then he goes downhill. He just says, "To hell with it." And he throws in everything. That book was so popular, a copy of it was found in the home of the [Heaven's Gate] people who committed suicide.

AC: Do you feel like the Indrid Cold story is bogus?

JK: Yes… Derenberger was another complex character. He was a pathological liar, to put it simply. His daughter called me a couple of years ago, very upset that some TV show had done something about him. He had given the whole thing up in the '70s or '80s, and moved to Ohio. People were always writing to me. They wanted to contact Derenberger because they wanted to contact Indrid Cold. Indrid Cold became a real entity to them, through the book.

AC: What about the people that said they saw the aircraft parked next to the interstate, in front of Woody's truck? Do you think there's a *part* of it that's real?

JK: I think his original story had some substance to it, because he was scared enough to go to the police. Nobody's going to go to the police with a bogus story. They might come to me or you with a bogus story, but they're not going to go to the cops. Also, two men who lived outside of Point Pleasant had pretty much the same experience. They were going to report it but their son came by and talked them out of it. I knew all the details and was going to use some of it in a book or article I was doing. [But] they got talked out of it.

AC: Switching gears, it sounds like you have a sense that we need to change direction as a civilization. Do you have a soundbite or a mantra for how to start that process?

JK: No, and it would take somebody with great leadership ability to have any affect. And of course, as you know, the Bible and Nostradamus and everybody are predicting that a man is going to come out of the Middle East and start this process going. So we're over there bumping off all the Arab leaders we can find.

AC: A lot of the old Sumerian tablets are over there being destroyed, too.

JK: That's another habit we have, of destroying so many of these ancient artifacts. When we finally arrived at Easter Island, they had a lot of writings carved into wood, because all they had were trees there. The early explorers destroyed all of the writings. Of course it would have been a job to interpret them (like cracking the hieroglyphs), but those slabs of wood should have been safely stored somewhere.

AC: Do you have any questions for me? If you were interviewing a person like me, who comes up 30 years later and says, "I had this experience," what would you ask?

JK: [I would ask] "Why are you doing this? Why are you still obsessed with this?" You've got to explore your inner self...

AC: Yes, and having spent a couple of years really interviewing people, traveling, and looking into it, I think I have come a long way with it.

JK: Well, this happens to many of the people who get involved, who would never think – in a million years – to get involved in something like this. It suddenly changes their whole lives, and they don't really understand what's happening to them.

AC: Harriet and I both, we've gotten into holistic healing. We're both doing new things. We have a lot of synchronicities in our lives, even though we haven't seen each other in decades. We saw each other only once in thirty years [yet] we had the same exact job (loading cargo jets). The same specific job... She was one of only a handful of women in the world to be a loadmaster.

JK: That's really interesting.

AC: But now we've totally switched, and we're doing something that helps heal. I think it makes a difference in a good way...

JK: Well, it has opened up the minds of many people, especially in terms of astronomy and people starting to look at the stars. There's a very good book that's been a bestseller for the last five or six years. It's called *The Elegant Universe*. I always recommend that as a starting point. You've got to understand the universe a little bit before you can get into this other stuff. We've had people chasing birds that are not bird experts. We have people chasing the Loch Ness monster, who don't know a damn thing about fish. I'd study the forms in the ocean and all before I'd really get serious about Loch Ness. Of course, now the British government has come out with a very firm statement saying that they have spent a lot of money at Loch Ness, and that there's nothing there. Well, that convinces all these people that there *is* something there.

AC: So would you say that your reason for getting into this originally was also a self-journey?

JK: Well, it started when I was very young. I had a very bad childhood. My mother and father parted when I was about 3 years old. In a sense, I'm an orphan who raised myself. I was reading my own books, and reading books on many subjects. By the time I was 17, I was really on my own, all by myself. I came to New York with 75 cents. It never occurred to me that this was a very dangerous thing to do. I just knew that I had to be in New York. This was where I was supposed to be. New York has been my home ever since. Even though I've traveled all the time, I keep going back to New York. I met a lot of fascinating people in New York itself, and around the world...

AC: Well, I think your *Mothman Prophecies* book certainly is fascinating. When I ran across it in '93, it totally put it all together for me. At least it got me thinking that I wasn't crazy...

JK: Right. That was a carefully done book. That was my intention. I really aimed that book at people who had had experiences, whether it was experiences with Big Bird, or small bird, or Loch Ness, or whatever. I've heard from thousands of them since. They know that they're not crazy, and they know that they are learning. It's a shame that the whole world doesn't go through a learning process, but they don't. It's only a small percentage...

CHAPTER 25

"Profound and tranquil, free from complexity,
Uncompounded luminous clarity,
Beyond the mind of conceptual ideas;
This is the depth of the mind...
"In this there is not a thing to be removed,
Nor anything that needs to be added.
It is merely the immaculate
Looking naturally at itself."

-Nyoshul Khen Rinpoche

Colvin, Andy – Grassy Knoll Radio interview 5 – April 28, 2006

"Vyz at Grassy Knoll Radio (GK): This is the Grassy Knoll. You're listening to AM1610 WDCX. This is segment 5 of a series we're doing with Andrew Colvin. His website is andycolvin.com and he is the producer of the film *The Mothman's Photographer*. [There's] a whole lot more information in it... In the meantime, Andrew, you've got a couple of little newsbites to discuss before we get into the meat of the matter?

Andy Colvin (AC): Yes, I've got several things from last time to revisit, and then some little fragments of things that happened this week. I'm going to try to blow through them. First of all, we talked about the anthrax coming out of Columbus. The original coverage was misleading at the time because the news was saying that it was the "Ames Iowa Strain," making people think it was from Iowa.

GK: That's right...

AC: I think that was *meant* to be misleading. The anthrax was from Ohio. It was the Ames strain but it was "weaponized," or refined, in Ohio. Another item is that the book on the CIA/art connection I mentioned is by Francis Saunders. It's called *The Cultural Cold War*. Basically, the idea is that the CIA infiltrated the art movement to take political messages out of art. In the middle part of the century, you had a lot of the Jack Kerouac "Beat" mentality going on, which was threatening to the Establishment. So, they secretly promoted these guys who were doing abstract art that had no political content. Here's a note about the DC Sniper. An interesting detail about the Bushmaster rifle they supposedly used... I don't know if a lot of people know this. We know about it here in Seattle because the snipers supposedly stole it here. Unfortunately, there is no way you could steal a 50-caliber Bushmaster from a gun store in Seattle. It's practically impossible. Guns like that are kept locked in the most prominent display cases. The provenance of the gun is also very suspicious. They could never pin down how the store got the gun in the first place. The Bushmaster rifle is made in Maine, and the owner of the company is a big Bush supporter. This is similar to the Diebold voting-machine CEO, who is also a big Bush supporter. I don't think I brought this up before, but we had some missing fetuses in my hometown when I was growing up. I've heard lots of stories from women in the area who told me that they got pregnant and then the baby, the fetus, would just disappear… The doctors would just call it a miscarriage.

GK: Hold on… I've got to stop you there. Did these women have aborted pregnancies or something like that? Are you saying that perhaps the fetus was extracted from them?

AC: We don't know what happened. They were sometimes months pregnant… The fetus just disappears…

GK: Holy mackerel…

AC: You know this is very common in the UFO abduction world. One of these women in Mound, whose fetus was taken, claims that she came very close to having a Virgin Birth. Now, I don't want to get anybody riled up here, but this is what I heard. And she's a credible person… This type of thing is not out of the ordinary for this phenomenon. It's very closely linked to the religious miracles that have spawned so many of our major religions. They all spring from this same unexplainable source.

GK: It's an Immaculate Conception type of thing.

AC: I myself had a girlfriend who lost a fetus. I wanted to bring this up because of the strange tie-in to *The Exorcist* movie. Apparently there are all these weird things that have happened to people who had some connection to that movie. At the time, I was dating this girlfriend. I had bought a car from Linda Blair's boyfriend, with whom I went to art school in Cincinnati. He had gone to Yale the year before. Linda Blair had been in this car a *lot*. The car blew up the day after I sold it. I had it for a year or so. The day after I sold it, it caught on fire. The dashboard and everything just caught on fire, while the guy was starting it up. He was really upset. He thought I had given him a bogus car. I told him I was genuinely sorry and that it probably had to do with Linda Blair… There was another strange thing, which occurred in 1981. Harriet Plumbrook got a message from a medium she was seeing, as part of a project for her college newspaper. She saw this psychic, named Medula, and the psychic said, "Give a message to Andy Colvin. His dad is here, and he says he has a protector." I sometimes wonder if that protector was watching over me when I was driving the Linda Blair car.

A woman I had known in Cincinnati, who was from the paranormal Bridgewater Triangle area of Massachusetts, once told me that she could see a dark silhouette hovering above her car. It followed her car around during the two years she was married to a troubled Navy husband.

GK: Can we at least say that Linda Blair's boyfriend extricated himself from the vehicle unscathed?

AC: Well, he later became a big Hollywood editor. He's worked on some really major movies, like the one where Jack Nicholson says, "You *can't handle* the truth." His dad was an engineer, by the way, like so many of these other guys. It was always kind of a mystery, what his dad really did.

Another woman I dated in Cincinnati had an interesting set of friends. Her best friend was dating a man whose father claimed that the CIA was monitoring their house at all times. They lived near Ft. Thomas, KY. There may be some connection between this family and the two MIBs who tried to break into my girlfriend's house in Ft. Mitchell (the scene of an "exploding entity" sighting). My girlfriend's father was in appliance sales, like Woody Derenberger and Tad Jones. I remember hearing a story that the father was forced to allow some of his product to be siphoned off by mobsters – from railroad cars.

AC: Okay, let's do the Swedish thing. I've been listening to some old Keel talks, getting them ready to be transcribed. He was very interested in Sweden and what was going on there. I found a couple of letters by Keel in a pile that I got from the Swedish UFO Museum, AFU. You could tell from the tone of it that he really understood the international scope of the conspiracy. Way back when, they had these Foo Fighters, these small things that were flying around military airplanes. They were basically UFOs. Keel was really interested in those. It kind of shows that maybe the military had certain capabilities that we weren't aware of. Maybe were using them against each other. These small UFOs would fly around jet fighters and track them, or make maneuvers around them.

GK: Would they be protective necessarily of US aircraft?

AC: I don't know... Keel had a strong presence in Sweden. One of their UFO guys came over from Sweden and fell in love with probably the most well known Mothman witness, Linda Scarberry. As I say, I was in contact with this Swedish museum. It was a random thing. I wanted to buy a contactee book on eBay. After I won the auction, I got in touch with this museum that happened to be selling the book. I told them about my Mothman interest. They said, "We'd like to have your video. Send it to us, and we'll trade you a file on Woody Derenberger that's got actual correspondence to and from Woody." And I said, "Great." Well somehow, Derenberger's daughter got involved. To make a long story short, I ended up getting a file that seemed sanitized. Half of the promised pages weren't there. None of the Woody correspondence to Earl Neff was in there. Most of it consisted of copies of the same basic AP newswire information, printed in various newspapers. So now we're having this squabble about why they didn't live up to their promises.

I never got the promised material. In what seemed to be punishment for my speaking out about this on the radio, the museum pulled the positive review of my series that had previously been posted on their website. The Neff files were donated to AFU by a Cleveland area UFO researcher named Bill Jones. In January of 2004, AFU received from Jones a donation of 2000 clippings that had once belonged to MUFON Ohio member Richard Lee, who had gotten them from Neff.

AC: But little synchronicities can happen while this stuff is going on. That seems to be how some of the research advances. I was listening to a JFK assassination tape regarding the connection with the Swedes. The CIA asset closest to Oswald, and with Jackie Onassis' parents, was George DeMohrenschildt. He was of Swedish nobility. Keel would go around investigating, asking people what the Men in Black looked like. He would show them "racial profiling" photos. He said that overwhelmingly, people identified the MIBs as being from Northern Sweden. They're called Laplanders. So you've got Swedes coming in, hooking up with the main Mothman witnesses. You've got Swedes perhaps *being* these MIBs. You have Swedes on Woodward Drive, in Mound. You have a proven connection that they were either spying on, or had some involvement with, the JFK hit.

In June of 2007, radio host Alex Jones received an anonymous list of the 2006 Bohemian Grove attendees. Included in the list was the King of Sweden, Carl XVI Gustaf. The following day after Jones posted the list, I read where economic historian Willi A. Boelcke estimated that almost half of Nazi Germany's iron ore had come from Sweden. This peaked my interest because it means that Prescott Bush, in his role as manager for one of the Third Reich's largest steelmakers, must have had close very business dealings with the Swedes.

AC: Of course, JFK kind of connects up to Mothman in other ways, too... I think I mentioned Union Carbide having the Martian landscape. That would have been in Mercury, Nevada, a place of interest to JFK hitmen and where Area 51 is located. Well, Keel mentions that Mercury, Nevada was taken out of Rand McNally maps.

The town of Sugar Grove, WV, has also been taken out of many roadmaps.

AC: Keel was also talking about the Roswell incident in these tapes. He thinks it was a Fugu balloon, which is the balloon that the Japanese would float over here and blow up. The Japanese were trying to just randomly kill people here on the West Coast.

GK: They used it in WWII, right?

AC: Yes, some of them hung around and didn't come down until '47. Maybe they were still secretly letting them up. Who knows? But Keel started talking about a Union Carbide product in relation to these balloons. He was saying that these early balloons had Bakelite in them, an early form of plastic. Like I say, I got this book on Carbide, and that was one of their first products. Plastic was their first big product. But it was very brittle... Oh, and this is totally random, but I just wanted to mention it. One of the people I interview in my documentary, Mercedes Yaeger, claims to have some strange psychic link to chupacabras. She also had a psychic experience about 9/11. She knew it was going to happen before it happened. She even had an abduction experience in the middle of our filming. She talked about it on film, the day after it happened. Coincidentally, before she moved to Seattle, she worked at Cantor-Fitzgerald in the World Trade Center. I was just blown away by that... By the way, Keel mentions in his tape that there were some weird rumors in New York in '92, about Saddam Hussein blowing off a bomb. This is right during the Gulf War. It's almost setting the stage for what happened ten years later with our invasion of Iraq... But this George DeMohrenschildt definitely had French intelligence links, even though he was a Swedish noble. He had Texas oil links and went to UT Austin to study petroleum engineering. He was even arrested as a German spy, but he got out of it... I was looking through my dad's Norfolk Navy yearbook and it turns out the French had an operation going on at Norfolk at the time of the Philadelphia Experiment. They had separate quarters at Norfolk for the French Navy guys, and the description of it just has that ring of "spy operation" about it. By the way, when he was in the Air Force, Woody Derenberger worked in the Air Signal Corps. I'm not saying he was a spy, but that's an area where they often have to have some sort of clearances... And did I mention that Derenberger worked at Union Carbide as well?

GK: I think you did. But I'll tell you what... It doesn't surprise us. Everybody seems to be working at Union Carbide!

AC: Derenberger, like Tad Jones, quit his Carbide job and became an appliance salesman. You have two guys there making that unusual switch. Ralph Jarrett, who helped Keel investigate Tad Jones, was also an engineer at Carbide. Jarrett probably knew Tommy Burnham's dad, who was also an engineer at the Tech Center at Carbide. All of these guys seemed to have contact with that Tech Center. But back to the Philadelphia Experiment... My father was there in '43 when it happened. I have a photo of him from that month in Washington, D.C. He was on some kind of special assignment in D.C. at the Bureau of Standards, according to my parents wedding announcement. A couple of weeks ago, I talked to my aunt in NY, Loretta Colvin Angus. She said that he had definitely gone to Philadelphia, at one point or another, and been based there. I heard testimony from DuPont supervisors, William T. Walters and Donald Stansfield, who had seen men burning – and disappearing – in Belle, WV. I think I mentioned it in the first episode. So you've got *some* evidence that these sailors were brought from Norfolk to S. Charleston, Belle, Nitro, and probably Pt. Pleasant, to work in the plants. Some of them seem to have been catching on fire and disappearing, as Philadelphia Experiment lore describes. They probably brought these guys, like my dad, over en masse to keep an eye on them. There is some strange connection to Montauk, too. It all started with a nightmare I had about my dad being in this chair and being really afraid, and mentioning something about cancer. This kind of ties into Frightwig... I feel that Frightwig may have been injecting people with cancerous substances. I feel like that dream was maybe a signal to me to investigate that angle. So this chair that my dad was in was of interest. I just recently found out that at Montauk, there was this thing called "The Chair," that people like Duncan Cameron would use to time-travel. Now, I generally don't put a whole lot of stock in every guy telling a story about Montauk, because the stories seem like they have disinformation embedded in them. But I found it interesting that this chair motif is an integral part of *their* story, too. I initially thought, "Well, that's just a little coincidence. No biggie..." But then I heard from an old friend from the early '80s (the one with the shadow following her car), who remembered a piece of art I had done. It had to do with my dad and a chair. She said that she had never forgotten that image because it was so sad and frightening. Oddly, I couldn't remember doing the image at all. It was amazing that she remembered it. The chair was a central thing in my drawing. Now, regarding the cancer thing with my dad... He got cancer about three years after the Mothman events. He was sent to Cleveland for care, which was kind of unusual. He recovered. They supposedly got it all out. But then he had an incident where he felt like he'd been jabbed by somebody during the night. And he got cancer in that spot.

GK: Where was he that he would have been possibly jabbed? Was he home? Was he on the road?

AC: It was at home in Mound. I think it's possible that they could have sneaked in, or drugged us with gas or something. It was so unusual, the way it happened. He *did* get cancer right there in that spot. That same year, there was a big push by Nixon to meld the Army Biochemical Warfare Division with the Cancer Virus Program. A guy from Charleston, the scion of the Laytons of Jonestown, once headed that division. Nixon is coming in and saying, "Let's beef up the biowarfare area, and let's call it our new 'cancer' research division." He's essentially saying, "Let's bring cancer into biowarfare." This was nearby in Maryland, which is where Harriet's family moved around the same time. The Frightwig suspect is a guy who definitely had knowledge of injecting people with cancer, and had done so on prisoners. He also links to some of the assassination teams that I've been talking about, too. He was definitely a skuzzy character, if you will, who would have had no qualms about jabbing someone like that. It may have been connected to an operation called CHAOS. Did I mention CHAOS before?

GK: You might have mentioned it, but we didn't do anything in depth about it.

According to documents in the appendix of "The CIA Doctors" by Colin A. Ross, a series of mind control experiments took place on Army personnel out of Edgewater Arsenal, code-named Project OFTEN. After testing many subjects, they perfected a chemical compound called The BOOMER. Boomer is also the name of the town in WV that spawned the Laytons of Jonestown. It is not known exactly what BOOMER did to people, but it probably either killed them (simulated a heart attack, etc.) or caused them to behave erratically, to the point of killing themselves or others.

AC: Operation CHAOS started in '67 around the time that these strikes were occurring at Carbide. Carbide had a strike in August '66, which lasted a few months. Pressure was mounting, just as the Mothman sightings started. The companies were probably moving to quell the strike, or to make things happen so that the strikers would give in. I think that maybe is why the Mothman started appearing at that time.

GK: Operation CHAOS was a government op?

AC: Yes, and it started in Greece, actually. The model for it started in Greece. You know, there are European connections all over the place here. The American CIA and the Greek CIA were quelling the labor unrest in Greece. They brought that model back to the States and started using it against workers and students here. The timing of the MIBs is very suspicious. One senses that they may have been training for CHAOS near Pt. Pleasant. One of the things I heard from the locals is that the Greek mob came into town just prior to arrival of the Mothman. That's a signal to me that there may have been a CHAOS-linked operation in the area.

GK: Can you explain what the tenets would have been of an operation such as CHAOS? What was the agenda?

AC: The agenda was to destabilize the peace movement, and then make sure that the peace movement didn't spread to labor or to the corporate world. In the Union Carbide history book there is a mention of this. It's very odd, the way they state it in the book. Like denial... They claim that "the unrest over the war did not enter the gates of the plant." To me it sounds like propaganda. I *know* it entered the gates of the plant because my dad told me it did. He told me there were guys talking about blowing up the plant. There were even Mothman witnesses who had visions of the plant blowing up, as the Gere movie indicated.

Did Mothman witnesses actually see the Bhopal disaster – which was caused later by worker sabotage – and not realize it? Were the men talking about blowing up the plant actually company moles sent in to identify rabble-rousers?

GK: Why would they want to blow up the plant? Was Union Carbide necessarily a purveyor of gas, or any kind of weaponry?

AC: At that time, they were controlling the nuclear industry. They had leases from the Atomic Energy Commission to mine uranium. I talked about the uranium towns before... Carbide was also making triggers for missiles. The heat-seeking "proximity missile" was a hot item at the time. Yes, they're a defense contractor making all manner of weaponry. They make a lot of raw materials, like plastics and chemicals, used to make mundane things *and* military things. They have very significant military contracts.

Carbide's longtime German partner, Linde, is a prime distributor of gases. Bottled Linde gas was featured in Werner Herzog's "White Diamond," a film about one man's dream to build a portable dirigible that could be used to mine pharmaceutically valuable plants from the tops of jungle canopies in Guyana. Guyana was the location of the former Carbide property that housed the Jonestown colony. Herzog's phone number was once in the Rolodex of an old friend of mine from Charleston, whose family owned mining land. At that time in the late 1980s, Herzog was considering doing a documentary on snake-handling churches in WV, near the Campbell's Creek gravel pit where Mothman was seen.

GK: Is Union Carbide still a big manufacturer of weaponry, chemical or otherwise?

AC: Well they changed the structure of the company in the '80s and dumped a lot of units. Then they merged with Dow. So Dow is now running the S. Charleston Tech Center, which has sort of switched its mission more to "data processing." This tells you it might have something to do with "data mining," since it's in the same state where they download the AT&T carrier signals. I think it's possible that they're dealing with that kind of thing at S. Charleston. I can't say for sure. But as a rule, they switch units around between themselves so much that it's hard to say who's doing what at any given moment. I unfortunately don't have the time or resources to investigate that part of it.

In the June 2007 issue of National Geographic, Dow placed a foldout advertisement that featured a map of the world's water resources and how they are all threatened in various ways. The placement of the ad seemed timed to coincide with similar fears spread by Al Gore's recent film on global warming. Like the "peak oil" scare rumored to be spread by oil companies to increase prices, the global warming scare is based on a creative mix of fact and guesswork linking earth temperatures to oil – thus justifying further price increases. Since Dow now owns Union Carbide and is most likely under the control of the Rockefellers, one can easily imagine an upcoming "peak water" scare to increase prices. My copy of the National Geographic ad arrived at the same time that Alex Jones posted an article confirming that "dirty bomb" tests were being set up in London. Any dirty bomb event would immediately poison nearby water supplies, and raise regional prices. This would ultimately benefit German companies like RWE, who have already bought up many of the water rights in WV and around the world.

The following issue of National Geographic (July 2007) featured a lead article on controlling malaria, the methods of which exactly mirrored those being concurrently foisted on West Coast cities for controlling West Nile virus. In Seattle, there was little public debate over the new proce-dures, which would introduce chemicals directly into lakes and streams via street gutters. Newspaper articles failed to mention which chemical companies got the contracts. The same July issue of the Geographic featured an article called "Swarm Theory," on how chemical companies and others were studying the group behavior of animals in an effort to better profit from recent energy deregulation. Many of the highlighted quotes indicated that groups could be controlled with less oversight than previously thought. One quote stated that the research was leading toward developing robots that could overrun a village in search of "terrorists."

GK: [It] would keep you running for a long time, trying to track down the core of all this.

AC: Let's see... It's almost time to switch into Maddox, or do a quick foray into the attacks on the Garuda line of reasoning, which is a shorter thing.

GK: Let's do the attacks on the Garuda.

AC: You see attacks on bringing out the truth about the Garuda in both East and West. In the East, you see it very sharply in the Buddhist world. There is a big schism between the Dalai Lama and Geshe Kelsang Gyatso, who is from a lineage that goes directly back to the Buddha. Kelsang's line, the Kadampas, believe that the Garuda is a living earth deity. They want to continue propagating that understanding. The Dalai Lama doesn't... He believes – or at least takes the official position that – the Garuda is a "superstition." It's hard to fight the Dalai Lama these days, because he's worked hard at bringing his message to the West... I noticed that on the fourth anniversary of 9/11, it was the Dalai Lama who was on TV all day. He was the guy who was helping us think about it, and process our emotions about it. So he's taking on a bigger role now. If you look back at how he got here, it's kind of interesting. The CIA helped bring him out of China. To give an example of intelligence agency interest in Buddhism, once upon a time I was in a certain Buddhist order. I was actually initiated as a priest in this Buddhist order. I was provisionally a priest, but I dropped out during the probationary period where you have to decide if you're still a good match (after they've revealed some of their secrets to you). It turned out that this order had intelligence connections. The leader of the order had been an officer in the Air Signal Corps in England. The official story is that he decided, out of the blue, to go AWOL in Sikkim (where Keel traveled) and become a Buddhist. He placed himself right there on the border with India, where all of the Dalai Lama's buddies were coming over the mountains. He became one of their main contacts. He eventually set up a huge Buddhist movement that revitalized Buddhism in India. To recap, an Englishman who was in the intelligence wing of the British military ends up revitalizing Buddhism in India. His second in command is the son of an admiral in the Royal Navy. The Dalai Lama moves to India, and sets up new facilities there. From then on, it's been this cozy relationship. That's sort of the Eastern part of it... Now in the West, just in my own personal experience trying to spread information about the Garuda teachings, I have seen a lot of resistance. Part of it is from people already having an ego investment in their own spiritual point of view. People tend to think of Buddhism as a competing religion with Christianity. But it's really not, because it's more of just a spiritual *practice* as opposed to a worship kind of thing. So, on the various web groups, there is resistance right away. There are a couple of major Mothman discussion lists that people go to, and they're both pretty limited that way. One of them seemed to be warming up to the Garuda teachings until the moderator, who is Catholic, could stretch no further than seeing the Mothman as a demon. It's kind of rough at times… The group that is the most resistant is the "local" one. It, too, has a Catholic moderator. We have had big fights on both lists over the possibility that the Garuda might be a benevolent deity - that there might be some relationship between the Messianic aspects of the Garuda and the Messianic aspects of Christ... However we are making some good progress in my new group called "The Mothman's Photographer." We're willing to look at the conspiracy angles as well as the Garuda teachings. We may

Large bird float carried by Mindrum and Colvin past Rockefeller Center, NYC, June 12ᵗʰ, 1982

actually make some progress in terms of finding out what's going on.

GK: I never know why Christians get all hackled up about somebody positing something. I mean listen, if we're grounded in what we believe and someone wants to come out and portray something, that's fine. I don't like the whole idea of censorship. The thing is, I know what I believe in, and the listeners know what they believe in. If somebody wants to come up and say something, fine. When you tell me that this individual was all upset about your views being introduced, to me it smacks of insecurity [and not being] grounded... You're not stepping on my toes whatsoever.

AC: One thing I forgot... This lady that remembered my drawing of the chair, this Montaukian chair... I went to visit her childhood home once. Her mom was a beauty queen like that former Miss WV, Patsy Ramsey (Jon-Benet Ramsey's mother). My friend Tommy, the Mothman contactee, his mom was also a Miss West Virginia... But I was driving up to see this woman who, by the way, lives near a NASA listening station in Massachusetts...

GK: It doesn't get any better, does it?

AC: On the way to see her in 1982, we stopped in New York City and got involved in the Anti-Nuke Parade. It was huge, with 750,000 people in Central Park. We carried one of the banners in the parade. It was this huge white bird that looked like Mothman. I have a photo of it that's going to be in the book. Some of the Mothman sightings were of a light gray color. Virtually white... One can almost say that we marched with Mothman past Rockefeller Center. Having those kinds of little synchronicities on that 1982 trip made me feel that there might be something to what my lady friend was saying, in 2005, about this Chair. That it had some important meaning... But let's move into Maddox. I want to at least touch on that. There is this name "Maddox" that comes up in the Mothman lore. Supposedly there was somebody on the bridge named Maddox who was killed, or almost killed. A threatening message was left with Keel that said something like, "Don't investigate this anymore or you'll end up like Colonel Maddox and his daughter." Keel then reported in *The 8th Tower* that a person with the name Alvis Maddox had been a witness in some high-profile UFO sightings in TX.

GK: That's a real individual? That wasn't a pen name or pseudonym?

AC: It turns out that there *is* a verifiable Alvis Maddox, and he was involved in the JFK assassination story. He was a Dallas deputy sheriff, noted for being with a key JFK witness when that witness died. The witness was Buddy Walthers, a Dallas policeman who had interviewed the Paines about their Nash Rambler. Jack Ruby had been seen picking up Oswald in it. Walthers had picked up the "extra" bullet in Dealey Plaza. This extra bullet was a crucial turning point in the whole JFK investigation. Walthers refused to change his story. He kept saying, "No, this was an extra bullet that was fired." So this Alvis Maddox turns up being on assignment with Walthers. Walthers dies as they are investigating a drug deal. Maddox only gets shot in the hand or foot...

GK: What was Maddox's end? I mean did he just die of natural causes later on?

AC: I don't know. I think he might still be alive. As a side note, Loren Coleman, the Bigfoot journalist, posted a file on a Colonel Maddox who had been in Vietnam and had worked for Bell Helicopter. I think Col. Maddox was in Laos or Cambodia, which kind of means he probably had something to do with the Phoenix program. There was a cell of people working at Bell who were reportedly linked somehow to the JFK assassination. In this cell were Michael Paine and his wife Ruth. They were Oswald's landlords. They owned the Nash Rambler seen leaving Dealey Plaza. They were related to Arthur Young, inventor of the helicopter. Young had been involved in the invocation of The Nine... There is a connection between Michael Paine and Sen. John Kerry. Paine's mother, Ruth Forbes Paine, is Kerry's cousin. I think they're first cousins... The investigator on that is Bruce Adamson. He's kind of a crazy character out in California. He is a former postal carrier who spent all of his time and money investigating George DeMohrenschildt. At one time, I thought that maybe the Colonel Maddox at Bell was the father of Alvis, the UFO witness/policeman. They're both from Dallas, sort of the Bedford area... By the way, I once dated a female artist who was from Bedford. She was German, and her father had been a US Air Force pilot... It interested me that I had a random connection to the Dallas suburb where these guys lived. Another "Maddox" name is linked to The Nine as well. Holly Maddux was the name of the woman who was supposedly murdered by Ira Einhorn, the Philadelphia activist and leftist scientist.

GK: Who fled to Europe after the alleged murder, right?

AC: Right. Einhorn, in an interview, said that he had worked on this "black box" technology with Puharich. He was really close to Puharich, the implant guy. According to Einhorn, they had access to all these silicon chips. They had a tie-in with a company that made really small chips... So there is a Maddux dying in relation to The Nine. Einhorn was set up. He was a patsy. Or so he claims...

GK: Do we know what happened to that case? Was it ever adjudicated?

AC: Well, that's the funny thing… We never heard anything about it once they caught him. And that's sort of the giveaway, isn't it?

GK: Yes, we do wonder when things disappear into the memory hole. And *that's* one of those cases that did…

As of 2007, Einhorn was in jail in central Pennsylvania, still protesting his innocence.

AC: Another Maddox is Charles Manson's mother. Her name was Maddox.

GK: Now hold on. Is Manson's last name really "Manson?"

AC: No, his mother's name was Maddox. And since the media won't specifically identify his father, he might as well be a Maddox. Supposedly his father's last name was Scott, an Army Colonel. It makes you wonder…

GK: Yes it does…

AC: Supposedly the father was a *Colonel* Scott. They are willing to identify the brother of the Colonel, Darwin Scott. Darwin Scott was murdered in '68, perhaps by the Manson family. He was brutally slashed. It could have been Charles Watson that killed Scott. Watson is another suspicious player from a Dallas police family. Watson *was* the Manson killer. He was Manson's right-hand man in the "Manson family." He was the real slasher. So Manson's "uncle" ends up slashed just like the Tate victims. There are lots of ancillary victims in the Manson case that have never been talked about in the media. This guy Scott died right on the border of WV, OH, and KY, only a few miles from Point Pleasant. That's where Levenda kind of gets this idea that Manson was from KY. Actually Manson was more from WV.

GK: Scott was slashed?

AC: Yes, yet we never hear the name of Manson's father. Why don't we know the first name of the father? I think it's very suspicious.

GK: Well that gives rise to the whole thing. We know that the Manson family was also used in certain hits on Gerald Ford.

AC: Certainly… Both hits were connected to Manson. We know that Manson knew shooter Sara Jane Moore from way back on Woodward Drive. And we know that Manson and shooter Squeaky Fromme were lovers…

GK: Wasn't Nelson Rockefeller in line [to be President if anything happened to Ford]?

AC: Manson was being used for all kinds of things. He was a police informant. He got credit cards all along for financing his endeavors. No one quite knows what *that* was all about. He got lots of help doing what he did. Watson may have helped set Manson up to take the fall.

GK: Was Watson's nickname "Tex?"

AC: Yes...

GK: I remember... All those murder headlines occurred right after my birthday in '69. I remember reading the Daily News and thinking, "This is so bizarre." Tate's husband Roman Polanski was into filming the macabre. It was almost like life imitating art, imitating life, you know?

AC: I know a cousin of Tate's. Sharon Tate was from Dallas. Her father was an Army officer. Her mother apparently "feared for her safety" long before the murders. Tate's cousin was in the Austin band I was in. He was one of the oil kids I was talking about earlier. He's a crazy character. That's just another little coincidence... And I'm sure this means nothing, but the Gulf of Tonkin ship that started the Vietnam War was *The USS Maddox.* Then, Vietnam ends up being the incubator for these ruthless Phoenix operatives who brought their ghastly trade back home.

GK: Now, was there a camp in West Virginia?

AC: I think it's possible... We have witnesses saying they saw men doing paramilitary training in the TNT area, where you had all of these bunkers. A hundred of these bunkers... Here is another unusual coincidence... A week before the Mothman sightings started, the second Jim Garrison investigation into JFK kicked secretly into gear. Here you have these paramilitary JFK hitmen from Louisiana suddenly being under scrutiny again. Their Louisiana bunkers had already been taken away during Garrison's first investigation. The Louisiana bunkers were, by the way, leased to an oil company having offices in West Virginia, called Schlumberger. They also have offices all over the world. The history of Schlumberger goes back to Europe. According to Anton Chaitkin, it goes back to the "British/Swiss intelligence connection" which spawned Benedict Arnold and the Tories. So suddenly the paramilitaries had nowhere to go, or were risking increased exposure. They needed a place that was isolated, which had a lot of bunkers. They could just go right up the Mississippi River to the Ohio River, and unload it right there. Pt. Pleasant's TNT area is right by the water. They could put the stuff in secure bunkers and start training again. The TNT area is also a toxic Superfund site, so there aren't many people in there. People tend to stay away. It was perfect for their purposes. I don't think the Mothman was there to scare people away. The Mothman *drew people in.* I think the Mothman was probably this deity showing up to give clues as to what was going on. It wanted an audience. Hundreds of people were coming to the TNT area. It would have cramped the style of any paramilitaries. So they probably used "muscle" in town to scare people, telling them to shut up and stay away...

GK: When you talk about the paramilitary exercises, I think back to JFK, with David Ferrie and the Louisiana Civil Air Patrol. Didn't those exercises take place in Louisiana?

AC: Yes, they did. You know, Ferrie was into the occult.

GK: Yes, he was...

AC: At the time of Mothman, there were occult groups seen practicing in the TNT area, too. People in robes, who may have been associated with a nearby Manson Family "coven..." You had dog mutilations. Everyone naturally assumed that this occult group caused the mutilations.

GK: Were Ferrie's training venues in Louisiana?

AC: Yes, Houma, Louisiana was where he was training at one point.

GK: Okay. So now we may have others in West Virginia. Can you name any

Comparison of Man in Black that Colvin randomly drew in the 1980s (left), felt to be associated with his father's death, to mugshot of JFK conspirator David Ferrie (right), a cancer virus researcher and CIA pilot speculated to be Mothman's "Frightwig" man.

of the towns that they might have been around?

AC: Phone records indicate Ferrie called Huntington, West Virginia. And we have people seeing a guy who looked like he was wearing a fright wig. Of course, if you know your Ferrie...

GK: He wore wigs...

AC: He wore a bright red ape-hair wig. He got the hair from the monkeys that he used in his cancer experiments. If you saw the movie *JFK*, you'll remember Joe Pesci playing Ferrie.

GK: Oh yes. He was great.

AC: Well, that's him. That's David Ferrie. He was a "wandering" bishop in the Orthodox Old Catholic Church of North America. These tangential lineages were used so that OSS/CIA guys could access churches as fronts for various activities. It gave them an excuse to be here or there, raising money, or doing whatever...

GK: I heard Levenda when he was on "Ghost to Ghost" talking about the Wandering Bishops... Ferrie was involved with these Wandering Bishops? Or was one?

AC: Absolutely... He was from Cleveland, by the way. He always wanted to be a priest from early on. He became a pedophile. He kept getting in trouble for his pedophilia, and therefore couldn't get into the church officially. The real bishops rejected him. So he ended up working for the CIA. Who knows who came up with the idea to use these wandering orders. They were started in the early 1900s, principally out of New York City...

UFO author Timothy Green Beckley stated in "The UFO Silencers" that Gray Barker was once tailed in his car all the way from Cleveland back to WV. The driver following Barker was wearing a priest's outfit.

AC: The Wandering Bishops had three major branches, but they all came out of New York originally. One was the Ofeish line, which was I think more Eastern Orthodox, or Middle Eastern. They stayed in New York, I think... But another branch went to Kentucky. One of the three modern branches was represented by a Kentucky priest who knew Ferrie. That puts Ferrie in the Mothman area. Suspiciously, that KY bishop, Carl Stanley, died the same month as Ferrie. Ferrie died in February of '67. Stanley had consecrated Ferrie into his particular order, thus giving Ferrie a little more "juice." It gave Ferrie the ability to "wear the robe." If you remember the JFK movie, there was a robe hanging there. Oliver Stone was making reference to the importance of the robe to Ferrie. But Ferrie was also into these monkeys. At least one witness, Judyth Baker, has come forward to say that Ferrie was experimenting on prisoners at a Louisiana prison. He was injecting them with cancerous substances. The monkeys came from "suicided" cancer researcher Mary Sherman. Baker also claims that she was dating Lee Harvey Oswald, and that Lee was also involved in that Angola cancer experimentation. Both Ferrie and Oswald were also involved in the Ochsner Clinic in Louisiana, which was doing cancer research. Basically that research was coming out of this whole other line of inquiry, which had to do with polio. Polio vaccines in the '50s were being contaminated with the "SV-40" virus, which causes cancer. Almost all the early polio vaccines had cancer-causing agents in them. It was a really big scandal, but it was eventually covered up. Ochsner was essentially behind it. He was the polio vaccine spokesman. He even injected his own grandchildren. They got polio from the shots, and one died. Ochsner set up this big clinic to try to find out how to reverse what had been done… Supposedly that's where Ferrie and Oswald got their training. There is a photo of Oswald and Ochsner on an old album put out by a right-wing radio station in New Orleans. Ochsner was well known as a right-wing supporter of dictators in South America. A lot of the dictators would fly their families up to New Orleans for care.

GK: Andrew, let me ask you this. I have a photo and I've lost it… I've left the place where I stored the photo… But there was a photo of Oswald and Ferrie together in the Civil Air Patrol.

AC: Yes, I'm going to have a little picture of that in my book. A good book to read if you're interested in the "cancer virus" topic is *Mary, Ferrie, and the Monkey Virus.* It's about Mary Sherman, the cancer researcher. She was a brilliant cancer researcher who was trying to figure out how to solve this problem of the contaminated polio vaccine. So she had all these monkeys that they were experimenting on. I think Oswald lived just a couple of blocks from the clinic. At one time, you could actually go there and see where they had their setup. But they were irradiating all these different mice and apes, to try and figure out what to do. Sherman ended up being murdered. It appears that she was actually fried by the radioactive machine they were using in the experiments. Somebody simply stuck her in front of it and shot her with the raygun.

Another theory, which is probably disinformation, is that the raygun was booby-trapped to kill Ochsner when he came into work the next day. Under this scenario, Sherman just happened to go in the night before and accidentally set off the trap.

AC: They dumped her body in her apartment and set fire to the mattress. Then it was all written off as "suicide by accidental fire." But there was no way that could have happened. Her arm was burnt completely off. There was no way a smoldering mattress fire could have done that. She lost her arm bone completely. It disintegrated, which takes extreme heat. But Ferrie ended up with her monkeys. That's the real story. *That's* why Ferrie had all these monkeys. The guy who wrote that Sherman book, Edward Haslam, happened to stumble upon Ferrie's old apartment. The monkey smell was still there, years later. Haslam's research, like mine and so many others, was led by weird coincidences. I think Haslam was put onto Ferrie by the fact that he went to school with the coroner's son. The coroner's son stood up in class one day and said some things that basically let everybody know that the fix was in on some of the JFK deaths. They were forcing the coroner's hand, as it were.

GK: We're going to hold it right there… Andrew, we're going to outro with one of the songs that I believe you're involved with, are you not? Manson Street?

AC: Yes, this is Manson Street, a song that I wrote with the oil boys in TX. This is on the soundtrack to the documentary. *[Music plays with Colvin singing]*

The air was hot, my heart was about to pop,
Clouds of chlorine gas had escaped and the whole valley coughed.
Next morning, the sky had partially cleared but
Those who had dared to take a deep breath, their lungs were seared!
This is Charlie Manson Street, chemical plants produce the heat,
Sara Jane Moore's hillbilly store, drinking from stills, raking the floor…

One room shack a lack a lack lack lack,
Weiners in a can for a snack snack snack,
Smoking from a pipe in the back back back,
Staring at a light so black black black.

Heinous house on a heinous hill, films by Roman Polanski,
Heinous dog on a heinous cat, heinous things perverted as that.
Running the pipeline, running for fear
Some kind of invisible trap could be waiting.
Playing with fire, making no sense,
Hunting with hound dogs, sharing in sin.

Heinous smoke from a heinous stack, dirt on the face, curve in the back,
Heinous boots with a heinous tread, milk's in a bag, mold's on the bread.
Heinous car on a heinous track, kids in the seat, guns on the rack,
Heinous nights in a heinous shack, heinous things we can't ever take back.
Heinous crime on my heinous head, bones in the stove, snakes in the bed,
Heinous sky that's a heinous red, the stuff in the air puts thoughts in your head.

"An extremely interesting but assiduously neglected phase of the Kennedy assassination and its 'investigation,' or whitewash, was presented in a story published in the NY Daily News of Nov. 10, 1963 by Joseph Cassidy and Lester Abelman. They related that Pres. Kennedy visited New York on the preceding day, shortly after Nelson Rockefeller had announced his candidacy. He stopped at the Carlyle Hotel, which is reportedly owned jointly by the Rockefeller and Kennedy interests. They reported that the Secret Service maintained the 'tightest' vigilance on a NY visit in recent years; and that no one, even newspaper reporters, were permitted to approach the President. No explanation has been offered, or sought by the 'investigators' for this extraordinary vigilance by the Secret Service in NY as contrasted with the lack of vigilance in Dallas. Was the service warned that Kennedy's life was in danger in NY? Did they have reason to believe that an attempt would be made on his life in NY? A clarification of this matter might throw considerable light on the unexpected assassination in Dallas."

-Emanuel M. Josephson, "The Truth About Nelson Rockefeller, Public Enemy No. 1: Studies in Criminal Psychopathy"

"There has been much speculation about the elites' plans to cull the human population. I lived in Huntington, WV from the beginning of 1995 until 1999. Huntington has a big CSX train yard with a few large buildings on it. On the same block, in close proximity, is a BASF plant. According to Google maps, this plant makes pigments and dyes. Fat chance that's all they make. I might be grasping at air here, but I wonder if there's anything ominous about this. There is much talk of transporting humans by railcar to the extermination facilities and detainment and work camps. BASF is one of the "Baby Bells" created when IG Farben, the company which made the Zyklon-B for the Nazi gas chambers, was broken up. I have heard both BASF and CSX mentioned in conjunction with conspiracy talk… At the time I lived there, a company in Huntington manufactured rail cars… One does wonder whether such a facility could be converted to manufacturing, say, boxcars with shackles, just as a chemical plant which manufactured dyes and pigments might conceivably be converted to manufacturing more ominous chemicals."

-Tracy L. Paxton, letter to Grassy Knoll

CHAPTER 26

My aunt, Gennie Gibson McKinney, was born in Mound and later lived adjacent to Devil's Hollow, above Fisher's Branch (original homestead of the Fishers said to have helped raise Charles Manson). Gennie is a devout Christian, a longtime member of the Roxalana Road Church, and a genuine saint. For a period during the 1970s, Gennie was America's top Tupperware saleswoman. She lived for many years on Woodward Drive, and was one of the first people to recognize and nurture my talent for observation. In times when my observations led me to the edge of the abyss, she had the heart and nerve to coax me back to reality. Gennie's married name, McKinney, happens to be one that shows up a lot in paranormal events. Her husband, Paul, fought in the Korean War, and was a lifelong employee at Union Carbide. The union he was in had a branch with a Masonic logo featuring an alchemical salamander and extremely hot flame.

McKinney, Gennie Gibson – Aunt Eva's Light – 2003

Andy Colvin (AC): My Aunt Gennie will now tell a story about my Aunt Eva Withrow.

Gennie McKinney (GM): Michelle [my granddaughter] who's a nurse at the nursing home where Aunt Eva was, called me at 12:30 and said, "Grandma, Aunt Eva passed away." So I walked through and through this house crying, because I hated to let her go. [She] was the nicest of my remaining relatives. I wondered if Aunt Eva [had gone] to Heaven. So I came into my living room and looked out the window. The sky was just as dark as it could be and I said, "Lord, please let me know if my Aunt Eva went to heaven." All of a sudden, a star appeared. It was one big star in the sky. There was not another star. And it wasn't an airplane, because it didn't move. It stayed right there. That was my sign. Aunt Eva went to heaven.

AC: Did it stay there all night? Or did it just go away?

GM: I don't know. I just closed my draperies. And then I called [my son]. I was crying. He said, "Mom, I don't have any way to get there but if you need me, I will find someone to bring me down." And I said, "No, I'll settle down…" But you know, she was my last aunt. I have no uncles left. My mom and dad are dead; my brother is dead; my sister is dead. It was just hard on me, really. It seems like I'm all that's left out of the Withrow family.

AC: I think Mom [Gennie's sister, Betty] said you guys were maybe ten or twelve years old [when this happened]. I guess you were out on Haines Branch. Mom said that there was a light above the graveyard [of the] church. She said there was a [light that had risen on the night a child had been buried].

GM: [Yes] Betty saw that. The Middle Fork of Poca River was where we lived, where our farm was. Near Rippling Waters pool... When [your sister Loretta] was born [they] lived in New York. But [they] came home and stayed with Mom and Dad [on the Middle Fork of Poca] for a long time, while your Daddy was in the Navy.

Author's mother, Betty Gibson, who saw strange lights on the Poca River near John Amos Power Plant, Raymond, WV 1984.

Recently, Mothman has been seen around Amos.

A vision of Gibson appeared to the author when she died in the late 1990s. A large owl squawked and flapped outside the bedroom window of her home near Panther Rd. for 3 days after she died. Her husband saw a black panther there soon after they first moved in.

The Poca River is a tributary of the Kanawha River. It therefore qualifies as a potential route for this phenomenon. One of the things I remember about my mom living on the Poca River was that she had a lot of visitations by owls. They actually nested in her yard. The family farm that my mother grew up on is only one valley over from Devil's Hollow. "Devil" place names usually mean there has been a history of paranormal activity in a particular area. Our farm was right next to a place called Rippling Waters, a famous watering hole. A mysterious church organization has recently taken over Rippling Waters and built a shrine of some kind next to the lake. The area has a long history as a place for mass baptisms. They once had a strange two-headed goat at one of the baptisms. Gennie actually gave me some old 8mm film footage of the goat. It's likely that this spiritual watering hole is linked into the Mothman grid.

AC: [Earlier you said that you] remember the Big White Owl [incident on Woodward Drive]. So what do you remember about the "big white owl?"

GM: I didn't live out there [until later]. I just remember one of you boys saw it two or three times.

AC: I didn't see it.

GM: Must have been Chip, then...

AC: I remember waking up. I had heard the commotion about the "owl". But Chip wasn't there. Chip and Dad weren't around. They were gone. So I went back to bed. The next day, they claimed that they had been out there fighting with this owl. But they hadn't been there when I went out to check on them. I always thought it was kind of a mystery. Since owl stories often have something to do with the paranormal, I thought that maybe they had disappeared into another dimension for a short period of time. That's what I always thought happened. I just figured, "Well, something weird happened and there was a glitch in time." They remember it as an owl, but nobody saw the owl but them. I think that was one of Chip's little brushes with the paranormal. He remembers it as an owl caught in a rosebush. But screen memories of owls (or deer) often manifest when someone has had missing time or an apparent UFO abduction. Harriet used to walk off when she was a kid. She would think she had been gone for ten minutes but her mom would say, "It's been four hours. Where have you been?" Harriet had been in a particular place in the woods. She would try to go back and find it, but couldn't...

Harriet Plumbrook (HP): Stuff like that happens all the time. My mom used to say, "You've been warned over and over not to run off." I didn't think I had.

Harriet and I both experienced symptoms typically attributed to contactees. She had missing time, scoop marks, and out-of-body experiences, while I had the jabbed finger, odd glandular disturbances, and strange blood cell composition.

AC: Have you had anything like that, Aunt Gennie? Anything strange or unexplainable?

GM: I believe we're sometimes forewarned of things that are going to happen... I think it was a sure sign, when I saw that star. I do! I believe that that was my sign not to worry about it. Aunt Eva was where she'd want to go.

AC: Talking about deceased relatives coming back... About four years after my dad died, I walked into the garage one night. I heard him clearly say, "Hello, Andy." It sent chills up my spine.

GM: Mercy, it would me too...

AC: I wasn't expecting it, so it kind of scared me. It was so long after the fact. I wasn't ready for it at all. But something like that *can* happen years later, even if you're a skeptic. And I *was* pretty much a skeptic about that sort of thing at the time. The realizations kind of sneak up on you.

GM: The Bible says that when Jesus went away, he said he wouldn't leave us comfortless. If I were to have something happen that would really get me down, I think I would [sense the] presence [of Paul, my deceased husband] patting me and saying, "It's okay..."

Gennie showed us a photo from her family album, with writing on the back. Gennie has several photo albums chronicling the history of the McKinney, Gibson, and Withrow families.

GM: Here's my Grandma Lucy. Lucy's father was a full-blooded Blackfoot Indian.

AC: This is a new piece of information. I've got to start studying the Blackfoot tribe now. Aunt Gennie seems very sure that it's Blackfoot...

GM: *[shows newspaper photo]* Here's Aunt Eva. Here's the Santa Claus that Aunt Eva used to have in her yard for years and years and years.

AC: Didn't she tie Santa Claus up with a chain, in order to keep people from taking him?

GM: It kept it from blowing down. It tells the story [here]. They sent a photographer there to do a story about it. Some little child had come by and cried, because that lady had Santa Claus tied up. The [mother] called the Daily Mail. They came and took a picture, and did a write-up about it.

AC: What's your theory about the Mothman? Do you have a theory about him?

GM: I don't know. I read the book. I don't know what to think about it. I'd like to really see him. It would scare me to death, but [I'd still want to see him].

AC: *[points to that day's newspaper]* I was joking earlier today. I predicted that, since Vice President Cheney is in town, they were going to plant some terrorism. It turns out there was another sniper shooting here in Charleston today! There's an article on Cheney, asking for money for Iraq.

A few weeks before this interview, Harriet had a dream about a pentagram. The next day, I sent her an email with a theory I had heard, about the DC Sniper slowly creating a pentagram over Washington, D.C., using the shooting locations to map out the shape. We were amazed by that coincidence. Her dream and the sniper's map... When the sniper was finally caught, it turned out that he was someone seen frequently in my Seattle neighborhood. The mosque that he attended was right around the corner from my house. The mosque was in a beautiful old brick building owned by Seattle's ben Gasser family. It was later torn down, despite a public outcry to preserve the building as an historic landmark. Early on, I had been asked to take photos of the building by a local architect, David Foster, who was spearheading the preservation effort. I had gone inside the mosque and been greeted by a group of Muslim gentlemen there. Since I felt a glint of recognition when seeing the D.C. Sniper on TV, I sometimes wonder if he was amongst that group.

CHAPTER 27

Neal Mindrum happened to be with me when I had a Bigfoot encounter in the Catskills of New York in June of 1982. We were traveling to the Anti-Nuke Rally in New York City. We had bypassed New York in order to camp near my uncle's place, near the Indian Point Nuclear facility. There, we had a late night encounter with what may been the Invisible Bigfoot. During one of my recent trips back to WV, I was traveling through central Ohio and was able to meet up with Mindrum in person. We met at the Williamson Indian mound and drove to nearby Wright-Patterson Air Force base. Mindrum is normally reclusive and extremely camera shy. It took a lot of patience, effort, and logistical support to get the following taped testimony.

Mindrum, Neal – 1982 Invisible Bigfoot/Global Hawk – 2003

Andy Colvin (AC): We're meeting here in Ohio, at Wright-Patterson Air Force Base today. It is the 35th anniversary of the vision that Tommy Burnham and I had of the Twin Towers – the precognition of 9/11. Why Wright-Patterson Air Force Base, you ask? Well, it's a well-known tale that the crashed saucer from Roswell was brought to Wright-Patterson and stored in Hangar 18 along with various other alien accoutrements. Whether you believe that or not is up to you, but it seemed like a good spot to meet and commemorate the 9/11 precognition. Neal, I mentioned to the folks out there that you and I were together in the Catskills, on Bear Mountain, when we encountered something in the forest. As I've read more and more about the invisibility of Bigfoot, I'm starting to think that *that's* what that was. What do you think?

Neal Mindrum (NM): It was 1982. We'd been driving for a great deal of time, so we pulled over. We decided we were going to crash on some sort of a dirt road. We pulled off in this area... We had sleeping bags in the trunk. Andy pulled the sleeping bags out. We started to create [a campsite] that would be fairly comfortable to catch some sleep. Before long we heard twigs snapping. Andy felt *the presence*. He became unsettled. It bothered me [too] so we got out of there.

This was all Mindrum was willing to say regarding that terrifying night on Bear Mountain. He was obviously a bit shaken up by having to recall the episode. I bought him lunch and that seemed to settle him down. After lunch, we ventured over to the Air Force Museum. By cracking some bad jokes, I was eventually able to loosen up the stoic executive. Along the way, I found an odd piece to the 9/11 puzzle in a museum display case.

AC: *[points to Air Force Museum display listing current Air Force command-ers]* Note the date that the Air Force switched commanders: only five days before 9/11! See right there? The AF Commander is one of the military advisors to the President. They would have needed the Air Force commander's compliance on any inside job on 9/11. Maybe it's related to Global Hawk technology. We just saw Global Hawk technology here at the Air Force Museum. It allows civilian passenger planes to be flown remotely. What if they had to get rid of the previous Air Force commander because he didn't want to go along with the plan? What do you think, Neal?

NM: Sounds plausible…

AC: *[to clerk]* Do you have any books on the Roswell UFO that is supposed to be kept up here at Wright-Patterson?

Clerk: No.

AC: No?

Clerk: Definitely not.

AC: No books on any of that stuff?

Clerk: I don't think [we have any]. If we did, they'd be in the "space" section.

AC: Where's that?

Clerk: It's right on the end here. I'll show you.

AC: *[jokingly nodding towards Mindrum]* My "dad" here is interested in it. He's right behind me. *[points to Mindrum]* This guy, my dad…

Clerk: Oh yes, we *do* [have a book on it]!

AC: Look at this! What do you think, Dad?

NM: Well, son... Do you think your mother would be [happy] if I were to spend her hard-earned cash on this? *[laughter]*

After finding the Roswell book, we saw an eye-popping advertisement – several minutes long – touting the technologies employed by the Air Force. There were lots of scripted shots of soldiers saving babies. Mostly however, it was real footage of planes blowing things up, flying upside down at tremendous speeds, and communicating with headquarters using sophis-ticated satellite communications. Strangely, there was a quick clip of a brain operation of some kind. When blended with the technology imagery, it gave the viewer the impression that implants were being used to link soldiers' physiologies to computers. Following the film, we discovered that the official mascot of the Air Force is the baby owl. There were many varieties of white baby owl toys for sale in the museum bookstore.

I frigoriferi General Electric d'acciaio

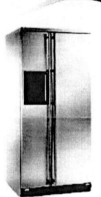

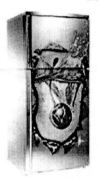

Le speciali coperture in acciaio inox sono realizzate in acciaio AISI 304: uno dei migliori acciai del mondo!

Con questo acciaio sono pannellabili tutti i frigoriferi General Electric: dal modello Side-by-Side con spigoli arrotondati sulle porte e sul top, al modello Top Freezer con porte bombate che ricordano lo stile degli anni '50.

Inoltre è possibile far riprodurre sulle porte - da un vero artista - qualsiasi disegno aerografato da Voi desiderato.

Scegliete un frigorifero General Electric pannellato acciaio, scegliete qualità, affidabilità e un design insuperabile !

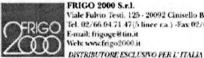

FRIGO 2000 S.r.l.
Viale Fulvio Testi, 125 - 20092 Cinisello Balsamo - MI -
Tel. 02/66.04.71.47(5 linee r.a.) -Fax 02/66.04.72.60
E-mail: frigoge@tin.it
Web: www.frigo2000.it
DISTRIBUTORE ESCLUSIVO PER L'ITALIA

General Electric

Italian GE ad from 2000, showing refrigerator manufactured with image of plane flying into NY's Twin Towers. Interestingly, the refrigerator on left has a cherry - symbol of the Islamic Moors - being submerged. GE, a Rockefeller creation, switched CEOs the week of 9/11. GE now owns AT&T (whose signals are "mined" in WV), Western Union (who built the "mine"), RCA (who supplied Montauk), and NBC (who made a Mothman special in 2006, and mysteriously received the "hate the rich" video from the VA Tech Shooter in '07)

CHAPTER 28

In 2003, I sat down with my niece, writer Sharon Moore, to get her testimony about Mothman. Sharon has had many different kinds of experiences, which are covered in different areas of this book. She is an integral piece of the Mound, WV puzzle. Sharon seems to have been zapped by the same force that touched Philip K. Dick, John Lilly, and Robert Anton Wilson. I suspect that her Celtic heritage has something to do with her visionary experiences. The Scottish Celts reportedly spent centuries in the Moorish land of Egypt prior to moving north. Sharon Moore's very name is suggestive of the Moorish influence that may lie at the heart of the ancient WV mound culture. Sharon is a natural-born mountain healer, frequently sought out by locals for her psychic skills. She is not related to Sara Jane Moore.

Moore, Sharon – Bed Bat Visits, Visions, Dreams – 2003

Andy Colvin (AC): *[Looking amused from inside of car]* There are lots of things I love about the Mothman phenomenon. You have these little coincidences that just get your mind going. Here we are in Dunbar, West Virginia. This is a sighting area mentioned in *The Mothman Prophecies*. When this interstate bridge above me was being built, there was a sighting of a silver sphere similar to the one seen on Woodward Dr. by Tommy Burnham. John Keel came here and found weird tracks off to the side that looked like wolf prints, which were later deemed unclassifiable. Oddly, they were animal prints that had already been seen at other sighting locales around the country. Keel also found one naked human footprint and some "Apollo astronaut" bootprints. It was a famous sighting, and very mysterious. A man with a black box was seen, and there were supposedly some threats made afterwards to Tad Jones, who had seen the sphere.

AC: *[Shifting camera to gravel pit under interstate]* Here we are at this overpass near the Tad Jones sighting spot. Note that we see a sign here that says "Shamblin Stone." Coincidentally, it just so happens that Mr. Shamblin, of Shamblin Stone here, now owns our family farm near Ripley. He now owns and lives on the family farm that my mother was born on, and grew up on. By the way, my sister Spring and I both had a dream about globes of light coming into the house and hypnotizing us. I wanted to know more about the globes, so I took Harriet up there to do a psychic reading of our old house. She said she *saw* us being interrogated by two men while we were all in a trance. There are instances within our family, and without, of people having the same dream. Spring and I have had the same dreams. This seems to be somewhat easy for people to accept. But Harriet and I appear to have the same dreams, too. We share dreams of being in a classroom where we're being taught things. But it's not any actual classroom from our childhood... We both realized that we were having dreams about this same place.

Is this shared dream business just a trick of the "ultra-terrestrials?" Are these really the same dreams?

AC: Sharon, the dream that you and I shared is about a railroad trestle in St. Albans. You had a dream of it first... Then, I had the same dream.

Sharon Moore (SM): We were talking about out-of-body experiences. I kind of thought that's what it was, originally. I had this dream that I was flying above this railroad station... I'd never been there and didn't recognize it. I was driving through St. Albans years later, in real life. Then, I saw it! I said, "*That's the place I dreamed about!*" There was one strange thing in that dream, where I think I was testing myself, to see if it was real or not. In the dream I went into a bathroom in the railroad station, and there was a sink [running]. There was steam over a mirror. I went over to the mirror. To see if anything would happen, I tried wiping the steam. And I wiped away the steam. To me, that is a kind of [proof] that I was really there somehow, physically. Does that make sense? I was trying to do something to affect something there, so I could figure out if it was real, or a dream. Then I was talking about that dream with you. I could tell by the look in your eyes that something was going on. And you said you'd had a dream about the same place!

AC: There were Mothman sightings in St. Albans, so maybe we're dreaming the Mothman's dreams, or picking up some electromagnetic signal connected to that spot.

SM: You mean dreams of flying around?

AC: I have lots of dreams where I'm flying around. I notice people's reaction to me in the dream. They're very afraid of me. It could be that I'm dreaming Mothman's dreams.

SM: In just about every dream I have, I'm flying at one point or another.

AC: In Gray Barker's *Silver Bridge*, he actually wrote some chapters where he describes it the same way. He feels that he somehow has a psychic connection to the Mothman.

SM: Well, you know, some people don't have flying dreams at all... Sometimes you'll talk about flying in your dreams, and people look at you like you're crazy. They've never done it. Yet other people do it all the time. There's some difference that makes some of us do it, and some not.

After a short break, Sharon's daughter entered the room and a slightly different discussion began. At the time, the two were living at the end of Patrick St. in Mound, where three large, white crosses have long been erected. The crosses face Blaine Island.

AC: We are at the crucial moment in the family dialogue. We turn to aspects of dream, and the symbolism of fire. A life in turmoil surrounded by fire... The interpretation of dreams... The cougar that keeps biting you... Tell me about that, Ariane.

[Sharon's daughter] Ariane Moore (AM): I kept having these dreams where there was a cougar. It would come up to me. I'd lie down and play dead. It would bite my neck a little, and then go away.

Harriet Plumbrook (HP): That's an animal guide contacting you.

AM: In one dream, it was futuristic. I had a laser and stuff, and I killed it.

AC: So in the dream, you killed the cougar?

AM: Yes.

HP: That could be exactly what the animal guide was trying to show her... If an animal repeatedly appears in your dreams, you're in a [time of] passage...

SM: She has a dream that she's lying in a plain bed, and the cougar is nipping at her. I think it means that she's too passive. She plays dead, instead of facing problems or hardship. She ignores it, and hopes that it will go away.

AC: Is that how you feel?

AM: Sometimes...

SM: So then she has an extra dream where she is older, in the future. She has a space gun, and she kills it. [My interpretation is that] she thinks that in the future, she'll be able to handle [things] better. And she's waiting for it.

AC: That sounds accurate. Is that close?

AM: Pretty much...

AC: Still, an "animal guide" could be trying to relay that very message, through an animal to which Ariane feels close. Sharon, are you still affected by your birdman, or "batman," encounter?

SM: I scream all the time in my sleep. Everyone knows... In the middle of the night, I'll just scream – perhaps with no reason – and run. Or I'll wake up in the kitchen or somewhere, and I'm screaming.

AM: *[Soberly]* Or outside in your underwear...

SM: Yes, I walk. I still walk in my sleep quite a bit.

AC: You said that one night you encountered a caped being above you in bed. Can you talk about that?

SM: Well, I had two different experiences in the same week. I know Mom remembers this, because just before that we went to [a New Age shop] and got a rock that was supposed to enhance your psychic awareness. I had two different experiences in a week...

[Sharon's mother] Loretta Colvin (LC): That's the same thing that happened to me, remember Andy? I saw two things in a week...

SM: The first one was a little bit different [than a winged being]. First thing, I woke up in the middle of the night. I felt something was watching me. I looked to the door. And just as plain as you're sitting there [I saw what] looked like a large black man. His skin was *really* glistening, like he was oiled up or something. He was really muscular and had big brasslike bracelets on his wrist. He wore a loincloth type of thing. His head was the head of a bull, with horns and red eyes. All of my life I've seen [hard-to-believe] things and [unusual] people. But this one was one of the more scary ones... I looked at it. I looked at all of its features. Then I told it to go away. I basically looked at it and said, "I'm going to turn my head and when I look back, you're going to be gone because I don't want you here. There's no reason for you to be here." So I did it. Then I looked, and he was gone. Well, a couple of nights later, I woke up again. This time, I could feel something above me. I didn't look up right away because this one gave me a more ominous feeling. The bull was scary looking, but didn't really *frighten* me. This one did... I finally looked straight up. It was just like a cocoon. Like the shape of a cocoon... It was kind of like a bat hanging upside down. I couldn't see really detailed features. It was more that I could just see the outline. It was either a cocoon, or something like a bat. When I looked up at it, I could see that it was, like, connected to the ceiling... It was right in front of my face! It was probably four inches from my face. And though I couldn't see facial features, I could just feel it right *on* me. And I screamed! I screamed and I told it to do the same thing as the bull. I was like, "Go away! I don't want you there." And it left. But this one left a little bit differently. It was almost like it disappeared in front of my eyes, like it broke into little pieces and disintegrated. [This] was a little bit different from the bull thing. When I was a kid, I would see people in my room. I still do that when I move into a new apartment or something. A lot of times I'll wake up and I'll see somebody walking through the wall, or something like that. I can see who they are, their facial features. I usually have to do a ritual cleansing of the house, and just sanctify everything and tell everything, "This is not where I want you."

AC: What were some of the beings that you saw as a kid?

Sharon Moore, who saw Mothman in her bedroom not long before 9/11, Mound, WV

SM: A lot of times I would see shapes. This sounds kind of crazy probably, but they were like geometric shapes, floating. Like a pyramid or a triangle...

These sound like the geometric shapes seen by author Philip K. Dick.

AC: Were they lit up? Did they have a light source in them?

SM: Yes. I don't know if I ever told mom these stories or not. She probably wouldn't have believed me when I was little. This was like [from 1971 on] when we lived in Dunbar. I remember seeing them when I lived in the attic there. I was probably five or six, so I had just moved from Woodward Drive. I grew up always covering my head with the sheet and just making a little hole where I could breathe. Because I knew that if I uncovered my head I'd see something. Until I became an adult, I never slept with my head uncovered. If I were looking, I'd see something! A lot of times it almost looked like neon, like a glowing neon light. I'd look up and it'd be in the shape of a triangle. It would just float there. I would look at it, and watch it, and it would just disappear. Or, it would be a circle or a square. I don't know why. They never scared me, really. It was just something I saw. It was an attic with, like, a pointed ceiling and little doors... A lot of times I'd wake up and I'd feel something coming. Then, one of the doors would open. I'd have to run, close it and get back into bed, because I couldn't go to sleep with it open. It would just slowly open, all by itself. I'd wake up right before it would happen. These things would happen *a lot*, too. There were so many that I've forgotten a lot of them.

CHAPTER 29

I met the following witness, Ed Oundee, at the 2003 Mothman Festival in Pt. Pleasant. He and his mother had seen Mothman in southern Georgia, just a couple of years prior. They were so impressed by the experience that they had driven all the way to Pt. Pleasant to find out more. They were both lucid and utterly believable. Their worlds had been turned upside down, and they wanted answers. You could see them nervously reliving the emotional experience. John Keel brought some levity to the situation by chastising them for not getting it all on film.

Oundee, Ed – 2001 Mothman Sighting on FL Border – 2003

Ed Oundee (EO): My name is Ed Oundee. I live in northern Virginia. Back in 2001, last week of November, we were coming back from vacation in Florida. It was about 2, 2:30 at night. We were driving on I-95. We had just got into Georgia. My mom was driving. I was in the passenger seat. My dad was sleeping in the back. There were no other cars on the road, just us. Off in the distance, right in front on the highway, about 100 yards away from us, 30 yards up, we saw *the thing.* Very large, at least 200 to 300 pounds... It approached us straight on. Our high beams were on. It kept coming towards the car. My mom started to slow down because we didn't know what it was. It kept coming, coming, coming. Strange thing about it, there were no wings. It was just a body in the middle of the air. It came directly over the car.

Andy Colvin (AC): Could it perhaps have had wings that were folded back?

EO: Yes well, I didn't see them [on approach]. But [my mother] said she saw wings. I was always near-sighted. It went right over the car, about 30 feet right over the car. We got a good look at it. It was just like a body mass, like if a bear didn't have limbs or arms... Not unlike a statue... I think it looked like a butterfly. It passed over the car. As it passed over the car I turned around, because I wasn't driving. It [then] had these huge wings easily spanning 5 feet long on each side. Probably 10 feet altogether... It didn't flap its wings. It just kept going, just hovering, all the way across until we lost sight of the thing. My mom could tell you more. She has better vision. She got a better look at it. Her details might be a little bit different from mine, I have to say. It's been about a year and a half, and I've been searching for somebody to tell. There really is nothing out there [on this subject]. I'm interested more in UFOs. I caught a picture of [Mothman] on the *Sightings* website... Both of us said, "That's it. That's what we saw!" Then I found some kind of a lead. I finally found that there was something [going on] over here [in Pt. Pleasant]. So I wanted to talk to somebody to see if we weren't the only ones who saw it. [Maybe] we can come up with an idea of what it was. I have no clue what it was.

AC: How have you felt since then?

EO: It shocked me.

AC: Have you had any changes?

EO: It *did* change my perception of what was "out there." I mean I don't believe in monsters. I don't believe in angels and demons. But this thing just blew my mind away. I've told many people, and every time I talk about it I get scared. I get chills in my back. And I don't know what to do. I feel like crying...

Mrs. Oundee (MO): Yes, like Ed says, I was driving. We were saying, "Wow, it's only us on this road, nobody's coming or going." My husband fell asleep. We didn't want to wake him up... We turned the radio [down]. It was a clear night. And then we both saw something, but we couldn't tell [what it was]. I was just waiting for this thing to come over. It was flying... It was just coming toward us, without moving its wings or anything... We started shaking. I tried to slow down so I [would] have more time to see it. It was coming towards our car, very, very, very close. It was just this big *thing*. You know, it wasn't a bird and it wasn't a man. It was just a big "thing" with red eyes... Bright red eyes... I couldn't see if it had legs or a tail... When it came over here, it went up, went behind. It spread [its] wings wide and continued going [without flapping].

AC: It was sort of gliding?

MO: It was just *magnetic*. We talked about it and we said, "How can it fly?" It wasn't flying [it was] floating. [But] this body should have been heavy, because it was big.

EO: You could tell it was very heavy... At least 200 pounds...

MO: It wasn't coming [fast]. It was just slowly coming toward you. It passed by my car, and went above my car... So after that, we just looked at each other. I couldn't believe my eyes. I told him, "My eyes, my brain are refusing the idea that I saw something that big, flying without using wings." We talked to my husband, but it's hard for someone to believe you. We don't want to discuss it with other family [members] because they look at you [incredulously] like, "yeah, sure..."

EO: It was just like a torso and a lower body, with no extremities.

MO: Dark, with red eyes...

EO: It didn't have a head.

MO: No plane, not even a helicopter [could move that way]. No one can explain to us what it was.

AC: Assuming it's a Garuda, it's considered to be a deity in Buddhism. If you look at some of the ancient Buddhist paintings, they show [different] demigods [like Garuda] floating at the very tip-top, above the Buddha. At the entrance to the other world is the Garuda, the Mothman... He is [a depiction of] the being you encounter when you pass on.

MO: My father is Buddhist... So you recorded someone else who said the same thing [as us]?

AC: Yes, I've heard many stories like yours. I talked to somebody here yesterday who described the same body structure, the fact that the wings were tucked and did not seem to be there at first. It actually screamed at him. Consider yourself lucky because if it screams at you, it hurts your eardrums. Literally... He said he was a football field away from it. It screamed and he felt the scream *push the skin back on his face,* even from that distance. It was like a bomb had gone off. It just shook him to the very core... It came at him, just like it came at you (and me, when I saw it).

EO: We got a really good look at it for about 30 seconds.

MO: Yes, it came to us. It was so big that we thought, "If that thing goes down on top of the car, it will smash the car..."

AC: Yes and if someone shot it, it probably wouldn't be hurt. It hasn't happened yet with Mothman, but people have reportedly shot Bigfoots. The bullets actually seem to hit it and go in, but then the thing runs off. Everyone chases it but they can never find the body. The Bigfoots seemingly dematerialize.

EO: That's the best information that we've heard. I tried to focus as hard as I could on the face, but I couldn't get the face. I got the body but I couldn't get the face.

AC: Each person is going to see it slightly differently because it's not that it totally exists *out there.* In a sense it only exists because you're seeing it. Every person is going to shade it differently. One may see it with red eyes, and one may not...

MO: This statue [of Mothman in Pt. Pleasant] has legs. But we didn't see any legs...

AC: Very few people have seen the legs. That lady who was in here earlier saw legs. It came down on her car and crushed the hood.

EO: We drove seven hours to get here, just to talk to somebody else that saw this. We've been alone with this for a year and a half. I mean I have nightmares...

AC: What are your nightmares about?

EO: Oh, just general nightmares. But I've always had them since I was little... My nightmares deal with school, when I was in college, stuff like that. Normal stuff... But we've been in this alone. I've been telling people at work and nobody has any idea. Nobody... I've searched the Internet almost every single night for over a year and a half, trying to find somebody else, so we don't think we're crazy. We weren't sleeping. And we don't drink [alcohol].

MO: It came to you. It came to you.

EO: It's been like a thorn in my side for over a year. We didn't talk about it at all, until last winter. I didn't want to talk about it. She didn't want to talk about it. It didn't make sense to us. It didn't make sense to anybody.

MO: We talked to my family. My sister, we told her… She says, "It's something that's hard to believe. Do you expect me to believe that?" I say, "Yes, because I *did* see it."

AC: So describe your interest in UFOs…

EO: Oh, I've been obsessed since I was a little boy with the idea of other beings outside of this world... I've always wanted to see a UFO. I didn't want to see this thing here… I mean this blew my mind away.

AC: FYI, you may start experiencing flashes of "knowing" what's going to happen next.

EO: I've always had that, my entire life.

AC: Any prophecy?

EO: Not prophecies. I have dreams of places I've never been to… Then six months, a year, two years down the road, I say, "Mom, did I ever tell you about that dream [of] that place I've never been to?" We'd be in some place like on a cruise or somewhere far. I remember in San Diego [that happened]. It was the first time [I ever saw it, but I had to say] "My god! I had a dream about this!" It's different from deja vu. [In my case] I have a dream that I remember [right after having it]. I think, "I've never been there before." Then I tell somebody. And then sometime in the future, it happens.

MO: It feels much, much better [knowing that we aren't alone].

EO: At least you [confirmed for] us that there *are* other people out there who've seen it recently. *[turns to Sharon Moore]* I mean you saw it too, right?

Sharon Moore (SM): It was above my bed, hanging upside down like a bat. *[gestures]* About this close to my face...

EO: Even more scary... I don't want *that* in *my* room.

SM: I wasn't scared. I just wanted it to go away. I turned my head and when I looked [again] it was gone.

MO: Was it flying?

SM: No, it was hanging like it was a bat, with its wings tucked up. Its face was right against mine. It was black. Strangely, it was more like a shadow. It didn't really have a lot of detail to it.

AC: It's showing you your fears. It's making you confront your fears.

MO: It's more like a ghost. [In] Florida we were watching the news that somebody had taped a ghost in Oklahoma, on a police video. We were talking about this in the car [when we saw Mothman].

AC: At that very time?

MO: [Yes] at that time!

EO: Right before we saw it, I told her, "My gosh, it's like the *Twilight Zone* or something. We're in the middle of nowhere..."

AC: So you were feeling it coming on... You probably *did* enter an alternate space-time zone...

EO: We *did* say it was like the *Twilight Zone*, because there was nobody there. No cars...

AC: I heard another story like yours, where the witness was driving towards Ripley, WV, on the new interstate. He feels like he's in the *Twilight Zone*. Things appear on the road. And he drives *through* them. A tree appears right in the middle of the road, and he drives through the tree. That's why I'm saying that these entities are not totally there. They *are* there, but only for a short time. They're sort of loosely put together, so one *can* at times pass through them.

MO: But I think it was a body, for real. Otherwise it would have gone through us!

AC: Yes, maybe, but it can dissolve soon after you see it. You may catch it in mid-stream. It can go from invisible to solid, and you can catch it anywhere in between. It may or may not physically affect you.

SM: Absolutely... It can disappear...

MO: That's the only explanation! [It's] got to be a ghost. Got to be a ghost, you know?

EO: [Yes] because it didn't have any wings when we first saw it. It was floating in the air. So that had to be [against physics]. Andy's explanation is the best... It was something that's not [entirely] physical. If it's physical, it has to have some kind of propulsion. Some kind of [flapping] wings, or legs... Something to keep it up in the air... [The evidence of propulsion] only happened *after* it passed the car. *Then* it had wings...

"So what do I mean when I say that our souls live on after death? To [use a] computer metaphor, we are born with an initial program, whatever has caused us to be born as we are gives us something to start out with - tendencies, inclinations, and talents. From that point on, we are like blank disks greedily storing input and data with each passing day. In time, our operating system is established. And then what? When the time comes to us to pass on, is that program - all that we have hoped for, loved and hated - gone? Of course it isn't. But neither is that program entirely functional. It is like a recording on a CD; while it does exist, it can do nothing by itself. [It needs a player or other] means to operate... Whether we live one life or reincarnate is not for me to say. But I do know that we continue on, and I do know that, for a length of time commanded by whatever forces in the Universe govern such things, each of us will exist as the simple spirit described above. Like a CD or a videotape, every part of us is there, waiting... Each of us is interconnected with the awareness of all other - we are in fact, part of one mass consciousness, as Jung predicted."

-Kosta Danaos, *Nei Kung: The Secret Teachings of the Warrior Sages*, p. 67.

Danaos was one of only five Western students chosen to study Nei Kung, a form of Buddhist meditation designed to increase ones power by storing up yin earth energy in the belly. Practitioners use Garuda kriss knives to speak with spirits, and have been filmed doing things that defy the laws of physics.

CHAPTER 30

"He who binds to himself to Joy,
Does the winged life destroy;
He who kisses the Joy as it flies,
Lives in Eternity's sunrise."

-William Blake

Colvin, Andy – Grassy Knoll Radio interview 6 – May 2006

"Vyz" on Grassy Knoll (GK): This is the Grassy Knoll on AM1610 WDCX. We have with us for our sixth segment, Andrew Colvin. He is the documentary filmmaker; the title is *The Mothman's Photographer*. We've talked about a lot in the five hours that we've had. To me, this is ever so more labyrinthine than the Kennedy assassination and all the personages involved in that. [Although] what we're talking about *also* relates to the Kennedy assassination. It's almost like the Kevin Bacon thing again. All roads lead to JFK. Andrew, thank you for coming back to the Grassy Knoll. I appreciate the time you've spent with us.

Andy Colvin (AC): Thank you, Vyz.

GK: I'm going to say something. Take it for what it's worth. Once upon a time, Andrew, I wanted to get onto this show all the guests that everybody *else* had on. I [later] said to myself, "It's nice that you want to run with the dogs, but what are you getting done?" Understand what I'm saying here. What I started to look for are people that have not been necessarily heard, but *should* be heard and have a greater venue. I started looking for people who haven't been talked about all that much. Now one might say, "Well, that [makes it] easier for you to get guests on," but they're very worthy [guests who just happen] to not have a stage. So when you wrote to me about Levenda, I didn't know if you were fishing to come on [or not]. But I certainly said, "Why don't you come on?" And you said, "okay." Here's the thing... I didn't have you on because you had some strange story that should be on Coast to Coast, but because I really do believe you've hit on something which I've always thought was out there. And that is the activity not only around the Mothman, but also in that whole area of West Virginia... I'm glad you came on. I hope you go on and on in other shows, and stay to the veracity with which you've portrayed the other [five] segments. Stay true to that... I think you will. I'm very glad that you're here. If you cut your teeth on our show and go on to some other place and get more business, that's good. I think that's really important, and I hope you do that. But I'm glad you're here. I'm glad we had the time that we did. If we don't do any more beyond these [six] hours, I wouldn't consider myself cheated [nor would] the audience... We worked through this labyrinthine situation... I think it's a great learning experience for both of us. I think the audience appreciates the honesty and the connecting of dots... I hope you're glad that you've spent the time with us.

AC: Oh yes, I have. It's been great.

GK: So, you know, whatever happens afterwards, that's fine. But I think you've been legitimate, and I think you have a great story. We could do *17 volumes*, the way this thing's going.

Vyz's prophecy turned out to be true, because we actually did end up doing 17 volumes of the show in 2006.

GK: So anyway, be that as it may... I'm off my soapbox. We're back to normal again. You've got a couple of bullet points that you want to speak to, some errata?

AC: Yes, thanks. Well, I've got... There's a noise there.

GK: *[laughs]* There's always a noise...

AC: Did you hear that?

GK: No, it's on your end.

AC: It blew my ears out.

GK: *[sarcastically]* It's the NSA listening on your end, brother, not mine.

AC: *[looks at caller ID]* It's this "SRI Research Company" that tends to call while I'm on the phone with you. I'm serious... It's happened three times now.

GK: Well, give them my number and we'll talk amongst ourselves. Alright bro,' go ahead...

AC: Well, I wanted to start off with a "shout-out." I haven't done any of that, but I want to in this case. My niece's daughter just had surgery. She's a budding young Mothman investigator. Her name is Ariane Moore. She's in West Virginia. She is actually in the same hospital where the trapped miner is now in a coma...

GK: I hate to admit this, but in the few days that we've done this, there was a third [mining incident] in West Virginia. There were three. We were wondering if the other shoe would drop.

AC: Right!

GK: Be that as it may, it certainly happened (the third).

AC: Ariane is the daughter of Sharon Moore. Sharon is in the video series. She saw Mothman in her bedroom around the time of 9/11. She saw a Moloch-like satyr that same week. Sharon also saw these glowing numbers in her room, in the early 1970s, which were very similar to what Philip K. Dick and John Lilly were seeing then. Sharon and Ariane help me when I go back to film. They're sort of my crew, and they also help with product sales and so forth at the Mothman festival. So I wanted to thank them. It makes me want to bring up a little point about hospital care, since we're on that subject. There's a lot of cancer in West Virginia, and obviously it has something to do with all the toxins that are coming out of the chemical plants. WV has all the major players like Dow, Monsanto, FMC, Rhone-Poulenc, Bayer, Union Carbide, Diamond Shamrock, Sinclair, and Dupont. Dupont operated the TNT area when explosives were being manufactured there. Dupont is the same company on whose property we had these Philadelphia Experiment veterans bursting into flames and disappearing.

Edward Haslam's research shows that corrupted polio vaccines caused the recent spike in soft-tissue cancers. Cancer is basically a virus that thrives on lowered immunity. Toxins lower the immune system so that viruses can flourish. In the 1950s, this was well known, but it has since been suppressed and forgotten. There were tangible connections between Ochsner, the man responsible for selling people on the bad vaccines, and Dupont. Ochsner also had a relationship with Maytag, a CIA-friendly appliance company within the realm of Tad Jones and Woody Derenberger. Additionally, Ochsner was a consultant for the US Army.

GK: Just as a little sidebar… There was a book written about Dupont called *The Nylon Curtain*. It actually got a mainstream publisher, and then all of a sudden it was what they call "privished." In other words, the publisher went ahead with it but they gave no public [support]. No PR, nothing… In other words, they published the thing and let it die. [It] was absolutely eviscerated. You can read about that story in the book *Into the Buzzsaw,* edited by Christina Borgeson…

AC: We have another witness in the video that worked for Dupont for 30 years, in Delaware. She saw a UFO. She is married to my brother. They both saw a large, black, discoid UFO out in Delaware.

GK: That's a good source…

AC: But the WV cancer scandal… I think the way they keep the lid on all the cancer is through the insurance companies. It dawned on me that this is what's going on. When I was deciding where to go to college, we knew a couple of players in the WV insurance world. A couple of families... I went to a meeting at the country club. I was more or less from the wrong side of the tracks, but I had friends who were members of the country club. I was in the accelerated classes at school. I remember a fraternity preparatory meeting for guys that were going to WV University. It was kind of the proverbial "we're giving you the opportunity to be set for life" deal. It was for real... It was a biased yet definitive social mechanism, like the phony National Merit Scholar debates I took part in. I remember standing in the soft glow of the country club thinking, "Okay, this is the point in life where I make that decision... Do I want to stay here with these guys and be a big fish in a small pond, or do I want to go out and see the world?" I eventually made the decision to go away. But it was an insurance guy leading this whole thing. We recently had a big problem in West Virginia with doctors and insurance, right? A lot of doctors were severely disgruntled. I think they even went "on strike," if I remember correctly. It was a big story back when the malpractice rates shot up. Do you remember that?

GK: Oh yes, sure.

AC: Doctors were moving out of West Virginia to neighboring states. I had a relative who was studying to be a doctor, who decided to go into Virginia to study. Apparently the osteopathic schools are better there. One of the guys he went to school with had a dad in the Agency. Someone had gotten hold of this disc that you can put into any computer, which allows you to change whatever information you want, without knowing any passwords. It will leave no trace. I think there was some joke made about them changing grades in the school computer. I don't know if it was really a joke or not, but...

GK: I'll go for that.

AC: That's just a little fun point... I think what they did in West Virginia, though, was they put pressure on the doctors *through* the insurance companies. I'll bet you that everything is tied to whether or not the doctors are playing ball with the chemical companies. I really think that *that's* where it all comes together. If your father is dying of a rare cancer there, you don't really get any support for getting to the bottom of why he has it. If he works at one of these companies, you kind of get stonewalled. And it wouldn't happen unless the doctors went along with it. And this is how they're made to go along with it, I think. They're probably given sweetheart deals on insurance *if* they play ball.

GK: Oh yes, I had a good friend who was a doctor. Back in the 1980s, he said, "The doctors, the good old GPs, the guys we trust like Marcus Welby *all* want to see something different, but our voices are just so loud." It is very difficult to beat at the bastion of the pharmaceutical-medical-hospital complex. You know what I mean? So you do have voices of reason out there. Unless they want to fall on the stakes themselves, they'll find themselves howling at the moon, and nothing more. So I agree with you 100%. I do believe there are a lot of physicians out there who want to do it the [right] way. But they're just so obstructed that it is not – let's be honest – going to happen.

AC: We mustn't forget the pharmaceuticals... An outgrowth of the oil companies... The Nazi flight capital that came out after the war, a lot of that went into the pharmaceuticals. Big Pharma is putting pressure on doctors as well. Getting back to the miners for just a second... When you have these mining stories, there's all this focus towards the miners. That's understandable... Mining is a gutsy profession and these guys *do* die of black lung...

GK: Very hazardous. No doubt...

AC: But I think it is focused on by the media because it reinforces the stereotypes they prefer. It takes the focus off of other issues, like these people who are dying from working in the chemical plants. Or in industry, in general... I mean the West Virginia chemical workers *should* be among those whom the rest of the world sees. They *should* get equal time, because these people are working in really difficult situations. I have a cousin who works with the "Bhopal Gas," the same gas that killed everyone in Bhopal, India. She actually handles this stuff through a glass enclosure with sealed rubber arm-gloves. There's no doubt that there's a super-high cancer rate there. I'd like to bring a little more awareness to that, in any way that I can...

GK: Well, you can have all the laws in place, but we all know the way things really work and that is, "shut up if you want a job." This is nothing new, and nothing's really changed. They can make all the laws they want in the world, but if they don't enforce them, it doesn't mean [anything].

AC: My heart goes out to the families involved with the Sago mining disaster, that were given false reports of miners surviving. Unfortunately, I think the media made use of it to divert from some other things that were going on. You see someone like Coretta Scott King die, and you see Bush there. It's great that he's paying respects and everything, but when you look at some of the things that have been done by his pals to the Black community, there appears to be some hypocrisy evident.

GK: Hypocrisy is us: U.S.

AC: There are a lot of diversions that go on. But while we're on the subject of the chemical plants, one little detail about the art-CIA angle is… Once Union Carbide merged with Dow, suddenly you had an "art lady" in control of Carbide. The woman who presumably owns a big chunk of Dow is a big art maven on the West Coast. She's Dede Wilsey, and she pretty much runs the art world in San Francisco. I mention her because she's had a high profile recently. Her stepson, Sean, recently wrote a book about his life with her. It really paints an unflattering picture of this chemical heiress… Most of the time we think of art people as having certain sensibilities, perhaps PC or environmental sensibilities or whatever, but no! In reality, the people who own these chemical companies are running the art world. Texas rancher types…

GK: Jeez…

AC: I don't think people realize that there is an unbelievable amount of rigidity brought to bear on the artists. The artists are seen by the elites as needing the most control, if you will. The artists are often going around, flying off the handle, really exposing things and doing art about it… The art administrators put the hammer down on artists doing political art. I've had many negative experiences with the "official" art world…

GK: But you know, Andrew, I would say that a lot of the foundations that underwrite artistic works [are the real problem]. People ask, "Why aren't you contributing to PBS?" I'm going, "Why? The Carnegie foundation already is… The Rockefeller foundation already is… The Macarthur foundation already is… They're all pumping money in like crazy!" So these artists are – wouldn't you agree – grabbed by the shorthairs by these conglomerates? The artists are not free.

AC: Absolutely, they are not. It really came to bear in the '80s when I was in graduate school. Believe it or not, I dropped out with one class to go from getting my master's degree. It was a political protest. I stated what I was doing in my work, that it was a political protest against the conservative budget cuts at UT. At the time, I just felt like that was the right thing to do. They were cutting arts funding across the board. I lost my teaching assistantship due to cuts. Reagan/Bush put the hammer down as soon as they got re-elected. That was it for me. I was furious. But there was no other protest to speak of. Everyone went along with the plan. I couldn't take it anymore… You know, I thought my protest was even better because I was only one class away. That made it mean something… I think people understood that I was serious about my position.

My work on the subject of budget cuts was taken down, and more or less held for ransom by the Dean. I refused to go pick up the art until it was returned to the university display gallery where it was originally taken down. The administration wouldn't budge, and neither would I. I let the university keep the artworks.

GK: Andrew, not to get into my life but I tell you what… I went halfway through a Masters in journalism, an M.S. degree over at Ohio U. in Athens… I had already worked for a newspaper (the Rutland Herald) and a couple of other places. I was [thinking] "*This* isn't journalism. This is, like, something *about* journalism." I hated it. I absolutely hated academia, and I left. I understand exactly what you mean because "reality" and what you're being taught in graduate school are always – not sometimes – two different things.

AC: I think my protest actually spurred me on to continue to work. I know so many "good" students who got their degrees and then stopped doing art. I felt like I had something to prove after that. So I've continued to work. If you're interested in reading about the art topic, I suggest people read Eugenia Macer-Story. She has several books that touch on the paranormal and the world of the arts. She bridges the occult, art, and UFOs. She is a great UFO researcher and painter. She has also written several plays, and even runs a magic shop in NYC. She has a lot of occultish things happening in her life. She's developed this theory that there are these real, live occultists out there who are trying to play tricks on UFO researchers. This would be similar to the stuff that was happening to John Keel.

Macer-Story even mentions that while she was first reading Keel's research, she got a threatening phone call on the street in NYC that was meant to frighten her. It had the effect of turning her off to Keel's research for many years, as it falsely made it seem as if Keel was connected to something diabolical. This is reminiscent of a fringe within the cryptozoology movement – itself of creation of British and American intelligence assets – that has tried to link Keel to all things demonic. The cryptofringe repeatedly suggest that Keel was the first to blend the Mothman with the dark forebodings of Indrid Cold, the Men in Black, and the Death Curse, when in fact it was Gray Barker who first melded such things together. There seems to be an underlying fear on the outskirts that simply writing or theorizing about a subject can cause some sort of occult phenomena, or untenable mind control. Sounds more plausible on Madison Ave. than Woodward Drive…

AC: The Keelian stuff was happening to Macer-Story. She was very detailed in the way she documented it. She gives the reader an amazing day-by-day rundown of these little things that *can't* just be coincidence. She's even got some great photos of things. She takes photos of these occultists that follow her. Various provocateurs have tried to get her ensnared in different things, yet she's always ready. She's a great warrior, if you will, in this occultic "good vs. evil" fight. She's got some strange photos of paranormal things happening right in front of the camera. It's an amazing body of work. One of the ideas she talks about is that Yale University seems to be the center of an occult art conspiracy. I've found this to be true in my experience. I had different professors along the way who were from Yale. They all gave me a hard time as soon as they found out that I was into the spiritual realm. The bias was just *so* definite… I throw that out because that's where Skull and Bones is from…

One UT professor, who had graduated from Yale, went so far as to penalize me for turning in a term paper five minutes late. I had finished the paper on time, even though one of my best friends had been tragically killed in a car accident that week. Despite my fragile state, he mocked me and told me that I was welcome to sue him, or the university. He threatened to fight me "all the way up the ladder." Since I was working two jobs and practically sleeping in my van to get by, he knew there was nothing I could do about it. Ironically, he was an expert in Hindu religious art, province of the Garuda.

GK: You can't find an institution more embedded with quasi-occult fraternities than Yale, with Skull and Bones (and others beyond that). You're right…

AC: I can start jumping around here with little points that I should have mentioned earlier. The woman who contacted me regarding the chair image that I had made… The Chair related to my dad and Montauk, if you will recall. I had gone to see her after we carried the white bird at the 1982 Anti-Nuke Rally. We also had a weird encounter in the forest on that trip. It seemed to be a Bigfoot. We didn't see it, but there was something there. It seemed invisible. That's the best way I can describe it. It was walking, and you could see the brush parting. It was banging sticks. Our hair stood up and we were just terrified. Unbelievable… We were up in Bear Mountain, which is in New York…

GK: Hold on. I've got to stop you, Andrew. You were up on Bear Mountain, New York?

AC: We were traveling through to Massachusetts from New York, and stopped there to camp.

GK: So this happened up in the Hudson Valley of New York?

AC: Yes, my uncle lives in Peekskill. We were on our way to see him. He lives right near the big nuclear plant there.

GK: Yes, it's Indian Point...

AC: Yes... One will tend to have paranormal encounters like this in series. There'll be two or three coincidences or encounters. These seemingly bring your attention to something. That's kind of how it works. I was reviewing some of Dr. John Lilly's stuff and found out that he had a whole cosmology kind of built around this idea of following coincidences. He even had a name for it, ECCO. It was like a control system, using synchronicity to inform and benefit mankind. Interestingly, Lilly identified a negative force that he realized was fighting the ECCO, called SSI (Solid-State Intelligence). He realized at some point that SSI was a human-based, electromagnetic mind-control system. Lilly was having strange things happen around 1973-74, like we did... One thing I wanted to mention about Geshe Kelsang's battle with the Dalai Lama. Kelsang has decided to have all his books printed in Chinese. He has over 40 books, probably more than the Dalai Lama. The Dalai Lama is kind of soft and gooey. Kelsang is sharp and defined. Kelsang's books really lay out the doctrine, telling you exactly what you need to do if you want to reach enlightenment in the traditional way. He says, "Here it is, 1, 2, 3, 4." He puts it out straight from the ancient belief system. His Kadampa books are now being printed in Chinese. This is a really big deal, because China has been fighting the Tibetans all the way. Suddenly, they're making a deal and allowing Kelsang to publish. He seems to think there's no reason to keep the "supernatural" Garuda teachings under further wraps when it could benefit millions of people. Here is another weird coincidence... Kelsang has a church here in Seattle. A woman who worked for John Lilly is now a priest in Kelsang's church. She told me that a lot of practitioners in Kelsang's group seem to be reincarnations of monks from Tibet who were killed by the Chinese in 1959. She said I had the "Kadampa imprint." There was a big slaughter by the Chinese that occurred in 1959. Thousands of monks were killed. I was born that year. She was suggesting that I had perhaps been one of these monks. There's a whole belief in Buddhism that you can direct your consciousness after you die. If you work hard at honing your skills, you can literally decide which parents you are going to be born to next. You can choose your parents beforehand. This sounds crazy to us in the West, but over there in these different sects, it's...

GK: Common knowledge...

AC: As you might expect, it is said that Kelsang has already chosen where he's going to be reincarnated. He already knows which couple that he's going to be born to after he dies. This relates to the Mothman in that we may have had a lot of monks deciding to be reborn in certain mountainous parts of our country, like WV.

The monks reportedly came here in order to get away from the Chinese. This might explain why "Oriental" MIBs were dogging Mothman witnesses with young children. The Oriental Men in Black may have been Chinese agents, sent to abduct reincarnated monks from Tibet. This process would have been of major interest to former Nazis involved in secret societies and to the Russians, who are heavily into the paranormal. It might explain why I remember our Woodward Drive MIBs as seeming to have both German and Russian characteristics.

AC: I asked the priest if a "reincarnation to America" trend was happening. She said definitely that it was. She said a lot of people in the Kadampa community feel that this is what happened to them. Or what they made happen... She said that the globes of light that people see in proximity to Mothman and Bigfoot are, or at least *can* be, the spirits of dead people. The more advanced the person was, or the more powers they had developed through meditation, the brighter their light would be.

GK: Would that mean that the Bigfoots are past souls? We think of Bigfoot as something detached from human beings. Is the scenario that you're laying out – according to [Tantric] paradigm – that these might have been past souls, manifestations of past human beings?

AC: She was talking about lights and the souls of people, not Bigfoot. Seeing lights as spirits is a common practice in Appalachia. It's not just limited to Buddhists. Some of these balls of light seem intelligent and will interact with you. Keel was in fact doing that, with a flashlight. These are energies that are often interpreted as being connected to a person who's in "transition," or between lives. But it could be more complicated than that.

The Chinese were still killing monks in 1966, at the time of the UFO sightings in Mound and Pt. Pleasant... The red-eyed creatures apparently do inhabit the same realm as the lights. They are often seen in conjunction with the lights. Sometimes these monsters are even seen carrying the lights, or "mound stars." The Garuda is often depicted as carrying a sphere of energy. Uri Geller was constantly telepathing to mysterious lights and UFOs. A star of the popular "YouTube" website, the mysterious Prophet Yahweh, successfully calls UFOs today, usually with video cameras rolling. I interviewed several witnesses who had experiences with recently deceased people and anomalous lights. Since many Bigfoot are described as having human characteristics, it is possible that they might manifest as lights, too, when they die. As a teenager, I had many strange dreams of glowing Bigfoots carrying crystal balls. In the dreams, they seemed to telepath to me.

In June 2007, a UFO channeler who had previously performed a psychic reading of my house asked me if I wanted a free energy healing treatment. At a crucial time in the treatment, I was envisioning Woodward Dr. and a satori experience I had there. This experience had helped me through my father's death. Following the session, I asked the channeler to describe any visions she had seen. To my amazement, she described the scene I had been remembering in detail, including the emotional aspects I had been feeling. Strangely, she added a detail I had not noticed, which was that a bat-human hybrid was watching from the background. Suddenly, I then remembered a vivid dream I had once had of Mothman in that same location. I began to sense that perhaps Mothman had been guiding my satori experiences all along, in order that I might better handle difficulties. Before the session was over, I myself saw a vision - of the psychic in a cornfield near railroad tracks, and at an "emerald" lake next to a mountain. When I described these to her, she knew exactly what the correlation was. They had to do with moving forward from a grievous loss she had experienced.

AC: One related example is my niece Sharon. She had a dream that she was flying into her mother's womb while her parents were copulating. It was so vivid that it seemed real. She noted the details, went to her mother, and told her the details. Her mother burst into tears because that's exactly what had happened... The place, all the details... Sharon had a vision of her birth. This is a real thing. Understanding the Buddhist worldview is difficult, I admit. It takes a while, but once you get it, it does make a lot of sense. At least in terms of seeing the body as an energy bundle... There's this consciousness that pervades the universe. It coalesces in places, and forms things. It forms sunlight, trees, rocks, water, and the human body from the same constituent parts. It animates those parts. Everything is made up of the same basic...

GK: Molecular structure...

AC: Yes. To abruptly switch gears... Believe it or not, a psychic predicted the identity of the Manson family, right after the murders... And the same guy predicted the Silver Bridge collapse. Did you know that? He did both on the radio.

GK: Okay, tell me about this.

AC: His name is Joseph DeLouise. He has a book called *Psychic Mission*.

He was a radio psychic who was friends with the famous psychic Peter Hurkos. Hurkos' powers, by the way, were lab-tested by both Puharich and Bigfoot hunter Tom Slick. DeLouise was famous in the Midwest in the 1960s. DeLouise predicted the collapse of the Silver Bridge. He was seeing visions of it two weeks before. He talked about it in depth, on the air. He even saw the floating Christmas packages. He did it on the radio in Gary, Indiana. It's documented... He even saw license plates of certain cars that fell in the river. After the Manson murders, he got a vision of Charles "Tex" Watson, who had insinuated himself into Manson's family and committed the actual murders. DeLouise knew it was a guy named "Charles Watson." He actually went to the Tate home and got vibes from the house. The police acted very strangely in how they handled the whole deal. They didn't go after the clues he offered. It's almost like they knew it was Manson, but were letting him stay out to do some other things. Manson reportedly was a police informant.

GK: But Andrew let me ask you this... I'm not letting Manson off the hook, but they were saying that they could not connect Manson to *any* thrusting of a knife into anybody. The whole thing seemed concocted. It was a strange, strange situation. Do you agree with that? I'm not discounting the fact that he was wacked [out].

AC: Yes. The interesting thing for me, personally, is that DeLouise's grandmother and *my* grandmother were from the same part of southern Italy. He says that there are a lot of psychic women in that part of Italy. The Italians are on my dad's side, but you've got the same thing on my mother's side. My mother is from around Devil's Hollow in Jackson County, WV. That's a psychic area near the acknowledged UFO hotbed of Ripley... Actually, Harriet's mom was right across the county line from my mom. They were about five miles from each other... One in one county, one in the other... There are a lot of women in central West Virginia who have these psychic powers. Moving along to another piece of information, one of the things John Lilly discovered was that a certain dose of Vitamin K, or Ketamine, causes the human brain to see specific kinds of entities. Lilly was experimenting with Ketamine. I've never tried it, but it's hallucinogenic. My Buddhist priest friend, the one who was once Lilly's assistant, actually took this Ketamine under laboratory conditions. She told me what happened, and what it was like. Lilly found that if you took it at a certain dose, you would hallucinate "aliens." You would literally see the typical grey alien. This is also paralleled in the telemetric laboratory work of Michael Persinger, and in the UFO research of Albert Budden. Budden's the UFO researcher who wrote a book about the electromagnetic part of the phenomenon, called *The Electromagnetic*

Indictment. He did a twelve-year study in Britain that found that when you get around magnetic sources like gravel pits, high-tension wires, power plants, and so forth, you tend to have a higher rate of paranormal experience. Also you will see more singular, idiosyncratic forms of entities that are totally one-of-a-kind. Budden cited Persinger's research with electromagnetic waves. Persinger found that when the brain is hit with certain frequencies, it hallucinates aliens. So it's not just chemically that aliens can be induced, but also electromagnetically. It's an electrochemical process by which the brain sees these visions.

Persinger reportedly worked on a still-classified MK-Ultra project called SLEEPING BEAUTY, involving the use of "telemetric electromagnetic waves" that could cause both real or imagined "childhood memories." The name alone suggests that unwitting victims may have been dosed with waves while sleeping. Given that we now know that alien visions (as well as cancer) can be induced by this method, one can see that it is likely that some recent "UFO abductions" are entirely synthetic. On the other hand, visions of birdmen like Mothman have been going on for centuries, long before the advent of such technology.

GK: Adam Gorightly talked about those who use amphetamines for whatever purposes so, yes, you're right on the same track.

AC: I've been listening to some Keel tapes. In recent years, he has started talking more about the government surveillance on him. He talked about it in his Mothman book, but it was edited to be somewhat vague. He has come out more with the fact that the government *did* tap people's phones and *did* harass UFO researchers. One of the things that they were doing in West Virginia at the time of Mothman was photographing houses and children. You'd be at home with your kids. The Men in Black would show up and take photos of your house and/or kids, and then never show up again. After taking the photos, they would just take off and never come back.

GK: "Sears" home photos?

AC: They were stalking children, too. This activity could have been an Operation CHAOS-type program for harassing potential progressives. No one's really studied the sociopolitical backgrounds of the Mothman/ UFO witnesses, whether they were union activists or not. Or if they were upsetting the status quo in some way at the office...

GK: That's a really good point. Has anyone ever really talked to them? And if they did, did they get anything out of any union organizers that felt targeted?

AC: Well a lot of people died (i.e. rare cancer, "lightning strike," car accident) or disappeared completely.

Mae Brussell and others reported that laser-type firearms, with ranges of up to a mile or two, were developed around the time of Mothman. Could it be that some of the ubiquitous "lightning strike" victims mentioned by Keel were actually killed by handheld laser guns?

AC: Keel told me this. He's talked about it in different forums, that there were people disappearing... A lot of teenagers, a lot of young people... He says that a lot of them were connected to the Braxton County Monster, which is not to be confused with the Flatwoods Monster. A lot of people confuse the Braxton County Monster, a Bigfoot-like creature, with the Flatwoods Monster, a robotic, alien creature from 1952. It's probably because Flatwoods is in Braxton County... The Braxton County Monster kind of went all the way through from the 1950s to beyond the Mothman era. People were seeing a Bigfoot-like creature. In those same areas, it seemed that people were also disappearing. Keel said that the police were keeping it quiet. He also said that in some of the later UFO flaps, like in '73-'74 and '78-'79, the police were being contacted by more Men in Black than ever before. The Men in Black seemed to be going to police *chiefs* and trying to coerce them in one form or another. This part of it could have been a government op. They seem to have been targeting police chiefs to make sure that any cases of disappearing rabble-rousers went uninvestigated.

In his 1979 "contactee" lecture, Keel espoused the view that WV officials were covering things up. He said that the identity of a local serial killer was an "open secret." Yet the young man involved was allowed to come and go from a mental institution (Lakin?), and was not arrested because he was from a wealthy family. The victims were written off because they more or less "had it coming."

GK: I'm definitely thinking of it from that point of view. But will you please go back to the two distinct "monsters" that were out there in that area, and what they were?

AC: Well, the first one was the Flatwoods Monster that occurred in '52. There were a series of UFO sightings at the same time, all over the Eastern seaboard. Coincidentally, one of the flight paths followed the same flight path as 9/11's Flight 77, over West Virginia. One of the UFO's supposedly landed. People saw a "robot." People got sick, and a dog died (but was never autopsied). It was big news. It landed in Flatwoods, WV, which is about 30 miles north of Charleston.

GK: Now I'm going to pump you for a reason that'll be obvious. Was that a strip that could handle a commercial airliner on touchdown?

AC: No, it just landed on a hilltop near the Elk River. The Elk River area is where the Mothman was first seen. There was no landing strip. It landed on a hill on a farm. People saw it crash land. They went up. There was this creature that floated out of it. It had red eyes and it was like a robotic thing. They found oily scrape marks the next day on the ground. Frank Feschino has written a book about it. The title of the book confuses the issue, unfortunately. He called the book *The Braxton County Monster: The Cover-up of the Flatwoods Monster Revealed*. Again, these are in reality two different monsters. But in this book you find out that they sent up an Army National Guard Intelligence Unit to investigate the Flatwoods landing. They were on the scene almost immediately that night, hiding in the woods. Remember, there were oily scrape marks found under the landing spot, evidence that they could have set the whole thing up. But getting back to the other monster... The Braxton County monster was, according to Keel, a Bigfoot-like monster that was seen all over eastern and central West Virginia. Even in Ohio... There are tons of these sightings even now. Keel basically thinks it's a Bigfoot... I twice had strange encounters in eastern West Virginia, when I was camping. In one case I saw a weird kangarooish animal that I had never seen before. It wasn't a Bigfoot. But in the other case, we were stalked all night in our tent by these screaming things. It sounded like a baby screaming, then a woman screaming. That's a common description of how a Bigfoot sounds. There were several of them. They moved around on the perimeter, where you couldn't see them. We huddled in our tent with a gun, terrified. A Bigfoot contactee recently told me, "Well, you had a gun. That's why they were hassling you." I don't know what to think about that.

GK: I'd rather have the gun. I'll take my chances.

AC: Here's a key thing I wanted to say, about the Immaculate Conception we had on Woodward Drive. It wasn't a birth. I wanted to reiterate that point. The person got pregnant without having sex, and then the fetus disappeared... The other thing was that we had some globs of jelly fall on our neighborhood in Woodward Drive. This "star shit" is famous in the world of Fortean phenomena. Some of it recently fell on Whidbey Island, WA, near the Navy base. We also heard some sonic booms in WV that were really unusual, plus we had the black panther sightings and the odd phone calls. All of his was in addition to the Mothman, UFOs, MIBs, and dancing lights. We had it all going on in that neighborhood.

GK: To tell you the truth, I'm a little envious. That sounds like a really great neighborhood to live in. Boy I tell you, we've covered a lot of ground. If you were to sum up the last six shows (and that's a little bit ominous to lay on you), what are we looking at? Is there something going on there? Was the X-Files right?

AC: Well, you have different key military facilities in the WV area. You have the Naval base listening to people's phone calls and guiding submarines. You have DISC (Defense Industrial Security Police), the Air Force Command, and NASA Security based there in southern Ohio, on the edges of Mothman country. You've got the helicopter base in KY, and key chemical plants and defense contractors in WV. But that's all separate from this ancient phenomenon that has spawned our greatest religions. The phenomenon uses creatures like the Mothman, Garuda, Thunderbird, and Bigfoot. They're almost the same creature in my mind. There are a whole host of paranormal and psychic phenomena that go along with them. All through history, you've had humans trying to tap into this phenomenon and understand it, learn from it. Some people who approach it are benevolent, some not. So what you've got now is an official sort of public/private financing of research into that phenomenon. They want to harness it and to use it for probably the wrong purposes. Remember, when you look at any particular part of this phenomenon you are not, as the natives say, seeing it all. You have to remain aware of just what you're looking at. Are you looking at the real phenomenon that's kind of neutral, perhaps beneficial, that inhabits the 8th Tower? Or are you looking at the lower seven towers, where people are trying to gain from it by exploiting others?

In 2006, I stumbled upon the work of Montauk researcher Peter Moon, who has found considerable evidence that the Moors from Europe predated the Native American population. In fact "America" comes from a Moorish name, Amexem. The Moors are believed to have understood and utilized the many mounds mistakenly attributed to Native Americans. The Moorish connection is kept secret. Today's Iraq War is just another in a long line of Muslim/Christian battles. This explains why the mounds were mowed down and occupied by Christian defense families like the Duponts. Supposedly the story about George Washington cutting down the cherry tree really refers to his selling out of the Moors during the founding of the US Constitution. A major symbol of the Moors is the cherry tree. The 15 or so interim "Constitutional Congress" presidents before Washington were almost all of mixed Moorish descent. Even Washington was part Moor, or Huguenot. He was a close friend of the Duponts, who later ran the TNT plant. Mothman's occupation of DuPont's TNT area seems to be a clue suggesting future vindication for the Moors, just as the Chief Cornstalk story seems to be about Mothman vindicating the Indians.

GK: Well I'll tell you what, this all began with you inquiring about Peter Levenda. But I thought you had (and I still think you have) a much better grip, and a much better story to tell. What you've brought to the surface is a dynamic and realistic background that warrants a lot of investigation and interest by our listeners.

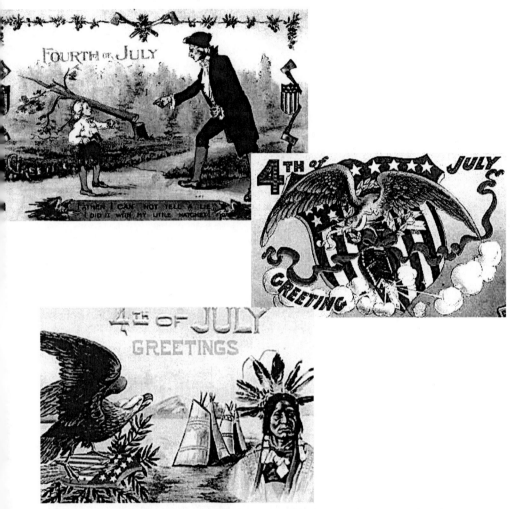

1908 Fourth of July postcard imagery derived from ancient Garuda symbols. Top image shows how George Washington's removal of the Moors' symbolic cherry tree with his "small" hatchet - indicative of a double-cross - helped build the new Masonic America, symbolized by the shield and winged hatchet. The middle image symbolizes Masonic mastery of the occult - the harnessing of the soul of ancient America. The lower image implies that the earth-worshipping Moors, symbolized by the crushed wreath lying the ground, were treated worse than the Native Americans, whose house remains.

CHAPTER 31

"When I examined these landing sites, usually the witnesses would describe something on three legs, on tripod legs. And we would find three depressions in the ground, where these tripod legs supposedly settled down. But then as I looked closer at these cases, I often found that there were two more depressions in the ground just like the first three, but some distance from the first three. We couldn't figure out if the thing only had three legs. Where were these other two depressions coming from? And then, as the '60s went on, they started playing games with these depressions. They said, "There's this nut (me) that's going around looking at holes in the ground. Let's give him some holes to remember." And so the holes in the ground became more and more complex. In one case that became very famous, the hole in the ground went down and then went this way [at a 90 degree angle]. You could dig it up and find that something had penetrated the earth in a horizontal direction… Crop circles have been around a long time. I was seeing them in Ohio and West Virginia in the 1960s. We didn't know what to make of them then. But now they're getting far more complex, just like our holes in the ground… Experts disagree as to what the designs really mean. But over and over again, we have games going on… It seems like somebody's having a lot of fun with this. It doesn't really have any meaning or purpose. I predict that after there's been sufficient furor over these circles, they'll stop, and something else will start up. We'll have a new mystery on our hands."

-John Keel, 1991 Lecture

Plumbrook, Harriet – Lake Hope/Camp Conley/SJ Moore's – 2002

Soon after I flew into Ohio in 2002, Harriet Plumbrook and I arrived at Lake Hope State Park. I was feeling jovial, as the depth and intensity of upcoming synchronicities was yet to sink in. It was easy, then, to crack jokes about the paranormal. Harriet and I were old friends from childhood. We had known each other in the crib, as they say. We had experienced many strange things as children, and had developed an odd sense of humor as a result. It's probably a coping mechanism of some kind… Harriet's father and my father were close friends. Both were military veterans, and both worked for defense contractors. Harriet's father survived the tumultuous times, while my father did not. Several of Harriet's family members were, and are, intelligence agents of varying stripes. When my documentary series was released on DVD in 2002, we were using her full real name. Unfortunately, this resulted in strange visits and threatening phone calls from Men In Black. We have since used a pseudonym for her in print and onscreen, in order to protect all concerned. When we first met up again in 2002, Harriet and I went to a campsite near Lake Hope in Ohio, where Harriet had seen a UFO in the 1980s. She described her sighting very matter-of-factly.

Harriet Plumbrook (HP): It was a circular object, with bluish lights all around it. So bright that it woke us up… It was like *lightning* that "stayed on." I jumped up and woke Chuck up. He said, "It's a *car.*" I said, "No, it's at the tree-tops." There was no sound, by the way. None at all… And instead of just shutting off, it faded out. You've got to understand that it was pitch black. No light at all… There was a glow to the area for a while after that. We kept hearing strange noises, like howling and screeching. Chuck claimed that he heard sticks breaking and thumping. The light was a blue you don't normally see. [It was] about 25 feet in diameter, is my guess. *[shivering]* Oh yes, *this* is where it happened.

I asked if she had experienced any "missing time." She recalled that in that day and age, no one knew about such things. Back then the thought of missing time simply never entered anyone's head.

HP: I just know that Chuck and I were sick the next day, like we had food poisoning. We were both sick to our stomach. But Kelly wasn't… And we *all* had eaten the same thing. Kelly did not see it. She was asleep. Dead asleep… She did not wake up. And it wasn't for lack of trying. We shook her and everything, to try and tell her. But she just wouldn't wake up. It was like she was dead.

As we prepared to drive out of the park, I mentioned that some people are not sensitive to paranormal phenomena and tend not to wake up, even though their unlucky mate might be up and about, interacting with whatever is there. I asked if she had heard a cracking sound at the outset, since that was what I had witnessed myself one night on Woodward Drive.

HP: Yes, that's what I think initially woke me up (as well as the light). I knew it was clear. The stars were out. I knew it couldn't be a storm. I'm a really light sleeper. Everything gets to me.

When we got into Harriet's Volvo, the conversation turned to Harriet's strong personal effect on electrical items, including her car.

HP: It took a long time for the engineers to figure out was wrong with the Volvo. I'd get all these messages on the instrument panel, telling me that something was wrong with it. But they couldn't find anything wrong with it. They checked all the relays. They tore apart the dashboard. They went through all bulbs and switches throughout the car. No problems whatsoever... When I went in for the diagnostic service, they emailed the engineers in Sweden. The only reply they got back was, "Some people are just like that. They have high electrical fields that disrupt the car's computer." Their final [analysis] was that I was causing it. They had seen it a few times from people with high electrical fields. When they told me this, I cracked up.

I jokingly asked Harriet if it was possible to purchase special insurance for potential damage she might do to electrical items. We talked about a bit of bad luck that Harriet ran into after she had her UFO sighting at Lake Hope. A possible occult "power object," a chicken bone, had been lodged in her tire. I wasn't yet aware that even my jokes would have synchronistic value. The interplay between tire companies, UFOs, and voodoo in the Mothman conspiracy would come up again and again in future months.

HP: Back there at the stop sign, the tire went flat. Chuck changes the tire; we take it to a gas station to get it patched and – lo and behold – what they pulled out of it was a *chicken bone.*

I joked that this proved UFO occupants like to throw chicken bones out of their vehicle, just like everyone else. The joke was on me when I realized I had left my pricey "Tri-Field EM Meter" at the haunted Hopewell Furnace, miles down the road. Luckily, the meter was still there when we drove back. I joked about the "ancient astronomers" who had built the furnaces, not realizing that years later I would find out that these same furnaces are part of the ancient knowledge system seemingly being revealed by Mothman. I joked about Indian feathers, outhouses (whose crescent moon is symbolic of the Moors), one lost glove, and V-8 can stuck in a wall, not realizing that every thought, object, and name I was encountering potentially held subtle clues. I was blind to the totalilty of the information being provided. We continued on to Pt. Pleasant, WV. Harriett gave an overview as we drove up Camp Conley Road, where so many of the famous Mothman sightings had taken place.

HP: This is where most of the UFO sightings were, at night. There used to be anywhere from five to ten sightings a night, from the period of 1966 to 1967, for a thirteen month period. Most of the families that lived here on Camp Conley Rd. moved away after the collapse of the Silver Bridge on Dec. 15, 1967. According to Keel, they were too traumatized to stay here after seeing that many UFOs per night. In the old days, the UFOs would follow the power lines all the way down to the river, where the power plant is. There were a couple of things in *The Mothman Prophecies* book that were incorrect, that kind of bothered me. But that may not have been Keel's fault. It could have been poor editing. It could have been anything. But these power lines weren't mentioned. They're not new. They've probably been here more than 35 years. And there is a massive power plant down there. It's huge, and it's never mentioned in the book. And since UFOs supposedly are sighted around power plants and power lines, it seems odd to me that that was never mentioned.

Next, we stopped by the Old Lakin State Mental Hospital, a creepy place with Mothman "sign" everywhere. It is right across the road from the New Lakin State Mental Hospital. In the old days, some of the doctors here were contacting Keel about UFO sightings "right over the hospital." Keel likes to joke that it wasn't the patients that were seeing UFOs, but the doctors. I noticed the phrase "Moth Bird 4 Ever" written in spray paint on the floor. "Death To All" was painted on a door. "Live or Die" and "Helter Skelter Lives," odd references to Charles Manson, were scrawled on the peeling plaster. Most chilling of all was the phrase, "I'm Watching," drawn below a bloodshot eyeball. The thought entered our heads that perhaps mind control experiments had taken place at this hospital. John Frick, a Maryland researcher who sometimes visits the area, would later make just such a claim on Bill Geist's "CBS Sunday" television show. Even though Frick only mentioned mind control as an extreme conspiracy theory that shouldn't be believed, his reference to it was mysteriously edited out in subsequent airings. Rumors still persist that MK-Ultra experiments were performed at Lakin on minority patients.

We drove on for about a half hour to Woodward Drive, where Harriet and I had grown up. Along the way we picked up "Fish" Ofeish, curator at what was then Sunrise Museum (now part of the new Clay Museum). Fish is an expert on creativity and learning. We wanted her to visit our elementary school and share her opinion on what may have been going on with the children on Woodward Drive. There had once been a Mothman sighting above Sunrise Museum, too, so I wanted to find out if she knew anything about that.

The first stop on Woodward Drive was the church and "medieval castle" at Zable Drive. I asked Harriet, who is a gifted psychic with "second sight," to give me her impressions of the castle. The first words out of her mouth were "it's haunted." I told her that at our high school reunion in 1987, I had interviewed several classmates in the yard next to the castle. The yard belonged to a classmate, Tracy Bailey, who now works at the Union Carbide plant a few blocks away. The plant is located where Woodward Dr. meets the Kanawha River. Longtime resident Donnie Fields stated in 1987 that the castle was "haunted by a witch who played organ late at night." As a teenager, I had heard the organ many times. I described to Harriet how Robert Godbey had told me, in 1987, about President Reagan's UFO sightings. Reagan biographers have since discussed some of these sightings. Reagan kept floating the idea that someday we all may need to "unite, if extra-terrestrials decide to attack earth." Harriet gave me her psychic impression of the haunted medieval castle on Zabel. She felt a "female presence" that was "a ghost," and the presence of a man who was "very much alive." I had not previously told Harriet of the "witch" who played organ. Harriet had moved away after 6th grade and did not know many of these details. We saw a neighbor, and Harriet asked her to explain about the castle.

Neighbor: There's a guy living there. He's about 60 years old. He's always lived there. His Mom and Dad used to live there. They used to own all this land. His mother passed on. Sometimes he seems strange, but he's really nice when you talk to him… People say a lot of strange things about him… I've been here five or six years. She used to play piano. You could hear it [everywhere]. I've heard a lot of things. He's got newspapers in there – stacked up to the ceilings – from way back. It's a mess. It's really not taken care of at all. He has really expensive stuff in there. Chandeliers and things…

Harriet had been correct about the presences in the house! Next, we drove about a block to the childhood home of Sara Jane Moore. I asked Harriet if she was picking up any "psychic reasons" why Sara Jane had taken a potshot at President Ford back in 1975.

HP: I think she was a bored, menopausal housewife who didn't have enough to do. Shooting Pres. Ford was the best way she could get attention. Growing up in this environment, kind of being a "nobody" in Charleston, WV [probably led her to need] some attention. She is always seeking attention.

I told Harriet that Sara, whose maiden name was Khan, had been a civil rights crusader when she was a young adult. She had led a protest to allow Marian Anderson to sing at the Charleston Opera House and stay at one of the "finer hotels" that then disallowed black guests. Ironically, Charleston, WV actually has a rich history of fostering progressive movements, such as black education and workers' rights. Booker T. Washington spent some important years there, and Mother Jones organized there. OSHA, the national agency overseeing worker safety, was formed as a result of the many deaths that occurred when Carbide was drilling the New River tunnel for its S. Charleston plant.

Harriet began picking up "bad vibes" from Sara Jane Moore's house. It is an old pioneer log cabin that has been there for decades. Our elementary school, Grandview, is next to it. I asked if the "bad vibes" that Harriet was feeling had to do with whatever made Sara Jane Moore later attempt assassination. All Harriet could say was that some of the vibes were very old, and some were very new.

We moved on to the Grandview building, where Harriet and I had attended 4th, 5th, and 6th grades. I started off with the most prominent thing I could remember about Grandview that might relate to Mothman. It was the fact that at one point, soon after we had taken IQ scores in conjunction with transferring schools, a film crew accompanied by an Air Force officer quizzed us. Harriet remembered this, and more...

HP: They were filming a documentary, actually. It was [being produced by] two "Ph.D. candidates." They were from an East Coast institution. I don't remember which one. But they had come here, and they were studying children of Appalachia. They had "heard" that there were some really bright kids here at Grandview.

Sara Jane Moore's House, Woodward Drive, Mound, WV

I asked Harriet if there could have been something going on, like genetic experimentation or tracking kids for future government service.

HP: Well, several of us had our IQ's tested here, and the rest of the general population of the school did not. They handpicked us and gave us IQ tests. *That* I distinctly remember. There were several "genius" IQs, which is unusual for the middle of Appalachia... Robert Godbey and I were pulled aside for special testing. They had separated Rob and I away from the group of other kids giving presentations. They kept us away from each other, as well. What they had me do was read a couple of pages of an encyclopedia, which was on Ethiopia. Then I was to get up to a black-board and draw a map of Ethiopia, and talk about it. And I did... I spit it back almost word-for-word. The woman said to her companion, "Oh my God, she has total recall." They had me sit down. They asked me a few more questions, like if I had any headaches or any other medical problems. Then they walked around me, and moved my hair away from my neck. They didn't say anything, but they pointed to the indentations that are in the back of my neck. *[shows two vampire-like scar marks to camera]* I was not born with these, by the way. There was no comment made in front of me about them...

"Fish" Ofiesh (FO): Harriet was not born with those two indentations on her neck?

AC: It's sort of like the X-Files, isn't it?

HP: I have no idea. [But] there were legitimate studies done on children back in the '60s. They said kids with higher IQs experienced more headaches. Robert has a higher IQ. I have a higher IQ...

FO: Robert has a *lot* of headaches.

HP: I have a history of them myself.

AC: I had two migraines last week...

HP: There were like five [genius] kids, but I know that they separated Rob and I.

AC: I helped Rob give his presentation. But they didn't seem too interested in my artistic abilities.

FO: You don't know who the other kids were?

HP: I don't remember...

FO: [Andy] do you have any idea?

One student was named David Hayson. Hayson lived right next to the Blaine Island Carbide plant, at the bottom of Woodward Drive. He died tragically, at age 11, of a rare form of leukemia. Was Hayson exposed to some chemicals, or perhaps to the radiation associated with UFOs, balls of light, or paranormal entities? Keels found these to be connected to a high white blood-cell count. As I mentioned, I myself had a dangerously high white cell count when I was 18, during the late '70s UFO flap in my neighborhood.

Safe with the belief that we were marginally intelligent, we toured the hallways of the school, which was then under reconstruction. The revolutionary "open classroom" design we had experienced as a result of Robert F. Kennedy's "Appalachian Project" funding had been rolled back. New walls had been built in order to create four smaller rooms instead of one big room. I recounted how I had come back to Grandview to vote in the early '80s, fifteen or so years after leaving it. As I voted, I saw all of the dinosaur drawings I had done years earlier, still hanging there. Soon after our Mothman encounters, I had somehow gained the ability to draw realistically, virtually overnight. As a testament of sorts to this strange development, my drawings still hung on the same mobile pegboard to which they had originally been pinned. Some of the same video equipment we had tinkered with as students was still in evidence as well. Having access to video equipment was almost unheard of in the late '60s. Robert Godbey and I had done "NASA" style presentations, which were broadcast over closed circuit TV.

I asked Harriet if she could "read" what Robert Godbey was now like. She had not seen him in 30 years. Harriet had already accurately described him physically, but I wanted more specific proof of her abilities. I asked her to describe any event she could from the trip Robert and I had taken to Egypt in 2000. Amazingly, she was able to "see" that I had restrained Robert, who is claustrophobic, while on a crowded train in Cairo. She saw that I had given him specific verbal commands to "stare out the window" as a way to avoid feelings of entrapment. To my relief, the tactic had worked. Robert had not bolted from the train.

Plumbrook, Harriet – Tour of Woodward Dr., Mound, WV – 2002

AC: I remember when we got into trouble at Sunday school here, next to Grandview.

HP: I was four, almost five. We were in Sunday school. You know how they're always talking about Jesus and all this other stuff... I decided to argue with the Sunday school teacher, who was a man. I don't remember what his name was. I told him that Jesus was just a person (not a prophet), that the planet was settled by aliens, and that all the great wonders of the world were built by aliens. I used big words that I'd never heard of. One of them was *paleo-seti*. Until I was 42 years old, I didn't know what that word meant. But I used it when I was four years old.

AC: Sometimes you would get phrases and concepts coming to you that were from elsewhere?

HP: Right. All I know is that he went to my parents. I was spanked and sent to my room for about a week. And we never went back to that church.

AC: Now, another thing that Harriet does is intuiting people's medical problems. She can even do this over the telephone. She can pick up on what's wrong with them. We'll go into that later. But what her rant did for me was, it got me out of Sunday school. Forever… I never had to go to Sunday school after that because of what Harriet said. I appreciated that. I mean don't get me wrong… I think Sunday school's a great thing, but it was greater to spend my summers running in the woods and playing basketball instead of being in the basement of the church over there.

This isn't exactly true because during my junior high school years, I attended Sunday school at a church on Charlie Manson's block. The reason I attended was because there was an older kid there, who was from a police family, who was very quirky and quite hilarious. He later became an expert of sorts on the underground scene in Charleston. Through him, I saw a different side of my hometown, one that I never would have thought existed. He could be seen four-wheeling through the hills on a dune buggy, following the pipelines. After my Volkswagen beetle spontaneously caught on fire in the early 1980s, I sold it to him and it was converted into one of his "Protector Bugs."

Following our visit to Grandview Elementary and lower Woodward Dr., Harriet, Fish and I traveled to upper Woodward Dr., where the Mothman shrine is located.

AC: You drove up Woodward Drive a few weeks ago just to check it out. What happened?

HP: Well, I remember getting near what they call the "top of the hill." I had my Mothman fluttering, right in the solar plexus (which is where I always get the feeling). I picked up Andy's vibration. Unbeknownst to me, Andy had lived someplace else on Woodward Drive. And it was at the top of the hill!

AC: *[pulling into driveway]* Okay, here we are at my family's second house on Woodward Drive, which Harriet somehow realized was mine as she drove by it. As we look, we see that a black cat has come out. An omen? It's growling. Look at this. It's coming at us!

HP: *[sees large, snarling black cat advancing menacingly]* For god's sakes, back up!

AC: *[frantically backing up on bumpy gravel driveway]* Fish Ofiesh is now in the back seat rubbing on protective clove oil! This is a mixture that Harriet makes. It's the kind of a mixture you want to have if you're out doing Mothman research. Can you tell us why?

HP: It offers protection! The Indians believe that the scent of cloves and cinnamon protect their spirit from anything evil or terrifying. And we *now* know that both contain properties that are antibacterial and antiviral. They can actually keep you from getting ill, even when you're around people that are sick. You rub it on your entire body.

AC: Didn't some of the people during the Black Plague wear it?

HP: Absolutely… The thieves would coat themselves in a mixture of cinnamon and cloves. Then they would go pilfer the bodies of those that had died. Steal their jewelry… They would never get sick themselves.

Mothman Shrine Location, Woodward Lane, Mound, WV

AC: Okay, we're back at Mothman Central, here at Woodward Lane... Our friend Timothy Thomas Burnham – remembered by some as the Vampire Boy of Woodward Drive – was a UFO contactee at a young age. He lived right where Harriet and I both saw what we think may have been the Mothman. I haven't really heard Harriet's version yet.

HP: My version's a little different than Andy's.

AC: Harriet's *is* a little different. Mine occurred up here... As we drive up, you'll see. On the left here is where we used to play basketball. Steve Slack lived in the house at that time, in the 1970s.

The young Slack spent his early years close to Boomer, WV, from where the Jonestown-linked Layton family hailed. Slack later became a river-boat captain on the Ohio River, traveling to and from New Orleans. One imagines that he became skilled at communicating with UFOs, using onboard searchlights. Slack's stepfather worked as a supervisor at an aluminum plant outside of Ravenswood, not far from Pt. Pleasant. The plant was more or less owned by the Mellon family, which has connec-tions to Carbide and to Timothy Leary's LSD experiments in NY. Leary's operation was raided by Watergate burglar G. Gordon Liddy, friend of JFK conspirator E. Howard Hunt. Hunt was most likely one of the "three tramps" in Dealey Plaza.

AC: Before Slack, our friend Tommy Burnham lived there. My sighting occurred right about in here. I was walking down this road when, on the right over here in the trees, something came out. Something tells me it was the Mothman. Why, you ask, do I think it was the Mothman? Because if we go up here a little bit and we look to the left, we see the Burnham's shrine in the driveway. Let us drive up here a little bit.

HP: Not a good idea...

AC: Oh, we're hearing it's not a good idea. So we're not actually going to drive up here. We're going to stop. But if you look right around the corner there to the right, there is the toolshed where Tommy and I built a shrine to the Mothman. Tommy started getting visited by aliens, who would land right over here in the grass. He would show us circular burn marks and tell us that *they* had come the night before. I think Harriet had just learned how to ride a bike...

HP: Yes... It was the day I learned to ride a bike. Tommy was crying hysteri-cally, begging me to believe him. He said that they had been to see him the night before, and that they were coming that night. He always knew when they were coming. He was just absolutely hysterical. He had taken me over to his house. It had rained. He showed me marks that were perfectly circular over in the field, right where Andy just [pointed]. There were marks. I guess you could call it like a tripod, the way they were shaped. There were three of them. Three circles… The object would have probably been about, say, 8 feet in diameter. [Again] he was hysterical, begging me to believe him.

AC: I can remember one night I stayed overnight with Tommy. In the middle of the night he wakes me up screaming, "They're coming, they're coming!" And so I call my mom and say, "Come get me, come get me!" You know what I mean? Next stop on our Mothman Tour is Harriet's sighting spot, which is about 20 feet further along the lane here. Take a look… It occurred over here on the right, in the trees. It was floating. Harriet saw…

HP: Well, for years, I wasn't sure *what* I saw. I knew I'd seen *something*. It wasn't a being like Andy's [in appearance, but] it glided and floated like Andy's. I don't think I really want to go into too much detail about what the being looked like. It bothers me too much. I never saw feet. It never touched the ground. It started out higher in the trees.

AC: How big was it?

HP: [It was] 7 to 8 feet. It was massive [and] tall [with] a very strange odor. A mustiness like a cave… It was overwhelmingly strong. [There was] also the smell of cinnamon. My being had eyes that were incredibly intense and inky. It was a broad daylight sighting, in the morning. Andy, when was yours?

AC: My sighting was at dusk. I saw what I initially thought was a person, standing like a tree over there. But when you look at the slope of the grade, it's so steep that no one could really stand there. So, whomever it was had to have been floating along.

HP: Absolutely…

AC: They sort of unfolded and came walking toward me. I was totally terrified and ran home all the way, a mile or two. Before I actually saw it, the birds all stopped chirping. All the crickets stopped, and I felt "the tingle." I knew someone was watching me. I could sense them. After a few more steps, I looked over. Then this thing steps out. It didn't walk normally. It was taking steps, but floating at the same time. It didn't really make any noise. It sort of seemed like it was half dead. It sort of didn't seem really alive. It seemed like something inorganic, or from another world.

HP: Did it try to communicate with you?

AC: It was like it was trying to say, "I'm here." The funny thing is that it reminded me of Tommy, as if it had some knowledge of Tommy or *was*

Vortex spot on Woodward Lane, where people saw UFO craft, lights, MIBs, and various entities. The author's film team encountered an energy field here that caused physical symptoms and dark visions regarding possible murders at Harriet's house and at Magic Island.

Tommy, in a different form… Perhaps it was an astral-projection of Tommy. It just felt connected to him somehow. If you go to the spot where I saw it and look in the other direction, you see the shrine. You see the toolshed that housed the shrine.

HP: It's very strange because I too had the tingling… The tingling started at the top of my head and went to my feet. And when I saw what I saw, no sound could come out of my mouth. My body would not move.

AC: Harriet had a different reaction. Whereas I could run, Harriet was frozen.

HP: You've got to realize that I was 7 or 8 years old. That's a very frightening thing to have happen when you're that age. For so many years, I blocked that out… My hypnotherapist believes that it's something I'm not willing to deal with yet, and that there's plenty more there. Much more detail… A whole other side to what happened… But I'm just not ready to go there yet. We're working on that.

We then discussed the brief visit we had made to the shrine location the night before. That particular visit had given us the opportunity to get re-oriented to the energy of the place.

Plumbrook, Harriet – Plumbrook Home – Mound, WV 2002

AC: It was pretty good that we were able to come here last night at midnight, on a full moon. We could feel it. I mean, when you walked by my sighting spot, you felt it in your whole body. I still feel it today.

HP: It's amazing. I picked up where your sighting was at the same time you did. Probably because I was picking it up off of you. It was amazing because you get that same feeling of electricity. It was very scary.

AC: Now another little synchronicity we have here is that Harriet's been dreaming about a neighborhood above Stonewall Jackson High School. She dreams she flies around over there. But she's never been up there – in real life – until today (or yesterday). So we get into town, and things work out so that Harriet is staying with someone who lives in the neighborhood she has been dreaming about. Then we find out that the daughter of the lady Harriet is staying with *lived in Harriet's house*, after Harriet had moved! The daughter happens to be an old friend of Robert Godbey's. We've never stayed with the mother before and we don't know her. It's pretty random... A seemingly random event resulting from a chance referral... In the course of following the Mothman trail, seemingly random events often become synchronous, and suddenly everything comes together. What can you say? It's bizarre. Harriet's having a little bit of a freakout as we realize that our random contact here in Charleston not only lived in her house, but *bought* her house. We will now show viewers that house, which looks abandoned.

HP: *[excitedly]* No one's living here now. Let's go in.

AC: *[hangs back, whispering to camera]* Now Harriet may not want to tell you this, but I'll sort of tell you. In this driveway that I'm pulling off into here, Harriet's dad was once car-bombed. Harriet's dad worked on some secret NSA projects back in the '60s. When the FBI investigated the car bomb, they claimed that a drug-dealing mob guy, Mr. Bruno, was supposed to have been bombed. Bruno lived next door. Supposedly it was an accident – a simple mistake – that Harriet's dad got car-bombed. He survived the bombing, but later drugs were found in the woods here. A suitcase full of heroin... Mr. Bruno was taken away on charges of racketeering. When Harriet went to research and find out what happened to him after he was put in prison, she could find no record of the arrest, even though it was originally reported in the Charleston paper. The official prison records are missing. I'm going to try and get Harriet to show us where she had another sighting, back on the hill behind her house. It was a cigar-shaped UFO. She believes she had some missing time. When she went back again to find the spot a few days after it happened, she couldn't find it. It was as if it were in an alternate reality. Here's Harriet's house. As you can see, it's not in very good shape. When you're on the trail of the Mothman, sometimes the smallest clues really matter. These would be names, numbers, and pictures that are at the site... What I'm going to do is just scan around. I'll bet there's something here that will connect up with the Garuda. The only package left in the house is addressed to a Mary McClung. We'll keep that in mind.

[A bird flies out from a nest inside the house, startling the team]

AC: Ah ha! We just had our omen. A bird flew out of this nest. As you can guess, it scared the crap out of us.

HP: Oh [expletive]! This was my bedroom back here!

AC: Our second name on a piece of mail is Kimberly Waite. Harriet will now explain how she found out there was no Santa Claus.

HP: Well, I was never allowed to get into this closet. My mom would always start screaming at me. I think I was eight or nine years old, which by today's standards is kind of late to find out there's no Santa Claus. I remember getting in here and on this shelf, covered up with a big towel, were all of our gifts... There's *a lot* of mail in here [now].

AC: Who was the person who blew the Santa Claus story for me? Harriet. She told me at school one day, "There is no Santa Claus." I didn't believe her but I went home and asked my mother. Sure enough, it was confirmed.

HP: Did I? Did I do that?

AC: Name number three: Jeffrey Melton. Melton was here in '93. Waite was here in '96. Mary McClung was here in October of '97. We need to find these folks and ask them if anything strange happened to *them* while living in this house. Okay, we've just found something in the attic.

HP: *[Holding framed nude portrait of Pamela Anderson from Baywatch]* I [suppose] this belonged to Jeffrey Melton?

AC: Pamela Anderson aside, one has to ask, "Why is this house abandoned?" And why so many renters?

HP: *[describing hillside in her back yard]* It's really grown over now, but this hill goes way, way up. There were rocks that stick out. Cliffs... I used to go up there and play. [One day] my mother said that I had *disappeared* for about two to three hours. [But] I felt like I'd only been gone about fifteen minutes. [I had gone] up there and I found a clearing that I'd never seen before. I could *never* find it again.

AC: This is where the house of the Italian mobster, Jack Bruno, once stood. Bruno supposedly was the actual target of the car bomb that found its way into Harriet's dad's car. Tell us about that event, Harriet.

HP: I remember the date: January 8th, 1968. My dad went down to start his car at the foot of the hill. It blew up. He was burned pretty badly on the leg, but otherwise was okay. He had a brand new, black Grand Prix. Jack Bruno had a black Lincoln Continental. The first thing my mom did was to call the FBI, since she was in the middle of being an informant (which I didn't know until recently) against this Jack Bruno. She told the FBI about it. They came out that day and said, "Somebody probably was trying to get Jack" and mistakenly got my dad's new car. But we don't *know* [whether] that is true because there were other vans and panel trucks at that time that just kept floating down this lane. They weren't FBI.

AC: Panel trucks? Like the panel trucks in *The Mothman Prophecies*?

HP: Yes.

AC: Men wearing coveralls, acting like they're working on power lines, that sort of thing?

HP: Yes, but at the time [we didn't know] that that's usually [indicative of] a covert operation. I had no idea.

AC: Didn't someone find a suitcase full of heroin?

HP: Yes, my mother did. In the path between the two houses... She turned it over to the FBI and became an informant.

AC: They never found out *what* exactly happened to Bruno after he went to prison, did they? Aren't the records missing?

HP: They are... He went to the Federal Penitentiary in Harrisburg, Pennsylvania, and spent a lot of time there. Later when I was in journalism school, I decided – just for kicks – to look it up, because we had to look for things for practice. I could find no record of him.

AC: Since we're here on the little Mothman lane, let's talk a little more about Tommy Burnham. What happened to him?

HP: First, he moved to North Carolina, and then eventually to Florida, to the Space Coast. From talking to his mother – I actually called his mother to try to reach him – I found out that he had received a full scholarship in Chinese, of all things, to the University of Indiana. She would not let him accept the scholarship. [So] he went to a smaller school in Florida, and got a computer engineering degree. Later he received a Masters in philosophy. Now he supposedly has his own landscape business in [FL].

AC: But he worked for NASA for a while, correct?

HP: He did. That's where he was a computer engineer for years.

AC: When we were kids, he always said that he believed in space travel. He actually told me that he had traveled before in a spaceship, and that he was going to work for NASA.

HP: Yes. I can confirm that. He used to say that all the time [too]. It was something that came up probably every day.

AC: It turns out that his mother, too, now works for NASA, for the Allied Space Command. Right?

HP: She is an assistant [of some kind] to the Director of the Center. Mind you, she is 66 years old and still working...

AC: She's a former Miss West Virginia, isn't she?

HP: Yes...

AC: Tell us about the phone call...

HP: I told her who I was... She said to me, "Oh, you sound all grown up." I started asking her questions about Tommy, and she started hedging right away. Then I asked her if Tommy would like to meet Andy and I here [in WV] because we were going to do the high school reunion thing, and wanted to see a bunch of kids that we went to school with. She very abruptly told me, "Absolutely not... He doesn't want to do anything like that, and furthermore wouldn't want to speak to either one of you." I asked her to give him my phone number, but I'm sure she never did. I doubt she even told him of the conversation. I just found it strange that this woman is protecting a 43-year old man.

AC: It *is* strange, isn't it?

HP: Yes, because she was [pretty] hostile about it.

AC: So what do you think? Do you have any theories? Do your Mothy senses tell you anything about it?

HP: Yes, she knows full well that we remember everything that happened when he was here. I think she was freaked out that we might start to ask Tommy questions. It's almost like she could sense it. She *knew* that we were up to something...

AC: What would make her not want us to see him? What bad could come of that, in her mind?

HP: I see two things. I think that she would protect him at all costs. She tried to keep him from going away to school. She always kept him close by, so that she could protect him. He was so emotionally fragile. Just a very emotionally fragile child… Also, given her job at NASA, there could be a host of things that she could be protecting. A whole cover-up about everything he used to say about being abducted…

AC: So you sense that maybe she knows something about what happened to him?

HP: I *know* she knows. But no one knew about alien abduction back in the '60s. It was just never discussed.

AC: Well, I know that she told *me* not to mention his alien experiences.

HP: Yes, I was told the same thing. To never talk about it…

AC: Of course, you never know if that's out of fear of being ridiculed by the community, or a result of belief in paranormal phenomenon…

HP: I just find it odd that someone who is living right in the middle of something so strange ends up working for NASA. I find that a little bit odd.

AC: A little side note is my next-door neighbor, the Cobbs… Their daughter married a guy by the last name of Dean, who also worked at NASA. His sons would come up from Cocoa Beach for the summers and get into trouble around Mound.

Plumbrook, Harriet – 1981 Protector Story – Kanawha City, WV 2002

Harriet Plumbrook (HP): The story I'm going to tell you [illustrates] how I used to be a total non-believer in this stuff. When I was 20, I wrote for the student newspaper, the *Ohio State Lantern*. Actually I was the editor. I decided to do a whole series on different religions. I decided to go to this Spiritualist Church because I had worked with a guy who went there. He was kind of strange and I thought, "I'm going to go, because he's always telling me that dead people are talking to *me*. He's always telling me what they're saying. He knows *too* many details about these people – who are dead – in my family." So I go to this church with him. It's in North Linden, which is a horrible section in Columbus. It's just rundown ghetto. The medium, her name is Medula. She's almost 100 years old. I mean they have to escort her in and sit her down on cushions. They turn all the lights off. It is just pitch black in there. [My friend] reaches over and touches me and says, "I want you to know that you're not going to be able to write this story." And I said, "Come on." He goes, "No, you're going to become *part* of it." And I thought "Yeah, whatever…

Just a bunch of B.S." Well, during the course of this conversation, spirits start coming through Medula. Her voice would change. You'd feel fluctuations in temperature. You'd feel air swirling around you. It was the weirdest thing. You'd hear things moving, and paper rattling. And lo and behold, "Andy Colvin's father" comes through! Mind you, I had not seen Andy Colvin since January of 1971. This is approximately November 1980. His father came through to tell me that he had a "protector." You know, I'm sitting there going, "what?" Nobody had mentioned his name to me in years... About two months later, in January 1981, we [reunited]. It was unbelievable. Andy was going to school in Cincinnati, and I was going to school in Columbus. His mom, who by then was remarried, came – out of the clear blue sky – to Columbus to visit my mom. Andy's mother said, "You've *got* to contact Andy. You have *got* to get in touch with Andy." And she *supposedly* didn't know about any of this stuff. Why would I need to get contact Andy? She said, "You need to see him." It's like she *knew*...

"Fish" Ofiesh (FO): So when his dad came through to you, did his dad come *through* the woman first?

HP: Yes.

FO: And the woman said to you...

HP: She said, "There's someone in this room that wants to talk to you. The man's name is Andy Colvin." I didn't say anything. I froze. She said, "The message is, tell his son that he has a protector, and that he's fine." [In other words] Andy has a protector, and his father was fine. [But] why me? Why him?

FO: And that's how you got in touch? Oh man, that's great!

HP: Lo and behold, all these years later, it's the same paranormal shit happening again...

AC: I thought about it for years, what the "protector message" was all about. I read *The Mothman Prophecies* and the paranormal literature. I knew I had to contact Harriet again. But I kept putting it off. After 9/11, I felt like I *had* to contact her again...

FO: Do you think it was your dad just saying that he was there for you, or do you think it was more prophetic?

AC: I think it has to do with me maybe having a spirit guide. For instance last night at the energy field, I didn't consciously think of my dad. But I was aware at some level that I've "got a protector." I therefore felt like I could observe the field, or perhaps interact with it a bit.

Another possible interpretation of Medula's message is that my father has a protector and is fine, in heaven or wherever he may be.

Sara Jane Moore and Charles Manson were known to frequent Van's Never Closed Market (above) on Old Rt. 60 in Mound. The rough Blue Moon Tavern (below) is where Manson's mother stabbed a man in the head with a broken bottle. The author's friends witnessed a strange murder scenario at the tavern. One patron killed another patron outside, then forced other patrons to place the body in the trunk of a getaway car - only to casually come back later for more drinks!

CHAPTER 32

[Colvin to camera] Berenice Abbott once said, "The photographer is the most up-to-date person in society, as the photographer is always turning the now into the past." Zola declared in 1901 that one cannot claim to have really seen something until one has photographed it. But in the Mothman country of central West Virginia, ideas like this are turned upside down. One finds that an unseen past lives on. Harriet, Sharon and I were able to go back to this same magical spot where we had seen things. Amazingly, this same energy was still there, still alive. In some ways it shows that there is an interface going on between the human mind and these energies. These energies aren't totally apart from us. They seem to be created in conjunction with our own minds. The Mothman teaches us that the paranormal is not really "out there," but in us.

Energy Field Event – Woodward Lane, Mound, WV – March 2002

During the "energy field event" of 2002, I decided to keep my video camera running. On tape, it was too dark to see the subtle energy field. But we did get an interesting audio recording of our sensory and emotional responses to the experience. These are our actual words as we encountered the three plasma beings of Woodward Drive.

Harriet Plumbrook (HP): [It] almost looks like wisps of smoke or something. I don't know how to explain it. It's in the center of the road.

Sharon Moore (SM): That way...

HP: He's right here, straight ahead of me. I feel his presence. It's male.

Andrew Colvin (AC): That's what I felt when I saw it (in 1973), that it was male...

SM: I can't feel that.

AC: [At that time] I felt it was maybe connected to Tommy.

HP: No, no. It's not of this world. [Can't] you feel it is [from the] beyond?

SM: Yes. I don't think it's *somebody.*

HP: I don't either [but it still] seems familiar to me.

SM: I don't have a particularly good feeling about it, but I'm not scared.

AC: This is where we used to play basketball. Here's the basketball court...

At this point I felt it necessary to blow air out from my mouth. I did it three times, resting a few seconds in between.

SM: There! [It's a] white light… White light… White light… Oh man, oh [expletive]!

HP: It is *very* strong.

SM: Oh! It's right up in that bend. Not very far away…

At this point I expelled air out 9 times. 3 sets of three…

AC: *[sees mist]* What's that?

SM: It's almost like it's *not there*. When we got up here, it went that way [and started] looking [back at us] through those trees. It's freaking me out. I can't look.

I gave three more exhalations here. The amount of energy that was coursing through us was intense at this point. Sharon began to wonder about the purpose of the visit. We hadn't explained anything to her prior, as we didn't want to influence her perceptions.

SM: What has happened here? What's going on?

AC: This is where I had my sighting [of Mothman].

SM: Right here?

AC: Like I say there was someone standing, like a tree, over there. And then they just started "moonwalking" out.

HP: This is the exact spot of Andy's sighting. Mine was up further.

SM: *[points to trees where she thought the plasma was watching us]* Is there anything up there?

AC: Well, that's where Tommy's place is. He said the UFO landed right over there.

SM: A clearing? I'm not going to look at those trees.

AC: We can walk out here. I think this is kind of a safe area, because we played basketball here a lot. I know that sounds stupid, but it just feels okay to me.

SM: [It was over on the extreme] left. God, it was right there. The closer we got up to the top [the more it moved] over to the left.

HP: We need to leave. Don't let it take control of you.

AC: I feel pretty good because I've been in this area so much. I've spent so much time here, been around this thing so much. Played ball here every day here for years. I know it's there, but it's just an energy [form].

HP: Damn straight, but I keep catching outlines of it.

SM: In the trees?

HP: Back over here, a little more towards the edge here. There it is again! Do you see it? Feel it?

SM: I felt it. Yes. Like a whoosh...

HP: It stepped out more towards the road.

SM: On the left side?

HP: Yes. Can you see low, glowing light? Because I can see some energy coming from it, whatever it is.

AC: Yes, I've been seeing that all along.

HP: Good, it's not just me.

AC: It's just, like, a fog.

HP: Yes...

Sharon buckles to her knees on the asphalt lane.

SM: Oh!

HP: It's okay... You alright?

SM: From the edge of the road, it went up. Shot up the hill...

HP: Something moved. That's for sure.

SM: It looked white. I saw white.

HP: That's what I see, too. I've never been able to really view [auras and] things [but] I can see this.

AC: *[points]* Now it's up there!

HP: It is!

AC: It just kind of [pulses and] gets brighter...

SM: Holy [expletive]! I just saw it. Like a flash...

AC: Yes, it just moved. It's just fluctuating.

HP: It's like plasma...

AC: It's just an energy field...

SM: Oh, god... Did you see it again? Can we go up there, to the very top, to the clearing?

AC: Why?

SM: I don't know. Why not?

AC: So are you feeling better?

SM: I'm fine. It's not scaring me... It's just human nature. It's overwhelming. I have to turn away from it [occasionally and then] I'm okay.

HP: Okay...

SM: Do you want to [go up there? Didn't] you feel like we should leave [earlier]?

HP: When we were standing *there*. I'm okay right now.

SM: Have you been up there?

HP: Oh yes.

SM: All the way up?

AC: Last night. We were in our car, though. We didn't walk.

HP: Well, we got out.

AC: And we felt the tingles.

SM: I'm interested to see what that is...

AC: Well, let's see. It might take a form. The form I saw was some kind of a dark silhouette. Harriet saw an alien. You don't know what you might see...

HP: Can you handle it [Sharon]?

AC: Once you get in the middle of that field, it can make you see things (if it happens to match your brain frequency).

SM: It's up to you guys.

HP: It's up to you [too].

SM: I'll try it if you want.

AC: What's your goal?

SM: I'm curious...

AC: [If we stay here, then] we're just observing it. There's a sense of safety...

SM: I don't feel like it's going hurt me. It just startles me. [I'm] pretty calm right now. Occasionally it's just like a jolt. I feel it, and then it fades away.

HP: Yes. I feel like that, too.

AC: Feel the tingles?

SM: Oh!

HP: [Feel that] little change in temperature?

SM: Yes.

HP: [And then another] little change again?

AC: Yes. That's why I got confused as to which spot it was. I think there are two energy spots in there.

HP: [This is] dead on [where I saw the robed alien].

SM: It's like a high elevation. Like you're up in the clouds or something... How to explain it? It's like the air changed...

HP: The fog's increasing.

SM: It's going in and around my lungs differently.

HP: You see it? Stare straight ahead. See the white?

SM: Yes, I just saw a flicker on each side. I have to look out of my peripheral vision.

AC: You guys want to take a look at the clearing up here?

HP: Just a real quick look. That's the spot that bothers me more.

A: It's to the left. The tool shed is to the left, where we've got the shrine. It's up this driveway around the corner. There's a house. [Tommy Burnham and] Steve Slack's house, right back in there.

SM: Where is [the energy] right now?

HP: There's something in the clearing. There's a mist. Do you feel it?

Having convinced ourselves that we weren't total cowards, our team decided to end our surveillance. We descended the steep, winding lane in silence. Harriet spoke up just as we got to our warm, comfortable vehicle.

HP: There was hostility in that place. I felt hostility there [earlier] today. That's what I was trying to tell you before...

Later that night, none of us could sleep. I ended up experiencing something akin to Kundalini, along with its evil sidekick, the "dark night of the soul." I received strong energetic signals that caused me to have visions about, and feel emotions around, some sort of drowning incident. It seemed connected to Harriet's old house. I told her all about it, as it was happening. Within hours, we would find out that someone living in Harriet's house had mysteriously drowned near Magic Island.

Moore, Sharon – 2002 Energy Field Event Recap – 2003

Andy Colvin (AC): Here we are, 2003, in Charleston, West Virginia. Last year we didn't get much footage with Sharon, but she was there when Harriet and I visited Woodward Drive at midnight. Sharon saw the energy field. We thought it would be good to have Sharon recap what she experienced that night. I remember the first thing was that we started walking up the hill, and you started feeling ill, with heavy breathing. And your necklace started burning.

Sharon Moore (SM): Yes, I wore my crystal necklace. I had no idea where you wanted to get to, as far as location. But about halfway up the hill, I started feeling a little heat there on my chest, where my gemstone was hanging. Then I was having trouble breathing. A lot of times when I'm doing tarot cards – or anything like that – I start feeling the energy. I start picking up on other things. I get short of breath, shaky, and jittery. That usually means *something's* going on. But I started feeling *that* way. As we got up close to this clearing (that was over to the left), I saw something dart across the road. It was more like a shadow. A shadow type thing... It didn't really have a shape. It moved... Further up the road I could see these wispy [things]. They weren't [horizontal] they were vertical, almost like figures without any real shape... Tall, slender things...

AC: Was it like a shimmery veil?

SM: No, they were separate. It seemed like there were maybe three people standing in the road. And there was something glowing white in front. Wispy...

Was the energy field acting as a sort of cosmic mirror? Was it was giving us energetic reflections of ourselves, in some other molecular combination?

AC: So you saw three figures with something in front of them?

SM: Yes, the shadow moved across, and that's what made me look. Then when I looked past that, it was like there were wispy figures of some type. I couldn't really make out a definite [shape].

AC: And the "glowing thing" in front of them?

SM: It was patches of light. Here, then maybe there. There were other things going on… The biggest thing was the feeling I was getting from it.

AC: Did they have gender, the three things?

SM: No, it was just more [ethereal]. It seemed more like what you would expect from a ghost or apparition. No facial features or anything… Just a fog-type thing…

AC: And the feeling?

SM: Most of it was the feeling. When we got up there and I [felt] that, it just really floored me. I went down… I sat down in the middle of the road. It wasn't really fear. It was just overdoing my senses. My senses were just being totally blasted out. I was picking up so much energy, and so much feeling. It was overpowering. It just made me really weak. I had to sit down. When I sat down, I tried to meditate a little bit, to try to relax. It was weird, because it sounded like everything got really quiet.

AC: It did…

SM: Yes, and I remember Harriet said the same thing. She thought that all of a sudden, everything stopped.

AC: That's when I looked back, and you were down on your knees.

SM: I stopped looking up there, and sat down. I closed my eyes and tried to refocus. That's what kind of made me feel so overpowered. But it wasn't like those things scared me or anything. Now, the shadowy thing did [scare me] a little bit.

AC: Is that the thing that you said went up into the trees?

SM: Yes, it moved across the road and just went into the woods. Then I started getting a real paranoid feeling, like I was being watched from the woods.

Could the shadowy thing have been Mothman, observing us as we faced our own plasma reflections?

AC: That's right where I saw the [1973] being, right where you say you saw that shadow dart across. That's exactly where I saw this thing jump out at me.

SM: Well, there was a clearing to the left where you could see [Tommy's] house. But I was more concerned with that corner lot there, where there were woods. That's where I felt something was watching us. And then we went further up the hill. I guess that was a clearing where Harriet had seen things. But yes, that's basically what happened.

AC: I've talked about what happened to me afterwards. Later that night I had a vision of somebody being murdered. Drowned... It felt like it had something to do with Harriet's house. It turned out that someone who had lived there *had* been drowned! But then three days later, I saw them dragging someone out of the river at Magic Island. That was *also* similar to what the vision had been. The vision I had was about Magic Island.

SM: So it could have been a premonition…

AC: Or a past event concerning this person who lived in Harriet's house and drowned. I didn't know which it was. I walked away not knowing what exactly happened. Did you have anything like that?

SM: No. What I've told you is [pretty much] it.

AC: I had an experience of spinal "kundalini" energy, blowing out the top of my head that night. Did you have that kind of thing?

SM: All my senses were just totally overwhelmed. I felt like I was electric… I couldn't keep my breathing under control. I just felt weak.

Plumbrook, Harriet – 2002 Energy Field Event Recap – 2002

Andy Colvin (AC): Harriet will now describe what happened to us when we were in Mound recently. We visited Woodward Drive at 2:00 am in the morning with Sharon Moore, and saw an energy field.

Harriet Plumbrook (HP): Sharon picked up on the exact spot where Andrew had his sighting. She had an amazing reaction. She had a stone for protection on her chest, a necklace… As we were walking up the hill, she started saying, "My chest is burning!" Andy asks, "Are you out of breath?" Because the hill's kind of steep... She says, "No, it's my stone burning me." And about that time, she gasped… She saw a figure. A long white figure...

AC: Then what happened?

HP: Well, she turned away from it. You went toward it, and it shot off to the left. I was able to catch a visual outline of it, which is a new thing for me. I don't usually do visuals. But she had clear visuals on it. We had the presence of more than one form of energy there. We know that much. But one of them was more dominant than the others.

AC: Tell us what happened when we went up to the spot where you had your 1968 sighting, a few feet further...

HP: She had an even more bizarre reaction. She had to sit down because she was so overcome with the presence. That it was [so] unbelievable... She sat down to catch her breath. During that time, there was about a 3 or 4 second lapse where all the bugs, all the little critters in the forest, stopped chirping. It was quite noticeable to both of us. Sharon composed herself, got back up, and started at it again. She could only take so much because she feels it so strongly – physically – that it kind of blows her away.

AC: Later that night, after we soaked up all of that electricity, what happened? Describe again just how it felt when you walked through the various spots.

HP: Oh wow, it was like sticking your finger in a light socket as a kid. I mean, it was just charging you. [Later] none one of us could sleep. It just pumped us up with so much energy. We got back to Sharon's place at probably about 3 or 3:30, and nobody could sleep. That's when you had your bizarre premonition or visual sighting. I don't know what you want to call it. It just came to you, something about my house further down the lane. You felt like something bad had happened there. It was such a feeling of terror. Your emotional reaction was one I'd never seen, nor felt.

AC: I had a feeling of death or murder. Then the following day, we found out something intriguing from the next owner of the house.

HP: The person that owned the house later on, after I'd moved, told us that a drifter had lived there. He pretty much took care of her place while she was in law school at WVU. She didn't make him pay any rent [since] there was lots of mowing and upkeep of the place. Apparently he had drowned in the river and nobody knew it for a while. It was in the paper. Somebody called her up and told her... Personally, I don't think that that's what you were picking up on. That may have been part of it, but something *else* happened there.

AC: Do you have any sense of what it was?

HP: Yes. It was a murder.

AC: You feel like a murder happened *at* your place?

HP: Oh yes...

Was this murder somehow related to the Aetna School building below, that had burned down decades before? I thought of the horrific story of screaming children, on fire. I had heard it from a cook who had worked at both Aetna-Dell and Grandview. One day in 1966, she had described the incident for me. I visualized the wooden building, which she said had vertical plank siding, as being covered in blood and flames. Could the fire have been the result of arson?

AC: The kind of stuff that occurred on the lane, with us walking through these energy fields, was mentioned in the Mothman book by Keel. He said that he went to a spot on the road one night, and felt terror when he walked through it. He kept walking back and forth through it. It was a very sharply defined area.

HP: Well, the same happened with us. We all three noticed that there were areas where the temperature varied. And I'm not talking about a breeze or something. There was no breeze this night. It was just hot and humid, with no breeze whatsoever. We were walking through areas that would be just really cold. Then you [would] walk back through the [hot] soupy air. And you'd hit another one that was really cold. [It was in] the cold areas that you felt the highest intensity of the tingling. No doubt about that... All three of us felt that.

Colvin, Andy – 2002 Energy Field Event recap – 2003

On a cold and rainy Seattle day, I gave this videotaped account of the 2002 "energy field event" to Sufi shaman Ken Alton. Ken made several contributions to my investigation. These are covered in the next book (Mothman's Photographer III). We were looking over a layout of our Mothman shrine area back in WV. The "map" was comprised of cups, saucers, and utensils on my kitchen table.

Andy Colvin (AC): We walked up the road (Woodward Lane) past Mrs. Atkins' house, across from Bethel Church. Right there at the corner of the basketball court, we all felt that there was a line in the sand, so to speak. Once you stepped across it, it felt like you were in a zone of electricity. It made your body feel agitated, like you were being shocked electrically. Also it seemed like the insects stopped chirping. If you stepped back over the line, it felt like you were no longer in the electrical zone. There was definitely a pressure difference. It felt like the pressure dropped once you were in the zone. It got colder once you crossed that line. So we sort of stood there for a while, stepping back and forth over this line. Then Sharon Moore's necklace heated up. She has a fetish necklace of a badger, which alerts her to danger. It was a very scary experience. It reminded me of the terror zone that Keel talked about in *The Mothman Prophecies*. And it seemed like this energy field – this mist that we saw – could sort of "read your mind". At least that's what we *thought*... Logically if something could read your mind, then the thoughts that you have – at that moment – are going to affects its behavior. It seemed to me like it was sort of an extension of my consciousness. Or ours... I sensed that if I had an attitude of peace then it would mimic that, and all would be okay.

In retrospect it's hard to say about these things. Sometime later, I found myself being told by a Qi Gong healer that I had picked up an "energy bundle" somewhere along the way. Bundles can permanently attach to your system and cause physical illness or emotional disturbance. The bundle was removed in front of an energy healing class. However, it alarmed a couple of onlookers, who wondered about which direction it was heading after departing my body. Apparently such bundles can go into another person nearby. For this reason, only experienced practitioners should remove them. Such a master is John Chang, who is featured in a book called "The Magus of Java: Teachings of an Authentic Taoist Immortal." Chang has been filmed doing things like setting paper on fire and driving chopsticks through thick wooden tables with only his bare hands. Chang is a talented acupuncturist who can be seen moving inserted needles just by pointing at them. He is also a master of the kriss knife, most of which have Garudas carved into them. People will bring Chang these "Garuda knives" whenever the knives seem to be "haunted." Chang then uses yin energy to communicate with the spirits inhabiting the knives. Films show him moving these knives on tables with just his mind, in a manner similar to Uri Geller and forks. This is yet another way that the Garuda can impart key information. Gurus like Chang are probably the reason "Garuda" is sometimes spelled "Guruda."

So I walked into the energy field right about here. I covered the distance of the court here, and came up to about here. Then the energy field went into the trees here, in front of Tommy's house. By the way, right behind these trees, where Tommy's yard is, is where Tommy saw the flying saucer. So we all moved up the road and came to the spot where I once saw a shadowy being.

There is much evidence that points toward this phenomena being a shapeshifting one. There are reports of witnesses seeing shadowy beings – like the one I saw – form out of black, swirling vapors. Swirling vapors are a standard occult format for calling forth entities. A small, dark "whirlwind" emanating negativity was seen by Harriet in her office in 2002. Harriet connected the appearance of the whirlwind to some MIBs who had made harassing phone calls to her soon after her Mothman interviews were released. One of the MIBs had even shown up at her office. This prompted her to begin using a pseudonym in relation to our work together.

We got to my 1973 sighting spot. Sharon really felt the intensity of the field at that point. We eventually moved up a little further here, to Harriet's 1968 sighting spot, where she saw what appears to have been an organic version of the Flatwoods Monster of 1952. That is, she saw an alien being in a cape, with sort of a point to the head. Like a hooded, monastic figure... She saw that right about here. It was sort of floating in the trees here. Sharon was down on her knees, just absolutely overcome with the energy. That's when the insects stopped completely. It was just this feeling of a vacuum. It felt like so much pressure had been taken out of the area that it was a vacuum. When you're in a vacuum, it's a situation where the extra pressure you have inside your body naturally wants to go out. So it has this feeling of expansion to it, with the electricity sort of flowing up in waves, and out.

We spent some time there roaming around the basketball court before we left. We sort of got comfortable with that feeling. We went home and that night, I experienced this energy that continued to become more and more amplified. It felt like it was coming up through my spine, from lower to upper. Just exploding out of the top of my head... I've been told that that's what happens during an experience of kundalini. The primordial energy that's normally locked in the lower spine just sort of comes out and opens all the chakras. When this was occurring, I was imagining scenes that seemed to be from both the future *and* the past. One of the scenes that stuck with me was one of someone drowning in the river. I saw in the vision that it was at Magic Island, which is in the Kanawha River where it meets the Elk. I also had a vision that it was connected to Harriet's house in some way, and possibly with a murder.

So... The next day when we go to Harriet's house, we found evidence that a lot of different renters had lived there. We talked to a subsequent owner of the house. It turns out that one of those renters had drowned. She didn't know exactly where it had happened, but she thought it was possibly near Magic Island... Three days later on that same trip, I saw someone being taken out of the river. It raises the question of: "Did I see the future, or did I see the past? Or both?" Time *may* expand out from the center. Oftentimes when you see something from the future, it affects the past. You can perceive it's anti-effect. Say you go out from the center to a future event. It occurs... Yet it has an electrical connection to a past event. It is counterbalance... In these paranormal places like Woodward Drive, the "veils" are said to be thin. And literally, we were seeing a shimmering veil.

This may connect to the idea of self-illumination, and how important it is in history. In earlier cultures these cosmic, sacred spots – where one could experience time in a non-linear fashion – were highly regarded. People were somewhat comfortable with undergoing life-changing events that open up their consciousness. When I was 14 years old and saw this shadowy being, my response then was to run. This time, my impulse was to observe, or approach if possible. I think the supposition here is that we – our unconscious – can create these situations to some extent. When you're in a place like this where the veil is really thin, it's apparent that your unconscious is being activated. Once you go in, your consciousness wants to create a situation where a rite of passage can occur. If you're an adolescent, say, and your unconscious wants you to expand or move to the next phase, it will maybe place a shadow being in front of you – or an alien, or Bigfoot, or whatever. Some kick in the pants that will blow your mind... The unconscious utilizes the power of ritual and visionary experience to bring you into the next phase in your life.

> *The Sanskrit word "bhu" is at the root of our phrase "to be," and indicates growth. Ancient peoples had no abstract concept such as "existence;" they merely measured beingness in terms of whether or not something had a growth cycle. Interestingly, bhu sounds like the word "boo," as in "boogeyman." Perhaps the boogeyman is really symbolic of one who forces us to grow by facing our fears.*

CHAPTER 33

Soon after we found out about the dead renter in Harriet's old house, we found the woman who had owned the house at the time, Nancy Sheets. Nancy went to my high school and is an old friend of Robert Godbey's. She has a great sense of humor, and knows where to get the best burgers in WV. As we shared lunch, she told us what it was like to live in Harriet's house. Not surprisingly, Nancy had "missing time" episodes and anxiety attacks. These stopped as soon as she left. She even revealed that whenever she walked by our Mothman shrine, she experienced strange sensations of tiredness that were "not physical."

Sheets, Nancy – Harriet's House and Missing Time – 2003

Nancy Sheets (NS): I remember his name. [The renter at Harriet's old house] was Jeff something... [His last name] started with a "C." He was my second renter after I went to law school. He drowned while he was living in the house. But not *at* the house... He drowned in the Kanawha River. I think he got drunk and just fell out of a boat. It was a little odd because it wasn't during Regatta or anything. But he died.

AC: Are they sure it was an accidental death?

NS: You know, I never looked into it. At the time I was just so relieved that he hadn't died on my property. It was kind of sad because he didn't really have any family. All of his things just stayed there. He didn't have any family or friends who came to collect his stuff. I ended up having to go out there and collect his things.

HP: Did they find his body right away?

NS: I have no idea. I probably could find out his last name. I'm sure there's some sort of newspaper article about it or something. You should be able to do a search of the Charleston Gazette. I know it was in the Kanawha River. At least that's what my next-door neighbor told me.

HP: Talk about your other renters that lived there...

NS: Well, when I first left for law school, I had a lady who rented the house for her daughter and her two grandchildren. They only lasted about a month...

AC: Do you know why?

NS: She didn't like that you had to turn the toilet on and off. I mean it's not an easy place to live, especially with kids. Just getting the groceries in and out on the [steep and narrow] road [is difficult].

HP: How old were the children?

NS: They were little... The whole reason she wanted to rent something out that way was because Grandview, at that time, was considered to be the best elementary school in Kanawha County. She wanted her grandchildren to go to that school.

AC: What year was that? In the early '90s?

NS: Well, law school lasted 3 years so, probably in August of '88...

HP: Were the Masseys still living there at that time?

NS: The Masseys lived there, as far as I know, through the whole time. I don't remember when Mr. Massey died.

AC: When she left, do you feel like she gave you the real reason?

NS: Yes, because the mother was raising hell with me, saying, "You didn't tell me this, you didn't tell me that. I'm gonna sue you..."

AC: Did you know the Masseys pretty well?

NS: I knew them pretty well because they had cherry trees, and I like to bake cherry pie. Every year I'd go over there and pick cherries. Their son kind of looked after things a little bit. Well, he acted like he did... He was kind of goofy. He would get concerned because, you know, people would show up at my house late at night. He'd have to come the next day and dip into why that had happened. Of course I had two big Rottweilers... I remember that he always wore a ball cap that said we needed more Border Patrol to keep the Ohioans out. He was just a real goofy guy...

AC: Did you develop a relationship with him at all?

NS: Not really close... I was probably only in their house three or four times [to see] Mrs. Massey. You know, just go in and have a cup of coffee or something... Plus, at that time you really couldn't get into their yard without jumping the fence. I think they were just so pleased that we kept the place mowed and that somebody was living there. It had been empty for a good while before I moved in.

HP: The two children that lived there... Were they girls or boys?

NS: Girls, both girls...

HP: Do you know approximate ages?

NS: I think the oldest one may have been in third grade. They were little… It was probably like the end of '85. [I lived there] through '86, '87, and most of '88. Right in through there…

HP: Did you know the neighbors on the other side of you?

NS: I never got to know any of those people. I really didn't know anyone out there on good terms, except the Masseys. The people that lived down the road in the "good house" were just so snooty, you know. It was like, "We're rich, and you're not." He was in the concrete business. [We all] wanted to give our road to the state so the state would maintain it. He put a nix on that whole thing. Then he tried to talk us all into just giving him so much money and then *he* would maintain it. He wanted to split it… It made me so mad. He wanted to split it equally, but he drove the farthest. I mean half the road was past me. The people at the bottom, I talked to them [just] once to make sure it was okay to park at the church during snowstorms.

AC: So that's the first [renter]. How many people lived there after [her]?

NS: Tom Tony lived there. He's a friend of mine. He went to Charleston High. He graduated in '76. [He's] like a year older than you are. He lived there for probably three or four years. He lived there when I graduated from law school, and then stayed there until probably a year before I sold it. I can't imagine that he had any real odd experiences there because I think he would have run away very quickly. He wouldn't think that was neat or interesting. But a lot of the time I lived there, I was kind of in a bad situation. I had a lot of anxiety attacks when I lived there, but nothing that I would attribute to the house. I always really loved that house. I liked where it was and that it was out [away from the city]. I thought it was cute.

HP: What would you attribute those [anxiety] attacks to?

NS: Dating an "a-hole…" *[laughter]* Needing to quit my job and go back to school… That's what I ended up doing. Living out there was probably more [than I could handle]. I was only making about seven or eight thousand dollars a year. Not a whole lot of money… There are times [during the summer] when, even if you mow every night, you can't get it all mowed. Sooner or later, you're going to have to pay some kid to help you do some mowing.

HP: Did you ever walk up and down the lane? Like did you ever have to park at the bottom and walk up?

NS: Yes.

HP: Did you ever feel any tingly feelings as you walked up?

NF: Probably every time, because inevitably I had a 20 lb. bag of dog food with me. *[laughter]* And I'll tell you in all honesty, I was drinking real heavy when I lived here. I hated walking up there. Once I could get to the top where you're talking about – that one driveway – it was [flat and] ten times easier. To me, just that first little bit was awful. It's just so steep. It just seemed like you were wore out and [yet] you had only begun. [But] I don't think it was physical [because] I was in really good shape then...

AC: Last night we went up there. We walked up that little short first part. We were exhausted. I mean we literally felt like we hit a wall of energy that made our spines tingle. It was absolutely bizarre.

NS: Wow...

AC: That's a spot where, years ago, I saw something that scared the living daylights out of me. I ran home all the way down to where Casdorph Road was... That's how scared I was.

NS: Man, that's a ways...

HP: Nancy, did your anxiety attacks stop when you left the house?

NS: I've never had another one. Have you ever had one? They're awful.

HP: Let me ask you something that may seem like a strange question. Have you ever found yourself having missing time?

NS: Missing time?

HP: Have you ever thought it was, say, two o'clock in the morning and all of a sudden it's four o'clock in the morning?

NS: Sure. [Back] then [I did]. I mean, I would go to bed at night and I'd be fine [but later] I would wake up and I'd be, like, huddled in the corner. I slept in the front bedroom, the one with the fireplace.

HP: That was my bedroom...

NS: I would wake up in that corner, down from the fireplace, nearer the second bedroom. I would always "come to" in that corner, with my head leaning against the corner. On my knees...

HP: Like frightened?

NS: My face would be wet. The front of my robe or gown or t-shirt would be wet. Like I'd been crying for hours. And it was always 4:30.

HP: You always [woke up] at the same time?

NS: I always woke up around 4:30.

HP: Did you ever have any strange scratches or marks on your body?

NS: Not that I would have attributed to that. I mean you were outside working so hard, and you [would get scratches]. You were always marked up when you lived up there. But I had this [sleep disorder] around 4:30 [precisely].

HP: And how often did that happen?

NS: Probably about once a week... [Maybe] not quite that often, but pretty often... Gosh, I feel like I'm having [an anxiety attack] now! *[laughter]*

CHAPTER 34

In the 1970s, a childhood buddy and I made a series of prank phone calls to the newly elected Gov. Jay Rockefeller. For punch lines, we used this strange phrase that we had made up. It stood for a magical, mysterious force that could not be pinned down. It was a shapeshifting word that had multiple meanings, along the lines of "God" or "love." Gov. Rockefeller actually took several of the calls himself, and was considerate enough to try to figure out what we were doing. He was cool and non-judgmental about the whole thing. It impressed me so much that I began to like him. Years later, the word we had used turned out to be a combination of the names of my son and one of my Kadampa Buddhist teachers. This teacher told me that following the invasion of Tibet in 1959, several Kadampa gurus engineered their rebirths so that they would be reborn in the US. By sheer synchronicity, I had stumbled onto the possible secret of the notorious baby-snatching Men In Black, which is that the MIBs – in league with secret societies and/or the military – may have been trying to abduct "gifted children" who were reincarnations of Buddhist masters from Tibet.

Colvin, Andy – Grassy Knoll Radio interview 7 – Spring 2006

Andy Colvin (AC): The phenomenon seems to have a moral code to it. I believe I mentioned this before. At the location of these sightings on our neighborhood street, there had been a school that had burned down. I still don't have firm info on the number of deaths there... But Puharich, in *Beyond Telepathy*, studied shamans quite rigorously. The shamans have a saying that "burning flesh fuels the spirits."

"Vyz" at Grassy Knoll (GK): Amongst those who are alive?

AC: Yes, the burning flesh "fuels" the area. We're kind of talking about a geomagnetic anomaly that's coming out of the Earth and influencing people. We're also talking about tragic human events (on the surface) that can influence the geomagnetic anomaly – creating a loop. Puharich's main thrust is that we have a psi-plasma field out there doing these things.

We might consider this psi-plasma field to be an energetic, morphogenetic grid made up invisible, crystalline shapes such as dodecahedrons and octahedrons – of infinitely varying size.

AC: Keel just calls it the superspectrum. It is this ether that transmits information faster than light. It's the superluminal state. This field is out there, and it passes through the Earth. It consists of positrons so small that if you dropped one, it would pass through the Earth and out the other side. Nothing like dirt, metal, or rock will stop it. It's too small. At that level, there's just all this space. Reality is just all space. And that's where the Garuda lives. The Garuda is the deity of spaces, frequencies, vibrations, and oscillations. All the areas between points... It's all the "negative space" in the artistic universe. The total absence of anything... The total absence of nothing... The Buddhists see the Garuda as symbolizing that. Interestingly, it is a winged being. People see this winged being, and wonder why it's there. Esoteric information is being transmitted through the ether, if you will. It tends to crop up more at times of crisis or massive social change. Andrija Puharich was a doctor doing research more or less on people, but he knew a lot about physics. Whenever you bombard an atom with radioactivity, you end up with an electron and a positron. The positron, for a split second, will fade out of this dimension and into the "anti-dimension." Then it "fixes" itself really quickly by bouncing back to our side. It's as if it is snatching energy from somewhere else, a place we cannot identify.

GK: A couple of things here, if you would. You said burning flesh. I have to go back to that. I guess it excites – arouses or whatever – spiritual activity. I thought you meant amongst those that are living... But you're saying that in that proximity, regardless of those who are embodied, you'll see some kind of increase in spirit. Is that right?

AC: Yes, you would see the energy stored in nearby fixtures like rocks and trees. I'm guessing that the fuel is *any* kind of flesh that's burning. There is a widespread indigenous idea that this will increase spiritual activity. The energy has to go somewhere.

Werner Herzog recently made a documentary about the Dalai Lama's Kalachakra Initiations at the place of the Buddha's enlightenment in India, the Bodhi Tree. Devotees slept on reeds of grass in an effort to transfer their dream energies into the stalks, for future ritual use. The Bodhi Tree itself played a significant role in helping the Buddha reach enlightenment, by channeling energy. The newly discovered "teenage Buddha" in India also meditates next to a tree. I had my own experiences with a tree entity that apparently followed me home and allowed my sister to photograph it. Citing the actual discovery of both metallic and wooden bones found underground, archaeologist Jim Brandon was of the opinion that fossils were not dead animals, but animals that the earth was in the process of creating. The animals rise to the top, just like trace minerals deep below the surface. Once at the top, they interface somehow with mound energies and become animated. The lower the bones are found, the more they seem to be hybridic. This suggests that a sifting or distillation process occurs as these "seed animals" migrate toward the surface.

GK: Okay, so it's not necessarily amongst those who are sentient and alive. It would probably increase the awareness or activity of whatever's in the ethos. or on the Earth in that particular area, so to speak... I'm assuming this is somewhat also fixed to a geographical area. In other words if it happened someplace in West Virginia, those in California aren't necessarily going to know about this. Or am I wrong?

AC: I don't know. Puharich doesn't really go much into that. But I just found several other things in his books that seem to illuminate parts of the Mothman story. About the winged being... I did see the 9/11 photograph you posted of that winged being. I saw it days after 9/11 occurred. I pretty much figured it was "photoshopped."

GK: Beyond that, are you saying that in times of crisis, it is not unusual for a sighting of a winged being to [occur]?

AC: That's right. So the question starts to become, "How do you interpret the sightings?" Are all the sightings related to some overarching message, or are they separate and unrelated? I'm not sure I have an answer that would satisfy the typical American. I do know that every time there's been a sighting recently, there seems to be some link back to the "internationalist" fascist conspiracy.

The concentration of the WV sightings seems to indicate that a central node in the "fascist conspiracy" was located there. The more recent sightings (in California, Alaska, Mexico, Yugoslavia, etc.) have been spread out and somewhat indistinct. However, there are still sightings in WV and Ohio, such as in the case of Emil Hach, who claims that Mothman visited him in his bedroom in 2005. Hach posted to Yahoo that he later spent some time in a sanitarium, where he told the staff about Mothman. Amazingly, the staff seemed nonplussed about Mothman, and indicated to Hach that it was not considered particularly abnormal to have seen Mothman. They had already dealt with several Mothman witnesses and found that most were just normal people trying to deal with a mind-blowing experience. Hach was told not to worry about it, and then released...

Following a break, my discussion with Vyz turned to Larry Flynt.

AC: I've always loved Larry Flynt, in a way, for his outspoken political views. One wonders about his shooting. You know, he got shot about a month after he posted a million-dollar reward for information on the JFK assassination. At that time, Flynt was involved with Mark Lane.

GK: Lane wrote *Plausible Denial…*

AC: Yes, and I guess you have to go pretty far back in the conspiracy world to know that he had this big feud with Mae Brussell. Lane was at Jonestown. He was there at the time it happened. He's been involved in lots of big cases that involve mind control or covert ops. Brussell was suspicious of his motives. Lane always seems to insert himself in these high profile cases where, subsequently, nothing much really happens towards finding out the truth. With Flynt, the same thing happened. Lane gets involved in this million-dollar contest and then Flynt gets shot, and everything kind of dies away. But Flynt was from northern Kentucky. Charlie Manson's mother was from northern Kentucky. She also lived in Charleston, WV for a time. Northern Kentucky was this gambling haven, going back to the old Ohio River days of the steamboats. It still carries on today with the bluegrass horse racing, gambling, and all of that. Some of the Mothman conspiracies may tie in with the Bluegrass Conspiracy. You even have Michael Aquino, the famous army mind-control guy, in northern Kentucky in the early '70s…

GK: Does he hail from there?

AC: I don't know, but he was stationed there for a time. There are so many areas to explore here for researchers. Anyone who's interested should just grab one and run.

GK: We dealt with Michael Aquino over a year ago, when we were doing the series with the Collins Brothers. I mean this is a serious individual who makes no bones about being rather dedicated to Satan. Are you in agreement with that?

AC: Yes. By the way, Anton LaVey was photographed with John Kerry. A cousin of Kerry's, Michael Paine, was Oswald's final landlord.

GK: Hold on, hold on, hold on… You know, Andrew, I love this. Whenever we think we're going to do an interview with any kind of central point, you can't help but get into all these tributaries that go out. That's okay with me. You and I could probably do segments for the rest of our lives and never cover the territory. But now it gets even better. LaVey was seen with Kerry, who [links to] Oswald's landlord?

AC: Ruth (Forbes) Paine, Michael Paine's mother, was John (Forbes) Kerry's cousin, according to researcher Bruce Adamson. So I guess Michael and Kerry are second cousins? Michael was married to the daughter of Arthur Young, the inventor of the helicopter. Young was in with LBJ's pilot. Young and Michael Paine link over to Bell Helicopter in Dallas. Some researchers think an airport facility frequented by Paine was one of the central planning locations for the assassination. Bell also employed Gen. Walter Dornberger, a former Nazi who ran one of the big camps. He was an executive at Bell. He came over after the war, in the Paperclip operation.

GK: *[mistakenly referring to Derenberger]* This is good old Woody, right?

AC: No, but it's interesting that their names, Derenberger and Dornberger, are similar. By the way, many Paperclip scientists went to Long Island, Ohio, and Texas. There are various links between the Ohio Valley and Texas, stemming from petrochemicals and the river trade. Not only do you have the Bhopal gas being made by Union Carbide in Charleston, WV, but you have the Bhopal gas being made by Carbide in Texas City, TX. Those are the only two places. The Texas City plant was funded by a joint operation between Union Carbide and Standard Oil of Indiana.

According to Charles Berlitz, a chemical barge embarking out of Texas City mysteriously sank a couple of days before the 1966 Mothman sightings started.

AC: By the way, Neil Bush worked for Standard Oil of Indiana. And Neil Bush lived in Lubbock when Hinckley, the assassin, lived in Lubbock.

GK: This is true. Would that be Scott Hinckley, John's older brother?

AC: I thought John lived there in Lubbock, too.

GK: Well, you know, he might have. Are we looking at the '70s, perchance?

AC: Yes, the late '70s.

GK: Okay, that's what I thought, too. We are agreed on the fact that the Hinckley family – of whose son, John, was a shooter in the Reagan situation – was very tight to the Bush clan, correct?

According to Jean Zeigler's book on the Swiss/Nazi gold connection, many of the major Nazis, like mind control doctor Josef Mengele, fled to towns in Paraguay like Encarnacion, along the Parana River... German is the main language spoken in Encarnacion, not Spanish. When it was reported in 2006 that George W. Bush had sent his daughter down to Paraguay to purchase a vast amount of land on his behalf, Internet bloggers like Howie Klein traveled there to find out exactly where the ranch was. While hard proof was impossible to come by due to State Dept. obfuscation, Klein seemed to think that ranch was located near Encarnacion. It just happens to be located above an extremely important water aquifer. This would assure ample profits for future Bush generations, particularly if there were repeated "peak water" scares. The area is sparsely populated, with almost no roads. This would make it virtually impossible to find Bush were he to flee any future war crimes charges.

AC: Right. One of the things that happened while we were away, you and I, was this anniversary of the Reagan shooting. Wasn't it the 25th anniversary? There wasn't much coverage, was there?

GK: No, there wasn't. [In] March '81, Reagan gets popped. Hinckley's the shooter.

AC: Bush was scheduled to appear at the Washington Hilton on the 25th anniversary day. Suddenly, his handlers realized that Reagan had been shot there, which might bring up some unpleasant correlations. Bush suddenly decides to go to Cancun instead, where he meets with Vicente Fox, whom he already vacations with for a week solid every year. Their families are very close. Fox and Bush have worked tirelessly to make sure that we have as many illegal immigrants coming over as possible. I guess there are some drug allegations as well.

The Bush family also reportedly vacations with the bin Laden family.

GK: Yes, that government is as famously corrupt as our own. Believe me, the drug runners have been very facilitous, as I know from the Westies (Irish "wise guys" in New York). I've stated this on shows before, about [Mexico] making sure that drugs got into the United States. And with the help of the military, during the days when they were funding Iran-Contra...

AC: Another thing that happened, only two weeks after the Reagan attempt, was the Pope getting shot. The shooter, Agca, became a media poster boy here recently, but then kind of disappeared. Didn't they just re-arrest him? Mae Brussell said Agca had links to the Bulgarian secret police and so on. She *connected* the Reagan and Pope attempts. She thought that the same organization did both shootings. Apparently it was tied to high-level Catholics like Alexander Haig, who were trying to apply pressure to the Vatican. Sure enough, there was a big shift in Vatican investments after that, to American companies. Some of these investments were for Trojan condoms and things, which aren't even supposed to be condoned in the Catholic world. So there was this worldwide crime network that tied not only into the church, but also the oil companies, drug networks, and different intelligence agencies. Collectively, they were behind scaring the living daylights out of both Reagan and the Pope.

GK: Nobody shakes the Vatican [i.e., the Jesuits]. I mean the Popes come, and the Popes go. The Jesuits are always there. That is an interesting scenario about John Paul getting popped. We've always wondered what that might have been, if it was done by the Bulgarians. The Eastern Orthodox Church has always been on the outs with the Vatican. I've got to bring that up with John Eric Phelps.

AC: They both seem to be involved with the Wandering Bishops.

GK: Oh yes, boy, I'll tell you what. I've got to have Levenda on again, because when I hear him talk about the Wandering Bishops, I'm saying to myself, "Man, aren't you talking about the Jesuits?" Honestly, I mean New York City, the whole thing. Good point.

AC: The Jesuits... Get this: November 11th, 1966, was the day the Mothman was first sighted. That's the same exact day that the Pope "called out," or confronted, the Jesuits. I just found this in one of Emmanuel Josephson's books on the Rockefellers. Josephson's name was thrown out on your show by one of your other guests. It was a Christian fellow who was talking about how the Rockefellers had started World Wars I and II, funded the Bolsheviks, and everything else in between. So I got about four Josephson books. He was a Jewish doctor from New York. He talked about how there were certain Jews who had given all their money to the Revolution in 1776. They had this patriotic zeal. He really disliked Rockefeller and wrote these muckraking books that have all kinds of interesting facts in them. They're a little outrageous at times, because he speaks in this Cold War terminology, calling people communists and so forth. But some of the points he makes are enlightening, like how the Rockefellers were behind the Museum of Modern Art. I think I already mentioned the art world. The manipulation of it by oil and chemical people like Dede Wilsey, the Dow heiress... Dow and Bayer are now the number one and two chemical companies, by the way. They're the ones who run the Carbide operation in Charleston now. You basically have the world's biggest chemical combine running the show in West Virginia today. Dede Wilsey was married to Al Wilsey, who was a big milk purveyor. The Rockefellers cornered the milk market early on. By the way, another big pasteurized milk purveyor was the great-grandfather, I think, of Loren Coleman's ex-wife.

My relatives in Fort Ann, NY, were dairy farmers who forever railed against the pasteurization process because it killed all the vitamins.

AC: When I was a kid, they always talked about what emergency supplies to have at the plants in case there was a big chemical explosion. Believe it or not, all they had for people was *milk*. They didn't have any health facilities in case there was an explosion or something. Just milk... The mantra was, "Give the guys milk and send them home!" I've started thinking that maybe that was all just a scam to sell milk. That's how ridiculous it gets when it comes to the Kanawha Valley and safety.

GK: Going back to the Jesuits...

AC: Tell me about them. I don't know that much about the Jesuits.

GK: Well, I'm not the initial researcher. Eric Jon Phelps and Charles Wilcox have written two books. Phelps has written *Vatican Assassins*. Wilcox has written *Transformation of the Republic*. In both cases, they've gone back and pulled out historical records. Wilcox, especially, goes back and pulls out correspondences that he happened fortuitously to come upon. Article upon article back in the 19th century, warning the United States citizenry about the intrigues of the Vatican and the Jesuit Order... This always sounds nuts [today]. I thought it was once upon a time [too, but] I found out that both Phelps and Wilcox were right. Across time and across centuries, there has been no other entity like the Jesuit Order. Everyone thinks it is spiritual when, in fact, it is military. That's why their head is called the Jesuit General. You want to talk about New World Order? You want to talk about One World Government? These are the characters. They are the ones who send down the orders. There is somebody who sits on top of the dunghill, and it certainly is Vatican, Inc. and the Jesuits – the muscle. The Vatican is just a pretty picture. Across time, the Jesuit footprints are absolutely erased. I'll give you one in particular, which is Burke McCarty's 1929 book called *The Suppressed Truth About the Assassination of Abraham Lincoln*. Let me just give you this as an example. She wrote in 1929, "At this moment, Jesuits are in Japan instigating anti-American sentiment for future war." Lucky guess? My point is that those who have the most to lose by exposure to their workings are the ones who must most completely hide their presence [from] media outlets, information outlets, books, textbooks, and mass information. I'm pinning it directly on a send-down from the Vatican and the Jesuit Order. The Jesuits are the muscle; they actually get things done. Does that help you at all?

AC: Sure... And there seems to be mild relationship between Mothman and the Phoenix program in Vietnam. They are namesakes, if you will. I think I mentioned that some of the Jesuit priests in the outlying areas of Vietnam were actually CIA. There was direct communication going on between them and the CIA. When the Sindona and Terpil scandals broke, we found the Vatican being accused of laundering proceeds from Golden Triangle product (heroin) indirectly connected to Phoenix...

Coincidentally, "Phoenix" was reputedly the secret code name for the Montauk mind control and time-travel operations. The aforementioned Vatican scandals involved CIA operations inside the Italian World

Trade Center, led by Clay Shaw, the JFK conspirator prosecuted by Jim Garrison. Shaw and David Ferrie were fanatically "Catholic," and good candidates for being involved with the Jesuits.

AC: I think I mentioned the secret cancer biowarfare research that was going on right around the time my dad got cancer. Puharich was working with Uri Geller at that time. I've read Puharich's book on Geller, called *Uri*. Puharich was traveling around with Uri, and all these crazy things were happening. They were supposedly seeing UFOs everyday. They would record tapes onto which this voice would appear and tell them things. This voice was called SPECTRA. It's very similar to Philip K. Dick's experiences with VALIS, and John Lilly's with ECCO.

Physicist Jack Sarfatti also claimed very similar experiences during the same timeframe. Sarfatti communicated with the orbiting UFO consciousness via something he called "The God Phone." Sarfatti, who worked directly with Puharich and Geller on remote viewing experiments, believed wholeheartedly in synchronicity and the advantage of listening to it. Sarfatti physically built several versions of the God Phone, searching for a workable model that could access both the future and past. It is basically a Montaukian time machine, like the one Keel envisioned during our 2003 interview in Pt. Pleasant.

AC: In all these cases, a disembodied UFO consciousness is thought to be circling the Earth in a spacecraft. Puharich was caught up in all this. I tend to think he was telling the truth for the most part, at least from his perspective. It's hard to know because he *did* have a lot of CIA contracts that he was working on. He may have been mind-controlled or manipulated without his knowledge. His research usually became classified the minute he did it. The fact that we have a couple of his books in existence, where he talks about his research, is nice. One would guess that this was purely an accident of the 1970s political climate. How open things were... His research got out. Today it would certainly all be classified, unless its release was a calculated set-up of some kind. Today we are given very little info on what these scientists are finding out about the paranormal.

One wonders if the government's remote viewing program was only publicized because such revelatory leaks couldn't be stopped. Once the genie was out of the bottle, selected insiders from the remote viewing program seem to have been allowed to break their secrecy oaths and then profit by writing books and lecturing. According to Peter Moon, remote viewing was stolen directly from Dianetics and Scientology. The many high-profile Scientology lawsuits, both before and after L. Ron Hubbard's death, helped fuel revelations that eventually leaked into public discourse. Unfortunately, the discourse seems to have been crystallized into criticism of actor Tom Cruise, a well-known Scientologist. This only serves to divert attention away from the more important issue of how government tax lawyers were allowed to take over, and completely distort, what was originally (according to Moon) a beneficial system of inner exploration.

AC: We're talking about a scientist (Puharich) with NASA and CIA connections, hauling around a UFO contactee (Geller) and doing a really close examination of him, trying to find out what's going on. In the middle of all this, Puharich leaves and goes back to Germantown, Maryland, very close to where this cancer-based form of biowarfare was being planned.

GK: Is that around Fort Detrick?

AC: Yes, about 15 minutes away... There, Puharich meets with Werner von Braun, former head of NASA Security. A cell within NASA Security has long been linked to the JFK assassination. Also, Puharich met with Edgar Mitchell, the famous astronaut. Today, Mitchell attends many different New Age conferences. He has been on panels at UFO conferences with Steven Greer, Robert Anton Wilson (playing skeptic), and the Rockefeller-funded John Mack. I actually went to a couple of these conferences, which essentially push the ET thesis to the limit.

An AP article from 6/25/07 stated that NASA would be allowing the National Institutes of Health and certain private businesses (probably pharmaceuticals) to use the new Space Station free of charge. Once it is completed in 2010, the station is expected to cost $1.5 billion a year to operate. At the same time, a DOE official named Jim Phelps, the developer of something called "Global Shield," was floating the idea in the UFO and conspiracy worlds that chemtrails were not dangerous, but designed to save people's live by casting certain protective chemicals across the sky. It seemed to be a play on the old idea – long sold to buffs and contactees – that the Sumerians were forced to mine gold in order to save the atmosphere on the home planet of the Annunaki birdmen. Much of Phelps work focused on events that had occurred at Union Carbide's K-25 plant in Tennessee. Phelps was apparently involved in developing various measures there to offset the ill effects of radiation to workers. His website is a unique blend of science and Egyptian mysticism. Phelps claims that the Egyptians' Eye of Horus symbol reveals their knowledge that radiation interferes with the functioning of the pineal gland, reputed to be the source of humans' psychic "third eye."

AC: Von Braun was CEO of Fairchild Industries, an aircraft company. Puharich was loosely affiliated with what later became Fairchild Semiconductor, the computer chip maker. Fairchild was more or less where the computer chip was invented. Puharich used their chips in experiments. I think he was actually sharing space with Fairchild at one time, up in Portland, ME. Von Braun's Fairchild Industries had links with LTV, a Dallas-based company...

GK: Hold on... Are we talking about LTV? I'll tell you what, my wife worked for LTV! Are we talking about what eventually became the steel people?

AC: With James Ling?

GK: Yes, Ling had the harbor [vessels]. He had the tugs and stuff like that. Is that right?

AC: He had all kinds of things going on. I recently read his obituary in the NY Times. I knew immediately that he was CIA because, in the Navy, he was one of these guys "recovering material from German subs." They were trying to break the German codes. He was probably one of the guys looking for an actual German codebox, in order to reverse-engineer it.

GK: What LTV did, through the '80s, when things got weird with steel and stuff [was diversify]. Republic got bought out. There were mergers and such. My wife, who worked in that industry, wound up working for LTV. So that's the same LTV, without a doubt. And it was Ling, there's no two ways about it. So he's in the mix as well, eh?

AC: Yes, you could tell by the very wording in the article that he was CIA. They were dancing around, trying to explain how things happened the way they did. He was in the Navy obviously doing spy work, but they can't say that. He gets out of the service. Next, he's supposedly selling stuff out of his garage. Within a year, he's got this burgeoning electronics company that goes on to change "the very way corporations organize." His influence on the corporate world was immense. But really what it amounted to was that he came up with all the new accounting scams that they're using today.

GK: Enron...

AC: Exactly... Ling may have been the guy who perfected the intelligence front-company concept, which sometimes involved looting previously solid companies. Like Greyhound, and others... And it's all Dallas activity... There's a ton of defense stuff going on there... Basically the mob from Chicago moved down there when they were run out of Chicago. That's the story, at least.

GK: That *is* the story. I won't belabor this, but my wife worked for Jones & Lockwell. They merged with Republic. Together, they were owned by

LTV. That's how that happened. They were most assuredly out of Texas, as you stated. I only knew them to be involved with things like tugs and harbor stuff, but it all fits in. Now I've got that straight. She'll be interested in hearing that, for obvious reasons. Weren't the mob bosses of Chicago and Dallas prominent in Kennedy's assassination? One was Marcello?

AC: Yes. You know, originally, Chicago had a mob structure that had some benefits, according to urban designer Richard Sennett. There actually was an old world, neighborhood street culture with lots of shops and different ethnics foods. This culture was based on traditional "mob" rule, which allowed the average person to go to the local mobster and ask for favors. Once the governmental bureaucracy took over, the favor-asking and grassroots give-and-take ended. People suddenly didn't have a way to really address their issues. Much of the street life in Chicago died. Today, you still have little pockets of it in some of the ethnic neighborhoods. Overall, power there seems to now be shared by the Catholics and the British.

GK: Also realize that when the Kennedy election was rigged, it was the bastion of Chicago and environs that threw it his way. Wilcox, in his *Transformation of the Republic*, recounts the Romanist element in upper Illinois and Wisconsin at the turn of the century (and into the 20th). The Romanist church definitely held sway up there, and probably did bring in the election for Kennedy. As far as the mob goes, I think they take their marching orders as well [from that same sector].

AC: To give a little personal anecdote about Chicago, at the time I was there (1978) I came down with a rare illness. This was not long before I took the photo of what may be a Man in Black in my yard. There were lots of UFO sightings occurring in Charleston then. But I was in Chicago for the summer, working one of the "co-op" jobs that the Univ. of Cincinnati sets up for students in the design program. I came down with a strange illness that they said was probably leukemia. I had some sort of lung damage, too.

According to a book by a member of the Bonnano crime family, one tactic of CHAOS-style operatives was to place small, radioactive "buttons" (procured from one of many DOE contractors like Carbide) in the car or home of a labor activist. If uranium or plutonium were hidden under a car seat or lounge chair, it would typically present itself in the victim as prostate or lung cancer, and not arouse suspicion. My father's cancer first showed up on the inside of his lap – an odd location...

AC: I was placed in the hospital in Chicago. I was put through some tests one morning that scared the crap out of me. Even though I don't think I have ever been abducted, or on the "alien lab table," it sort of felt like it that day. Soon after that, I just sneaked out of the hospital and went back home to WV. I saw my country doctor, who told me, "Don't worry about it. You'll be fine if you rest." I changed schools. I went to Marshall University, where I happened to study journalism with Ralph Turner, the reporter who had originally covered the Mothman. He was a great professor. He opened my eyes to a lot of the ways the national media brainwashes people. I looked at my blood in biology class later that year. I still had a huge amount of highly irregular white blood cells. The professor drew the different kind of cells you might see and said, "If you have any of these, pack up your stuff. You're not going to live much longer." And I was looking at them, right there in my blood. The worst possible white blood cells you could have... It was a very scary moment for me. Somehow I just blocked it out, moved on, and was able to recover.

I may have pushed my recovery program a bit. Within months, I had walked on to the Marshall basketball squad and was playing at a fairly high level. But it wasn't long before I suffered what amounted to a career-ending injury. Prior to the injury, I was being groomed as a backup for guard Greg White, who was am absolute magician at handling the ball. We spent hours playing one-on-one, trying out new tricks on each other. Greg often entertained crowds at halftime, spinning balls on all of his appendages at once. Greg later coached Jason Williams, aka "White Chocolate," who won an NBA championship with the Miami Heat in 2006. Williams, who is from Charleston, picked up White's tricks and applied them by becoming known as possibly the NBA's most entertaining white player. The Kanawha Valley seems to have a tradition of nurturing players with great moves. Could this be a holdover from the days of WV's ancient Moors?

AC: It turns out that my weird blood problem is very common in UFO contactees. But I don't have any memories of UFOs at that time, other than one or two dreams.

My best guess for when I might have been exposed to "UFO radiation" is either around 1971 when my father got cancer, or 1973 when I experienced the tree entity, poltergeists, and Glowing Bigfoot dreams. I also had a strange experience in 1974, when I was painting a large prop for a Stonewall Jackson homecoming game. Our school was a powerhouse in football that year. In fact, we won the state championship the following year. The homecoming event was therefore somewhat noteworthy. I did a painting of a black Cadillac, the car of choice for MIBs. Around that time, I had an intense dream that occurred while sleepwalking. I have a memory of standing in our front door, seeing "sparklers" twirling high above the driveway. The event seemed to be triggered by two different buzzing sounds, simultaneously heard in each of my ears. Coincidentally, Montauk researcher Chica Bruce said her entire family once saw something similar, twirling in broad daylight. She called it a baton, which isn't all that different from a sparkler. Strangely, the MIB car I painted appeared in a marching band presentation involving a majorette – who happened to be my sister, Spring – twirling flaming batons.

AC: Then there was this crop circle that I photographed outside near my house in 1979. This was before crop circles were generally known. I didn't know what it was. I just knew that it looked very unusual, and the area seemed to vibrate. I was taking timed exposures of it. It was very dark out, but the snow was glowing. In one of the negatives, there's this dark human shape that shouldn't have been there. I'm wondering if maybe I got exposed to something there. My spine was tingling at the time. You can almost see the energy in the photograph. You can see a ring of energy like a whirlpool *(photo on page 441)*. Puharich talked about this... Psi-plasma takes the form of circular vortices similar to superstrings. Its basic importance is that it "moves" electrons. Without such movement, there would be no resulting physical manifestation in space. Without activity in the psi-plasma making electrical particles spin, you wouldn't have anything happening. You'd just have purgatory, I guess. But these vortices remind me of a drawing of Ezekiel's Wheel from 1000 years ago. Puharich's vortex drawing looks just like the drawing of Ezekiel's Wheel. Ezekiel's Wheel is depicted with a winged being – with four faces – standing on it. This is reminiscent of the Thunderbird. Of not being able to see the Thunderbird in its totality at any given moment... In a sense, what I'm doing with my Mothman photo book is trying to represent the Thunderbird in more of its totality, using all these different images.

GK: Great!

AC: Anyway, I was in this hospital with this weird blood disease in Chicago. My girlfriend at the time was from northern Kentucky. A few weeks earlier, I had been sleeping in her basement. I woke up out of a deep sleep. I instinctively realized something was wrong, and went to the window. It was a sliding glass door with access to the outside. There were two guys coming in, with masks on. They had broken the light outside, and were coming in to do harm or steal something. Somehow I had woken up knowing this, before they'd actually gotten into the house. I turned on all the lights, grabbed a steak knife, and the guys ran off. My girlfriend then told me that a couple of years earlier, they had done a séance and used a Ouija board in that room. They had all had a vision of some supernatural being. A group of girls had seen this thing. Some of them had their necklaces burned off when the being "exploded." I mean these were serious heat effects. That could have been where I got the radiation exposure that landed me in the hospital. Especially if those masked men were paranormal entities of some kind…

GK: There's *something* going on here. You know what I mean? I'm not making fun of this in any way, shape, or form. Something's going on. I love talking with you because of what you've been through. What you've researched goes in a million different directions, and very deep down every route. It's got to be talked about. [Just] what in the world is going on? You've seen these things. You've been in touch with people. You have complete credibility. What are we dealing with here? Is this the elephant in a dark bedroom?

AC: It's the psi-plasma, I think. It's very isolated, and yet it's very generalized at the same time.

GK: We're dealing not with flesh and blood, as it would say in scripture, but principalities of darkness. Those who rule the air… But we're also dealing with those involved with it on a governmental or bureaucratic level. We are dealing with the supernatural, let's face it. The supernatural is not theory; it is real. So we're dealing with that, but we're also dealing with those who are walking the Earth and are empowered. Are you okay with that statement?

AC: Yes. The interesting thing about Puharich is that he was really looking at how this stuff operates scientifically. The so-called supernatural – at least in terms of telepathy – is proven in the lab. It has absolutely been proven, time and time again.

GK: Sure…

AC: Puharich had cages where he would place famous psychics. He would test their abilities to project and receive information, in and out. I think that's where the legend of Montauk comes from. At Montauk, they supposedly had the Chair that could amplify thoughts, and send those thoughts into the psi-plasma. Those with psychic abilities can pick up such signals.

This might account for the messages that I've gotten from my deceased father. The Montauk operators may have had lists of servicemen who, like my father, had been at the Philadelphia Experiment, sailed on the paranormal S.S. Franklin D. Roosevelt, and worked somewhere in the vicinity of Brookhaven on Long Island.

CHAPTER 35

"The Garuda is the celestial hawk in Hindu mythology which hatches from its egg fully developed. It symbolizes the awakened state of mind, Buddha-nature. It destroys the Five Snakes, which represent the physical and psychological diseases to which all sentient beings are prey. Garuda holds the 'knot of eternity,' which portrays the indestructible quality of meditation and its discovery of shunyata' (emptiness or Void). The Garuda holds in his claws a quotation from the Sutra of Manjushri: 'The proclamation of truth is fearless.'"

-Chogyam Trungpa, from "Garuda III: Dharmas Without Blame"

Colvin, Andy – Drawing of Harriet's 1968 Creature – 2003 video report

Andy Colvin: *[to camera]* I just thought I would share this letter from Harriet that she wrote on the one-year anniversary of our contacting each other once again. In it, she says she had "a vivid spontaneous memory" of the creature she saw on Woodward Drive.

Harriet: "This was the clearest visual I've had since my initial hypnotherapy session. Very vivid details of the face... There is what appears to be a coffee stain on the face. The base color of the face was [similar to] putty or a dingy caulking material. The skin is porous and seems to have texture, like someone who had bad acne at some earlier time. It's odd what triggered this memory. Someone sitting in front of me in class was wearing the brown color of the cloak of the alien. I'm not at all freaked-out by this but seem, instead, to welcome the vision for further exploration. The odd, strong odor came back to me. It was overwhelming... It was a musty, mossy smell but at the same time unlike anything I had encountered before. The odor itself was hypnotizing."

About the smell factor that Harriet mentions in her letter. I was just back revisiting the Mothman shrine area in Mound, here in May 2003. One of the things I noticed was that when I went by the spot where Harriet had seen her creature, there was a definite smell at this spot. Others were with me, and they noted that smell as well. It was a mossy, cucumbery smell. When I got to Harriet's place later, I smelled the same smell on her. It was as if she was subconsciously recreating – in her daily environment – that same smell from the sighting spot. I recently heard about experiments that were done to scientifically discover the most attractive smell to the opposite sex. It was a cucumber-based smell, mixed with something else. This spot on the lane seems to be hypnotizing people with smell. There are no gardens nearby, either. This is a very steep part of the hill, nothing but trees and brush. But the smell was really strong. It was there for several days. This seems to be the same smell that Harriet remembers. My sister Loretta remarked that the smell reminded her "of childhood." The role that smell plays in this phenomenon is intriguing. It helped bring the memories back to Harriet…

In her letter, Harriet said, "I heard a voice. It was telepathic… Strong and commanding… Directing me to urgently leave at once with this being." She felt paralyzed. She couldn't move. Her feet were glued to the blacktop. "It seemed to glide through the air and spoke to me without moving its mouth," she said. The creature was telepathically trying to get her to come with him. *[shows image]* When I saw this image of the Flatwoods Monster (it's a little doll that they made in honor of the monster), I sent it to Harriet because it seemed to resemble her drawing of the creature. When she saw the drawing she said, "Oh my God, *that's* the thing that I saw." So what we have here is Harriet seeing something roughly similar to the Flatwoods Monster of 1952, but in 1968.

> *Harriet later clarified this in early 2007, on the Grassy Knoll Radio program. She explained that her creature was not robotic like the Flatwoods Monster – and therefore wasn't the same. However, this still doesn't explain why two creatures so essentially different – a robot and anthropomorphic angel – would look generally similar in size and shape.*

This is a hat that I found in Albuquerque when I was there recently. *[displays hat from Pueblo Cultural Center]* These are your "three shamans" on the front. Synchronistically I received a similar three-shaman item, a necklace, from Harriet. These could be the same three beings that we saw on Woodward Lane in 2002, or that visited me in a dream two weeks before I read Olga Kharitidi's book *Entering the Circle*. Her book is about these three Russian shamans, and how they help humans heal themselves – and *other* humans – through the dreamstate.

> *The "Guruda" is said to manifest as three beings, each representing one of the three major Buddhist traditions: Hinayana, Vajrayana, and Mahayana.*

Is it possible that these three mythical beings have been visiting us for eons, resulting in symbolisms ranging from the aforementioned shamans to the Holy Trinity of the Christians?

Plumbrook, Harriet – Colvin Home + Dunbar/St. Albans – 2002

Andy Colvin (AC): Here we are in Dunbar, West Virginia underneath Interstate

64. Right above us is where there was a famous sighting in 1966, by Tad Jones. Can you tell us about it?

Harriet Plumbrook (HP): A very religious man (as the story goes in Keel's book) got a surprise when he was going to work one day. A spaceship landed in front of him, and a person got out of it. This happened approximately five miles west of Charleston, which is right where we are, near the Dunbar Bridge.

AC: What did the guy see exactly? What kind of craft was it?

HP: It was an egg-shaped craft with three legs… [It was] a tripod type of landing… It landed within 50 yards of him. He did approach it and get closer. He had a real hard time dealing with the whole thing…

AC: Now that we're here in this spot, are you picking up anything?

HP: Yes, it wasn't the first time this area's been visited. And it won't be the last.

AC: Do you get a feeling that this craft was related to the actual Mothman creature that was seen on the Elk River?

HP: *All* of this stuff is related. All of this phenomenon, whether it be the Mothman, Stickman, UFOs – or whatever type of strange paranormal experience – is related.

AC: There was actually a Mothman sighting in Dunbar. Didn't it land on somebody's house near here?

HP: Yes. In Dunbar, it was sitting on a family's front porch. There was also a sighting down the road in St. Albans. Both of these sightings took place just right off of US Rt. 60. [During] the one in St. Albans, it was actually sitting on a woman's roof.

We headed for Woodward Drive, in nearby Mound. It was a steaming, unbearably hot summer day. We left some water for my brother Chip, who had hiked with his wife up to the Big Rocks, an old Indian spot high on the ridge overlooking our old house. Some incredible things happened while we were there. Harriet and I felt extremely cold locations within the trees overlooking our house. These were areas where some of us had sleepwalked at night. Harriet picked up some verifiable psychic details of a possible Colvin family hypnosis session with MIBs. Unbelievably, an unmarked helicopter flew over the house soon after we began taping.

AC: The Mothman Tour 2002 continues at the Colvin homestead here in Mound, WV. Harriet is feeling the forces already.

HP: Big time… Big time…

AC: *[whispers to camera]* Harriet is sensing an animal presence. Here we are at the scary ravine next to our house, which everyone agrees is *scary*.

HP: I associate this [psychic impression] definitely with Sharon… I see her as a child. I'm guessing about 5 or 6 years old. I see her wandering off into here, like she's being summoned. She walked back here by herself. She's wearing a nightgown. It's got a ruffle around the bottom, light pink… It kind of has a cinched neck, and a bow right here. *[gestures]*

AC: *[shocked]* That's her gown!

HP: It is?

AC: I remember that. I have a picture of it… You know, one night when I was in college we were having a family gathering. I stepped out by myself, and looked this way to where we are standing now. And I felt a terrible evil presence. It was overwhelming. It was almost calling me to it, to disappear into another dimension… That was the feeling I got. It was like a David Lynch movie.

HP: Evil…

AC: Look, a black helicopter!

> *A dark, unmarked helicopter flew over our old house at this point. I was able to get some video footage of it. In all the years I lived there, we never once saw a helicopter go over our house. While this may be a common occurrence in big cities, it is – or was – very rare in our area. Not long after this helicopter event, I was contacted by a woman from the Pocatalico River Valley, who had been experiencing paranormal phenomena. She told me that there had been sharp increase in "paramilitary" air traffic along the Pocatalico, and in areas outlying Charleston. We had a boat cottage on the Pocatalico River for many years. My mother grew up on a tributary of the Pocatalico.*

AC: Here's the area where my sister claims a UFO landed around 1954… So, you're feeling overwhelmed?

HP: Yes, I'm shivering!

AC: It's 95 degrees folks, and Harriet is *shivering*. So you're getting a sense that Loretta was visited?

HP: Yes. [They] are actual memories…

> *Harriet checked out the landing site for the UFO. There was a large circular area of dead grass, about the size of a typical UFO. Even though it was just an impression left from a swimming pool that had been*

removed, it still spooked us a bit. Were the new owners subconsciously moved by unseen forces to put a swimming pool exactly at the landing spot of Loretta's UFO?

AC: My sister Loretta actually remembers a flying saucer parked right there, above those steps. She claims that in broad moonlight she saw a UFO parked there. She even mentioned little green men coming in and going through her belongings, her shelves or whatever... She saw black panthers on the hillside over here. Oftentimes these black panther sightings are actually more akin to a psychic encounter, like a lot of Bigfoot sightings. Sometimes the Bigfoot is seen but then disappears mysteriously, as if it can go between dimensions. Bigfoots are also seen coming in and out of UFOs. In our case, we kind of have the whole gamut going. We have nightmares about Bigfoots. We have real sightings of UFOs. We also have nightmares about various alien beings and a lot of these brand new black cars going up and down the road at night... MIB cars... There was one incident that occurred in the house here. Well, I won't say it was an incident. It's another nightmare, I suppose, of a Man in Black coming to our house and hypnotizing all of us... If you look at the house here, these steps on the right... That's where the Man in Black came up. We saw little balls of light in our living room there, which is next to that door.

Author's former home near "top of hill" of Woodward Drive, Mound, WV 1999

My sister has also had this same "balls of light" dream. She remembers being paralyzed. I remember being paralyzed. I remember the whole family being paralyzed and interrogated in the living room. My theory is that because of the NASA and NSA subcontractors in the neighborhood, MIBs were used to check people out. It's possible that real spies came to our house, drugged us, put us in a hypnotic state, and tried to find out what we knew – or didn't know – about our neighbors and any secret projects. The MIBs could have been Russian, or they could have been American. We don't know… You seem to be picking up some vibes about it, Harriet?

HP: Here's what I'm intuiting. I can see you sitting on the couch. Spring is sitting on the couch, too. Your mother and father are there. Loretta is there, but she's not on the couch. You're being interrogated by two men. I think it kills your Russian theory, because they're not speaking Russian. They don't have an accent.

AC: What do they look like? Do they look "Oriental?"

HP: They're different. They're not like anybody you would see around Charleston, West Virginia. You can definitely tell that they were foreign.

AC: Were they interdimensionals, astral projections, or real people?

HP: They were real.

AC: There are documents proving that drugs were used to interrogate people in the '60s.

HP: I just see you all sitting in a stupor.

AC: How did they administer the drugs? With gas?

HP: They may have [used drugs] but I don't see it. It doesn't mean it didn't take place. Your eyes are all wide open. You're listening intently to them. You're answering questions that they're asking. But you don't have any information.

AC: That's what I remember.

HP: Well you've never told me that, so… It's interesting. There were two of them. Very high cheekbones, very odd-shaped face, deep dark set eyes… I guess you could say they look a little Oriental. They're definitely *different*… Strange colored skin… Very strange… Pale-ish, yellowish, ashy, grayish… They're speaking to you in almost monotone, which is a technique that is used in hypnosis. That's how you induce the trance. Very little inflection in the voice at all…

AC: Do you know what they're asking about?

HP: No, not picking that up. [But] they told you that you *wouldn't remember*.

AC: But I did!

HP: Yes, I guess you did! I see something in the room... There's something shiny, like glowing... It's like strings of something hanging down. I just see light that keeps reflecting off of whatever that is... Strings of something hanging down...

AC: Like they used balls of string and medallions to hypnotize us?

HP: No, I just see something that looks like beads... I don't know why I see that...

AC: No you don't...

HP: Yes I do.

Fish Ofiesh (FO): What is it?

AC: We had beads hanging in one of the windows...

FO*: [amazed]* You did not...

AC: I swear to God! We had beads hanging in the window between the living room and the kitchen.

HP: Right... It's an opening. It's between two rooms. It's like a window.

AC: We also had chairs in front of that. I remember some of us sitting in those chairs with the beads behind us.

HP: That's why I'm seeing them. I keep seeing light bounce off of them. The room is dimmed. They don't really have the lights on. It's dark, isn't it? But they're talking to you about *light*.

AC: Are they trying to find out what paranormal things we may have seen, or are they trying to figure out if we know about secret projects?

HP: They're asking you about the paranormal. It's all I really pick up. What they were interested in is paranormal.

CHAPTER 36

"What we know as culture gets packaged and delivered by one
thing: symbols."

-David Carradine

Colvin, Andy – Electromagnetic Control/Sara Jane Moore – 2003

Andy Colvin: *[to camera]* Here is a Scientific American article about the
exploration of electromagnetic frequencies to change human behavior. They're
coming up with little modules that they can use to pulse a signal through
your brain, to enhance one's work performance. Of course the corporations
would just love to have this. They could use it for any job that puts people
into a bored state of mind, or stresses them to the point where they become
very tired. This device could be used to temporarily speed them up. It's sort
of like a form of speed. An electromagnetic speed... In this article, they talk
a bit about the history of this kind of experimentation. They don't really talk
too much about the experimentation process itself because that would entail
talking about how those experiments were done. The history, as claimed in
this magazine, doesn't go back much more than 1985. Although they admit
that this kind of research has been going on since "the early 1900s," they don't
really talk about experiments in intervening decades. Of course during that
intervening time period, we had all kinds of various Nazi experiments about
how to affect the mind with various electrical items. The Nazis were really big
on it.

Following the war, a lot of these German scientists came to the United States.
Japanese doctors came over, too. Further experiments were carried out by
our government. It appears that some of this experimentation may have
been done on people who are so-called "UFO" experiencers. I just heard a
recent interview with Walter Bowart, a pioneering writer about mind control
research. He wrote a book in the 1970s called *Operation Mind Control*, which
informed a whole generation of researchers about the various ways that the
government has experimented on people. A lot of this experimentation was
going on in the '50s and '60s, during the height of the various UFO flaps.
There are some people now coming forward to say that their experiences
weren't alien in nature, but military. These covert operations are now popularly
called MILABS, or "military abductions."

It's always important to consider the question, "Was it a manmade event, or
was it a natural event?" In Point Pleasant and Mound, it seems both were
going on. While it is clear that some of this stuff is indeed coming from

"another dimension," some of it may be simulated – or *stimulated* – by manmade technology. For instance, if certain towns – like the completely hypnotized one in NJ, investigated by Keel and Sanderson – *were* bombarded with electromagnetic frequencies, it might have caused people to lapse into these situations where natural paranormal events *could* manifest. Walter Bowart is saying that UFO research is now the "cutting edge of mind-control research." If you really want to get to the heart of mind-control technology today, he says to "look at the UFO phenomenon." You have to look at what is *really* going on, in any particular "paranormal" situation.

There was also some interesting stuff in the UFO Round-Up during this first week of September 2003. There was a big blackout in London. There was another UFO seen over the Northern Ohio area, east of Cleveland. This is where the recent New York City blackout supposedly started. Here's an article: *Mothman Curse Topples a Bridge in India*. Right after the premier of *The Mothman Prophecies* film in India, there was a big bridge collapse. There are lots of ponderous things going on every day.

Here's an article that caught my eye. It's the June '76 issue of Playboy magazine, with a "chilling" interview with Sara Jane Moore, called *The Real Reason I Tried to Kill President Ford*. You know, I've read this article and there's *never* a real reason given. It seems as if Moore has some really big secrets. Actually, she does divulge a few things. She basically says that she was set-up by the FBI, and that Squeaky Fromme helped set her up. Playboy asks, "Why hasn't your version of events been more widely publicized?"

> Sara Jane Moore: I get so mad. I made statements and nobody printed them. Are the members of the press forgetting that many of them have, in the past, told me I was sensible, reliable, accurate, honest, and reasonable? Even likable? To badly paraphrase Shakespeare, is it that the mistakes and frailties of men live on in the press, while the good is often interred beyond recall? There are two or three things I feel I ought to say to people, particularly about the callous, deliberate, manipulative techniques of the FBI, whose agents are not – as I had always believed – impartial investigators, but instruments of political action, using people as expendable tools for the repression and harassment of honest dissenters. I wrote a poem about the FBI. I'd like to read it to you:
>
> > Said the FBI, you are our mother, help us. If they truly love the people, how could they deliberately cause such anguish?
> >
> > Said the FBI, you are a patriot, help us. If they truly love the people, how could they deliberately

cause such chaos that tears at the very fiber of our
community?

Said the FBI, you are moral and Christian, help us.
Well, if they truly love the people, how could they
steal and kill and bomb?

So, I went out among the people as your agent, to
look for the kidnappers, to look for the killers, to
know the thief, to find the bombers.

And I heard from the kidnappers who, even in
their running, had a message of concern and love
for their brother...

And then they died in flames, your flames... You
are parents and yet you killed and over-killed.
Where was your concern for the anguished mother
or innocent kidnap victim?

You are the killers, killers of hope, killers of
freedom, killers of children. You are smug, protective and self-righteous.

Yes, I learned to know those you call thieves, who
take back for the people that which was torn from
them, first with whips, then with oppression in the
name of progress through profits.

And finally, I found the bombers, and embraced
them as comrades, and now with flames, we speak
our love. And our hate.

Perhaps Sara Jane's poem says a lot more than she was able to say in her interview... While the Mothman phenomenon can bring concern over warnings of
impending doom, remember that prophecies are sometimes meant to be wrong.
If we begin to recognize prophecies for what they are – as tools for positive
change – we may *truly* survive.

"I saw that Mothman creature just materialize out from a wall.
I am dumbfounded to this day about that. Since it apparently
doesn't have to follow our laws of physics, I think that it is more
than just some trans-genetic being. It is maybe from a different
dimension, and perhaps its physical likeness operates at some
odd frequency unique to its place of origin. At least that's what

I think. I can't verify that. I only saw what I saw and puzzle over it often. It's too bad some systematic science isn't applied to these sightings. To myself, and others in my family, it is as real as anything else is…

"Most people do not take it seriously, and I don't blame them. It is a bit weird. But it is a real, recurring sighting. That is why, when I explained it to three [different] psychiatrists in the last year, they didn't prescribe me a thing. Nurses have even come forward to tell me that a Mothman sighting is a common report. My story of the Mothman barely raised an eyebrow. I was even told that there should be a diagnosis code for it. It's that common. Nobody does anything about it, and it seems likely nobody ever will. It is categorized as a paranormal issue.

"Most credible scientists will not stake their reputations on chasing ghosts. It's too bad. I think that it warrants a serious investigation employing the scientific method. And the fact that this thing broke laws regarding breaking and entering [into my bedroom] I suppose is insignificant? What else do these things do, besides staring people down and freaking them out? Apparently there are ceiling-high, black-winged beasts with great, big glowing hypnotic red eyes wandering - at will – frightening people. Yet there is no official inquiry into it."

-Emil Hach, 2007 posting to Internet

CHAPTER 37

"In the universal Mind, all [aspects of] time "wake up." All times [exist at once]. Those in the [collective] Mind who think they have a [individual] mind are not in the Mind, because the Mind has no [specific] time. Infinite consciousness, which lives in infinite soul, carries on from parents to children... Everything you see, all that you hear, everything you're told, and the way you're told it, impresses your minds within... The way you are is [simply] the programming they have given you... We emerge [from the unconsciousness of infancy] to brag about [how] we know things, for another gold star on our paper from the teacher, or preacher (who only loves money and all the spirit that flew into the money)... The existence of the soul is locked in the bank – the infinite bank – that pays all debts when they come due... And we all learn to take our place. Like the resurrection of perfection in the past, it is the children who carry the hopes and vibrations that sneak past the door, in and around the night, when the bedbugs bite."

-Charles Manson, writing to his son

Plumbrook, Harriet – Manson Home Reading, Mound, WV – 2002

Andy Colvin (AC): I think I've tried about ten ESP test locations on you so far, Harriet, and you've been right every time. Let's see if you can find Charlie's house, or what was reported to be Charlie Manson's house.

Harriet points to it as soon as it comes into view.

AC: And once again, Harriet gets it right, folks! And I can prove it because I've already got photos of this place, which she has never seen. Instantly, she knew which one it was. Tell us about it. How do you feel this sort of thing?

Harriet Plumbrook (HP): I feel it right here in the solar plexus. Certain things like death, destruction, mayhem, people that are murderers, people that are basically evil... It'll hit me like a stabbing pain. It grabs me and twists... The minute you turned the car around [from] looking at the bus from Seattle... The minute we turned the car facing this way, where my solar plexus could face it, it *hit*...

AC: Truly amazing... We were driving around yet couldn't find it. And then we saw this charter bus parked back here. It says "Seattle" on it. For those who don't already know it, I now live in Seattle. *[gestures]* This is Charlie Manson's childhood home. Decades ago, when I first heard that Charlie had lived down here at the end of Woodward Drive (where it meets old US Route 60), I didn't know which house it was. I came down one day and looked for it on my own, thinking I could maybe get a sense of which one it was... I rarely tried ESP back then. But in that instance I did... I picked this house. Someone else verified it later. So I actually found this house using psychic means, as Harriet just did. Here's the window of Charlie Manson's old place. That American flag is a patriotic note. Now I'm standing in front of Charlie's place. If you turn and look in this direction you see Discount Jewelry and Loan, which used to be "Van's Never-Close Market." Van was shown on the news in the early '80s, discussing how Charlie and Sara Jane Moore were friends as kids. They used to come into his store holding hands, and buy candy.

I was friends with a local news anchor at the time of Van's interview, Kathy Brennan. We met at Marshall University's journalism school. Kathy introduced me to a woman from Sissonville, who told me she had seen strange lights over the high school there. Years later, a female student at Sissonville High would make national news for being suspended over wearing a t-shirt that criticized Pres. Bush.

AC: What do you think about all this, Fish?

Fish Ofiesh (FO): Pretty cool...

AC: How does Charlie Manson play into the Mothman thing? It's kind of hard to figure out. It seems like there's a connection, but we can't quite figure it out. Maybe it has something to do with the national security state, mind control, and the occult?

FO: And Charlie? Yeah...

AC: Now that you're sitting here, Harriet, and you can look at his place, what can you tell me about the connection between Manson and Sara Jane Moore? You sat in front of her house and did a reading. You picked up some details. Can you tell us anything about those two? For one thing, it's never really come out in the media that they were friends. It's only sort of hinted at by the fact that Squeaky and Sara Jane both shot at President Ford, two weeks apart.

HP: The only thing I can tell you, that I pick up right now [is that] they definitely knew each other. There's no doubt about it. It's the same feeling...

AC: They both were in California. They both were involved in popular murders, or attempts at murders...

HP: They *definitely* knew each other here.

AC: Van, who owned the pawn shop, remembers them as being friends and coming in together.

FO: Really?

AC: But Moore, when she's interviewed, will not talk about Charleston at all. In fact, she won't even mention the name of Charleston. She tries to keep the city completely anonymous. She doesn't even mention her hometown in interviews. For some reason, there's a lot she just doesn't want to talk about. And Charlie is the same way. When they try to pin him down, he dances away. He was into a lot of things in Hollywood involving prostitution with famous people. And drugs lurk in the background of those killings, too. In other words, they were more like mob hits than genuine, grassroots "helter skelter." This is probably what he doesn't want to talk

Charles Manson's House, Woodward Drive/Old Rt. 60, Mound, WV 1984

about. If he does, he will probably be killed in prison, or see his children harmed.

HP: Charlie's powerful, but there are a lot of other people out there that are more powerful… Charlie acts tough, but Charlie's scared. There's a lot of fear that comes out of his house. Charlie doesn't understand why Charlie thinks like he does. He rambles, and he doesn't even know why he rambles.

AC: Was he experimented on in prison, with drugs or behavioral techniques?

HP: Absolutely, both… He was a guinea pig. A human guinea pig… It started before prison.

AC: When did it start? Did it start here on Woodward Drive?

HP: I see someone roughly the age of 12, 13, that I'm intuiting to be Charlie at that age. It started then, shortly before his first stint in a reformatory. He was messed with *really* bad in different reform schools, more his mind than anything else. We know that. That's fact.

AC: He was a Scientologist for a long time, and claimed to have reached the highest level of Scientology.

HP: The man's actually brilliant. I'm intuiting that he has a high IQ.

AC: His way of speaking makes people think that he's a nutty hillbilly, because of his grammar. But the concepts are advanced.

HP: The concepts are so far beyond where he *should* be, because this guy is totally from the wrong side of the tracks. But if you ever listen to an interview with him, he speaks so much wisdom. It's hillbilly wisdom, but it's incredible wisdom. It's something that he wouldn't have learned from the street, if you ask me.

AC: Most people are going to say, "Huh? Charlie speaks wisdom?" Can you give an example?

HP: He seemed to understand that the government was messing with everybody. I'm intuiting it from this house. He seemed to understand that the government was one big game. He wasn't so eloquent when speaking about it, but he understood the concept of it. He understood what was happening to him. He understood that he was a guinea pig. He also understood that he was helpless to stop it. Charles Manson is not a threat when he gets back out on the street, as far as murdering someone. Charles Manson is a threat because of *what he knows*. Charlie's knowledge is far more dangerous than any weapon in Charlie's hand. I don't know much about Manson. You're the expert on Manson. I'm just telling you what I'm intuiting from being here.

AC: Does it have to do with his occult knowledge?

HP: It has to do with that, but it [also] has to do [with the] context, with experiments that were done on him [in his] his teen years. Mind control experiments…

AC: He talks about that kind of thing in his interviews. He says that for years, they've been giving him drugs and "messing him up."

HP: Right… He's honest about that. He is telling the truth. I'm intuiting that those were government-sponsored… He was actually hand-chosen as a guinea pig.

In a mid-1990's BBC documentary, Manson implied that he was first put into a reformatory by the American judge at Nuremberg. This would have been Judge Robert Jackson. Jackson was known for giving assurances that there would be strict monitoring over the immigration of Nazi scientists into the U.S. after WWII. But according to Linda Hunt, author of "Secret Agenda: The U.S. Government, Nazi Scientists, and Project Paperclip, 1945-1990," Jackson's boss, Undersecretary of War Patterson, didn't really believe Jackson was interested in catching Nazis. The Paperclip Nazi smuggling was still active during the Mothman era. The demise of the Paperclip operation only came about just as Werner von Braun's career began to wane in the late 1960s.

Jackson is widely considered by legal scholars to be one of the greatest Supreme Court justices in history, known particularly for his vivid writing style. In 1943, Jackson authored the majority opinion in West Virginia State Board of Education v. Barnette, 319 U.S. 624 (1943), which overturned a public school regulation making it mandatory to salute the flag. One wonders why someone so powerful and influential would have been involved in Manson's early life. The time period for Jackson's involvement with Manson would have roughly paralleled the end of WWII. Interestingly, famous mind-control psychiatrist Ewen Cameron, whose horrific "psychic driving" experiments at McGill Univ. were sponsored by the CIA and the Rockefellers, also attended the Nuremberg trials. This would have brought the mad scientist into direct contact with Judge Jackson.

Carl H. – Manson/Mothman poetry – 2003

Carl: *[Phone message from fellow researcher]* Hello Andy, my name's Carl H. and I live in Ohio. You recently sent me your DVD on the Mothman. I have some information that you might be interested in on the Serpent Mound, the crypto-explosive uplift that it's on, and some other information. I have some stuff that Manson sent me years ago. Some of his poetry... I forgot that he had lived down in West Virginia. [Manson's poetry] refers to *hawk's claws* and some bizarre stuff that I'm pretty sure relates to Mothman.

I have some odd, possibly Woodward Dr./Mothman-related (unpublished) poetry Manson sent me in his own hand... Also odd events that happened to me in Egypt, Europe, Pacific Islands, etc. that are parallel to things you noted... As an Ohio boy, born in May of 1960, I too have had some odd sightings locally... One in particular was returning from a trip to Three-Mile Island in 1979. At dawn, on a foggy road near Salt Fork State Park, we passed – at 10 mph – an 8' tall being clad in solid black, walking on the roadside. The creature's hands were level with the passenger door *top* as we passed! Huge!

The stuff Manson sent me is another crazy story of subterfuge. He sent me several handwritten poems and letters on his Mothmanish letterhead... In 1981-83, while in Europe, I was interested in Robert Anton Wilson's stuff. The rule of the road seems to be that the apprentice who begins to trod this path begins to pile up one synchronous event after another – overlap after overlap – that until closely scrutinized, seem totally unrelated. It becomes frightening and almost comical, too, as one computes the infinite probabilities of so many non-related relations, synchronicities, repeating deja-vu's, and recurring [numbers like] 23...

A bit of critique though... By assigning a Republican/George Bushian master-strategist plot to all disasters large and small – from J.F.K to Manson to 9/11 to the low-life DC snipers – you remove chaos theory right out of all equations (i.e., no randomness in human sociopolitical events). It is all a grand series of manipulations, schemes, counter-schemes and cover-ups... You conveniently dismiss the fact that we do live in a world teaming with losers, underachievers, misfits and just plain dumb people who *do* go on shooting sprees and think nothing of sleeping it off in a rest area! Hell, our prisons are teaming with millions of these bright fellows...

> *I include Carl's last paragraph because this is a common response of many who think that the conspiracy, or institutional, theorist is not considering the random stupidity of others. I think most conspiracy theorists do consider this. Many also understand that the stupidity of the general public has helped lead to sociopolitical events being manipulated by organizations operating completely in secret, as effectively pure conspiracies. The hierarchical nature of corporations, built on military tradition, has the advantage of having already canonized institutional secrecy. These are among what sociologist Erving Goffman called "total institutions." The*

current White House administration has teams of researchers busy re-clas-
sifying older, previously declassified materials. Today, we have technolo-
gies that didn't previously exist. It is now easy to spy on people, point EM
devices their way, and make them hear voices. With a little effort, they
can make the victim shoot certain people, bomb things, or hijack vehicles.
Remember the Boomer drug and its variants... One can no longer assume
that the "lone nut" isn't an artificially created pawn in the game of terror.
The nature of the field of play has changed. From now on, every time one
of these strange stories plays on the news, it is incumbent for researchers to
balance the usual "that's a lone nut idiot" impulse with the question, "is
this a stragetic event that is furthering some political agenda?"

Plumbrook, Harriet – Blue Moon Tavern, Mound, WV – 2002

Andy Colvin (AC): Here we are in the vicinity of the Blue Moon Tavern, where Charles Manson's mom used to hang out. You're noticing some things here?

Harriet Plumbrook (HP): Yes, there's a major substation behind us, next to Union Carbide and, of course, all the power lines that lead into it. If you think about it, these would go real close to Manson's house, and ours as well. Also, there's a gas line in here... All are indicative of electromagnetic fields, which is associated with the phenomenon that we are researching.

AC: Here we are at the Blue Moon parking lot. They're doing some remodel-
ing. This is where Manson's mom broke off a bottle and stabbed a guy in
the head with it...

HP: And stole all of his money... And had to leave the state...

AC: She stole Charlie's money, too. I guess he beat her up as a result. Then
they went to Indiana together, where he ended up in reform school.
There he was raped and put on the "highway," as he called it.

HP: And it all started right here... See that? *[points to her car window]*

At this point we see the car window next to Harriet go up and down by
itself, three times in a row. This is the unexplained electrical phenomenon
that the Volvo manufacturers in Sweden were talking about in relation to
highly charged individuals, like Harriet.

AC: I see that! The window is reacting to Harriet! Harriet said she felt weird,
and now the window goes up and down by itself. She is not touching
it in any way. Now she's trying to close it. She just hit the stop button.
Okay... Finally, on the third try it stops. It started by itself. It didn't seem
to want to stop...

Some researchers think that Manson was programmed while studying Scientology in prison. Others think it may have occurred via contacts with Esalen Institute or The Process Church. It's possible that Charlie received periodic programming from overlapping sources. Charlie's Nazi programming has always seemed to be at variance with some of his other beliefs like the Universal Mind, Christ Consciousness, peace and love, etc. Keel referred to 1950s UFO contactees being contradictorily programmed with both New Age and fascist ideologies, just like Manson.

Plumbrook, Harriet – Elk River/Roane County/Walton Mtn. - 2002

Andy Colvin (AC): Here we are in good old Roane County, West Virginia, land of the psychic CIA women. You have an interesting story about your aunts, who grew up here?

Harriet Plumbrook (HP): Yes, my mom is one of eleven. There are 7 girls and 4 boys in the family, and they all went to Walton High School. My mom, a couple of weeks ago, just out of nowhere mentions that her life would have been totally different had she "taken that job with the FBI." I said, "What?" Then she tells me that she was only 16 when she graduated from high school, and that her parents would not let her go off to Washington D.C. by herself. Then I find out that my aunts who worked in Washington, D.C., my aunt Barbara (who's now deceased) and my aunt Joanne (who worked initially for the Department of Agriculture, and then for the CIA), were also recruited out of Walton High School... A couple more ended up working for the government, but I don't know that they were recruited in high school. They were recruited in college. Like the one that was the head of the China Lake Naval Weapons Reserve...

AC: Now we are in Clendenin, WV, site of a famous Mothman sighting. You say your stomach is giving you psychic Mothy "vibes?"

HP: Indeed it is. A sighting took place [here in] late November or early December 1966. It is documented. I just can't tell you at the time which of those dates it is. It was around the time of the first wave of sightings in Point Pleasant. There was also one in St. Albans the very same day.

AC: So what is it about all these sightings taking place on the Elk River?

HP: There's definitely something to the Elk River. I can feel it.

AC: When you have your astral projection and/or remote viewing dreams, do you dream a lot about the Elk River?

HP: I do...

AC: And you dreamed about it before you ever saw these certain parts of it that we've seen on this trip?

HP: I do, and I did. It's very interesting [that] in a neighborhood that I've been "flying" around in [or] projecting around in for [a long time] and writing to you about, it's *all* looking down on the Elk River… I didn't realize that [before]. I've told you about seeing the river, not knowing it was the Elk River. I'd never been there before…

AC: Now here we are in Walton, West Virginia, the heart of Roane County. Any theories on why the CIA, FBI, NSA (and whoever else) come to this town to recruit people?

HP: That's a good question… I don't think it's just to offer them a better life away from here, I really don't. I think they're picking and choosing very willfully here. I think that maybe they're picking people to be mind-controlled or something. People here would never suspect something like that. Politically, everyone in my mom's family is so far to the right that it's not even funny.

AC: Just how far right are they?

HP: They're so conservative [that] they don't believe that the government should help with anything, or anybody. There should be no social programs. Everybody is on his own. They're pro big business. They don't care what kind of an ass of a Republican might be in office. They'll support him, just because he's a Republican.

AC: Things aren't always apple pie and ice cream on Walton's Mountain…

Colvin, Andy – Video Field Report, Nitro, WV – 2003

Andy Colvin (AC*): [to camera]* Okay, here we are in Nitro, West Virginia. It has an interesting history. It was named Nitro because this is where they made most of the nitroglycerin during the war years. Today, it's known for being one of the two places in America where they make the gas that killed everyone in Bhopal, India. My first cousin is a supervisor in the division that handles the gas. She tells me that she actually reaches her hands into the plastic arms and mixes the stuff up. Of course if the least amount of it gets out, it just kills thousands of people. She and her husband both work with that deadly gas…

In addition to having Mothman sightings, Nitro is a town that recently made cult news headlines. This is where the Clone-Aid Foundation, which was set up by the Raelian cult, started their first lab to clone a human. *[gestures]* It was here, in what was once the local high school. It's now a community center. I don't know exactly what connection the Raelians and human cloning have with Mothman. But anytime you get these cult stories that, for some reason, become big and then turn out to be false, you wonder if it wasn't just a disinformation campaign to muddy the waters of a particular issue. In this case, they seem to have come up with a bizarre, fake story that's full of holes, in order to discredit any future instances of real cloning that might leak out accidentally. It gets people's feet wet in regards to a particular issue, so that when the cloning or whatever actually *does* come around, people are more blasé about it.

For some reason, the Raelian cult reminds me of the Heaven's Gate cult. A lot of people don't remember this, but the Heaven's Gate cult was in the news long before they performed their function of killing themselves the same week that the Martin Luther King family announced the innocence of James Earl Ray. This King announcement was big news. There had already been a mock court trial set up by William Pepper (Ray's attorney) that showed that, had Ray gotten a fair trial with all the proper evidence, he would have been acquitted. The evidence was very flimsy. It was obvious that he was set up by the intelligence agencies. So when this announcement came out – this really earth-shattering news that the King family suspected the government – the Heaven's Gate cult suddenly decides to kill themselves! Although they killed themselves a day or two before the public announcement by the King family, the media held off on the story so that they broke on the same exact day. When you turned on the TV, instead of seeing the King family saying there was a government conspiracy, you saw the Nike shoes on dead people. It just completely obliterated the King story.

> *In 2006, this type of misdirection was also used in relation to suspected pedophile John Mark Karr. Karr just happened to groggily stumble forward and falsely admit to the Jon-Benet Ramsey murder on the same day that a federal judge ruled that Pres. Bush's secret NSA wiretapping was illegal. Patsy Ramsey had died only weeks before. The Ramseys had familial connections to WV. The NSA has a long wiretapping history in WV. As if to drive the point home, the Tri-State Airport in Huntington, WV was shut down on the same day because a Pakistani woman carrying no explosives triggered the explosives detector. The media used the non-event to justify the banning of liquids on all planes by associating it with the London "Liquid Hijacking" arrests from a few days before. The London arrests, which were the result of a yearlong investigation, just happened to coincide with the defeat of Senator Joe Lieberman in the Connecticut primary election – considered to be a watershed moment for progressives. The Pakistani woman was caught at the same WV airport where a plane full of untraceable weapons linked to KY drug dealers was once seized. As of 2007, the Transportation Security Administration*

seems to have settled into permanently forcing passengers to carry only small, 3-ounce toiletry containers, which typically cost twice as much as the larger containers used before. This benefits Ohio companies like Proctor & Gamble and Kroger, who make or sell such toiletries.

The Raelian cult may someday echo Heaven's Gate. Maybe they're going to play a future role. They've now entered the consciousness of the public a little bit. We've now heard about them trying to clone people. They're obviously nutty. We've seen their leader, a French race car driver, on TV getting all frustrated with Geraldo Rivera's questioning. So the stage is set for the Raelian cult to fulfill their destiny. *[gestures]* Well, it looks like we've found it. This is the building where Clone-Aid is supposed to be. This would be your old high school turned community center. It happens to be in the same building with the Nitro Police Department, the Nitro Genealogical Society, and something called Ra Security. Interesting…

Plumbrook, Harriet – Lowe Hotel Beings – 2003

Andy Colvin (AC): Well, the Mothman Festival is over and Harriet just remembered a tidbit, here, as we sort of try to recover. She remembers what her father said when the Silver Bridge collapsed on December 15th, 1967. He said to her that *that* would be the worst way to die…

Harriet Plumbrook (HP): Yes, so cold and icy. He actually died on December 15th in 1995. I never thought two things about it until the *Search For Mothman* documentary reminded me yesterday. They showed all the packages floating in the river, and they said it was the coldest day of the year. There was lots of ice and snow, and there was a crust of ice on the water. My father had made the comment that that would be a horrible time of year to die. If you had to go, why then? Then he turns around and ends up dying on December 15th. It's just a strange coincidence.

AC: So last night in the Lowe Hotel, where Keel and others were staying, you had another energetic spiritual encounter?

HP: Yes. They had moved my room. I was in the smallest room in the hotel, Room 336. The thing about Room 336 is that it has no windows. It's just sort of tucked behind a stairwell. It was a really teeny, stuffy [room]. It felt claustrophobic in there. This happened at about 3:20 a.m. this morning. I looked at my watch. I kind of left the bathroom light on, just so I could see around. I couldn't stand the idea of no natural light. I felt something like a hand, starting at about my forehead, rubbing all the way down and touching me… It stopped at about my abdomen. I felt this electrical charge and a buzzing ring, which started in my ears. My head started spinning. Unfortunately, whenever I get a feeling like that, it never amounts to anything good... I was afraid of what I might see. I just lay there for a while. My head just kept spinning, and the buzzing wouldn't go away. There was such a charge in the air. Just a really creepy feeling... I guess [whatever it was is] friends [with] the "people" I saw the night before – the three "light entities."

AC: Speaking of which, the night before, when I was in my room, I felt a weird energy in the room. I sat down and meditated on the floor. After a while, I started getting these images of three people sort of talking to me telepathically. It turns out that Harriet, at the very same time, was seeing three wispy lights in her room.

HP: Yes, and they distinctly had three different colors. There was a green, a violet, and a gold. They were in the far corner of the room. I wouldn't say that they were "human" forms, but you could see that they were associated with form. They were very much visible to me, with a very high charge on my personal field of electricity... Not a menacing presence at all, but definitely a very strong presence... One sat higher, and two sat down lower. You could see their light fields kind of blend into one another.

CHAPTER 38

"What is the nature of mind like? Imagine a sky, empty, spacious, and pure from the beginning; its essence is like this. Imagine a sun, luminous, clear, unobstructed, and spontaneously present; its nature is like this. Imagine that sun shining out impartially on us and all things, penetrating all directions; its energy, which is the manifestation of compassion, is like this: Nothing can obstruct it, and it pervades everywhere."

-Sogyal Rinpoche

Colvin, Andy – Grassy Knoll Radio interview 8 – May 2006

"Vyz" at Grassy Knoll Radio (GK): You're probably hearing this on June 9th, 2006. You're not going to believe this, Andrew, but this is #8. Are you okay with that?

Andy Colvin (AC): Way to go!

GK: We do thank Andrew Colvin for coming back. His website is andycolvin. com. You know that he has the documentary called *The Mothman's Photographer*. He's been on a number of times to talk about all the phenomena that's going on in and around the Ohio Valley. Especially around West Virginia... It's been a while since we spoke. Now let me tell you, Andrew... First of all, the Cleveland Cavaliers are dust.

AC: I was really hoping Cleveland would beat the Detroit Pistons. Cleveland is one of the hubs of the Mothman conspiracy, and close to my heart for that reason. An interesting thing about that basketball series was that I heard them mention that the Detroit athletic coach uses a cucumber-based mixture to deal with injuries. This reminded me of the cucumber issue during our little jaunt back to West Virginia in 2002. At this place where all these sightings occurred, there was the smell of cucumber in the air. We couldn't pin it down. We figure that it's some plant growing there. I don't think it's a cucumber plant, but it smells like cucumbers. Harriet remembered the smell from childhood. By the way, the cucumber plant smell is the most powerful aphrodisiac. They did some research about five years ago, I think it was, and found that cucumber was the scent that most of us were attracted to at a really deep level. I'm wondering if that smell has something to do with this process of seeing entities. If you've got a field of energy that is storing itself as memory in surrounding objects, it might use smell to either attract more energy, or release it.

Puharich actually did some telepathy experiments with psychics holding objects, and found that objects do indeed hold memory. It is testable. This is why people can solve criminal cases or find missing persons by holding objects owned by the victims. I'm thinking that this could also extend to the olfactory senses. These kinds of stimuli can trigger certain responses in the brain.

GK: With regard to cucumber, apparently it's got a lot more going for it than people realize. Medicinally, it seems to be an excellent food. It's almost always involved in juicing. When people apply it to their bodies, it's not without good reason. But you are saying something about the smell of cucumber…

AC: It was a specific lab test to find the most potent sexual attractants for both sexes. It was a fragrance test for perfumes, trying to decipher what smell *really* works the best. Cucumber was the one that I remember. There's a health angle to this, especially in terms of the Native Americans, who feel that Thunderbird witnesses make good healers. Discovering healing substances can be "part of the process" for entity witnesses. One of the Bigfoot/UFO witnesses I interviewed became a master herbalist. He talked about how you'll usually have both the poison and the antidote growing close together in the forest. They are spin-offs of each other. Two sides of the same coin… This sort of relates to Puharich's theories about the four basic psi-plasma vortices. The first one creates the second, with a swirl in the opposing direction, and the two create four, at right angles (aka in "another dimension") to the first two. A lot of people have seen these black, wispy vortices. They are smoky things. Harriet saw one in her office, in fact. That was the same week that she had some MIB activity. When it became known that she was involved in my project, some strange things started happening. She got threatening phone calls and a visit from a strange guy in a black jacket. I saw a report that someone saw one of the smoky twisters coalesce into a figure reminiscent of what I saw coming out of a tree on Tommy's property. These psi-plasma vortices appear to be able to create matter. Basically, they consist of "positive" swirls going one way and "negative" swirls going the other. Positive-negative… There's an "anti-dimension," too. Each positive and negative swirl causes opposing spins in what seems like another dimension. This can happen either at the submicroscopic level, or at sizes too large for us to observe. Or right in front of our eyes… But as I said, it looks very much like Ezekiel's Wheel.

GK: Yes… We talk about a lot of things, and lay out somewhat of a framework. I'll go down a side street and not get back again for the rest of the show, but I'll deal with that. Nobody seems to be upset about it.

AC: By the way, the Greek letter "Psi", as in "psi-plasma," is the 23rd letter. Its symbol is very similar to the outstretched arms of the Garuda. It's much like the Christ symbol, too. There's a bunch of stuff that relates to Psi that I found very synchronistic this last week.

GK: What about the 23rd letter and the synchronicity you find there?

AC: The Greeks tapped into this phenomenon. They had a whole pantheon laid out to describe it. Apollo is one god who is very similar to Christ. Some speculate that he was a real figure (Apollonius) and maybe Christ wasn't. These kinds of debates go on, but the symbologies of Apollo are very similar to both the Garuda and Christ. By the way, the number 23 is important in the Masonic world, linked by Robert Anton Wilson to Sirius and a host of other esoteric beliefs. Again, that 23rd letter is Psi, looking very much like the outstretched Garuda. The 24th letter is Omega. If you put the two together, you have the Garuda holding the two-headed snake. You see this symbol everywhere, in different forms, even today. There's something very important about those letters and the symbology behind them. Today, what used to be called "the ether" is called "psi." The etheric medium for psychic phenomenon has a basis in Greek symbology. And there's something about that Garuda. I've already established that Buddhists and Hindus consider the Garuda to be the god of spaces, vibrations, and gaps. The same is true of the Greeks. These references synchronistically come up in modern day explorations. With Keel, it was "Apol." He kept getting calls from this telephone entity called Apol, which is short for "Apollo" in my mind. Keel was communicating with him.

Apol was the basis for Richard Gere's scary telephone scene in "The Mothman Prophecies" film.

GK: Andrew, we've got some questions that people wanted to ask you. May I throw one at you?

AC: Sure…

GK: It says, "Does Andy believe that time is plastic in certain ways? For example, if there was a great deal of trauma in a location, does it have a way of reaching back in time as well as forward in time?"

AC: It's absolutely possible. Maybe it's not provable yet, but the physicists seem to think it is likely. It's a good explanation for why someone like Tommy could see this vision of 9/11 thirty-four years before it happened. We talk about this in the documentary. I interviewed a Filipino shaman here in Seattle, Ken Alton, who felt like I had perhaps traveled back in time – or was connected to some energy that traveled – and caused my sister's 1973 photo to morph and exhibit what now looks like a Garuda in the window. He believes that people can affect photos that way. And you know, bizarrely enough, this is another one of Puharich's experiments. Puharich proved that psychics *could* affect film emulsion. Alton described it as dropping a stone in the water. A traumatic event is like something dropping in the water. You have the ripples going out in all directions, through time. Time is an abstraction for us. It's almost what they call in Buddhism an "indeterminate." It is something that's probably not knowable or answerable, like the question "who created God?" Time is not something I dwell on too much, but I think a ripple from the stone was seen on our trip to WV in 2002. We were at our vortex area. You can hear all of this in the field recording. We're talking about what we're seeing. I was the person in the lead. I probably soaked up most of whatever it was. The others had on protective devices, like stones and amulets, to absorb the energy. But I just took it straight on. I had a kundalini-based vision that night, of a drowning in the water at this spot in the Kanawha River. Three days later, there was a drowning there. I happened to come upon it. I thought to myself, "Well, that's a precognition you had." But then I found out that there had been a collapse of a bridge there 100 years before that had killed some children. There were some legends about it and so forth. I'm not sure if the vision I saw was one from the past, or one from the future. It got me thinking along those lines. It sort of becomes difficult to tell if you're seeing a ripple from in front of you (in time) or from in back of you. You're just feeling it coming through the psi-plasma. This is sort of how it works. People just pick up these things from the ether. But there are definitely physical rules to it that can be studied. Puharich was doing that.

On June 11, 2002, I received an email from Harriet where she predicted that I would be involved with a momentous paranormal photo. This was exactly 20 years, to the day, from when Neal Mindrum and I encountered the "Invisible Bigfoot" on Bear Mountain, NY, and then carried a huge Big Bird past Rockefeller Center (the following morning). A couple of years after Harriet's email, the possible Garuda in my 1973 kitchen photo was found by my young son.

AC: I wanted to clear up one thing that I said last time. At that time, I wasn't sure what Puharich had decided about distance – how distance relates to ESP. I checked and found that, generally, the further away you get from something, the weaker the signal gets (if only slightly).

GK: It comes down to the idea of time and whether it's malleable. I'm not deep into this whatsoever, but there are a lot of people who think that within the realm of quantum physics, you can jump ahead in time or go back in time. It makes all the science fiction stuff look plausible...

AC: This reminds me of the collective unconscious. People wonder about human will versus fate. Versus destiny... Once you get into time, you start getting into various issues. If you know what's going to happen, is there really such a thing as destiny? Or can we change it? This *does* come up in this phenomenon. You're given messages about the future. Sometimes they are rather abstract. I'm struggling with this right now. I was given advance notice about a couple of things. I know they are coming. I know *something* is coming, but I don't know exactly what it is. How do I interpret that? How does one deal with that? Can one have an effect on that, or is destiny locked in? I think this thing about distance and ESP kind of explains it. You do have an influence on it, but the further away you get from a particular vortex, the weaker your ability to manipulate it. Look at the collective unconscious. We are all just a wave on an ocean of consciousness. You *can* affect things, but you're limited in how much you can affect it. Oftentimes, the researcher is challenged to do something. He is given a mission of some kind... I can definitely say that that's true in my case. I've been following this stuff for a long time. While I've been doing this particular project for only the past five years, I've been studying this *kind* of thing for decades.

GK: So as a researcher, you kind of have to stand back and *do nothing* to affect the outcome. Is that the situation you find yourself in? I mean we've looked at this as the province of science fiction for a long, long time. Would it be true that if you go back and delve into things, Andrew, that you might be presented with a situation whose outcome you [could] alter?

AC: Eugenia Macer-Story writes a lot about this kind of internal dialogue. She seems to conclude that you shouldn't try to do too much. Maybe you don't *really* want to change it, because what you change it to might be worse.

GK: Yes, you have no way of knowing.

AC: I just wanted to throw this other name out: Anna Genzlinger. She was one of Gray Barker's prospective authors. She was interested in the Philadelphia Experiment and Carlos Allende. Allende contacted a UFO researcher named Morris K. Jessup, who then mysteriously died in 1959. One day, Genzlinger was reading about the Philadelphia Experiment in a Berlitz book. Suddenly she had a flash that Jessup had been murdered. She ends up writing a book that Barker never actually published. This is a woman who just out of the blue starts to feel like Jessup is speaking to her from the other side. Not only can you get a message from an entity or a semi-deity, you can get it from a specific person. In this case, someone who's been murdered... Genzlinger felt like Jessup was speaking to her from another dimension. She knew details about him that she could never have known. She was getting them from him somehow. It's pretty gripping. Well, maybe "gripping" is not the right word...

GK: [Tell us more about who] she was getting messages from.

AC: Morris K. Jessup's first book was *The Case for the UFO*. His second book was *The Expanding Case for the UFO*. He was a great astronomer who did a lot of great research. He's part of the Philadelphia Experiment pantheon, if you will, having been under the employ of both the Navy and the Rockefellers (we think).

GK: Okay, here's [another] comment: "I'm told that the Fort Thomas Military Post in Northern Kentucky has an Engineering Reserve Unit there, and a Psyops Unit. My dad told me that Jack Ruby used to live in Belleview, Kentucky, and ran a nightclub." What do you know about that?

AC: Well, it reminds me of the girls in the basement who saw the entity and had their necklace crosses burned off from around their necks. This occurred in Fort Mitchell, not far from Ft. Thomas...

GK: What do you know about Ruby being in or around those environs?

AC: I don't, but it certainly makes sense given the gambling history of the Ohio Valley. It was extremely dangerous in the beginning, in the Indian days. People were lying in wait along the banks. It was one of the most dangerous places to try to travel through to the West. Everybody basically ended up going up north through western New York, and over to Cleveland. Otis K. Rice's book states that there were four major routes through WV. Certain ones were scarier than others. The one through the Kanawha Valley was the worst. The most wild... It was truly a frontier mentality.

GK: The Kanawha River... Does that run from West Virginia into the Ohio?

AC: Right, and it's about 35 miles from where the Kanawha meets the Ohio to where I lived. Further up, it got really hard to navigate, so eventually they had to dam it.

GK: Why is that? Is that through mountainous terrain?

AC: Yes, there were minor gorges and falls.

GK: That rings a bell to a certain extent. Do people use that river today as a rafting venue?

AC: That's another river, the New River, which runs into the Kanawha. You have world-class whitewater rafting on that river, further up where it's not dammed. So yes, the Kanawha would have been pretty wild and treacherous in its original form.

GK: I seem to remember that because, when I was in graduate school at Ohio U., somebody did a story on the Kanawha River. I wasn't really paying attention. I'm assuming it was whitewater rafting or kayaking.

AC: I'm hoping to get back there and check out the Wayne Forest area to see if a plane crashed there on the day of 9/11. That's our next step. That's the missing link in the conspiracy. The researchers seem to have gotten Flight 93 figured out pretty well. Of course such revelations have – as usual – been matched by official propaganda from the other side. In this sense, I imagine that the new *Flight 93* movie is completely filled with misinformation…

GK: [Filled with] garbage… I don't think that 93's been figured out, but I've been thinking about what you told me [about it having] made a turn above that Ohio Valley area. I'll be honest with you, Flights 93 and 77 are both planes that nobody knows what happened to. We're not going to get into the whole thing about what went into the Pentagon, but the behavior of those planes in the area [is a mystery].

AC: When we were in WV filming in 2002, we didn't know about this, but there were red-eyed creature sightings in Wayne National Forest that year. This is not long after 9/11. Think of 9/11 as that stone dropping in the water. You're going to have big ripples, or signals that have significant psychic, geomagnetic reverberations. The waves go out. We can almost predict the modulation, or distance in time between paranormal flaps, and figure out when the next wave is coming through. Keel was very good at predicting those waves. He said that they tend to come every five years.

GK: What does that really mean? I mean, predictions can occur, but what is it about the passing of time that makes a certain 5 or 10 years dictate events? I'm a little lost here, but go ahead and tell me what you think about the passing of time and the stones dropping in the water.

Keel may have been intimating that this is partly a subjective process. That there has to be an individual reference point of some kind when considering waves or cycles… Keel described it as a "learning process" that witnesses, abductees, and contactees go through. He lamented that not enough people may be going through the process in order to save Earth from things like future ecological destruction. My sense is that the

Garuda and other deities will continue to manifest until mankind enters another cycle of higher consciousness. Of course, the pendulum will swing back at some point. This is a sobering thought. The contemplation of this cycle of higher and lower consciousness leads one to the sensation of emptiness. One realizes that one has no control, and that we are merely a product of undulating universal forces. This sense of futility is a kind of psychological encounter with the Void. It can be as frightening as an encounter with the Garuda. Some escape the fear of the unknown by becoming "scientific" materialists railing at the very thought of the supernatural.

AC: Some of these things, such as creature sightings in Wayne Forest close to 9/11, are simply suggestive. Where *do* you start your clock? If it's every five years, where do you start? I have a letter in my possession from that Swedish UFO group, AFU. It is one of two papers in the file that weren't repetitive media accounts. It was a 1973 letter from Keel to one of the Swedes, where Keel predicted that there would be a big wave in '78. Sure enough, in Charleston, West Virginia, and in other places, there was a wave peak in '78. And the late 1960s flaps were about 5 years before the 1973 flap...

GK: This is something that we're just posing. We're extrapolating from a question that was asked by a listener. In the time we've got left, and that's really not a lot, consider [this comment]: "We should try to get Andy to talk more about the Philadelphia Experiment, and when he says his dad was there. Does that mean, on that day? Or does it mean that he was there on the Naval Yards?" Did you want to speak to that at all, Andrew?

AC: He was in the vicinity, stationed there at the time. To preface, this is another one of those things that came up very recently. Before that, I only I knew that he had been in Norfolk sometime during the war. That's all I grew up knowing. Last year, in 2005 (I don't remember the exact date), I was leafing through this old Navy yearbook that he had. And there it is! It was printed at that same time (late 1943). I'm just saying that this is another one of those things I can point to, personally, and label synchronous. The more I look into it, the more things like that I find. When you combine my father's being there with the fact that I knew a couple of other people who had seen men catch on fire and disappear, it *seems* to relate to the Philadelphia Experiment. I was then able to guess that maybe the Navy brought some of these guys over to West Virginia en masse. Like I say, Dad would not talk about it at all, so I can't say if he was right *there* on Aug. 12th. But here's the thing about the Philadelphia Experiment: it wasn't just one event on one day. There were at least two major experiments that we know of. In the first experiment, which started in Philadelphia, the ship disappeared, was seen in Norfolk, and reappeared again in Philadelphia. But they did it again about a month later. After Einstein came back and looked over the data, they tried it again from Norfolk, not Philadelphia. They actually had a convoy of 130 ships passing the test ship. How many people on how many ships saw it, we don't know. Charles Berlitz implied that there are many people out there who saw it and contacted him. They all would know some part of the story. He felt like the story was kept alive not by the media (like so many of these stories), but by working class people who had been there, or knew something. It was a grassroots kind of thing.

GK: So what did happen there? Did something disappear?

AC: Yes, the ship in Norfolk (the Eldridge, or DE173) disappeared and came back.

GK: And came back?

AC: Yes. And this is where Carlos Allende comes in, because he was on one of the ships in the convoy.

GK: What is he doing there?

AC: He was a Merchant Marine. He saw the ship appear and disappear. He talked to Gray Barker about it. That's kind of where it links back to Mothman, through Barker and the servicemen who ended up being employed in Belle, S. Charleston, Nitro, and Point Pleasant during the Mothman era. Barker was a UFO researcher from Clarksburg, WV, who was interested in the Philadelphia Experiment. All I can say is that my father was stationed there in Norfolk. A lot of those men probably heard a fairly accurate version of the story, even if they hadn't actually seen it themselves.

GL: What about this Montauk Chair?

AC: I haven't done a lot of research on the Montauk part of it. Things seem really far out. I can say that Puharich was probably the prototype. If you're going to point to any scientist who worked on a Montauk Chair-type project, it's Puharich. He pioneered putting psychics in Faraday cages, electrifying the cages, and testing their abilities with various frequencies. God knows what all he was doing. One of the things he throws out, offhandedly, in one of his books is that he stumbled onto the exact frequency that caused cancer.

GK: If you could identify that, you could eradicate cancer. Isn't that true?

AC: Boy, I don't know. I think you could certainly cause cancer with it.

GK: I'm thinking that if there was one frequency that was generated, there's probably a frequency that can negate it.

AC: I've heard about this Chair in a couple of articles on Montauk, by both Alexandra Bruce and Adam Gorightly, That's about it.

GK: What is the connection then, between the Philadelphia Experiment and Montauk?

AC: Well, to simplify it, Montauk is considered to be a continuation of the Philadelphia Experiments, in another location.

GK: With the goal being what?

AC: Time travel... By the way, there's some weird connection between Montauk and Mark Hammill, the Star Wars guy. That was one thing I was titillated by, I guess.

GK: How'd you come up with Mark Hammill?

AC: Hamill's father was military intelligence, and Hamill supposedly produced the Philadelphia Experiment movie, using a pseudonym. That was in Gorightly's article...

GK: Going back to the Philadelphia Experiment and its relation to Montauk, can you give us some kind of continuum, how they connect? What are their purposes, as far as you know?

AC: Well, the Philadelphia Experiment was exploratory, I guess. Berlitz believed it was an accident of sorts.

GK: A scientific accident?

AC: Yes, they were testing for one thing and got another. The second experiment was considered to be successful in terms of the scientific knowledge gained, but very unsuccessful in how it damaged the men involved. It became a problem, so to speak. I'm not sure how much of a connection there is between Philadelphia and Montauk, beyond the personage of John von Neumann, who led both. There are a lot of people out there who say there is a connection. Similar kinds of Project RAINBOW experiments were apparently tried at both places. Montauk was also connected to Brookhaven Laboratory, out where Keel was chasing MIBs... There are a couple of guys who do some time travel within the Montauk story. They claim that they went back to the Philadelphia Experiment. It is pregnant with these difficult-to-follow trains of thought regarding time. It's just not something I'm prepared to vouch for. What I'm trying to do right now is to work with what I know personally. Doing interviews with people that I know and can vouch for... I'm trying to present those, and add that to what's already out there.

GK: What does the Montauk Chair mean? What is that about?

AC: It sounds very similar to Puharich's experiment of placing a telepathic individual in the center of this electromagnetically isolated cage, then amplifying his telepathic signals. I think in terms of Montauk, they did *more* than that to the psychic. They gave them drugs and hooked them up to other machinery. It was mind control. As Puharich's research progressed, he started influencing the remote viewing movement quite heavily. He knew Puthoff and Targ and those guys at Stanford, who started doing time travel with remote viewing. Some of the Stanford scientists were Scientologists who, according to Peter Moon, ended up using L. Ron Hubbard's techniques in their remote viewing experiments.

GK: What year was it that he began, or accelerated, the idea of remote viewing?

AC: It would have been right after the Uri Geller experiments at Stanford in '71. They did a lot of that military research in the Bay Area. There are apparently ways to time-travel with your mind. This was one reason for having these world-class psychics. There are remote-viewers who have come out and said, "Oh, I contacted aliens" or "I went back in time" or "forward in time." To give it the benefit of the doubt, I'm going to assume that it's possible. Now again, this appears to be a question of how much influence one can have. If you went back in time, how much influence could you have? I don't think you could have that much impact because there is always the question of your proximity to the original event.

This would explain the need for strong amplification of the psychic's thoughts, as rumored to have occurred at Montauk.

AC: A lot of this stuff seems to be ultimately uncontrollable. There are human factors that create unpredictable results. How much of this can be applied to normal warfare, or corporate warfare, or whatever it is they use it for, I'm not sure...

GK: I'll tell you what, we've touched on a lot of bases. You also had a line of thought that you at least wanted to broach before the show was over. What was on your mind? Is there anything you want to avail us of?

AC: I'm just looking down at my notes. I could just grab the first thing I'm seeing.

GK: That's cool. When you said you had some stuff scribbled down, I was thinking, "Okay, let's take a look…"

AC: One of the transcriptions I recently took note of had to do with a witness that we see often in the documentaries, Marcella Bennett. I interviewed her and her sister. Although the sister didn't see the Mothman, the sister saw balls of fire when they were kids.

GK: Now hold on a second, people will say, "Transcription? What's going on?" So why don't you explain that a little bit before we go any further.

AC: These are two of the witnesses from my documentary. All of the interviews are being transcribed for a book.

GK: Okay…

AC: The sister uses birds as talismans. This is similar to what I was saying on WING-TV. There are certain ways one can utilize this phenomenon. There are also areas you want to stay away from because it's too risky. I'm not sure how healthy something like astral projection is for people who don't have a strong shamanic tradition behind them. If you have a support group and a clear field of benevolence or good karma built up, you could do it. But there are some things I suggest people not do until they've been prepared.

GK: Agreed…

AC: But this is an example of looking at a Mothman witness and finding something exciting. In this case, one of them actually uses birds to get what she wants. She has a special relationship with birds. She uses them as genies. She gives the birds her wishes, and claims that they come true. There are a lot of little things like that in the documentary. People saying that they do these kinds of things… One guy claims he can fly. He doesn't fly now, but he claims that he did when he was young. His name is Tony Whyte. His whole family is interesting. They've all got unusual experiences. These experiences seem to run in families. The Whytes are a featured family, you could say, in the series. Levitation is, coincidentally, something that Keel claims to have seen happen in Sikkim.

GK: We only have a couple of minutes left. How did you want to wrap this up? What is this musical group you're in?

AC: It's I.V. League.

GK: I.V. League… I love it.

AC: It turns out that there is now a hip-hop group that has the same name. You can buy their t-shirts on the web. I thought about buying a bunch of their t-shirts and giving them away as our t-shirts. Just kidding…

GK: Listen, let's bring it to a close and we'll be back again. I'm telling you, this is segment 8, whether you like it or not. This is Vyz. You've been listening to the Grassy Knoll…

Intelligence assets David Ferrie and Lee Harvey Oswald getting paramilitary training in Louisiana in the 1950s. The two worked together on cancer experiments seemingly organized by US Army Biowarfare, whose director at the time was father of WV's Larry Layton, Jr. – the convicted Jonestown mind control doctor.

CHAPTER 39

In one of our more far-flung adventures, Harriet and I traveled to the remote mountains of eastern WV and checked out the gates of the secretive Naval command post that Harriet's dad helped build in the 1960s. Today, it is guarded by black-clad troops carrying what look like NATO assault weapons. NATO guns have their ammunition clips on the top, not the bottom. When we were parked near the gates, our video camera malfunctioned in a way that it never had before. Prior to approaching the gates, we stopped in nearby Moyers, WV, where we discussed one of the attempts made on Harriet's father's life.

Plumbrook, Harriet – Sugar Grove Naval Base reading – 2002

Andy Colvin (AC): So this is where the second attempt on your dad's life was made, by attempted car "accident."

Harriet Plumbrook (HP): Actually, this was the first attempt... This was in approximately 1965, in Moyers. *[gestures]* This is Moyers, WV. There isn't much to it... He was run off the road by someone, and spent about a week in the hospital in Elkins. Then another week back in Charleston...

AC: Now that you're here, do you have a sense of who did it? Was it the Eastern Bloc or was it the Americans?

HP: I think it was the Americans.

AC: Why?

HP: Well, I'm just kind of feeding off of your own tack of paranoia here. I mean this van sitting here is just all too suspicious.

AC: *[videotaping into rearview mirror]* Okay, here's our probable listening van. We've already scoped out one van. We asked them for directions. Tell us what happened.

HP: They asked us *who* we were going to see, as opposed to *where* we were going to go.

AC: This one here is a "Verizon Wireless" van.

HP: Followed closely by an "Asplundh" truck...

AC: There are lots of trucks around here with lots of gear on them. And roads that aren't marked very well...

HP: At all...

AC: Probably to try to keep people away from the secret installation... They're probably listening to us right now. Tell us a little bit about what we're going to see in Sugar Grove. Your dad worked there, right?

HP: Yes. He never talked about it. All he said was, "it's an installation." Whatever an installation is...

AC: Today we know that it was part of the top-secret Echelon project, eaves-dropping on America's communication networks. Practically everyone knows about it these days. But back then, it was pretty secret.

HP: [There were] times when he wouldn't come home for weeks at a time, because they wouldn't let him.

After driving around on unmarked roads and visiting an odd artist's studio that had macabre sculptures of Mothman, mutilated baby dolls, and bloodied Disney characters on the front lawn, we finally found Sugar Grove.

AC: So now we're here in Sugar Grove, WV. We're sort of following the Mothman trail. We know that your dad worked here, had a car crash here, and was car-bombed back on Woodward Drive. We're trying to find out if there are any psychic links of note as we visit these spots. Can you tell us what is here at Sugar Grove? Most people probably have no idea what is here...

HP: Well, specifically, no. But I know that there's some type of high-tech listening station [here that] can listen in on all types of conversations. Microwave, radiowave, all kinds of stuff... It's a receiving type of station.

Harriet casually remote-viewed the facility and said that she saw screens guiding craft in the world's oceans. She also said that we were being watched and listened to by the security guards at the gate. When I checked my videotape of the gate later, I noticed an odd overlapping of imagery indicative of some sort of electrical interference. The guards at the base and at the housing complex wore full tactical assault gear. Locals stated that they themselves did not mix with the base personnel at all. The base had its own schools and entertainment. No one seemed to know about possible eavesdropping at the base. All that locals would admit to knowing was that the base is a communications center for "sending and receiving messages."

After having some wonderful chicken-fried steak and cherry pie at the Cabin Inn in Brandywine, we headed back to Charleston by way of Flatwoods, in Braxton County.

AC: Before we talk about Flatwoods, one thing I wanted to bring up is this random connection between the WTO protests, in Seattle, and the Mothman. In reading one of the Mothman books, I found a reference in the appendix to an address in Seattle. Basically it said, "If you're a paranormal investigator, check this out." It was a list of spooky attractions across the country. So I went to this location in Seattle. It was the only actual address listed for the state of Washington. I found some references onsite that seem to tie in with the Mothman. For instance, I found the quote, "Big Brother is watching you," which turns out to be something Harriet's dad always used to say to her. I found the word "shadow" drawn in the concrete, along with Harriet's initials. There were also Masonic symbols there. Incredibly, there was something that could be construed as the Mothman drawn on the door of this particular Seattle address. And it just so happens that this address is the same spot where, during the WTO protests, police and protesters repeatedly clashed. This was sort of the boundary line between the two sides, right at 905 E. Pine. Almost as a joke, I asked Harriet to remote view that area in Seattle and see if she could locate which address it was. And she did it. She accurately located 905 E. Pine. She also said that something appeared to have occurred on the 3rd floor of the building. A few weeks later in one of the Seattle tabloids, *The Stranger*, there was a reference to this building being haunted on the 3rd floor. It had once been used as a music building for Seattle Central Community College. A student had committed suicide on the 3rd floor.

Plumbrook, Harriet – Flatwoods, Braxton County, WV – 2002

AC: Here we are in Flatwoods, WV, home of the famous Braxton County Green Monster, not to be confused with the Braxton County Brown Monster. It's the Mothman Tour 2002. The choice is yours, Harriet: paranormal or normal?

HP: Looks like it could have been normal for *this* area. The actual sighting took place in 1952. There was more than one sighting in the area. There was one in Sutton, which is down the road, and one in Gassaway, which is a little further to the west. Actually a dog that was exposed to this Flatwoods thing died. Several people saw a creature about 7 feet tall, with large, dark eyes. They became violently ill after being exposed to the craft that it stepped out of, indicative of radiation…

AC: So do you think this monster is related to your monster?

HP: Yes, I do. I have the distinct feeling that it is.

AC: Do you think there's an energy field that exists in this area, that perhaps relates to Woodward Drive?

HP: Oh yes... It attracts them like flies. No doubt about it.

AC: Okay, here we are at what we think is the location of the original sighting of the Green Monster, on this farm here... Harriet, what do you think?

HP: Well, I've got the creepies. It was somewhere off of the main highway that I got the creepies... I feel sick to my stomach. Sometimes I'll get that if I come through an area that's known to be a site of intense radiation.

AC: Maybe we should do a quick rundown of the electromagnetic the spectrum. We should do a measurement using the Tri-Field meter. Okay, we're going to take some readings here to see if we're picking up any fluctuating levels of ambient radiation or electromagnetism. Jeez, it's almost off the scale! *[beeping sounds]*

HP: Andy, I think we should get out of here. This thing's going nuts!

Creeped out, we piled back in our vehicle and headed on down the Elk River. Along the way, some men dressed like hobos tried to get me to come down and talk to them under a bridge. We decided to do some filming in our car, away from the bridge.

AC: Well alrighty... We've fled Flatwoods. Now we are in Gassaway, West Virginia. In the background we have some live Mothman soundtrack music, sent to us from *The Mothman Prophecies* film soundtrack band, King Black Acid, out of Portland, OR. Wasn't there a famous sighting here in Gassaway, home of the rare paddlefish?

HP: Yes, at about the same time as the one in Flatwoods. There was a sighting approximately 4 days later in Gassaway. Someone also became violently ill, and described the same being...

AC: What are your Mothy senses telling you?

HP: Creepy... Big monster was here.

AC: You've been talking about getting a tattoo. Is this the place where you'd want to get that tattoo?

HP: Well, I don't think Gassaway would really have a tattoo shop... But I'm thinking that at the end of this whole thing, I ought to get something that says something like, "The Mothman Tour 2002."

AC: This *is* the 50-year anniversary of the Flatwoods incident.

HP: It is indeed...

Plumbrook, Harriet – Mineral Wells, WV – 2002

AC: We have gone over some mountains and are now in the Ohio Valley, on Route 2. We are in the holy land, where the waters have special properties: Mineral Wells, West Virginia. Give us the goods, Harriet.

HP: Okay, on November 2nd, 1966, right up the road here, Woody Derenberger had a visitation right on the highway... A guy by the name of Mr. Cold stopped to see him on the highway, and gave him all types of UFO information. Told him where he was from, and told him he'd see him again... And see him again he did, several times... The guy became quite a celebrity, with people camping out at his farm in Mineral Wells. Eventually the celebrity caused him to get a divorce and move away, and never be heard from again.

AC: Where was Indrid Cold from?

HP: Lanulos, so he claimed... From some faraway galaxy... He told Derenberger that he would have severe physical withdrawal symptoms after he spoke with him. Every time he spoke with Cold, he would have splitting migraines where he would almost pass out. [Cold first] landed in front of the car. [The ship] looked like a stovepipe chimney. There were other people who witnessed this, and who came forward later to verify his story. They, too, had passed the craft on I-77, on November 2nd, 1966...

AC: Here we are at the Willow Island Plant, about 15 miles north of Parkersburg, on Route 2. Some of these plants are nuclear. Some are apparently not guarded very well. Is that right?

HP: Yes, that's right. It's such a terrorism concern nowadays, but it should have been back in the '60s, too, when all these UFOs were flying over them. This is definitely a *visited* area. A repeatedly visited area... Back in the '60s, when all of these sightings were taking place, most of what was seen followed Route 2. The lights exactly followed the river.

Plumbrook, Harriet – Sistersville/Paden City, WV – 2002

AC: Here we are in Sistersville, West Virginia.

HP: Sistersville has an interesting paranormal history. It all started in 1897 with the Great Airship sightings, which were mainly in Texas. But there's recorded history of an airship sighting here, in Sistersville. In the spring of 1967, there was a Mothman sighting here. All during the time from November '66 to December 1967, UFOs, globes of light, etc., were seen here... Hundreds of witnesses, all documented... There is a lot about this in old newspapers in Texas. Most of the witnesses believed that they saw a cigar-shaped object land. Supposedly in [Aurora] Texas, one of these airships crashed, and an alien was given a Christian burial... But when that grave was dug back up, it had already been robbed.

AC: One of the things you notice about these towns that have had significant sightings is that they often have strong Masonic orders.

HP: Yes, most every town we've been in has an Eastern Star, which is the women's side of the Masonic lodge, *and* a Masonic lodge. To me, that's just a little too much of a coincidence.

AC: Well, a lot of towns have Masonic lodges. The interesting thing is that in one of Keel's talks, he mentions that some people believe that secret societies have somehow interfaced with this phenomenon, and that *these societies* are the ones who go around in vans abducting people and doing genetic experiments. It's part of some ritual occult "working."

HP: Yes, and two other authors that have touched on that are Kevin Randall and Jim Marrs. They also believe the Masons are involved somehow with the UFO phenomenon.

AC: I don't know if I mentioned this before, but another thing Sharon Moore told me was that she has the same dream that I have, about a train trestle in St. Albans. I have this dream a lot. Often my mother is there. I was shocked when Sharon said, "Yes, I always have this strange dream about St. Albans and a trestle." Then Sharon talked to her mother, who *also* says that she has a similar dream about St. Albans! So we're kind of kicking around this theory that if you've seen the Mothman, or he's come into your life in some way, you might thereafter have a "dreamstate interface" with him. In other words, wherever he has materialized, there might be an energy field available for us to pick up on. Maybe we subconsciously astral-project there later, without knowing it. Or we have some feeling, intuition, or knowledge about that spot because something in us has been physically touched by the energy there.

We pulled into the town burger joint in Paden City, WV, which sports several Native American wall displays. One of them is an elaborate "dreamcatcher." We sat down at the table beneath it. We soon met a strange man wearing a "grey" alien shirt, who knew several locals who had seen UFOs during the original Mothman flap. Since we were on break, we didn't have our equipment set up for filming. Immediately after lunch, however, Harriet recounted what he had told us about his own UFO sighting.

AC: So what did that guy say? I didn't get much of it on tape.

HP: He said that at some time during the '80s, he saw a bright object. He couldn't tell any shape or anything. It was mostly bright lights…

AC: Was this in Paden City?

HP: Right, that's what he said. He was on his way to work one day. When he got to work, he was an hour late. He'd never been late in his life. He doesn't remember anything else. He had a friend who thought he was basically playing a joke with the missing time story. They went out with another friend, who lived near these power lines where he had seen the object… While they were out there, they all three saw the same object.

AC: And now 20 years later, this guy is wearing a UFO shirt. Interestingly, right behind Harriet on the wall here, someone has hung a moth drawing. Harriet is now saying that her Mothy senses are tingling.

HP: I feel like I'm in *The Twilight Zone*. In fact, I *know* we have stepped into *The Twilight Zone*. We weren't even going to stop here… Then we run into the UFO man.

We left the burger joint and headed towards Wheeling, WV, childhood home of UFO researcher Budd Hopkins.

AC: We're about a block away from the Paden City Tasty-Freeze. We see that we are in Wetzel County. The name Wetzel is a name that shows up frequently in the UFO world. It's an unusual name, yet it shows up a lot here.

HP: Yes, that and about half dozen other names have been mentioned frequently… Wetzel is definitely one of *those* names.

AC: I have on my Mothman T-shirt. We just went into Wal-Mart, where we ran into a Mothman witness at the returns desk. Harriet, what happened there?

HP: *[laughing]* Well, John Keel was right. He said that any time you put it out there that you're involved in the paranormal, you're always going to get a story back. Somebody *always* knows something about it. Our clerk said that she was with her boyfriend and another couple in a car. They had just watched the Mothman movie at someone's home. Driving back on the backroads to wherever they lived, this huge Moth-like creature hit the windshield. She said she screamed… They all kind of freaked out. They never got a real good look at it. Andy's done it again. He needs to stop wearing the Mothman shirt.

AC: She seemed pretty credible. Very lucid…

HP: She did… She seemed pretty normal. She didn't offer any explanation of it. One thing you'll notice with someone who's telling you a big story is that they'll try to explain it. She offered no explanation.

AC: Keel said that for every one witness that comes forward, there are hundreds that don't come forward.

HP: Right… And he wasn't just speaking about the Mothman, but all the phenomena that he's investigated throughout the years. That is definitely the case… It was much worse back in the '60s at the time the Mothman was going on, because people were really afraid of being labeled a crackpot. They are still afraid now, but not as much as they were then. People are a little more open now. But it's still one of those things they kind of have to step into. It takes a little bit of courage to step up and say, "this is what I've seen."

AC: Why do you think things have changed?

HP: I think it's a combination of two things, actually. First of all, our society's a little more open. We're not as afraid of being labeled a loon. And second of all, this phenomenon touches everyone. Everyone has an experience like this [in their past]. When you've got this many numbers of people stepping up and saying they've had an experience, it just makes others want to step up and say the same thing. But like I said it's just vast, the numbers of people coming forward now….

AC: One of the things I think I forgot to mention was that yesterday, as we were leaving WV, Ariane Moore showed me a sword that she had picked up in someone's attic. It was one of the medieval swords that they use for those Renaissance reenactments. She asked me to look at it because it had a face engraved into it. I looked at the face and, sure enough, it's the Garuda! It even has the two snakes… Garuda is sometimes shown with two serpents, grasping one with each claw. The caduceus symbol has the two snakes going up the winged staff. Ariane just randomly found this Garuda sword. It even has little feathers etched in. An amazing little synchronicity there…

Plumbrook, Harriet – Salt Fork State Park, OH – 2002

AC: We're passing through Salt Fork State Park in Ohio, the last stop on the East Coast Mothman Tour. Tell us about the significance of this place.

HP: It's about five miles north of Cambridge, Ohio. What is significant about it is that there have been [at least] thirteen Bigfoot sightings here, spread out over probably fifteen years.

AC: A lot of people think that Bigfoot is seen the most in the Northwest, but that's not true.

HP: Right... Actually the state of Ohio has the highest number of sightings of any state... Close to a hundred that are actually investigated per year... Some of those are discarded, some aren't.

AC: It seems like you're pretty interested in seeing a Bigfoot. How does it connect up with the Mothman?

HP: I've said this all during this journey... *All* of this stuff is related. I think that it's just another way for these beings – or whoever's visiting us – to reach us, and let us know that there's something else out there besides us.

AC: What about the stories that Bigfoots are guardians of underground caverns where small, robotic aliens mine minerals?

HP: That is a prevalent theory in the UFO community, because most of these Bigfoot sightings are in conjunction with a UFO. In fact, in about sixty to seventy percent of them, there's a UFO or some type of strange light seen in the area.

AC: What about the psychic Sasquatch? There are several researchers who now believe that the Sasquatch is a psychic being who can move between dimensions by materializing and dematerializing. That explains why you can find Bigfoot tracks in the snow that suddenly disappear.

HP: Yes, and in about half the sightings that I've read about in the state of Ohio, that is the exact thing that people have said. They'll see it, and then it actually dematerializes before their eyes. It doesn't disappear off into the woods; it disappears *right in front of their eyes.*

AC: If you come across a Sasquatch it is usually by accident. They generally won't approach you. Supposedly they can read the human mind.

HP: That doesn't surprise me, because in a lot of the UFO-related phenomena, they say that these creatures can read your mind. Alien beings can read your mind. Plus they can create screen memories....

AC: Screen memories... Can you explain that to people?

HP: Well, that's when the "aliens" implant a memory into your subconscious, to make you forget the whole experience. I mean let's face it; it would be pretty traumatic to have them come in and use you as a guinea pig.

AC: A lot of witnesses, after they go into hypnotherapy, realize that the original screen memory masked being abducted in a van by some guys in military uniforms.

HP: That could be possible, too.

Plumbrook, Harriet – Bush Mansion – Franklin County, OH 2003

Andy Colvin (AC): Okay, so next we're heading to the mansion of Prescott Bush, the grandfather of our current President. It just goes to show that Ohio, Mothman Country, is really the center of a lot of powerful interests. Can you speculate on these connections at all, Harriet?

Harriet Plumbrook (HP): Well it seems that wherever the Bushes turn up, weird things start to happen. Everything from paranormal phenomena to murder, mayhem, and destruction…

AC: Do you think it's a cultural thing? In Ohio, you have a lot of Mothman sightings throughout history. Do you think that plays into the way society here has evolved? Here we have reports of the Bushes worshipping this giant stone owl Moloch at Bohemian Grove. It almost seems like they're secretly in tune with the phenomenon.

HP: I think that they're definitely aware of it. I think this kind of thing is definitely reported to the White House. It's kept very quiet. I think that we've more or less undergone a spiritual rebirth around here, because of it. People are just much more open than they used to be. They realize that there is something higher than themselves out there, that they are part of a larger whole…

AC: Are we now passing the Victoria's Secret corporate headquarters?

HP: Yes, this is Victoria's Secret. Columbus is home to The Limited and Limited Brands, which would be Victoria's Secret, Abercrombie & Fitch, Limited Too, Bath & Bodyworks. You have big cornfields and then you have The Limited.

AC: There are some huge corporations that have started here. Can you name some other ones?

HP: Well, you have Battelle Industries, which is a big think tank. A pretty scary place that has gotten into some psychic and other paranormal phenomenon… If you read a lot of that type of thing, you'll see the name Battelle come up over and over again. The Limited is about the largest. It employs about 22,000 in its various divisions. Actually the State of Ohio, through Ohio State University, employs about 30,000. There's also Acu-Ray… Nobody's really sure what the heck Acuray does. We have Chemical Abstracts. We know that they're involved in deadly weapons and that kind of thing. And DCSC, Defense Construction Supply Center… The Navy actually runs it and houses it, but it supplies all the Armed Forces. It's been here since the early 1900s. It's near the airport. Just about everything you can think of is stored there, from ammunition to tanks to body bags. Lots of body bags... In fact, when I was a loadmaster for Evergreen Air, DCSC brought a bunch of body bags out to us and we flew them over to Korea. I lifted two million body bags on a Boeing 747.

AC: I thought I'd talk a bit about Prescott Bush as we arrive here and get close to the mansion. I don't know that much about him. I've read a few articles. It sounds as if he was known as "Hitler's banker." He was a banker in New York. I guess he started out in Columbus. This is their ancestral home.

HP: Right. He started a company known as Buckeye Steel, which is on the south end of Columbus. He also had interest in what they call Jeffrey Mining and Manufacturing. The Jeffrey family owned it, but he was the financier. He was really the person behind it. The Jeffrey family was kind of the front to it. The way I've heard the story is that he more or less financed many large businesses that started in Columbus. Perhaps started a couple of the banks... But that's never been proven one way or the other. The major thing they started in Columbus was Buckeye Steel, which has just been recently purchased by a Canadian company.

AC: In his capacity as a banker, Prescott was funneling money. He was a main conduit for American monies that were being given to Hitler. He was brought up on charges six or seven times. If you read some of the New York Times articles from that era, they said things on the front page like: "Sen. Prescott Bush Indicted For Trading With Enemy." Here we are on Mann Road, Franklin County, Ohio. Secluded... Pretty far away from the city. We will see where the Bush family empire started. Here we are... We can't see the house. It's set back a ways.

HP: The only time you can really see the house is in the winter.

AC: Here's the front gate. Are you getting any psychic impressions?

HP: Very interesting... I'm getting that this wasn't a happy place. Not a happy place at all... That "white picket-fence" happiness was not the case here. It was an unhappy home. They put on airs that they were a stable family. They weren't... I don't know much about the woman Prescott Bush was married to, but I'm definitely picking up that she was unstable. It was a very chaotic environment. *Very* chaotic... I don't like what I'm picking up there. It is really an uneasiness. They were never really satisfied with the [place] and were unhappy... Maybe that's why they moved to Texas.

AC: Shall we drive in?

HP: No way. I know those people, or know who they are. My mom knows them really well. I wouldn't do it, no way. This is an area that's watched very heavily. If someone pulls that crap, they go straight to jail…

On July 24th, 2007, the BBC reported that in 1933, Prescott Bush and a group of bankers conspired to have Gen. Smedley Butler overthrow then president FDR and implement a fascist dictatorship based around the ideology of Mussolini and Hitler. Butler played along in order to determine who was involved, but later blew the whistle. The media blackballed the story. In 1936, William Dodd, U.S. Ambassador to Germany, wrote a letter to Roosevelt in which he stated:

"A clique of U.S. industrialists is hell-bent on bringing a fascist state to supplant our democratic government, and is working closely with the fascist regimes in Germany and Italy. [These] industrialists had a great deal to do with bringing these fascist regimes into being. Industrialists [who typically] ignore laws designed for social and economic progress will seek recourse to a fascist state when the institutions of our government compel them to comply with provisions."

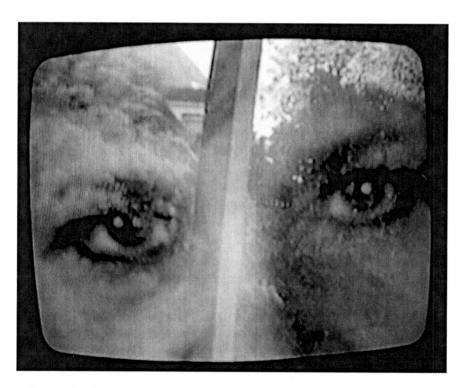

Still image of psychic Mothman witness Harriet Plumbrook, from the Mothman's Photographer paranormal reality series.

CHAPTER 40

Tom Ury is another popular Mothman witness whom I had the pleasure of interviewing. The first thing you notice about Tom is that he is extremely likeable. He has that mixture of sardonic humor and sense of justice so unique to West Virginians.

Ury, Tom – 1966 Big Bird sighting – 2003

Andy Colvin (AC): When you had your sighting, Tom, I was 7 years old. I built a shrine to the Mothman because I thought he was cool. Sure enough, the friend that helped me build the shrine later saw him. I saw Mothman, and my sister and niece have also seen the Mothman. Building that shrine seemed to start a chain of events. We've all seen him now. Or different forms of him... What did you see?

Tom Ury (TU): Being the eternal skeptic, did you and your friend convince each other to see it? Not that I'm a psychologist or anything…

AC: I think that's a valid question. I would say that that would be more possible *had* my experience been limited to just *that* time period. I don't think Tommy made anything up, because he went so far into it. I mean he had so many strange things going on: UFOs, aliens, abductions, plus Mothman and prophecies. He told me this all was happening but I didn't connect it to Mothman. I was just thinking, "You're crazy."

TU: A lot of people have seen the Mothman, not The Bird. I separate the two.

AC: Okay... That's interesting.

TU: [The Mothman witnesses] have seen things… It might be an omen of something to come. What I saw was a bird. But I guarantee the wingspan wouldn't fit in this room. I saw it in the daytime, stone sober, going to work. I had 150 miles to drive [on the] busiest day of the year. I had nothing to prove by even reporting what I saw.

AC: It wasn't humanoid? It was all bird?

TU: It flew over my car. Maybe 150 feet over my car, and made big circles… But there was no man form to it at all, nor body. I couldn't see any legs. It was airborne all the time I saw it, so…

AC: What happened in my family was that the years passed by, and little paranormal things happened. We would talk about them, "Do you remember this? Do you remember that?" And nobody put it all together until we read *The Mothman Prophecies* ten years ago. I'm reading this book and suddenly, I'm realizing that *everything* in this book happened on Woodward Drive. All of it...

Sharon Moore (SM): The first lady we interviewed [here at the festival] lived in the same area near Woodward. She had it going on, too.

TU: I'm sure that people who've said they saw Mothman saw *something*. I'm not one to call somebody a liar, or [say they are] crying wolf. They saw something. Heck, what it *is* is a mystery. The bird? There is *no* bird that I've ever read about as big as the one I saw. [A local pilot] tried to catch it in an airplane over here at the airport.

SM: Well if it was a bird, how did it get in my room? If it was a physical bird, then how could it have gotten into my house?

TU: What you saw and what I saw are two different things. Yours was at night... Mine was the first daytime sighting... These may be two different instances that just happened to occur at the same time. I don't know...

AC: The Native Americans say that the Thunderbird always appears to each person as only one aspect of itself. So if you see it, you're not *ever* going to see the complete form of the being. You're only going to see an aspect of it. *You* may see it as all bird. To the next person that sees it, it looks more human. But they *are* related. The Natives say that the two are related.

TU: I'm skeptical, but I'm also open-minded. I've never seen God [either] but I know He's there. Two tours in Vietnam will do that to you...

AC: Your sighting... Did it change your perception of life, or God? What sort of a psychological effect did it have on you?

TU: I'd probably say none at all. [I've] tried to put it out of my mind. You know, I saw what I saw. I've had a standing offer for 37 years: I'll take a lie detector test on what I saw, if these people who saw a man with wings will take one. I haven't had a taker yet.

AC: Would you say that it made you more spiritual?

TU: No, it was something I saw, that I can't explain. To me, the bird was just as big a mystery as Mothman. I never saw Mothman. I saw a huge bird that was too big. Bigger than any bird I ever heard of... So, maybe it *was* a spiritualistic thing appearing to me, and the pilot (a week or two later).

AC: It's interesting... My first sighting was very similar to yours. I was in a car. I saw something. It wasn't a huge deal and I wasn't that afraid. But the funny thing was that very soon after that, I suddenly could draw like Picasso. I couldn't draw at all before that. I still don't know if the two were really related, but it *seemed* like they were. It seemed like the sighting made me believe that things other than the normal were possible. I think I just told myself, "I can draw if I want to. Why not?"

TU: I've never seen a UFO. I'm not saying they don't exist. If it changed anything at all, I guess it gave me a little better sense of humor. You sure do take a lot of ribbing. And I didn't take as much as most people. I was a respectable businessman. I had no reason to make up a story. I lived 150 miles from here. I had no reason to fabricate a story, or imagine anything.

AC: The Natives say a similar thing, that if you've seen the Mothman, it will often turn you into a sacred clown. A person who has an odd sense of humor... Humor is a good way to deal with seeing something scary that shouldn't exist...

TU: When I knew it wasn't going to come *through* the top of my car, I wasn't afraid anymore. There were a few strange occurrences along with it. I was driving a road that I never took before, because of the *detours* on Route 50. Just meeting Gray Barker [was strange].

AC: What was he like?

TU: Nice man, but weird...

AC: There's something about Gray's book, which you have here today, *The Silver Bridge*... Most of the book is a nice accounting of what happened. He really did a good job. He interviewed people. He tells the story very nicely. But there are a few chapters in here where he writes like *he* is the Mothman. Do you know what I'm talking about?

TU: Oh yes... Like John Keel says, it's a "celestial fairy tale."

AC: It still rang true with me somehow, though. I think he really expressed the psychological aspects artistically. A lot of people I've been interviewing are telling me about this psychic stuff, this ability to sort of see the future and connect with other things. I sort of think Gray Barker did that. They call him a hoaxer, but I think he was describing a deeper truth at times, even if that wasn't his immediate intention.

TU: Well he was – I found out later – a noted science-fiction writer. He had a lot of fun with the book. He knew a lot of things. He used a lot of what they call "journalistic license." [But he was] a real nice man... I was a little bit perturbed by what he and John Keel wrote about me... I've got a copy of the original article in the newspaper...

AC: What sorts of things have been written about you, that aren't true?

TU: Here's the original article out of the newspaper, "Oh That Bird, It Was Seen Again." It says that I was driving back, and I saw a huge bird that circled over my car for about a mile or two at 7:15 in the morning. It *does* say that I reported a bird, that I was going 70 mph, and that it was keeping up with me. Now here's what John Keel writes... You can tell he took the basis of his story from this article. But talk about journalistic license: "On November 25th, a young shoe salesman named Thomas Ury was driving along Route 62, just north of the TNT area, when he noticed a tall, grey, manlike figure in the field by the road. Suddenly, it spread a pair of wings and took off straight in the air, like a helicopter." Now, there's nothing in the original article about "man-sized," or "going straight up in the air." I did say that when I first saw it, it was coming over the trees. [But] what helicopter? Like you see in these Sylvester Stallone movies? I knew it was a bird as soon as I got a good look at it.

AC: I want to be there when you point this out to Keel.

TU: Jeff Wamsley, he's been a little bit skeptical about letting me meet Keel. [But] I realize that he's making a living. [I'm] just trying to get the story across on The Bird. I think The Bird story is just as interesting as a man with wings.

Tom suddenly thought of Faye DeWitt's interesting Mothman story.

TU: A woman came up to me and she said, "I saw Mothman one time." I said, "You did? Where? Do you live around here?" She said, "No, I came up from North Carolina."

AC: I met her.

TU: Oh did you? The one that [avoided] the bus wreck? Now, my hair stood [on end when I heard that]. It kind of got me. And then last year, Marcella Bennett told me her story. We rode to Kittanning, Pennsylvania, where they filmed the movie and the Unsolved Mysteries segment. Jeff knows I'm a skeptic. I sat in the back. Donnie Sergent and Jeff were in the front seat. Marcella and I were sitting in the back. It was a four or five hour car trip. I said, "Okay, let's get it over with. Let me hear your story." And I'll tell you, it was pretty convincing. That's the reason I can't call the people who've seen the manlike figure liars, crazy, drunks, or anything else. I saw what I saw. They saw what they saw. [Are they] related? I don't know. We'll find out one of these days, though.

AC: *[quoting Maddie Bennett]* Yes, when we go to the other side...

TU: I better get out of here and see if I can catch Keel. If you hear somebody yelling, you'll know I found him! *[laughter]*

CHAPTER 41

"There is a Yeti in the back of everyone's mind; only the blessed are
not haunted by it."

-Old Sherpa saying

Colvin, Andy – Grassy Knoll Radio interview 9 – June 2006

Andy Colvin (AC): I'm reading the book on Nelson Rockefeller and the
Amazon. Are you familiar with that book?

"Vyz" at Grassy Knoll Radio (GK): No, but I like the fact that you're reading
it. You know my feelings towards that family.

AC: It's called *Nelson's Conquest of...*

GK: Would that be the woman that he... Never mind...

AC: It's called *Thy Will be Done: Nelson Rockefeller and Evangelism in the Age
of Oil.* It's by Gerard Colby. There are a lot of interesting things in there
about Nelson that I want to touch on.

GK: What year was that, by the way? What year was the first copyright?

AC: 1976.

GK: I'd love to get my hands on that baby.

AC: Colby is the same guy who wrote *Dupont: Behind the Nylon Curtain.*

GK: Jeez, that's right. That's the guy whom Kristina Borjesson writes about in
her book *Into the Buzzsaw.*

AC: I'm just going to go through some things that are on this completely
messy and scribbled notesheet.

GK: You go, brother...

AC: Let's start with the last thing that I read last night. Colby is talking
about how the Rockefellers were using religious groups to basically take
over South America. That's sort of what the book is about. Here in this
passage, Colby connects that endeavor with intelligence work:

*One Rockefeller associate was a CIA veteran William Kitner. He was the
epitome of the intelligence operative, a spook who filtered easily into all
social and political levels, moving in and out of a labyrinth of clandestine
circles. Kitner owed his rise at the Pentagon to Nelson Rockefeller, first*

as a member of Nelson's staff, then serving as Chief Aid at the top-secret Quantico Seminar…

AC: These Rockefeller guys give top-secret seminars where they talk about Army policy. Kitner worked in the Rockefeller Brothers Fund "Special Studies Project" as an aide to the Joint Chiefs. He was head of Long-Range Planning for the Army, as well as the Foreign Policy Research Institute, a think tank in Philadelphia. He began advocating the use of private, voluntary organizations – including religious personnel – in Cold War operations. This is a guy who would have interfaced with the Wandering Bishops quite well. These missionaries in South America were basically bringing troublesome tribesmen in, using language study as an excuse. The plan was to infiltrate, control, and basically get rid of the indigenous people. They did the same thing in Asia.

GK: I swore I wouldn't do this, but I'm going to ask if you can give me a quick capsular comment about your take on the Wandering Bishops. If it's too long, don't worry about it.

AC: I don't know nearly as much about them as Levenda does. That's his thing. I'm just speculating that maybe these churches and priestly orders are being manipulated by right-wing politicos. You see it with these missionaries. On one level, you have really sincere and honest Christians helping the natives. But at the top, you have guys flying guns in on missionary planes, like Pat Robertson supposedly does.

GK: We love Pat. We love Pat a *lot*. Pat's a phony. I'll say it.

AC: If I were to make an encapsulated statement about religious orders, I would advocate a Buddhistic form of renunciation. Take back your own personal enlightenment. Don't think that a church hierarchy, or corporate hierarchy, is going to be able to…

GK: Save you?

AC: I'm not going to say that missionary work is unnecessary, because the sincere ones do good work in a lot of areas. Some of these missionary aid organizations are great.

My great-aunt Eva worked for a mission to Appalachia called The Mountain Mission. Charles Manson's grandmother was affiliated with the same organization. My sister, Spring, was a missionary nurse in Haiti. She adopted a Haitian baby (named Andrea) whose 20-yr. old mother, Lucie DuPrema, had been tragically killed following childbirth. Voodoo witch doctors accidentally dropped Lucie into boiling water while trying to cure her of an infection that they mistakenly believed was caused by evil spirits. In reality, the infection was caused from giving birth in a dusty field. My sister wrote her Masters thesis about related matters in 1998, entitled "A Descriptive Study of Ethical Dilemmas Encountered in Nursing Administration, and Resources Used for Ethical Decision-Making." Spring surveyed hundred of nurses about their jobs and found that: 1) in most hospitals, there are not enough nursing staff on the floor to give adequate patient care, due to downsizing and purposeful understaffing; 2) patients are not insured enough to get full care; and 3) many staff are incompetent, including doctors. The thesis was published by Bellarmine University in Louisville, KY. When I searched for the thesis there, I found that it had been transferred to a Dublin, Ohio repository called Online Computer Library Center (OCLC). When I checked the OCLC database, I found that my sister's critical analysis of Big Pharma's impact on healthcare was "missing." Dublin just happens to be the worldwide headquarters of Battelle, the enormous think tank involved in Project Blue Book and various chemical, pharmaceutical, and "managed care" schemes. In 2007, Battelle began partnering with a company named Sypherlink to create a massive data-mining system for the government, called "Information Fusion Solution." The press announcement for the merger stressed that the system would be able to quietly lift information from various sources without a trace. This suggests to me that they might be making use of PROMIS-style "back doors" secretly embedded in the software of most databanks. One of the stated goals of the system is to give government agencies "significant time and cost savings for deployment of critical national security initiatives." Does this mean that Battelle will be involved with rounding up dissidents in the future? Will they be making use of robots to do so? To trigger such a scenario, will they once again allow their anthrax to get into the hands of "terrorists" mailing packages to liberal Senators and news agencies, as happened after 9/11?

AC: That's just a little something to keep in the back of your mind. Control your own enlightenment. That's about all you can control, ultimately. That's kind of what the whole Mothman experience means to me. It's this force that is available to you at different levels. The 8th Tower, or 8th Sphere, is the so-called "top." You want to be at least conversant with the airy energy of the 8th Sphere. But my point about this Kitner is that you have the Rockefellers directly interfacing with groups similar to the Wandering Bishops. You have sincere religious organizations that just happen to have secretive levels imbedded in them, doing questionable things. This William Kitner sounds kind of like an early "neo-con." He argued for the adoption of the counter-insurgency doctrine at *all* levels of government, military and civilian. He rejected peaceful co-existence as illusory. Violent co-existence was his reality. He basically believed that only military officers should be in the government. Only the military could provide proper economic development in the Third World. This is a guy who's moving through all levels of D.C. culture. I'm sure there are many people like this today. It's probably even worse today.

GK: This also very reminiscent of an individual by the name of James Burnham, who's probably the forerunner – along with Strauss – of being preemptive, saying the communists are the bad guys and we ought to be there before it happens. I'm going to take a look [on the Internet] for Kitner while you speak. This is reminiscent of the doctrines that seem to come in after WWII, to keep the fires flamed so we could never let our guard down. And the military-industrial complex could keep on humming…

AC: Also in the same paragraph, it jumps to how Kitner's "militarized development" thesis gave a "theoretical foundation" to the "civic action" programs of unconventional warfare, tested in the Philippines by General Edward Lansdale. Lansdale was the Phoenix assassination leader who had an interest in using "gypsies." The gypsies come up in the Mothman lore. Some of the MIBs looked like gypsies. Some looked like Laplanders and some were said to be Greek, which possibly meant that they were Operation CHAOS people. Maybe Lansdale was involved in Operation CHAOS?

Coincidentally, one of the villages near the paranormal site of Fatima, Portugal, is called Chaos. There have long been Virgin Mary sightings in and around Chaos.

GK: I also believe Lansdale was seen as a particular problem for Kennedy in those days.

AC: Yes, and then you have Lansdale in Asia, working with the Lansky mob guys, bringing drugs back. You mentioned Ruby had this gambling place in northern Kentucky… Lansky had a casino there at one time, too. I found this in one of Michael Collins Piper books.

GK: Funny you should mention that…

AC: Ruby and Lansky were partners in a gambling casino called the Colonial Inn. Ruby famously claimed to have been injected with cancer, by the way. This whole bluegrass drug conspiracy was tied in with SE Asia. Almost all of the Army guys are trained in Kentucky. Every Army trainee is going though Kentucky. That's one reason we have so much of this covert stuff going on there.

GK: Does Fort Campbell, Kentucky, ever come up in any of these surreptitious goings-on?

AC: I've been keeping an eye on Ft. Campbell because they have the helicopters there. That's the big helicopter fleet base.

GK: The big black ones?

AC: Yes, and Bell Helicopter, out of Dallas, has a direct line to Fort Campbell. We've already connected Bell Helicopter to various JFK, Paperclip, and MK-Ultra (mind control) guys. By the way, try not to confuse Woody Derenberger and Walter Dornberger. Those are two different guys. Derenberger is the contactee. Oddly, they have very similar names. Could they be related? General Dornberger came over from the Nazi camps to help lead Bell Helicopter, just as Werner von Braun led Fairchild and NASA Security. Nelson Rockefeller was pleased with this reorganization of the Pentagon around counter-insurgency. "Counter-insurgency" is basically code for "Phoenix Program." They relied on assassination. It's actually a rebirth of the old assassination methods from 1000 years ago, where you selectively target and assassinate.

GK: Imagine that...

AC: The reason I'm interested in that is because the Assassins, or Hashishans, not only used killing but mind control. Mind control came from these pseudo-religious assassination squads. In the Orient, they would trick the initiate into believing that they had died and gone to heaven. They would give them a few weeks of glorious, sumptuous debauchery in Heaven...

GK: That's right. You took the words right out of my mouth.

AC: And then take "Heaven" away... Then they would say, "Go kill so and so" to get your privileges back. My point is that "the phenomenon" seems to do this, too. It's a carrot and stick thing. Where did this idea come from? Is it a synthetic product of the Orient from 1000 years ago, or is it an older, more natural and constant kind of thing. I can tell you from experience that the phenomenon tries to trick people. It even gives them assignments. For instance, Anna Genzlinger was led to study Morris K. Jessup by hearing Jessup speak to her from "the other side." This brings us to *Paranoia* magazine from Spring of 2002, Issue 29. It's an article by Andy Lloyd on the "Dark Star," Nibiru. It's the 10th Planet idea, which we hear lots about. Zechariah Sitchen has talked about it.

GK: Planet X, yes...

AC: There are some interesting connections in this article. I've often felt like the flying Anunnaki people, who ruled Sumeria, are connected to this Mothman phenomenon. Lloyd discusses the Theosophists, by the way. The Theosophists are where we get some of the UFO contactee language.

The noble ideas that the Nazis latched onto were Theosophical ideas. Lloyd mentions the Theosophical branch of Symbolism, and the Rosicrucian branch. These are basically Western ways of looking at the phenomenon. Lloyd says, "According to esoteric lore, the 8th Sphere is a neutral oracle that gives people messages. It's a shadowy spiritual plane occupied by beings intent on dragging down degenerate spiritual forms on earth. It seems that this realm is the one accessed by mediums, who erroneously believe that they are contacting departed souls." This raises the question of whether or not you're getting a bonafide message. They use that same misdirection pattern in mind control, I do believe. But let's say it's happening organically in real life, and someone is getting a message from the psi-plasma. They may think that they are being given a vital task of some kind. The person may even be tricked into believing that they might die if they don't perform the task. This could happen to you when you're driving in your car through Nevada. You see the flashing lights that put you into a trance, and later believe that you received a message. A lot of people experience this kind of thing. They have these great missions that they're on. In a way, I have to admit that my research on Mothman is like that. It was spurred on by that kind of thing. The important thing is that we look at our programming. Not just our TV programming, but also our mass media programming… Look at these very subtle kinds of programming. That's really the key to your own personal enlightenment. In Lloyd's comments above, I'm interested in the ambiguity of that middle sentence that says, "The 8th Sphere is a shadowy spiritual plane occupied by beings intent on dragging down degenerate spiritual forms on the earth." Now, that could certainly be interpreted as "the 8th Sphere is bringing down a demonic force." But if you read it another way, it says it's "taking down," or disarming, any degenerate spiritual forms. This kind of ambiguity has led to the polarized arguments you see in the Mothman, Bigfoot, and UFO worlds. Are these demonic beings, or are they angelic?

GK: What are [these] older texts [that Lloyd is referencing]?

AC: Older "Masonic" and Rosicrucian texts stemming from the Hermetic traditions of Egypt… All of these systems of symbology are interconnecting. They all seem to first come out of the Middle East and Northern Africa. And from there they traveled to Europe, as recent genetic history research shows. As a photographer, I like to look at all of the different pieces, and mix and match different combinations of possibilities. You really start to see repetitions of symbols in different cultures. They start to mean something at a very deep, unconscious level. Like for instance, they have an image in here of the Holy Trinity. It says that the pagan god Ba'al (in the middle of the trinity) is probably the Dark Star that everyone is talking about. Basically, Lloyd is equating these ancient theories and symbols to astronomical events. They're apparently mirroring each other. The idea is that if you look at these older texts, they will tell you things about astronomical procession. This reminds us of the Hindus' Kali Yuga, which states that we undergo a 26,000 year cycle. During that cycle, the galaxy turns just once.

GK: Let me ask you something if I could. It just came to the top of my head. Did you ever encounter any data that stated there were Mothman sightings in and around the Chernobyl disaster?

AC: Supposedly that's not true.

GK: Shall we say it's unconfirmed? Go on with what you're doing. I'm sorry…

AC: Lloyd has a quote in here from an initiate in one of the early secret schools. A little over a century ago, there were some revelations made. There were some major arguments going on within the secret schools. It says here that the secrets disclosed pertained to a far deeper level of knowledge than had hitherto been made available. In a nutshell, what was made public during this conflict in the schools was that our moon was a counterweight to another sphere, which remains invisible to ordinary vision. Lloyd is thinking that this is the Dark Star. This invisible, counterweighted sphere is, in esoteric circles, called the 8th Sphere. Here we have a slight variation in the symbology. Instead of imagining Keel's 8th Tower, we imagine the 8th Sphere floating out there in another dimension. In this 8th Sphere, entities supposedly live. They can come down and influence earth. One of the most resonant archetypal symbols is that of the Lost King, the supernaturally aided monarch who, having completed his tasks on earth, does not quite die. This is very similar to the Garuda story. After the Garuda kills the serpent, the serpent doesn't die. It can work either way. There's this constant battle going. The yin and the yang, good and evil… The supernaturally aided monarch retires into some other dimension, where he bides his time until the needs of his people dictate his return. Again, this is a messianic script very similar to the Garuda (and Christ). These same ideas are in every culture, not just the Southeast Asian or Native American. The European tradition, too, is chock-full of birdman symbolisms. Lloyd has a picture of the triple-headed alchemical dragon, Azof, whose various serpentine tails culminate into a strange Trinity. The Garuda also has serpents, as well as the Christlike outstretched arms. Even the alchemical entities of the Egyptian tradition have the same symbolisms. There they connect to the solar disc, the winged disc that you see on WING-TV when you go to their website. The solar disc is symbolic of Nibiru, the Dark Star. In Buddhist depictions, you often see the halfway-visible Garuda floating in space above the Buddha. The Garuda is a kind of dark star, too. He's bridging between dark and light. This alchemical dragon trinity is an interpretation of a messianic godhead, prior to Jesus Christ. The middle figure in the trinity has two serpents like the Garuda, but looks like an Anglo-Saxon knight.

Garuda sculpture showing birdman bridging space between human nervous systems, or spinal columns, represented by "lotus cobras."

In the Western tradition, we have the Black Sun, also called the Black Virgin. This is a feminine force shining invisibly from the center of the earth. This belief has resulted in earth-energy worship at sites where Marian visions have occurred. Shrines, grottos, barrows, mounds, menhirs, and dolmens (stones) were typically erected in the West wherever the "Virgin Mary" was seen.

In the East, such things are commonly venerated at stupa, pyramid, and cave sites. There, the entity is called Guanyin. She is considered to have been the Buddha's teacher. In Chinese art, Guanyin is often depicted standing atop a dragon, accompanied by a bird, and flanked by two children with warriorlike capabilities. In "The Mothman Prophecies," Keel described a female Mothman seen in Vietnam in 1967. This Mothgirl was completely black and did not reflect light (like my tree entity from WV). She seems to fit the description of the Black Virgin.

In France, the Black Virgin is worshipped in August of each year. This was Aleister Crowley's favorite time, the Dog Days. According to Maurice Guinguand and Beatrice Lanne, the Black Virgin has been venerated for centuries, calling her "the feminine diviner of positive telluric [earth-energy] forces, and record-keeper of lost subterranean riches." Can the Black Virgin lead us to the mysterious Book of Records, thought by Edgar Cayce to be buried underneath the Sphinx? I once dreamed of reading such a book beneath an amusement park, and then experiencing enlightenment.

On p. 61 of "Celestial Secrets: The Hidden History of the Fatima Cover-up" by Fernandes & D'Armada, we see a depiction of a Marian being from 1978, associated with an "oval object" not unlike the telepathic eggs reportedly unearthed in the land of the Garuda (Indonesia). The Virgin Mary image looks surprisingly similar to the corn goddess of the Hopi Indians, as depicted in Katchina dolls. I once wrote a graduate paper regarding the evolution of the Hopi "paho," or baby toy, into the sacred Katchina dolls so famous today. The Hopis decided to begin using synthetic materials in their dolls following WWII, which boosted sales tremendously. The Hopis have been greatly helped by their willingness to selectively adapt to modern ways. The Hopis were also one of the tribes of great interest to the Rockefellers.

GK: Would you call these legends, myths, or folklore?

AC: This is a note I made, that wasn't necessarily meant for the radio. It says, "The birds have mastered the ether." Birds fly around, so it's natural to connect birds with lighter, less dense molecules. Taking this simple fact further, to the realm of the supernatural, is a "natural" progression. We see the bird as supernatural because of its ability to do what we cannot (without the use of extra gear). Buddhists feel that objects manifest from this bird-dominated ether. Again, the Garuda rules that space. Those spaces between points... He can fly through... Buddhists feel that the supernatural is not just occurring in your mind, as when you telepathically link with a supernatural entity. It is also physical. They believe that you do see the vision. Say you're driving. You see the lights. You maybe see the Bird, or Birdman... No problem... They just take it further. They believe that the universe is built from that same "supernatural" process. It's mostly out of our hands. It's the "all-is-one" idea. We see the symbolisms and physical manifestations *because* of the underlying etheric reality, not the other way around.

Etheric processes have created, and are running, our bodies and objects, beyond our conscious control. Forms arise out of consciousness organized in infinite layers.

GK: State that one more time for me.

AC: The psi-plasma that Puharich studied is *forming* material. It consists of these super small particles that are so small that they're mostly empty space. When they pick up a superluminal "charge," they spin. They then create energy bundles (called "skandas" in Buddhism) that join together and form material objects.

GK: Let me stop you right there. What would that mean? And this is not an easy question, I understand. But if those physics were true, what would that mean about reality?

AC: Well, I've been editing these little clips that were transcribed from the video series. I was talking about a *Scientific American* article on holograms. The article states, "Quantum physics says the entire universe might be a hologram." In fact, they go so far as to say that, even though we live in a three-dimensional universe, we actually are only experiencing reality *two-dimensionally*. Now, holograms sort of do the reverse. They are essentially two-dimensional; yet give the appearance of the three-dimensional. So physics is starting to say that what you're seeing in front of you *is an illusion*. It appears that one's experience, or that which we perceive, is on the skin of reality. After the ether has spun, this formerly empty space has coalesced to form something. You are seeing that every day. You're seeing what light is reflecting off of. But you're not seeing the reality below it, which is space. Everything is happening on the skin. Inside, reality is all space. A *lot* of space... It is space that occasionally releases energy. The heat of the energy bubbles up and out, as a kind of visible yet psychic sweat. When you're driving down the road in the desert, and you see those anomalous lights on the horizon, that's like the sweat of the psi-plasma leaking through a pore in the skin of reality. Hey, I like that metaphor!

GK: That brings it home to me.

The above example makes me wonder what the brain is doing when it looks at a hologram.

AC: The Buddhists and physicists are both saying that we're made up mostly of empty space. In the note mentioned above, I go on to write, "If you think about how vision works, two-dimensionality is the format. Even though things appear three-dimensionally, when I'm photographing I'm accessing a part of my mind that sees two-dimensionally." For photographers, that's a basic kind of thing you have to learn to do. You have to realize that certain subjects might look good when you're there, but will look like crap when printed on the page.

AC: The brain is always going to interpret things two-dimensionally.

GK: That is true. That *is* true...

AC: You have to choose your subject matter accordingly. If you bite off more than you can chew, that lovely three-dimensional scene is just *not* going to work in the flat, two-dimensional format.

These ideas are encapsulated in the old photography dictum, "The secret to good photography is knowing what not to take pictures of."

GK: This makes some kind of sense. You said something about the leakage through our world. I asked this of Adam Gorightly, regarding those lights I saw... Is there a possibility that something tapped into our earth, which I just happened to witness? I know that's a pretty pathetic way of positing that statement, but do you know what I'm saying? Did I see something that was a leakage from another sphere into our own?

AC: Yes, I think so...

GK: All right... Now, at some point, if you're "on the path" as they say in Buddhism, you're going to try to start integrating that knowledge. At some point, you stop seeing it the old way you saw it before, and start to realize that the [new way] is just part of our reality, too. Are you saying that if my mindset had been different – more evolved or whatever – that what I saw might have had a different impact on my brain?

AC: Probably... But it's a subjective thing. Call it "getting in touch with what's really there." They call it "rigpa" in Tibet, which means seeing reality. This is different than seeing a *set of concepts* you've been told is reality, or believing the stories that you've made up about reality... It's about getting back to the process of really looking at your own programming. Eliminating the filters, so that you can nakedly perceive what is really happening...

GK: The only reason I bring that up is that we talked about what happened to me [and the lights. So] one of the explanations might be that something from another realm, or plane, slipped into ours and we just happened to be there to go, "Oh, what's that?" Is that somewhat approximating the [truth]? The thing that struck me about what you just said – and I don't think this is anti-Christian or anything – is that we have no idea *what's* out there. I talked to you about witnessing the flashes... I was with people who are not fools. We all wondered what it was all about. You talked about that leakage, which I thought was very interesting. I guess I hung onto that because that made some sense to me. It really came home that we witnessed something from another plane. Is it possible that we witnessed something that wasn't meant for us to see?

AC: Well, the other plane is in *your mind*, too. That's kind of what I was talking about before. The shift in *point-of-view* is what the Buddhists are after. It takes years to do it. You have to continually use these symbolisms to do it. You then start to see that the anomalous event is also within your mind. That mind is not localized within the body... Because of the psi-plasma, your mind is the universe, literally and scientifically. Not just in a flaky, hippiesque way...

GK: I got you.

AC: Scientifically, the positrons of the universe are passing through your brain. You are it, and it is you.

This is expressed in the Buddhist saying, "I am that."

GK: And we are all together...

AC: Let's bring in John Lennon!

GK: Alright, let me nail you down again and then I'll let you go free. What we saw – be it the Nevada Desert or behind a house in Teaneck, New Jersey – was that reality? Was that really a physical reality that others might have seen? Or was that just for us?

AC: It could have been either. Some of the lights are going to be seen by other brains in a group, and some aren't. It's the infinite variety that's always happening. There's no doubt that these lights can morph. Their molecules change to allow entry into our visual dimension. Then they go back out again.

Invisible "interdimensional" creatures are probably always there. Their seeming to "leave" is simply a drama played out in our heads. The playwright, if you will, is our limited ability to see the wider range of visual frequencies.

GK: Does that say anything about the mentality of the people involved, or is it just happenstance? Go ahead, say it straight.

AC: There does *seem* to be a selection process whereby certain people are going to be more likely to experience it, yes. Keel sort of figured that out. They were generally menstruating female teachers of gifted children, who drove Ford Galaxies. Or ex-Catholic males in a personal crisis of some kind…

GK: That would fit the bill. We weren't in crisis, but…

AC: By the way, this doesn't mean that the events are not physical at some point. It's just that they change and become seemingly nonphysical to us. Electrochemically, you have classes of people with certain blood types. It is entirely possible that a given UFO would more often choose a certain type. But it is also common to *think* that you've been chosen. A lot of people do.

GK: It's not a status thing, it just happens?

AC: Yes, it just happens, and it's very natural. It happens to a lot of people, and it's very old. I had this other note I wanted to get to. It's kind of a switch, but it relates to what we were talking about before. In the city of Copan in Mayan country, there is a temple that I saw in a documentary recently. It had what they called "a god" issuing from the mouth of a bird, with two snakes above it. I saw this and said, "That's the Garuda!" The Mayans were telling us that what we now call "Mothman" is God, or related to God. The Mayans were saying that God enters our world from the mouth of The Bird. In Buddhism, it's kind of the same way. The Garuda isn't necessarily a god. He's more like the background format, or the medium. The ground on which it is all happening… Enlightenment would be the Buddha, or the Christ, or this particular Mayan god that was issuing forth from the mouth of the bird. In some ways, it's very prosaic and simple. Birds fly, so they symbolize empty space. And creation comes from empty space. It's almost that simple to me. But again, because of people's brains and how we're all so intricately wired, the leakage from these pores in the skin of reality has all kinds of unusual effects. So how does this leakage, this slate of inspired prophecy, start to get into politics or conspiracy? The question of whether or not you're going to get a slew of clues from the psi-plasma has to do with the intensity of the particular situation. You're going to get a lot of clues if the particular situation is dire enough. That's what these old texts seem to say. You're more likely to see a materialized vision of this bird when you are in a dire place, situation, or time (relative to your understanding). If it's a minor crisis, you might see it and experience just a simple clue. But if it is dire enough, you might experience a series of clues about an entire ongoing process. A lot of the 1960s and '70s clues seem to be pointing in the direction of the military-industrial complex. If you had to point to a cartel that was really responsible for destruction of life forms on earth, they're the guys. They're the ones who are cutting down the rainforest. I never really knew until I looked at this Rockefeller book. They have systematically encroached on the rainforest, buying up huge sections of it, starting on the edges going inward. Nelson had million-acre ranches with a quarter of a million cattle on them. Did I mention this last time?

GK: No.

AC: He was also interested in genetically mutating beef. Combine that with the need to test live animal tissue for locating underground resource deposits and, bingo, you've got a good excuse for engaging in cattle mutilations. I'm not saying that Nelson is responsible for every single cattle mutilation, but it's very suggestive. Like a lot of things in this story, the perpetrators seem to be mimicking natural processes. I say "natural" because there *are* some cattle mutilations that appear to be unrelated to helicopters or guys with millions of dollars trying to make the perfect steak. Some of the cattle activity *does* seem paranormal. In *The Dyfed Enigma* by Ted Holiday, he talks about a herd of cattle that kept moving, or being moved. They were literally locked in at night. They could not get out; there was no way. And yet every night they would be found a mile away, wandering. Something was picking these cattle up and moving them. There were no mutilations in that case, however. There was no end product or result. It was just an unusual glitch in time/space. So again, even in cattle mutilation, you have to look at the situation and ask, "Is this the real phenomenon or the synthetic one?" In *Dyfed Enigma*, they had another interesting thing going on. You know, there's this big controversy around Mothman. People are always asking, "is this phenomenon demonic or not?" Here's evidence that it's not demonic, and that it's just presenting different manifestations. In addition to the Dyfed cattle mysteriously moving, you had these scary Men in Black. The silver-suited, 7-foot tall versions… They're called the Spring-Heeled Jacks. It's a version of an MIB that has tremendous leaping ability.

GK: What's an MIB? You mentioned an acronym there. Was it MIB?

AC: Yes, Men in Black... At Dyfed, which is in England, there appeared to be time-travelers, or interdimensional guys, who probably weren't faked. They were pretty scary. They were very frightening, like in Pt. Pleasant. The animals were very frightened. Any animal that would come into contact with these MIBs would be damaged for life. They would never recover. It seemed demonic. Well, believe it or not, they were *also* seeing the Virgin Mary in the mirror of a cabinet there. *Thousands* of people came to see it. There were articles written about it. It was a real thing, happening on the same farm as the MIBs and the flying cattle. You have what people would clearly consider a benevolent Catholic miracle alongside very scary and destructive beings. This appears to be the same phenomenon creating both things. With this Mayan temple I described before, here's another little strange coincidence. I happened to study at the Univ. of Texas with the lady who broke the Mayan code, Linda Schele. She's no longer with us. She was probably the best teacher I ever had, in terms of pure intellect. She was nothing more than a fine art painter who went down to Mexico on a vacation, and eventually ended up breaking the Mayan code. Why? Because she had this natural visual ability... I have a term for this. I call it "blind learning." Some people are just able to see and understand things. They learn things without being taught. They tap into the creative force.

Schele focused on teaching people how to teach themselves. She did not give grades based on whether you took a test or knew a set of predetermined facts, but whether or not your desire to learn had been demonstrated.

GK: One would think that they have a predisposition to do this...

AC: It's related to telepathy, I think. I've noticed that a lot of people changed by paranormal experiences are not only picking things up from the "ether," but they are putting things together very originally, in this blind-learning kind of way. Maybe they're just learning...

GK: Telepathically?

AC: People *can* learn that way. You don't necessarily have to be taught something. You can be taught how to teach yourself. As they say in the education business, try and "teach kids how to learn." That in itself goes a long way.

GK: She could have had some precognition, or whatever. When she came upon this, it just struck a chord with her...

AC: I wish I had known more at the time. I could have asked her specifically about the Garuda, and if it is the same creature that they call the "flying jaguar."

GK: By your use of verbiage, am I to suppose that she's dead?

AC: Yes, she died. But I never met someone who had such an open mind. When one was in her presence, one literally could *feel* the power of her intellect. She had something. It was almost a divine presence.

GK: What year did that take place in?

AC: 1986, 1987… My experience with her was very similar to the experience of studying with Sogyal Rinpoche, a Tibetan lama whom a lot of people have read about. He has a book called *The Tibetan Book of Living and Dying*. When I first met him, I picked up some kind of transmission. There's a process in Buddhism where you can download enormous amounts of knowledge, wisdom, and the like from a guru in a very short time. Like in minutes or seconds (usually after a certain amount of preparation)... They have various teachings and transmissions. They'll usually have a ritual, and then this downloading occurs. But it can also occur spontaneously. I don't know how much of this stuff has gotten out to the average American, but it's a pretty amazing process. It's fascinating, and probably a major reason why there were so many intelligence agents infiltrating the Buddhist world back in the '60s.

GK: [We can] go even beyond that. Hitler had solicited a number of them who were found dead upon the Russian invasion into Berlin. That's a known fact. There were scores of Buddhists found there, for whatever reason…

Were the Berlin monks from the same sect of blue-skinned, psychic monks mentioned in Peter Moon's Montauk series?

AC: Getting back to that thing about burning flesh and how it "fuels" the spirits… Ted Holiday had this thing about sacrifices. He felt that there was something to this whole ancient tradition of sacrificing humans to these entities.

Could a secret belief in the need for sacrifices explain why secret societies seem to hover around events of mass destruction, war, and terror?

AC: Scott Corrales, the chupacabras researcher, feels that these chupacabras entities might be "gods of some kind." In the old days, they used to leave out people in the desert. Instead of pulling their hearts out like the Aztecs did, they more or less just put them out in a field…

GK: On the fringe of town, and "let the wolves have at 'em…"

AC: Right, but it wasn't the wolves that got them. It was these entities…

GK: That's the same thing you hear from Rome as well so, yes, that resonates.

AC: I kind of didn't want to bring it up because it gets some people fired up. For instance, I did a men's retreat with Michael Meade, who's kind of the new Robert Bly of the men's movement. I tried it out. I wanted to see what the movement was like, and if it matched the stereotype in the media. They had an African shaman there, Malidoma Some, who escaped from a Catholic mission that had abducted him when he was just a kid. He has a different relationship to sacrifice than we do. There were some Catholics in the crowd that got really worked up because Malidoma was trying to explain why animal sacrifice was beneficial. I can't remember how he said it, exactly, but it seemed to be a convincing argument. To make a long story short, there *is* a reason for it. He was basically saying that if you're not going to perform sacrifice in a ritualized manner, then it's going to be done in an unritualized manner.

GK: Wow... Okay...

GK: We practiced making a fetish at that retreat. I can't really talk about it because it's supposed to be secret but, when it was happening, I seemed to know the next steps in the process *before* they happened. That was really...

GK: Weird?

AC: Yes. He was leading us through the ritual process of how to make and work with power objects. I was doing the steps before he said them. He would say, "Okay, the next thing is," and I was already doing it. I felt like I was accessing a part of myself that had done this in a previous life or something... Before we move on from the Paranoia article, though... Andy Lloyd also gets into The Nine! It was interesting to find this, and see The Nine from another point of view. Actually, I think a better way to say it might be "The Council of Nine." He says here that the Council of Nine originated from Blavatsky and the Theosophists! This gets us back to the Paperclip ex-Nazis and the contactees who were being given these Theoso-Nazi ideas. Puharich, when he was following Uri Geller around, suddenly started being talked to by the Council of Nine. Geller would go, "The Nine say we need to drive out to such and such place. Let's go." They would drive out there and turn the tape recorder on. A voice would start talking on the tape – supposedly from the UFO – saying, "We are the Council of Nine." It's interesting that this whole Nine business with Uri Geller was started by a Hindu man, named Vinod. Vinod was a Hindu mystic who hooked up with Arthur Young, Puharich, and some heavy hitters in the science community. Vinod started them on this path of the Council of Nine. But it was an idea that came from 50 years before. I don't know if they knew that or not.

GK: Probably not…

AC: But it's carried on into the UFO phenomenon. Lloyd talks about how The Nine has influenced various UFO researchers today. He says, "The [UFO] message that has been emerging over the last hundred years appears to have been coming from the Council of Nine, a shadowy group of spiritual entities who base their personalized archetypal imagery upon the ancient Egyptian gods. The information itself has been derived through channeling and psychic communication of various types." As I say, sometimes the messages occur on tape recorders or other devices, like cameras. Then, the tape (or negatives) will disappear supposedly. That's where I start to get a little skeptical. But you never know…

GK: No, you don't…

I have had things mysteriously show up on film, such as the kitchen entity photo of 1973. I have also had negatives disappear mysteriously, such as the shot of the anomalous figure in a crop circle outside my house in 1979. Since these could easily have mundane explanations, they may be in a different class than the receiving of long, disappearing tape messages.

AC: Lloyd continues, "What interested me here is the tie-in between the alleged source of the ET revelations and the shadowy realm of the 8th Sphere." The question sort of becomes, "Is the Council of Nine really from the 8th Sphere?" Is it *really* the neutral oracle, or is it one of the entities from the lower 7 rungs of the Tower? If there is any truth to timeless psychic communication, it *is* possible that the Theosophists were describing the Annunaki from the Sumerian story, taking on the guise of the Council of Nine. If you know the Annunaki stories, you know that they're not good guys. They're bent on enslaving people and making them mine gold, and all kinds of strange things. Some people believe that these are the guys who built the pyramids. Lloyd wonders, "Are the ancient gods attempting to orchestrate an increasing belief in their own presence within the solar system? Are their intentions malevolent or not? To attempt to access these beings by channeling or other forms of mediumistic communication can only be dangerous and foolhardy. We must find our own way as a race, and not succumb to the temptation to seek the answers beyond our natural sphere of understanding." I would agree with this. Lloyd continues with, "The Dark Star is a physical entity, and it will be found one day, possibly fairly soon." I think that, as we go through this 26,000 year cycle, we probably do encounter a particular astrological body only once in that time period. The encounter would probably occur either at the "bottom" or "top" of the cycle. Apparently every 13,000 years, we're sort of in an Enlightenment age, and then

13,000 years later we're kind of at the bottom – in the Dark Ages. This is the old Hindu idea that we're constantly going through this cycle. It only *appears* to us that we've just been here for a few thousand years. We've actually been here much, much longer. The span of time is so great – compared to our personal lives – that we don't see what's going on. We are literally having great societies rise up and decay, over and over again.

GK: That's interesting.

AC: The Dark Star and the 8th Sphere would fit in with that.

GK: Yeah, it would…

AC: It's just a natural process. If you look at us on the Kali Yuga calendar, we are heading out into a new stage. We're still kind of at the bottom though, generally.

GK: The bottom of what?

AC: The bottom of the scale. It makes a loop, and we're just a few hundred years, maybe a couple thousand years, out of the Dark Ages. The bottom…

GK: If we're at the bottom of something, are we on the verge of climbing out, ascending to a better time?

AC: Yes, but it's such a drawn-out time that…

GK: We may not see it right now.

AC: We may not see the benefits of the upturn because it's going to take another ten thousand years, probably.

CHAPTER 42

During the filming of the Mothman's Photographer, I visited with the Whyte family several times. Their family is originally from Mothman country, but they migrated west during the postwar years. In many ways, they symbolize the typical "Mothman family" in modern America. Even though they moved away from the Rockefeller-controlled regions of Appalachia, they still grew up in a Texas town dominated by the Rockefellers and Ohio agribusiness. Even today, they work in industries (medicine, banking, philanthropy) that are dominated by the Rockefellers. They have had a variety of paranormal experiences, some of which echo or shed light on my own experiences. The Whytes are wonderful people who like to barbecue, bake pies, and hike. They seem like "family." Karyn, the oldest sibling, began having psychic experiences during a childhood course in the Silva Mind Control Program. Today she is a nurse, Zen practitioner, and proud mother of two.

Whyte, Karyn – Silva Mind Control Event – 2003

Karyn Whyte (KW): I was in Silva when I was 8. My brother Randy was 6. It was in the early '70s. We went through the whole course together. Our parents took us... They didn't have a children's course at that time. It was designed for adults, so we just went along and did everything the grownups did. One of the last things you do in the course is "readings" on people. I forget exactly what they call it, but they give you the name and age of a sick person, and your job is to diagnose what it is. You know that there's something physically wrong with these people... I had a name and an age on a person. You go into your relaxed state. I wasn't getting anything. Nothing... I wasn't feeling anything. One of the techniques that they use is to tell you to "put on," or pretend like you're putting on the head or body of the person. When I did that, I really felt like I *was* this other person. I wasn't saying things like "this person is very sad," or "this person is having mental problems," or anything like that. Instead it was, "I am really really sad. I'm in a dark place. There's no windows here. Nobody is coming to help me." And I just felt desperately depressed and sad. I started crying. It was very intense. Really intense to me, as an 8 year old... But this is what they told me to do, right? They told me to diagnose this person, so that's what I did. I was kind of conscious of people coming around while I was doing it. The instructor said, "Okay, I think that's enough. You should take her head off now." So I took her head off, and I was back to myself. It was like we were two people at one time. It was really weird. Very unusual... I've never experienced anything like that again. It was strange afterwards, how people reacted to me. You had gone through this whole program, right? I think it's 6 weeks long. At the end, I actually did what they were trying to achieve. But it freaked them out...

Andy Colvin (AC): Did it freak out the instructor?

KW: It freaked out everybody! The instructor said things like, "Well, you had an interesting experience," or "something special happened." I don't remember exactly what it was. But people looked at me like, "What the heck was that?" I don't know what it looked like from the outside. But I know how it felt to me. It was *different.*

AC: Haven't you had other experiences like that?

KW: Well, actually, one time I did. Now that you mention that, my mother-in-law...

AC: What year was this?

KW: This was 1991, so I was well grown up by then. My mother-in-law's sister had died the previous year, in the Spring. Six months later, her sister's husband met a new woman, and was marrying her a few months after that. It had been within a span of a year. I was at the wedding. I never knew the sister. I didn't have any real emotional investment in her, so I was just sitting there watching the wedding happen. All of a sudden, I got a wave of emotion and I felt like I was her. I *was* my mother-in-law. I heard a voice saying, "My sister! My sister!" I really felt what she was feeling at that moment. I know I did. I looked over at her, and she's just sitting there. I had just met her the year before. I didn't really know her very well but I thought, "Wow, I just learned something about her today," About what kind of control she has over herself... Which I obviously don't... I've got no emotional control whatsoever. But that was real. *That* was something real. But I think that was the last time.

Since Karyn was crying at this point, I tried to change the focus a bit.

AC: Someone else we've talked to during this film project, Mercedes Yaeger, has the same thing happen a lot.

KW: Oh really? I don't... It's not something that happens all the time. Whenever something like that happens, it's unusual. You know that something different – something unexplainable – has happened.

AC: What do you think is behind the mechanism of this phenomenon?

KW: I've got no clue. I don't know. I don't have any explanation for it. I just know that whenever things like that happen, they're real. As far as science understands it right now, there's no physically measurable explanation for it. We can't quantify it. I'm not saying it's *not* quantifiable, just that right now we can't.

AC: It makes sense that you've gone into the healing arts as you've gotten older. You were asked at a young age to intuit someone medically and you did, in the most profound way.

KW: Oh, I never said what was wrong with her, did I?

AC: What was wrong with her?

KW: She was in a mental institution. She was in a mental institution for severe depression, and had attempted suicide. Maybe they shouldn't have given that person to an 8-year old…

AC: They were obviously doing some strange things in the Silva program.

KW: Yes, and they still do that. At least in the 1980s they were…

AC: Have you had anything happen in relation to your Buddhist practice? You're one of the few people I've interviewed who has a Zen practice.

KW: Do I ever have any paranormal sort of experiences on the cushion?

AC: Yes. I've been talking a lot about Buddhism and how Buddhism explains the phenomenon so nicely. I mean modern science doesn't have all the answers. Buddhists actually have the Mothman, or the Garuda, in their pantheon of deities. They've studied all the various processes that involve psychic activity, precognition, etc. They almost have it down to a science. Especially the Tibetans…

KW: Zen is originally from China, then it came to those other countries. But I think that even at the core of Tibetan Buddhism, it's not different from Zen Buddhism. There are lots of gods that are visual or physical representations of different states of mind. Those are *really* teaching tools. It's sometimes easier for people to experience something if they can see it, or attach a name to it. But I think the core of all the Buddhist traditions is still the "dropping away," becoming your essential self, which…

AC: Doesn't exist…

KW: Yes. "Self" is not a word you use.

AC: In Tibetan history there's a story of an ancient standoff between the most famous Chinese monk and the most famous Tibetan monk, to see which path would be the one that Tibet would take. The Chinese practitioner was using what we could say was more of a "Void" approach. This story was in a book by Alexandra David Neel. Neel sneaked into Tibet, disguised herself as a man, and studied their traditions. She felt like the

Chinese approach was superior. It was more of a female, or "emptiness," kind of approach. But the Tibetans declared the Tibetan the winner. His approach was more of a male "doer." The Tibetans decided to say, "Go ahead and *have* all of these visualizations, *believe* that there is something physically there that you're dealing with." In Chinese Zen, however, it evolved more into a "what's *not* there" kind of approach. Does that sound right to you?

KW: Yes. That makes sense.

AC: Neel was saying that she felt like the Tibetans were kind of being hypocritical, that they would give "emptiness" lip service, but when it came down to it they still believed in manifestation. When she actually looked at the transcription of the debate, she felt like the Chinese had won hands down, because the Void is actually the core from which everything else arises.

KW: Right. And so what's the point of the rest of it, except as a teaching tool? I think that's why Tibetan Buddhism has more popularity here in the States than the other varieties, because it is so charismatic. It's pretty to look at, and gives you something to focus on.

AC: So you had a visualization the day before Christmas?

KW: Yes, Christmas 2002... I was sitting there making pies and cakes, missing my family and people who have gone, and thinking about my grandma. I wanted to make this cake that's eggless, milkless, and butterless. It has no eggs, milk or butter in it, and it was always one that she made at Christmastime. But I couldn't find the recipe. It wasn't with my regular recipe stuff. So I started feeling sad. I couldn't call her on the phone and ask her how to do it anymore. I was sitting there feeling sorry for myself, and all of a sudden I visualized and heard in my mind, "look in the Betty Crocker!" So I went and looked in the Betty Crocker cookbook. And it was in there! I had punched holes in it and put it in the Betty Crocker cookbook, on a separate piece of paper.

AC: It wasn't a Betty Crocker recipe?

KW: Right. It was her recipe, but I had stuck it in the Betty Crocker cookbook. At that same moment that I gotten the visualization and the sound, I also thought, "That's odd, that's not the way I usually remember things." And then I found the recipe. At that same exact second, my son came around the corner. He had a soda pop. He held it up and said, "Cheers from heaven!" Here's number two... This was way back in the '80s. I was at work and I was typing, kind of in a zoned-out state just typing away. All of a sudden, I saw this picture of the scene out of my grandmother's living room window. It was what you would see if you looked out of her living room window. I mean it was just like I was *there*. I also got this bad feeling at the same time, like something was wrong. As soon as I could, I called my mother on the phone and said, "have you talked to Nanny lately?" And she said, "No, not lately." I said, "You need to call her. I'd feel better if you called her to make sure everything's okay." So she called her. Everything was [supposedly] fine. Nothing happened... But a couple months later, my grandmother told everybody that she had been diagnosed with breast cancer. She hadn't told people right away what was going on, because she didn't want anybody to worry about her until she knew what it was. That moment that I had seen the [vision] was the moment that she found out that something was wrong. She was outside, but had run inside to get the phone. She had leaned over the couch arm to get to the phone, and she felt a sore spot. That was when she realized that something was wrong. And [what I saw] was what she was seeing at that moment.

AC: You got that image...

At this point Karyn's daughter interjected that she herself is telekinetic and psychic, and that this is a source of happiness for her. Karyn's husband then joked that the girls should focus on trying to telekinetically manifest hundred dollar bills. Further joking ensued, concerning how family members could use psychic warfare tactics on each other.

AC: The Tibetans have a legend about a sect of blue-skinned monks, who got that way from ingesting a mineral thought to increase psychic power. The color blue also comes up with my sister and her contact experiences. She sometimes spontaneously goes into a trance and enters a blue room where they have blue "jaguar" people. This seems to happen to her following the sex act. But she's a "weird bird."

KW: Well, this doesn't have anything to do with sex. My brother, Randy, and my dad had this similar sort of strange experience. I don't know what you want to term it, but they both had an unexplainable event. The way I had remembered it [when I first told you about it] was that Randy had seen this blue figure. After I got home, I was thinking about things because [I cried] on tape and it was an intense experience. I thought, "Wait..."

AC: A lot of people cry on tape. It's a cleansing experience.

KW: I'm not going to cry this time. But I remembered, when I got home, that I had gotten these two experiences confused. I said before that we were both in Silva together, and that part of Silva is inviting a spirit guide to help you. That [spirit guide] was his blue person. You "open a door" and there is someone there. Randy's guide was this blue energy body. He said it didn't have a sex. It was just like this blue energy. I had somehow gotten those two things superimposed in my mind, that [blue spirit] and his experience with the entity that came into his room one night.

AC: So how do you feel about your brother Tony's explanation that it's more or less "all in the mind?" His gist seemed to be that this was all connected to people's perceptions...

KW: It's possible, sure... I really just think that it's unexplainable. I think that there might be [a state] other than physical or mental. Something in between... Maybe there's something that is neither tangible, nor totally esoteric...

AC: Could it be the "clear" state? In Tantric Buddhism, the clear state is said to be in between void and form. There you have "clear beings" that are sort of translucent. They have an ethereal body.

KW: It could be in that realm. I believe in the ethereal body...

AC: The old Bon tradition in Tibet has those three basic outlines. One can move between them. Some beings in the middle state would be similar to ghosts. But it's also a dimension of clarity where you can travel astrally.

KW: Maybe that's the level that all these experiences occur on.

AC: The clarity allows for fast travel *and* also allows travel through time. In our everyday conscious state, there's so much crud separating us that we can't accomplish much psychically. Our conscious mind is too filled with sensory input.

KW: Yes, and maybe these experiences are somewhere in between, where there's some overlap between those dimensions, or realities.

CHAPTER 43

Randy Whyte is always extremely reluctant to appear on camera. He leaves the area the minute any camera starts rolling. He is a modest, talented professional who once survived an Army stint in the steaming jungles of the Caribbean. While on an island known for its many chupa-cabras and UFO sightings, Randy got a flesh-eating virus on his arm. He was eventually sent back home to a delighted family. One Halloween night, I caught him at just the right moment when he was willing to talk on camera. The following interview transpired. Randy reluctantly agreed to its inclusion in this book. I applaud him for his courage.

Whyte, Randy – Childhood Alien Visit – 2003

Randy Whyte (RW): I was asleep in my parents' house. I was awakened by lights in my window. I sat up in my bed and looked towards the open door. The room was dark. The hallway was dark. Looking around from the corner of the room was an entity with the classic oval eyes, underneath a dark cowl. The only thing I could [actually] see was the head. But I could perceive a body behind the image. From that point [on] I didn't see anything else. Yet I knew somebody was in my room. I felt someone walking towards the bunk beds. My room opened up onto a courtyard, and there was a streetlight across the way. I could often see what was in the room. I didn't really see anything in the room, but I knew it was there. Then the bunk beds swayed… There was a ladder towards the end. I felt the bunk bed shift, as though someone was crawling up the ladder. Obviously, you know what that feels like… I couldn't see anything at that point. But the covers moved…

Andy Colvin (AC): The covers moved, too?

RW: You could feel the weight on the mattress of the bunk bed. At that point, I didn't really think about anything else. I just kept thinking [about that]. Then, I'm just *in my room* [after some time has passed] trying to figure out what happened.

AC: There was, like, a skip of time?

RW: [Yes] and then I went to sleep.

AC: Did you sleep a really long time?

RW: I slept until the morning, yes. It was a normal day after that.

AC: Any changes in your life soon after?

RW: Well, I thought about it all the next day. *All* the next day… I was captivated by this event that had just happened to me.

AC: Didn't your dad mention something about it at the breakfast table?

RW: No, it wasn't the breakfast table. It was the dinner table… I had gone to school. My dad had gone to work. My dad mentioned that something strange had happened to him last night. I said, "Really? Me, too…" He said that he was awakened in his room with the feeling that somebody was in the room. He lay in his bed in a wakened state, not really moving, just trying to perceive what was around him. He felt that this *something* was directly above him. He reached up and he grabbed it! He felt something move away from him. He *chased it* out of the room. Then he went back to bed. But he felt it another time that night, too.

AC: So it touched him somehow? Made contact?

RW: It was touching him. It came to him.

AC: He felt that it wasn't right. Didn't want the intrusion…

RW: He felt that there was somebody in his house. It was the wrong thing. He was going after them.

[Randy's brother-in-law] Craig: What I find really interesting is that after this really intense event, there's some [amnesia]. You can't quite account for some time. All of a sudden, you just fall asleep. These things happen and then you just fall out. I had that same experience. I still don't know what it is…

AC: Do you think this thing runs in families? Craig, you married into Randy's family. Your wife has had some experiences that are paranormal in nature. Do you think people come together and get married because they have these experiences?

Craig: The Clan of the Abductee? Yes…

RW: It beats the hell out of me why I fell asleep. I can't imagine why I did it. It was an unnatural event in my house that night, yet I went back to sleep. It changed the notion that there is a "normal."

AC: Do you think you were sort of headed in one life-direction, and then switched into another direction at that point?

RW: No. It's always been me. They did what they did. I am what I am. That's all that I am.

AC: Can you talk about "otherness?" You were saying that this gave you some insight into otherness.

RW: Otherness is just other than what you see in front of you. There's a whole world behind it. You know, there's just a whole *other*.

AC: Does it bleed over? Do you think there are measurable rules that govern the way it bleeds over into the not-otherness, the normal?

RW: No, I think all things have their own intentions. That's one of the things I understood after they came into my room that night. They had their own intentions.

AC: Do you think they listen, or react? Do you think that when you give a response, that an interplay goes on? Or do you think that it's completely one-sided?

RW: They had their own intentions. It was an unknown.

AC: Did they want something from you? Or was it more observational?

RW: It was more observational. They were just there. I think they didn't come back because my dad and I woke up that night.

AC: That would seem to be a case where your awareness affected their response. I've always believed that your response dictates where it goes.

RW: I think it didn't come back because my dad and I woke up that night. If we had slept through it, they would have been back again.

I spoke with Melinda Whyte in August of 2006. She is the wife of Randy Whyte. As we have seen, Randy experienced alien visitations and other paranormal phenomena that were confirmed by his siblings Karyn, Tony, and Kathy. I was fascinated by the fact that Randy and Melinda own a Makah "Thunderbeing" mask that hints at the telepathic and hypnotic abilities of Thunderbird-human hybrids. Melinda described their recent encounter with what may have been Sasquatch. As a side note, a UFO, near Loring Air Force base in northern Maine, once followed Melinda's father in his car.

Whyte, Melinda – Invisible Bigfoot Encounters? – Sept. 2006

Melinda Whyte (MW): We were on the 101 outside of Newport, Oregon. There was nobody around. Randy pulled over and kind of gave me a look. I know that look. I've only seen it one other time. It is just one of those "let's get the hell out of here" looks. So we sat there and he's got this weird look on his face. We were on bikes pulled over on the side of the road. We got to our camp that night and Randy said, "I have something to tell you. There was this really suspicious stench, a really vulgar smell." He said, "I didn't want to tell you because I didn't want you to be scared." And I said, "Well that goes without saying." He said, "I saw this pile of feces about a foot tall and it had berries in it. It wasn't from elk because elk leave pellets. I saw *something big*, too. But I never said anything…"

Andy Colvin (AC): Until you have a Bigfoot body to test the dung against, you don't know what it came from. All you can do is identify it as "unknown." Was anything else going on? Was your car parked nearby?

MW: Nope, there was nothing. We were outside of Newport and there were no cars. No one had passed us for a long while. It was kind of remote. It was one of those twenty-mile stretches where there wasn't a lot going on. It was a pretty dense, thicketed forest with a little clearing off of the side of the road… But there was another situation we got ourselves into… This was in Orleans City. I don't know the name of the forest, but this is a road off of 101. The [main] road was really dangerous, so we took the side trip. This was probably about a 1000-foot climb in about a mile and a half. It was a pretty steep climb. It was about 4:00 in the afternoon. It was just very remote. It was just one of those areas that has the hair on the back of your neck standing up. You're kind of on alert, knowing that there's "otherness" around you. We didn't say anything about it until we were out of the forest, but we kind of sensed that we had company. I had that feeling for the entire trip, actually.

AC: That's happened to me two or three times. I've actually heard the screaming outside of our tent. You get an electrical charge that stays with you the whole time you're there.

MW: On the backroad that we were on, I [physically] felt what you are talking about. I was thinking, "It's interdimensional. It goes in and out." I was laughing about it because it's too much of a cliché, you know? We were in a densely forested, remote area in Oregon where no one really goes very often.

AC: I think this stuff can manifest very fast. In the Bermuda Triangle, they recently discovered that these planes tend to disappear when a certain kind of multifaceted cloud quickly forms. It comes up from the ocean, accompanied by an *unseen* electromagnetic cloud, and melds with the plane. It's a disturbance that just comes up and disorients the space-time continuum of the area. The planes disintegrate, or go into some other time zone or dimension.

MW: Is that an explanation, then, for what I experienced?

AC: Well, I think these entities and electromagnetic forces are connected. There can just be a little happening – an electromagnetic happening – in a spot, which probably occurs over and over again. These beings manifest, are seen, and then go away.

MW: I've always wanted some evidence. I think if you open yourself up to it [it can manifest]. With the stresses of your daily life away from you, you're open to new possibilities, to new things… Talking about energies and how they can switch really quickly, here's another scenario. In 2000, we were on our way to New Mexico. We decided to take the coastal Route 101 down through Northern California, and then cut across to Redding. We took the road that turns off below the Redwoods. I don't remember the route number, but it comes across to that little town below Mount Shasta with the Bigfoot monument that everyone jokes about. We were between that little town and Redding. It's very remote. You could see Mount Shasta. We pulled off to go to the bathroom. As we walked about a quarter of a mile into the woods off of the road, we both had this feeling about the area. It just wasn't a very happy place. Randy looked at me and said, "Let's get back to the car as soon as possible." I don't really know what that was all about, because it seemed to me that Sasquatch wouldn't project negative energy. We just weren't sure *what* it was that we were feeling. The strong vibrations… Is that unrealistic?

AC: No, that's how I usually react, too.

MW: Is it?

AC: Well, yes.

MW: But why should we be afraid?

AC: I don't know.

MW: Randy asked that question, "Why are we afraid?"

AC: When I go back to the spot where all these things happened to me, I'm usually afraid. Especially if I'm by myself… I *can* walk up there alone, but I'm still nervous. It's on a country road in WV. There was an old school there that burned down. Some kids got killed. There might be some ghostly stuff going on there.

MW: The Indians from a long time ago thought the Sasquatch was [supernatural]. So maybe that's what we were picking up on. The West Coast is a very big area, with a lot of different tribes. So maybe it could be a population thing. But that's as close an encounter as I've ever had.

AC: These vortices and paranormal entities can be dangerous. They can unintentionally hurt you just by shining their light. You can get things like radiation poisoning and electromagnetic burns.

MW: So what do you think the chances are of having these experiences? Every time I go to Oregon, I feel that way in certain areas. What do you think are the chances of me actually having an encounter?

AC: I don't know.

MW: Did you ever go to Eugene? Have you ever been to the Canyon River Valley and some of the areas around there, where the Cougar Hot Springs are? That's a very electrically charged area. We spent a four-day weekend there. That was a really strong area.

AC: Just go with your feelings. *That* can be beneficial.

CHAPTER 44

"Imagine a world in which generations of human beings come
to believe that certain films were made by God, or that specific
software was coded by him. Imagine a future in which millions of
our descendants murder each other over rival interpretations of
Star Wars, or Windows 98. Could anything – anything – be more
ridiculous? And yet, this would be no more ridiculous than the
world we are living in [today]."

-Sam Harris, author (1967-)

Whyte, Kathy and Tony – Dad's Alien Visitation – 2003

Andy Colvin (AC): We've already spoken to Karyn and Randy Whyte. Now
we're going to speak to their younger siblings, Kathy and Tony, regarding
their father and brother's experience with "aliens." Would that be how you'd
describe these entities?

Kathy Whyte (KW): Sure...

AC: Okay... It seemed like there was a bit of disagreement earlier, as to whether
your father had scoop marks?

Tony Whyte (TW): I was thinking maybe the scoop was an inoculation mark.
But really, it was in the wrong place...

AC: Could you show us where the scoop marks were?

KW: [points] They were here, on his calf.

TW: From what I recall of the story, it seemed like there were hooded figures
that came into the rooms of both my brother and my father. That's all
they seem to remember. I try to be a skeptic but honestly, it's hard to be
skeptical about this. It was confirmed by both [of them].

KW: They had the same experience. Dad remembers waking up and seeing
someone at the end of the bed. He woke up because he felt like someone
was staring at him. He said, "What do you want?" And they didn't say
anything. He described it as a hooded figure with red eyes and just a
black space here. [points to facial area]

TW: I've heard the story many times. When I was about twelve or thirteen,
I started [researching it]. This is back in the days when the Internet was
not really [all] there yet. But they had bulletin boards... There was a
bulletin board system that would have alien stories. I read *Communion*

by Whitley Strieber, which my dad was into. I got the impression from *Communion* and from the stories I heard from my dad and brother that this was a humanoid figure. But why should they be humanoid? Because they're humans! They're time travelers. They're at a different point in the future when their gene pool is no longer big enough. They have to come back and get fresh genes. Fresh DNA...

AC: That's the story that one hears a lot, yes.

TW: That seems to be it. Otherwise, it doesn't seem to make much sense. I mean aliens could [or should] be *any* sort of lifeform...

AC: Jim Keith said that he thought the alien face was a composite of the simplest elements of the human face. If a person has a mind-blowing experience that they can't fully process, they'll piece together a face to fill that memory in. That usually would be a face similar to an alien face. The brain simplifies complex situations and complicates simple ones.

TW: It could be a "collective memory," a collective unconscious thing where so many people repeat something that it becomes implanted in *your* mind. Whenever you don't know exactly what happened, it becomes your [default image]. A lot of people seem to have planted memories like that. I definitely believe that.

AC: Randy described it as an alien that came to the foot of his bed.

TW: The hooded figure went to both rooms.

KW: The next day, Dad came home from work and said to Mom, "I had this really weird experience last night. This hooded figure came to the end of my bed." Well, actually, I guess Mom was there...

TW: But she doesn't remember any of this.

KW: She was there in the bed next to Dad. He asked her did she see it, and she was like, "see what?" So they went back to bed. Then Dad went to work, and Mom stayed at home and had her [normal] day. Mom said that Randy asked her about who was "in the house last night." She had him describe it. Then when Dad got home [she compared notes and found that] they had the same description of the entity.

TW: As far as the alien thing, it seems like the chances that a completely different lifeform would be interested in abducting and experimenting on humans – past the first stages – are pretty remote. It seems like they'd have to have an interest in our species to come back again. Any sightings would seem to have a human purpose.

KW: Maybe we're pets to someone.

TW: As far as us being of great interest to a completely alien race, I am definitely very skeptical of that.

AC: So what did Randy see after your dad died?

KW: Well, from my understanding of it, Randy saw Dad. Dad came to him, like he [later] came to me. Randy got a phone call at work that Dad had died, and immediately went home. He wanted to meditate. So he sat down and calmed himself. Immediately, Dad was *there*. Dad asked, "What's going on?" Dad was very confused. He said, "All I remember is spinning." At this point in time, Randy still didn't know that Dad had [been] in a crash where he flipped two and a half times over. Randy said, "Well, Dad, you died." And Dad felt very relieved. He said, "Oh, that's what happened. Okay, alright..." He had the answer, and he was ready to go on. Randy described a light that he saw. He described it to me as "the most beautiful thing you've ever seen in your life." All colors, and all combined into one... I don't know exactly how to describe the light because he's the one who saw it. But he said that it was indescribable. The most beautiful thing he's ever seen in his life...

AC: Was the light in the room, or in his mind?

KW: In the vision... You know, here's Dad with him, and a light in the distance. Dad wanted to rush on into it. Randy said, "No, Dad, you've got to stick around. There are some people who might need some help with this. We might need you to be here for a while." And Dad said, "Okay." I don't know exactly how it ended... Karyn was very upset, of course. She went upstairs to her room and started trying to calm herself and meditate. When she did that, Dad was there. She was confused. She was like, "Dad, why? Did you kill yourself? What happened?" And he said, "No, Karyn. It was just an accident. It was just something that happened." Karyn was a bit consoled by the fact that he didn't go off the road on his own. Dad said that he loved her, and said some other things to her. Then he said, "You give that boy a hug for me," meaning [his grandson]. At that moment [his grandson] was coming up the stairs. So Dad went to Karyn after he had been to Randy. Then he came to me. He has come to Tony in his dreams. Dad has come to me in my dreams, too...

TW: I wouldn't say that it was an experience that connected me with another level or spirit plane. I feel that it was something that came from me. I feel like a lot of stuff that people explain as being from the afterlife, or some sort of supernatural phenomenon, is just their mind compensating for things. And honestly, I think if Dad were here, he might say the same thing.

KW: It's inexplicable. But I do know that Karyn and Randy have more psychic ability than I do.

TW: I don't believe that for a second.

KW: Well, I think that they have trained it better because they actually took the Silva Mind Control course in the early '70s. She and Randy know how to tap into their powers more.

TW: Not at all!

KW: Well, that's my opinion. I feel that Karyn and Randy handle the supernatural and spirituality a lot better...

TW: I feel that the urge to explain things sometimes makes things come to the surface of your mind. The alternative is really scary. People don't like to consider the fact that perhaps everything means nothing. [Perhaps] there is no real afterlife. It's a very human thing to try to make meaning out of all this. It should mean something, perhaps, but maybe it really doesn't.

AC: Certainly the sages say that it's Maya. That it's illusion... The very fact that we can say, "I am in this body," means that we are *not* in this body, in a sense. Part of us is just pure consciousness coming through the body. Nobody knows if you can say such things without a body

KW: Yes, that's the big mystery.

AC: You can try and make the argument through pure logic. That's what the Tantric practitioners do.

TW: Frankly, I don't believe it. How could you be self-aware without a body? How is it possible? What would you be aware of? Isn't everything related to your physical being in some way?

AC: Waking consciousness is related to the body, yes, but there's also the unconscious...

KW: You know, my niece said something funny the other day. She said, "I'm glad you exist, Aunt Kathy. I'm glad you exist, Uncle Tony." And she said, "I think I didn't exist once. I remember what it felt like, but I don't remember what it looked like."

TW: And that's exactly what not existing feels like. It feels like nothing because you aren't existing. You know?

AC: All I'm saying is that the traditional Buddhist idea is that consciousness is the source of things, not the other way around. Things do not make consciousness happen. Everything that's happening right now – that seems to be a manifestation – is really an illusion. There's really nothing happening. It's all just a visual manifestation of the Source. So death is, in a sense, an illusion from that angle.

TW: Because you think we spring from an eternal source?

AC: The eternal source is consciousness, occurring right now.

TW: And it's not possible that maybe it's just a freak occurrence of molecules and elements and things that come together and spin off to form different things?

AC: I tend to think that the "freak occurrence" of molecules forming things came *after* the formation of consciousness.

TW: That's not to negate any spiritual feelings you have, but isn't it possible?

AC: Well, earlier you were proposing that it's connected with us. If you take that same kind of idea to its full extent, and view it all as in the mind – as coming from The Mind – you get into an area where it's just about consciousness coming through. The body is just a manifestation of that consciousness.

TW: Right. Like how do you know you're really living or dreaming, that sort of thing.

AC: Yes.

TW: Virtual reality…

AC: Some people who have taken hallucinogenics, or been injured or traumatized in certain ways, have had experiences where all the senses were taken away. Apparently things still happen in the mind, even when all your senses are taken away. That's one hint that there's some other stuff going on. Or "nothing" going on…

TW: I've definitely had those experiences. I think the most profound thing that I've ever come to is the fact that *nothing* means *so much*.

AC: The Void…

KW: Anyone who "knows everything" should know that they know nothing.

AC: Well, the Void is everything. It is probably the underlying phenomenon of all this stuff that appears to be happening. The opposite of voidness is all this stuff. In Buddhist cosmology, the Garuda is the first being to arise from the darkness and become manifest. That's why I think the Mothman is so important. In the ancient Buddhist tradition, he is the first guy up to "bat" in the game.

TW: Okay, but what is the Mothman? Why would he manifest?

AC: It's a birdman. It's the flying aspect that is important. Part of us flies in our dreams and is wrapped up in that. The best bridge between body and pure space is a body that can fly.

TW: That's why he has wings...

AC: The wings symbolize that morphing, creational process.

KW: I love to fly in my dreams. I can make myself fly in my dreams. I mean I can decide to dream about flying.

TW: I do it the same way in every dream. I kind of jump and push off. Then, it's like I have air tufts that come out underneath me. And then I make an arc and come down.

KW: I kind of bounce up and down and then go straight up.

AC: Do you have the same landscape recurring in your dreams?

TW: No. I can be anywhere and fly.

KW: The only [UFO] thing that's ever happened to me is that I have seen a very strange green light. I was traveling with a friend of mine. We were coming back from the beach, in an area outside of Seattle called Renton. Isn't that a suburb of Seattle?

AC: There have been sightings in Renton this year.

KW: Really? Well, we were in Renton and we were driving down the highway. All of a sudden, a beautiful little green light started following us. Oh, it's giving me goose bumps! It started following our car, you know, just along the side of our car. Then it just shot off. And I was looking at it in awe. This was probably like 3 or 4 seconds that it came along, followed the car and then shot off. I looked at my friend and said, "Did you see what I saw? I saw something really weird." He described it as a light. It was a green light that followed close to us.

AC: About 5 years ago, there were media reports of a giant green fireball traveling down the interstate where you were. There was even a ball of light that came through our property. We were away on vacation at the time. Our renter in the back house said an orange ball of light came through her house. Another renter saw a string of "linked" UFO lights above our house in broad daylight. There have been lots of things like that in Seattle.

KW: Oh my, that is so weird.

TW: Weird things happen, and you can't always explain them.

AC: Whether or not it connects to aliens is a completely different thing.

TW: Whenever something is an unknown, it's tempting to try and define it via some sort of previously identified phenomenon. I don't necessarily think that aliens would have a huge interest in us. But I don't doubt the existence of aliens...

KW: I don't doubt their existence.

AC: They may not be extra-terrestrial, but terrestrial.

KW: I don't doubt the existence of something else out there in the universe. I mean we would have to be terribly caught up in ourselves to think that we're the only organisms...

TW: Exactly. It seems awfully self-centered, doesn't it? If they have an interest in us, it's probably because they *are* us...

KW: Or descendants of us...

AC: Yes. A lot of ancient tribes and religious groups seem to have the idea that we mated with aliens at some point in our history. According to them, we are part "winged being."

TW: They just found more evidence that there might have been life on Mars. It's possible. I mean who knows? Our planet's been around for a long, long time.

KW: This is a huge, huge place, you know? This is a huge universe with a massive amount of space.

TW: But why would an alien race take an interest in the human race?

KW: Out of curiosity… Why would we take an interest in single-celled organisms and start looking at them under the microscope? Why would we take an interest in something strange to us, and study it?

Whyte, Kathy & Tony – Flying Around the Spirit Tree – 2003

Andy Colvin (AC): Do you have any events in your life that are anomalous?

Tony Whyte (TW): Sure, I have weird stuff that happened. But I think they're all explainable.

AC: What were some of those things? And what's the explanation?

TW: Some were precognitions... But I think that might just be intuition. I do have distinct memories of flying as a kid.

AC: Memories of *dreams* about flying?

TW: No…

Kathy Whyte (KW): No, this is a weird thing.

TW: No, I remember actually *physically* flying.

KW: From our wall, to the roof…

TW: And not just flying over the countryside, but flying in my courtyard, from my wall to my roof… I kind of made a dipped, curved trip across the way. It was like I was on a string or something. Like I was tethered… I don't think that has anything to do with aliens. But it *is* possible that what I remember might have been just a dream.

KW: I think that we share a certain energy.

AC: Have you shared any dreams?

KW: No, but things have happened before [that are like that. For instance] Tony and I were in a conversation, and somebody was asking him questions. I thought I knew the answers to them in my head. [Amazingly] he said the wrong answer; the answer that I had in my head! He said the answer and then he was like, "What? No, that's not right. I don't know why I just said that." Then he went on through the conversation and the lady asked him another one like, "What's your sign?" I'm thinking (wrongly), "It is Virgo." And he pops out, "Virgo." Again he goes, "What? No, it's Leo." I mean that kind of freaked me out. The other supernatural things that I've had happen had to do with ghosts or dead people. Some things like that…

AC: What were some of those?

KW: They mostly had to do with my father. One of the things happened right after he died. Tony and I went down to the crash site (where he died) with my mother, and we were standing out there in the field. I had this huge, overwhelming feeling of being lost and not knowing where my father was. I started worrying where he was, and if he was okay. We got back into the car and started driving back. I was just asking the world, "Dad, where are you? Do you still exist? Are you going to be around anymore?" And I saw him in front of me. I had my eyes closed and I saw him. He said, "I love you, Kate. Everything's going to be okay." And he hugged me and I felt his warmth – and it was cold outside. I felt the shirt he was wearing. I knew what shirt he was wearing. I felt that. I *know* that he came to me. I've had a couple of other times where I felt like I really wanted to talk to Dad. Once I was feeling alone, standing by a fire and looking up at a tree. My Dad always told me about tree spirits, so I think about tree spirits. I thought about my Dad and just asked, "Dad, are you around me anymore? Are you still here?" This was three years after he had died. All of a sudden the wind in the bottle that I was holding made a "whooo" sound…

AC: What did he say about tree spirits? I've been discovering things about trees.

KW: He really believed in tree spirits. He told me in a letter about tree spirits, that they were ancient beings and that they communicated. He asked if I would say "hello" to a certain tree of his in a certain forest…

AC: A real tree in a real forest? Not in an alternate universe or anything?

KW: Yes. He told me to go out and find a tree that I felt drawn to, and to sit down and feel the tree, and touch the tree. To tell the tree spirit to pass a message along saying "hello" to so and so… I can't remember what forest it was where he had met his own tree spirit. He found it backpacking when he was younger. He was asking me to ask [whatever] tree spirit I found to pass along a message to [his earlier tree].

AC: What thread ties these paranormal things together?

TW: I think the common thread is that humans are experiencing it, wanting to relate it all.

CHAPTER 45

"There once was a man in China who liked pictures of dragons. His clothing and his furniture were therefore accordingly adorned with dragons. This deep affection for their kind was brought to the attention of the Dragon Lord, who one day sent a real dragon to stand outside the man's window. It is said that he promptly died of fright."

-Yamamoto Tsunetomo

Colvin, Andy – Grassy Knoll Radio interview 10 – Summer 2006

Andy Colvin (AC): Did I mention that somebody had seen Mothman on the border of Florida and Georgia? I was interested in why there had been a sighting there. It didn't make sense from a symbological point of view. But it *was* after 9/11. The witnesses, the Oundees, are in my documentary. I now think we have a clue as to why the sighting happened. It may have been because of this Diebold conspiracy. Do you know anything about that?

"Vyz" at Grassy Knoll Radio (GK): You mean with the bogus voting machines?

AC: Yes. This is perhaps another tentacle of the Octopus. Mothman sometimes seems to be pointing towards such things. A Diebold synchronicity happened when I was filming in 2002. Around the time we got to Jackson, Ohio, they had a plane crash there where the Diebold CEO was killed. Jeff Wamsley, organizer of the Mothman Festival, had a record store there at the time. We were trying to interview him on camera. The crash got me thinking about Diebold. Then in 2003, I found out that Mothman had appeared to Ed Oundee and his mother, near where an investigator into Diebold had been found dead. A technician named Clint Curtis, who worked for Yang Enterprises, a NASA subcontractor, had come forward saying that he was asked to change votes by hacking the Diebold voting machines. According to Curtis, the person who asked him to do it was a Republican Representative named Tom Feeney. Feeney was a pal of Dick Cheney's who had once been Jeb Bush's running mate for Governor of Florida. Ray Lemme, a seasoned Florida DOT inspector who was investigating the scandal, was found dead. The media doesn't want these Diebold scams to be investigated for various reasons. In this case, it might prove that Bush operatives stole the presidential election in 2000. Also, such revelations might eventually point to a control center in Ohio. Lemme, this potential "Votescam" whistleblower, seems to have been terminated. It sent a message. But they made it look like a suicide.

GK: Oh, what a surprise...

AC: Here's another connection to Diebold... Again, these are little things in my life acting as ciphers. I knew this woman in '81. I talked about her. She is the woman from Massachusetts, named Bonnie, who remembered the chair drawing I had made... She once had Mothman following her around, and her beauty-queen mother was seemingly tracked by a secret society throughout life. I did a photo of Bonnie in '81 that involved a Diebold ATM machine called "Jeannie." It turns out that Jeannie is Bonnie's middle name. I showed the ATM photo to some people. It's going to be in my photo book. One person, whose opinion I respect in such matters, said it is probably the most unusual picture they have ever seen. And it's got a Christian theme to it. I've always been dealing with religious concepts. And that photo was sort of prophetic. I think we're kind of linked with people and future events in this way. Anyway, I wonder if Mothman sighting wasn't signaling about what happened on the Florida border. They took the victim, or his body, across the line to Georgia, because Georgia doesn't require autopsies on suicide victims.

GK: Was he in Ohio and brought down to Georgia?

AC: No, the investigation was happening in Florida.

GK: I see. So they brought him into Georgia. That makes sense...

AC: It's probably tied in with the drugs and everything else going on in FL.

GK: You got it.

AC: So they take him all the way up to GA. That's a long drive to dump somebody. That's the kind of thing I'm talking about, though. These linkages, even though they're kind of ethereal, or conceptual...

GK: Do have the thread...

AC: They can tell you things. Another little coincidence... I talked about Harriet seeing a laser shoot down a missile over the coast near San Francisco. She described the details to me at the time. More recently, these details were synchronistically corroborated by another case. I happened to find a guy on the Web while just browsing. He was a UFO witness from the '60s. He was in the military. In addition to seeing a laser shoot down a missile, this guy had seen a sphere swirling around the missile prior to impact. This was what Harriet had seen. To both of them, it looked like a laser marking pin. I sent her the guy's story. It turns out that the guy is actually teaching a class that Harriet's son is *currently* in, at Bradley University! I thought that was pretty amazing. By the way, when Bradley played Pitt in the NCAA tournament, if you looked at the little electronic scorebox in the corner of your TV screen, it said "Brad Pitt." I emphasize Brad Pitt because Keel likes to joke about how, in the Mothman movie, Brad Pitt would have made a better Keel than Richard Gere...

AC: Due to a completely random coincidence, I happen to be old friends with a lawyer for Brad's production company. When I went down there to see my friend a few months ago, he informed me that he had recently had a slew of paranormal experiences in Hollywood. I'll touch on them because they are fascinating.

GK: Do it.

AC: He went to a Hollywood party. This was a really hip party for stars, lawyers, and executives. The kind we all fantasize about... In Hollywood, there are a lot of people who traffic in spiritual phenomena. Somehow, my friend got involved in a ritual that involved taking South American herbs amped with pharmaceuticals. They were mixing organic and synthetic substances to create visual experiences. This kind of reminds me of Michael Persinger's work. He's the guy who discovered that, at a certain frequency, the brain will imagine an alien. We're kind of wired that way. When this frequency is bombarding our brains, we will start to hallucinate aliens. It can also be done with drugs, too. Lilly did it with Ketamine. Grof did it with LSD. This is what happened to my friend after he took the special Hollywood mixture. He started being visited by an alien being. Now this is a lawyer from the Midwest. A very practical, non-flamboyant person... It almost destroyed his life. He was running outside to try and catch the alien that he was *sure* was hanging around his house. He said that he was totally tripping for at least a month, and was in an altered state for several months. We're talking about weeks of hallucinations. He finally recovered. But like so many people who go through this "alien" contact, he embarked on a journey of synchronicities. When I was at his house, I could feel that a synchronicity was about to happen. I told him, "One will probably happen now. If I go over to your bookshelf and just pull off a random book, I'll bet we find out something interesting."

GK: It's called "Lucky Dib."

AC: I often research this way. I have my stable of books and I'm always buying more. I'll just go grab one, open it up, and see what's there. It's incredible. It works... Anyway, I pulled out a book, and it was *the* very book that had gotten him through the entire hallucinogenic alien experience! It was a book by Ramana Maharshi, an Indian sage who realized the connection between geomagnetism and enlightenment. When he was 14, Ramana decided to leave home and go stay at the base of a particular mountain. He then stayed in the same spot for the rest of his life. This reminds me of when Tommy said to me, "Hey, just stand in that spot and you will have a psychic experience like none you've ever had." Well, this guru did that. He said, "This is where I need to be. Because I've just experienced some form of enlightenment here, I'm going to stay here for the rest of my life." A whole movement built up around him, and now there are several books about him and by him. But this lawyer friend of mine used the words in Ramana's book to regain his sanity. Coincidentally, I had just ordered that same book before embarking on that trip! It was in the mail to me at that exact time. This is how synchronistic it was. The book I had just purchased was the book that had gotten him through this mind-shattering experience. In his copy were many scribbles. He had changed the subject of the book from Maharshi to himself. Keep in mind, this book is basically Ramana's personal story. Ramana was telling the story of how he reached enlightenment. My friend put his own name in there instead of Maharshi's. He changed all the words around to fit his own life. Then he read that to himself over and over again, until he got through the long hallucinatory phase. And it worked. He's now totally fine. He's got two kids and a great practice...

GK: It worked out. Wow...

They don't call it Kali-fornia for nothing. Incidentally, Birdman sightings have been reported near a Malibu cliff shrine dedicated to the Hindu God Kali (namesake of the Kali Yuga calendar). Shrines with Kali themes are still being discovered, buried under vines in the Hawaiian Islands. In fact, one was discovered just days before we filmed segments at black panther sighting areas on Maui. The story of our Southwest and Pacific adventures can be found in my next book, The Mothman's Photographer III.

AC: Puharich did a lot of different research. One thing he found was that objects hold memories. I don't know if I mentioned that last time.

GK: Explain how that happens, please.

AC: Visualize the psi-plasma coursing through everything. Connecting everything... Remember that this plasma has intelligence. It can literally hold ideas and information. That's essentially how we hold ideas in our minds. This is widely understood in the indigenous world. In fact, some shamans will project their lifeforce into an object at death, in order to continue on in spirit form. I don't know exactly how it works, or why anyone would really want to do that, but they do. As we all know, these psychic techniques are also used in criminal investigations. Joseph DeLouise realized that Charles Watson was the killer – not Charles Manson – prior to the Family ever being found. DeLouise picked it up from the house, from objects. Puharich did that kind of research. I think someone in Puharich's sphere could have used his "black box" technology on UFO contactees in the Mothman area. Puharich is important. He had these ties to the CIA, the Navy, and to the Hudson Valley, where the Rockefellers live.

GK: Oh yes…

AC: This is all very close to Iron Mountain, which was an entity that was working with Union Carbide to store uranium files and such…

GK: Hudson, New York… The *Report from Iron Mountain*… People argue whether it was true or not. I think it was true, without a doubt. The government freaked out when it came out. Johnson's administration went, "Oh no, this isn't true…" But it's like, "Yes, it really is." Now, let me say this. That facility was supposedly in Hudson, New York, on the east bank across the Rip Van Winkle Bridge from Catskill. Now, having said that, what do you know about what might have taken place? Are you just talking about some document that bears the name Iron Mountain, or are we talking about a facility on the east bank of the Hudson to keep the elites from getting nuked.

AC: I've seen references to Union Carbide being the corporate entity behind the success of Iron Mountain, the facility in Hudson. By the late '60s, it had already been around almost 20 years. Iron Mountain was, among other things, storing uranium documents for Union Carbide. Carbide was developing the Bomb. Iron Mountain was a physical place where they kept some things associated with the Manhattan Project, and beyond. One gets the impression that they are doing data-mining there now. But in that transition period, they were putting out technical reports. The *Report from Iron Mountain* is one of those reports.

GK: You're saying that they actually did testing wherever Iron Mountain should be. Is that correct?

AC: No, storage… It was physical storage for documents and supplies. They started in 1951 in Hudson. They were storing things for Union Carbide that had to do with uranium development and/or making the bomb.

The proximity of the Indian Point Nuclear plant might have prompted a need for such storage. One imagines that Defense Industrial Security

Command would have had a close relationship with such a high-security facility.

AC: The important fact is that they were partnering with Union Carbide. Helping Carbide with its radioactive processes... Carbide was making the pure nickel spinners for creating the isotopes needed for enrichment. It's interesting that they all were in close proximity. Puharich's home (in Ossining), Iron Mountain (in Hudson), the Rockefellers' home (in Sleepy Hollow), Carbide (in Tuxedo Park), the Army (in West Point), Indian Point (in Peekskill)... Then you the Hudson Valley UFO sightings of Whitley Strieber, Budd Hopkins, and John Mack...

GK: All I'm going to say is that what you've said about Iron Mountain is very provocative.

AC: One thing I don't want to forget... There is this idea in the occult that in order to ritually invoke certain entities, two 6 to 8 year old children are required. I think I got that from Eugenia Macer-Story,

GK: Whenever three or more are gathered...

AC: We had two (me and Tommy) building a shrine to Mothman, plus Harriet. My question is, "Was this being manipulated? Was Tommy being coached into having occultic ideas?" I don't know. But getting back to your flashing light... You had talked about seeing a flashing light. That's a very common trigger for UFO contactees and abductees. They'll see a flashing light at first. After that, all manner of hallucinations can occur. Again, these hallucinations can be partly physical. An entity can appear and be physical for a time. It may even do damage that others can observe. It's pretty clear that that can happen. Bigfoot can manifest, and it can leave tracks. Then it goes away. Believe it or not, Puharich *did* flashing light experiments. He found out which frequencies trigger certain kinds of hallucinations. He used them on a psychic who was a friend of Peter Hurkos. Puharich found that at certain frequencies, predictable things would happen. Apparently it launched the hemi-sync visual technology that we have today. With hemi-sync, people put on headsets and experience different programs for changing brainwaves in (supposedly) positive ways. Puharich was the originator. He did exhibitions of this stuff for the Navy. Hurkos, who was a very famous psychic, volunteered to be the guinea pig in some of these exhibitions. According to author Douglas Valentine, the Navy had all sorts of links – drug and otherwise – to Meyer Lansky and the KY mobsters. Puharich knew Werner von Braun, as we mentioned. Werner von Braun knew Tom Slick, the Bigfoot investigator. Slick knew Puharich, too. In fact, Slick and Puharich did experiments with Hurkos, some involving using him as a courier and/or psychic reader of mail. They were obviously up to some kind of spy activity, and had certain needs for a good psychic. As I said, Hurkos was put through the flashing light test. At a certain frequency, Hurkos would see a swirling pattern. When I read the descriptive details, it reminded me of a pattern that I see occasionally. Say you've just closed your eyes to rest. You see this slowly swirling image with millions of little sparkling jewels, and it's slowly turning. It's not the normal configuration you see when you close your eyes.

GK: [Is it] the "thousand points of light?"

AC: It feels like I'm looking at the underlying matrix. It only lasts for a short time. I've had this happen just a few times. I think that there's a natural way to enter into these states. Puharich went to the trouble of setting up elaborate tests to figure out exactly how to trigger these. One gets the impression that he wasn't happy about all the ways this could be used by other people. I think he was a pretty decent guy, because the CIA burned down his house in Ossining. It seems he got into a feud with them about some of their behaviors. They were classifying all of his research and he wasn't able to really do much with it. He would start, and they would finish. He was kind of getting jerked around. So I'm not trying to pin all of this stuff on Puharich. He was a brilliant guy who did a lot of really groundbreaking research. We were talking earlier about Iceland and it's possibly being the Thule Ultima, the Nazi form of Heaven…
In the 1970s, Puharich held a worldwide conference there that focused on psychic science. They published a book called *The Icelandic Papers*. If you want to get a glimpse of really hard-to-understand physics involving the mind, go check that out. One important thing that he discovered was that dehydration increases conductivity of electricity in the human body. This actually increases psychic ability. Another thing he found was that negative ions increase ESP. Negative ions are greater during a thunderstorm (when the Thunderbird is said to fly). Puharich literally started bombarding dehydrated psychics with negative ions, in order to find the perfect blend that would increase their telepathic abilities. He also amplified their signals at different Hertz rates. These were experiments designed to discover how to make a person project consciousness more accurately. These may have led directly to the Montauk Chair experiments. Someone in the agency probably took Puharich's research and started monkeying around with people at the facility on Long Island. I often wonder if it's Brookhaven more than Montauk, because Brookhaven comes up in Puharich's books as being a place where he might meet someone like von Braun. And Brookhaven was funding some of Puharich's work.

Peter Moon has edited a book on the subject called "The Brookhaven Connection." The book's author, Wade Gordon, calls Brookhaven "the most top secret research lab in the world." Not only does the book claim to tie Brookhaven to Montauk, it also attempts to link Brookhaven to The Philadelphia Experiment, the Majestic-12 documents, the Roswell Crash, and the JFK assassination.

GK: Is it a coincidence, or are we looking at the real deal? [What was] your father's feeling about being involved with the Philadelphia Experiment, or the Montauk Chair?

AC: I think there may be some weird connection with the Montauk Chair. But my dad didn't actually say that... He was on Long Island, though. From some of the strange messages I've gotten, it appears that there might be something linking the Montauk Chair and my dad. It's hard to say... I won't speculate too much on it until I know more.

GK: I understand that. Of course, people have asked about it. Do you think you'll ever find out more?

AC: Yes, I do. Absolutely... By the way, Puharich found that fear stimulates the sender of a telepathic message. This is a very interesting fact. It could have huge ramifications for guys like Bush, who are trying to scare everyone all the time. It could really increase the psychic processes whereby the psi-plasma (symbolized by Mothman) is relaying prophetic messages to and from individuals...

In the future, people may figure out ways to send messages telepathically to others, beyond the bounds of government surveillance.

GK: That [fear] *is* taking place with the propaganda we're seeing today. I don't mean watching network news... I don't even have cable. My outlets are very few. But, if what I'm watching can be extrapolated across all those myriad channels, are we not seeing [brainwashing] to the max?

AC: Absolutely... It's tricky, though. The trickiness enters in when you're trying to manage the use of the two basic stimuli, fear and relaxation. In the body, fear relates to adrenaline, and relaxation to acetylcholine. Puharich was studying the balance of these two chemicals. He would basically induce fear in the psychic, and then see what would happen. He started figuring out how the cell voltages were changing with the fear. He tried amping up the voltage. Then you start getting into what's happening in the nerves and how they're sending messages. Basically with the nerves, you have a gap there, and the messages are traveling across the gap. Relating it to symbolism, the gap is where the psi-plasma is. Where the Garuda is... Other entities are in that gap, too. There is voltage going across the gaps. The interesting thing is that some membranes will only pass certain signals. They will only pass, say, a fear (adrenaline-based) signal. Other ones will only pass an acetylcholine-based signal, resulting in the relaxation of a given muscle. Other membranes can pass one or the other, depending on the direction of the flow. It gets complicated once you get into examining the different combinations of stimuli and response. But what Puharich found was that shamans and yogis stimulate both systems at once. They basically get into a trance by taking stimulants *and* relaxants together, in high doses. Tobacco and alcohol are commonly used, but there are other substances than can be used as well.

Olga Kharitidi, M.D., the Russian psychiatrist who wrote the book Entering the Circle, *found that the tobacco and alcohol combination is still used by the "dream healing" shamans of the Altai Mountains of Russia.*

AC: This combination allows enough control, at the molecular level, to get the conscious mind into deep contact with the psi-plasma. When the shaman gets properly amped-up in both areas, he or she will typically pass out for a time. As their system starts to recalibrate, it leaves islands in the brain. These are areas that still have the amped-up charge. It is those high-voltage islands that communicate with the psi-plasma and allow the shaman to see through space-time, and perhaps manipulate reality. Speaking of manipulating reality, one example might be the picture of the Garuda that my sister took. I really suspect that this is a picture of some genuine phenomenon, resulting from the manipulation of the psi-plasma. It doesn't necessarily mean that the Garuda was standing in that kitchen window in 1973. Maybe it was some sort of holographic image of the Garuda. All we know is that somehow, that image coalesced onto that film. I'm kind of stunned that we have this photo showing the real creature, or else its hologram or facsimile, yet no one is interested in investigating it. The people making all of these documentaries about Mothman could care less. They just play some scary music, interview a couple of witnesses, and go home. Regular folks shouldn't necessarily care, but you'd think these producers would.

On 1/9/07, psychic Eugenia Macer-Story stated on Adam Gorightly's radio show that she feels the Mothman is the Garuda, and that the Garuda is trying to educate us as to its existence and workings. A talented artist in many fields, Macer-Story cited an "astral drawing" she once made of the Garuda. At first, she simply began drawing a woman experiencing a shadow figure, similar to that seen by John Keel, Sharon Moore, Loretta Colvin, Chica Bruce, etc. Suddenly, she lost control and drew a full-blown Garuda instead. This seemed to symbolize to her that the Garuda uses the guise of a shadow person. Could a "cooled-down"

Garuda become a Man in Black like Indrid Cold, or is the entire Indrid scenario just a complicated set-up designed to make us think that the Garuda is demonic? Due to MIB disinformation, Macer-Story said she had disliked and misinterpreted John Keel for several years in the 1970s, thinking he was a practicing occultist and/or demonologist. She also stated in her radio interview that "intelligent" light spheres and orbs probably manifest as Men In Black. In lower Manhattan, she has photographed many Men (and women) in Black following her. Could these MIBs somehow be related to the 9/11 attacks?

AC: It's strange, but in that picture my sister took of the Garuda and me, there's an upside-down 7-Up glass.

GK: What's the 7-Up glass?

Image of Colvin in kitchen (left) taken by his sister in 1973. Note Garuda-like reptilian bird face in lower left of window. Just a few days after Colvin publicized this image, a Bigfoot photo contest was launched by Loren Coleman, in conjunction with Hasbro. The eventual $5000 winner of the contest, Pennsylvania teenager Erik Starn, entered a photo much like this - a window shot from the inside. Coleman reported that Starn claimed it was "Mothman" looking in from the lower left corner.

AC: It's just a glass that we had. I'm also wearing a West Virginia Tech shirt in that photo, which may be a clue of some kind. I imagine that a lot of these Army biowarfare guys went to school there. The 7-Up glass comes up in Puharich's book on Uri Geller. Geller felt like he got messages from the 7-Up glass. It was highlighted as an anomalous 7-Up glass. It meant something to me when I read that that my 7-Up glass had some other meaning. That's how minutely coincidental this stuff is.

Speaking of coincidences... At this point in the interview, I glanced at my computer screen. There, I had the "slide show" screensaver running, showing random images from my photo collection. The very photo we were discussing popped up.

AC: Believe it or not, that picture just came up on my computer screen, on the screensaver here! Oh by the way, Tom Slick, one of Puharich's CIA contacts, was involved in the Patterson Bigfoot film investigation.

GK: The Patterson film?

AC: Yes, the 1967 Roger Patterson film of Bigfoot... It has been in the news recently. Greg Long wrote a book saying it's fake.

GK: What's your feeling about that film?

AC: It's always looked sort of fake to me. That's all I can say. It could be a CIA guy in costume. Tom Slick was a CIA asset and a leading cryptozoologist. There are probably others like him. The top guys in any field are the ones they usually recruit.

GK: When I look at the object in its environment, whatever I see seems real. It seems like it's correctly placed, etc. My question is, "What am I looking at, as far as that particular humanoid?" If that humanoid is something other than what we are, then we've got a situation here.

AC: I think it's probably a guy in a suit. However, I also think it's possible to take a picture of an entity. I'm just not sure that the Patterson film shows a real entity.

GK: Exactly... That particular video shows something obviously *in* the woods with foreground, background, etc. But is that somebody in a monkey suit? That's another question...

AC: In amongst the Puharich material, I wrote, "Maddie Bennett uses 'the force,' via birds, to get what she wants." She claims to use the birds as genies. Not only do we have scientists in the lab saying that you can get messages from an object or another being, but this down-home mountain lady is using it to her advantage in her daily life.

GK: Restate that. She's saying that birds are…

AC: She talks to birds, basically. This is a woman whose sister, Marcella, had one of the closest encounters with Mothman. And Maddie had some experiences with UFOs as a kid. Today, as an elderly lady, Maddie gets messages in advance about upcoming occurrences. She can ask for things, using a bird as a medium.

GK: Did you capture this in your documentary?

AC: Yes.

GK: Wow… Why don't you talk about that? We've not said anything about the documentary. People should know that if they want to scrutinize the information you have to impart, it really would be nice if they had your 5-part DVD.

AC: Yes, it's five 6-hour DVDs. You can also get that in MP3 audio format if you like.

GK: What does that mean to people? MP3 usually means audio.

AC: Right, yes… You can get the video, or you can get the audio. Some people don't want to watch TV because of time constraints. If they happen to be in their car a lot, they can just listen to the interviews there.

GK: Alright, so you have two different formats. You have a DVD that can be watched at home, and you have an MP3 that they can pop into their CD players and listen to as they're going somewhere. Great… That's really important. So go ahead with the information about this, because a lot of people listening probably haven't heard you before.

AC: Go to andycolvin.com, or go to eBay and do a search for Mothman.

GK: How close are you to [finishing] the photo book?

AC: It seems to go on forever, but we're almost there. It's being published by the Cincinnati Conceptual Art Museum. If you just go to Amazon and put my name in, you'll see the book. In addition to the anomalous image that my sister took, there's another image that I wanted to mention. Gray Barker had a description in one of his interviews about the Philadelphia Experiment. He did a poem about the Philadelphia Experiment where he talks about this "heat mirage" that people would see around the sailors, either when they were on the ship during the original experiment, or later. Before they would catch on fire and disappear, you would see a heat mirage around them. This kind of spontaneous combustion occurred at the Belle, WV, DuPont plant, to guys who were probably ex-Norfolk sailors like my father. The anomalous picture in question was taken after my father was dead. It was in the field next to our house at the top of the Woodward Drive hill. There's a heat mirage around this person, or thing, that I photographed. I was taking a photo of a crop circle that was in the field. It was an old circle, but I took the photo anyway. There's this being there. You can literally sense the psi-plasma bending the view. That's the best way to describe it. The psi-plasma field is going in a circle around this being.

GK: Okay…

AC: Getting back to Ted Holiday, who wrote *The Dyfed Enigma*… He also wrote *The Dragon and the Disc*, which talks about the connections between the Garuda, dragons, and UFOs. He indirectly hints at the politics of church and state. The king always sent out his knights to slay the dragon. This is symbolic of the destruction of the pagan culture. The attempted destruction of knowledge about ancient psychic processes…

GK: Fair enough…

AC: Holiday mentions some UFO research done in Puerto Rico. They found that UFOs are generally seen 30 kilometers from the center of a geomagnetic anomaly. They're not usually seen closer than that. They circle the geomagnetic anomaly. That really clicks it in for me. You've got this geomagnetic node that actually behaves like a giant atom. The "electrons" swirling around this node are what we have come to know as UFOs. They only swirl around the edges, at a distance of about 30 kilometers. Now apply this same concept to Charleston, where we lived. Take the cities of Point Pleasant and Charleston and place them on an appropriately sized imaginary circle, where it's 30 km to the center. When you do that, you find that the center point might include Liberty, West Virginia. It just so happens that there is a guy who claims that in Liberty, WV, NASA has been studying a vortex. You can check this out. I'm not making this up. The guy's name is William Dean Ross. He's kind of a strange bird. He pops on and off various lists and blogs. He wrote an article called *Catch a Falling Star* that goes into this story. He worked at Carbide's Institute, WV facility doing research in conjunction with WV State College. Institute is where the Germans and the Rockefellers were making synthetic rubber during WWII. This is also near the site where Tad Jones saw the UFO, as discussed in *The Mothman Prophecies*. It's very close to where I lived, and it is next to Dunbar, where there were two or three Mothman sightings. Institute is a critical link in the Standard Oil global chain. Ross says that NASA and the NSA are using WV State College (which is in Institute) for research, and that he was part of the team. He claims to have filmed these forays out into the countryside, to this vortex. NASA is apparently trying to move beyond Puharich, studying inner space as well as outer space.

GK: Things go bump in the night in West Virginia, believe me. I'm not a naysayer whatsoever. Things are a bit weird there.

AC: Here's a scribble. It looks like I've written down the source as Michael Clark. It says that the Rockefellers *oversaw* the Special Virus Cancer Project, which ran from '61 to '78.

GK: Where did that take place?

AC: It was in Maryland. Have you heard of Leonard G. Horowitz, M.D., by the way?

GK: Len Horowitz? Absolutely!

AC: He's written about this for a long time. I always read his articles. Apparently he just posted this on Rense. I'm not a big Rense fan or anything...

GK: [Me either] but Len's a pretty straight shooter, I would like to believe.

AC: The article by Horowitz is about the origin of AIDS being related to this Special Virus Cancer Project. I mentioned earlier that Nixon was really pumping money their way right around the time my dad got jabbed. This was the same time that Puharich went to Maryland, and Harriet's family moved to Maryland. Now we have a Rockefeller connection to that. Horowitz just comes out and says that the Rockefellers were overseeing that project, or were funding it somehow.

GK: Exactly...

AC: So there you go. Another reason why they might go to WV to jab people, or pull some shenanigans with cancer research... Rockefeller was the new governor. They could easily mitigate any revelations that might come out. If somebody screwed up, they could easily cover it up, like Jeb does in Florida.

GK: Agreed... You've been very fair about this. In the early shows that we did, I thought I might push you about the whole idea of Rockefeller influence in West Virginia. Not that you know about it, or necessarily want to talk about it... But we talked about the X-Files always referring to West Virginia, having things happen in West Virginia. I'm glad you're saying this, because something's going on there. It *has* been the province of the Rockefellers for over a century. Would you not agree? In fairness to you, you're looking at a very big manuscript in which not everything you wanted to happen did. That's what you're dealing with. There's a lot of stuff out there. We can all deal with little blips and bumps in the road. But the fact that you would come forward with this information is *huge*. I'm going to tell you right now, people are going to be very, very interested in this. I'm going to guarantee you that. I'm just so happy that you came on and spent the time you did. If certain radio producers don't want to download it into their particular broadcast network, that's [their loss]. I'm really glad you came forward like you did, and as repletely as you did.

AC: You're welcome.

GK: This *has* to be told. Not many people will do this kind of thing. Man, this is great. I'm happy. As far as your notes go, you told me you had [some] shows left. This would be the first of them. How are we doing as far as you being on track?

Anomalous Figure in Crop Circle, Mound, WV 1979

AC: It is possible that we could maybe get it done in another couple of hours.

GK: Hey, it's your time. I want you to profit by it. As long as you want to run, I'll run. And long may you run...

AC: For me, it's not necessarily pointing fingers at this person or that person, in terms of who pulled this conspiracy. There's always going to be another conspiracy for Mothman to divulge. It's about the process of becoming comfortable with, and encouraging people to use, this psychic process. Through the psi-plasma, we're linked to forces that can – if carefully approached – perhaps be utilized without endangering ourselves. It's the process of being on the Path. I relate it to Buddhism because, to me, that's such a practical way of looking at life. Everything is preparation. Life is preparation for the moment when you merge back with the superspectrum. Understanding the psi-plasma is important in terms of getting your own frequency right. "Getting your mind right," as they say in Southern parlance... *Look* at the process. Look at your programming. Take back your own enlightenment. Take back your spirituality. Take responsibility for it. That's what's important. It's not about busting somebody, although that probably needs to be done with some of these guys. Fighting them would be such a large and abstract process. The most practical way for most of us to "fight back" is to learn from the symbolisms available to us. Take from them what you can. It's about giving back to your Self.

GK: I'll only say that I appreciate the fact that you are illuminating an area of American life that is not really known about, for obvious reasons. And that's always a problematic thing. The fact that you've come out and done that, and are willing to offer a solution, is pretty good stuff. Andrew, like I said, I appreciate the time you've spent. Hours have flown by. I'll be sad to see you go, but I know you have other things to do. Other projects... Can I assume we'll talk in the very near future?

AC: Sure. Thank you very much.

Note: Further interviews with Grassy Knoll can be found in our next book, The Mothman's Photographer III. Check www.andycolvin.com for more information.

BRAVE MOUNTAINEERS

Born in the country, and I like that country smile

Of the little girls and boys, they remind me of a child that I knew,

And a big harvest moon that shone by suppertime in the dusty afternoon.

And I need to be there, when the autumn wind goes singing

Through the trestle we would climb…

Like brave mountaineers, we never were much bothered by time.

Born in the country, and I like that country song

We played for just a nickel every time we got to town…

And I bought you a dime diamond ring…

In the hayloft we would play we were princesses and kings.

And I need to be there, when the world gets too heavy

And the shadows cross my mind…

Like brave mountaineers, we never were much bothered by time.

Born in the country, and I like that country way

Of the uncles and some cousins and the card games they would play,

While the young ones slept overhead

Beneath the quilts that mother made when all the prayers were said.

And I need to be there, when the autumn wind goes singing

Through the trestle we would climb…

Like brave mountaineers, we never were much bothered by time.

And I need to be there, when the world gets too heavy

And the shadows cross my mind…

Like brave mountaineers, we never were much bothered by "time."

-Gordon Lightfoot

BIOGRAPHY

Andy Colvin was born in Charleston, WV, in 1959. Andy and his family and friends had encounters with the supernatural birdman popularly known as "Mothman." Colvin found that he could draw, paint, and take photographs after these encounters. He was recognized as an artistic prodigy at his elementary school, where his drawings still hang.

After his father died in 1972, Colvin supported himself by doing portraits at local fairs and illustrations for local businesses. He became known for working in semi-trance, capturing the essence of his subjects in unforgiving media such as India ink, gouache, and watercolor. Word traveled fast about a teenage "Mothman artist" who could draw with either hand, and who rarely looked at the paper. In 1973, Colvin's sister unwittingly took a picture of him with what appears to be a Garuda in the background. In 1979, Colvin unexpectedly took a photo of what may be Mothman's alien sidekick, Indrid Cold.

Colvin is now a photographer, filmmaker, and writer who has been interviewing witnesses to strange events for over two decades. Prior to making documentaries, Colvin wrote music and worked on commercial films, in art museums, and in photographic studios. He has shot documentaries on several subjects, including the Seattle WTO protests, the McVeigh execution, and Generation-X "Slackers." Colvin's work has been seen or heard in all 50 states, and in several foreign countries. His 32-hr. paranormal reality series, *The Mothman's Photographer*, has won fans throughout the world for its down-to-earth approach to potentially solving one of the world's greatest mysteries.

Colvin earned a BFA in photography/design from the Art Academy of Cincinnati in 1982, and studied graduate photography/film at the University of Texas at Austin from 1982-1989. While in Austin, Colvin studied with world-class researchers like film scholar Louis Black (founder of SXSW), anthropologist Steven Feld (collaborator with Mickey Hart), and renowned Mayan art expert Linda Schele (who broke the Mayan code). Colvin's 1980s Mothman photo series gained him sufficient acclaim to allow collaborations with some of New York's most famous artists. Colvin is a founding member of the Austin Film Society. In the late 1970s, Colvin studied at the celebrated journalism program at Marshall University, and was an announcer at WFMU. While at Marshall, he tutored with media icons Ralph Turner (who originally reported on Mothman) and Matt Lauer, now of The Today Show.

Andy Colvin now lives happily with his wife and son in the Pacific Northwest, next to a haunted Native American schoolground, near a Thunderbird Totem.

Verplanck Colvin, the "John Muir of the East," whose books and incredible feats of winter surveying created the Adirondack Park and kept most of NY from being sold to Canada by the same "World Bankers" later involved in financing Hitler. Colvin also discovered the tiny, swampy source of the mighty Hudson River which had previously eluded explorers for almost 300 years.

LIST OF PHOTOGRAPHS